# Let Me Make It Good

# Let Me Make It Good

## A Chronicle of My Life With Borderline Personality Disorder

**Jane Wanklin**

Mosaic Press
Oakville, ON. - Buffalo, N.Y.

Canadian Cataloguing in Publication Data

Wanklin, Jane, 1955-
Let me make it good
ISBN 0-88962-627-8
1. Wanklin, Jane, 1955- . 2. Borderline personality disorder - Biogra-
phy. I Title.
RC569.5.B67W3 1997    616.85'852'0092    C97-931834-3

Published by MOSAIC PRESS, P.O. Box 1032, Oakville, Ontario, L6J
5E9, Canada. Offices and warehouse at 1252 Speers Road, Units #1&2,
Oakville, Ontario, L6L 5N9, Canada and Mosaic Press, 85 River Rock
Drive, Suite 202, Buffalo, N.Y., 14207, USA.

**MOSAIC PRESS**, in Canada:      **MOSAIC PRESS**, in the USA:
1252 Speers Road, Units #1&2,      85 River Rock Drive, Suite 202,
Oakville, Ontario, L6L 5N9           Buffalo, N.Y., 14207
Phone / Fax: (905) 825-2130        Phone / Fax: 1-800-387-8992
E-mail:                                    E-mail:
cp507@freenet.toronto.on.ca        cp507@freenet.toronto.on.ca

**MOSAIC PRESS** in the UK and Europe:
DRAKE INTERNATIONAL SERVICES
Market House, Market Place,
Deddington, Oxford. OX15 OSF

Mosaic Press acknowledges the assistance of the Canada Council, the
Ontario Arts Council and the Dept. of Canadian Heritage, Government
of Canada, for their support of our publishing programme.

Cover and book design by: Adam Sherwood
Printed and bound in Canada

I would like this book to be dedicated to Dr. Michael E. Milo,M.D..,Dr. James D.F. Harris, M.D., Dr. Farida Spencer, P.hd, and Judith Carscadden, RN.

For the memorials, I would like it to read: "In fond memory of Angela, Darren, Dennis and Pamela. Your friends miss you."

For the acknowledgements, I would like to thank my mother for her unwavering support, love and encouragement, and my father for being there for me. As well, my brother, Jim, who showed me that with determination and hard work it is possible to reach what often seem like impossible goals and my grandparents unconditional love.

Other kudos I would like to include are Mary Beth Skeoch, one of my oldest and dearest friends, who never gave up on me, Mike Guest, who taught me to stop worrying and love the computer and Margaret McLeod who helped make my time in the L.P.H. more bearable. Last but not least, I thank my affectionate and lovable cat, Julius.

I sit at my table and wage war on myself
It seems like it's all for nothing.
I know the barricades, and
I know the mortar in the walls breaks
I recognize the weapons. I've used them well.
I've a rich understanding of my finest defenses:
I proclaim that claims are left unstated.
I demand a rematch.
I decree a stalemate.
I divine my deeper motives.
I recognize the weapons.
I've practised them well, I fitted them
Myself.
It's amazing what devices you can sympathize, empathize.
This is my mistake. Let me make it good.
I raised the wall and I will be the one to knock it down.
Reach out for me, hold me tight, hold that memory.
Let my machine talk to me. Let my machine talk to me.

R.E.M.
*"World Leader Pretend"*
*(Reprinted with permission)*

# INTRODUCTION

This book explores the world of a person diagnosed with Borderline Personality Disorder and the havoc it has wreaked on her, her family and her friends. It is an attempt to make some kind of sense of it all and to come to terms with the past and the people involved in it.

Many of the patients discussed cannot speak for themselves and I feel a responsibility to be their voice.

As you read this document, some of its content will infuriate sicken, and repulse you. The language gets quite salty at times, but many of us involved were angry and scared a great deal of the time. Therefore we used the verbal tools that were at our disposal to express these feelings.

My book is an attempt to make some kind of sense of it all. I hope those who read it will realize that mental illness is something that can happen to anyone regardless of level of intelligence, economic status or family situation.

This is not a work to either exploit myself or any of those with whom I came in contact over the years but rather to document the kind of reality that often hides in the shadows and whispers haltingly in quiet, reflective moments.

It is important to record some of the atrocious things that went on in supposedly "progressive" Psychiatric Institutes in the 1970's, before the Mental Health Act was instated. I am not hungering for any kind of unhealthy revenge by writing about wards like the Behaviour Modification Unit in the London Psychiatric Hospital, but rather to record history as it actually happened.

Most of the world would rather not think about the mentally ill or what they have to live with every waking hour of their days. Perhaps after reading this book, one of you will not avert your eyes as you meet an obviously sick person mumbling and muttering as he or she approaches you, with dishevelled clothes and a blank cast to the eyes. You may even pause for a second or two, look that person straight in the eye, and smile as if to say," I know you're here. You matter."

Then, perhaps, my four decades of residing in Hell will have been worth it after all.

**Jane Wanklin**

# Chapter One

# *Childhood Threads*

As the afternoon slid soporifically toward evening, I lay motionless and numb under a white blanket. Threadbare curtains shaded my room from the sun's glare, and the institutional bed felt stiff and immobile under my pathetically shrunken body. Breathing was difficult; each small, staccato gasp fought to escape lungs that had nearly ceased to function.

Sweat beaded constantly upon slightly twitching hands as the process of withdrawal from life unfolded and I knew, with the stilted emotions of the semi-conscious, that I was going to die.

There was no fear, no twinges of wild panic fluttering against my protruding ribcage; simply a delicious, comforting rush of calm. It was almost over. The starvation process neared completion and it felt right. It was not, despite everything I'd been taught and had read over the years, a bad thing.

Here, in early November of 1993, I suddenly snapped out of suicide mode just long enough to reflect, somewhat sadly, upon the inescapable fact that thirty-eight years of fierce and stubborn struggling from within a self-destructive psyche were about to end like this: Quietly, uneventfully, and in a small observation room at the London Psychiatric Hospital.

Why did it have to be this way?

\*　　\*　　\*　　\*　　\*　　\*　　\*　　\*

The first few years of my life certainly fell far short of notable or exceptional. I was born on April twenty-second, 1955 in London, Ontario, a comfortable, nondescript city which was, and still is, completely overshadowed by the flashy cosmopolitan mystique emanating from Toronto, a scant one hundred twenty miles east.

I learned to talk quite early, at six months, but was a little slow with the walking thing. (Mom always said that it was because I spent all my time sitting around and yakking). I developed a rather precocious fascination with words and language and would either be rapturously in love with the sound of a particular word, or I'd simply hate it. I was also a snotty little bitch at times, giving my poor mother a look of total disgust at three when she suggested that I scribble on old newspaper. I guess I expected an expensive sketch pad from the art store or something.

My parents had married in February of 1954, when my mom, Marion Jean, was a twenty-seven-year-old registered nurse, and Dad, James Malcolm, a year her senior, was employed at theUniversity of Western Ontario. According to Mom, they'd been very much in love at the time of their wedding, but things had fallen apart soon afterward, within a year, actually. She'd had second thoughts about the marriage a week before and wondered grimly if she'd be able to tolerate Dad's long periods of silence.

But Mom wanted children, complete with the suburban house, manicured lawn, picket fence; the whole nine yards. Remember this was the mid-1950's and women's minds were supposed to work that way then.

Well, after being the sole object of my parents' affection and devotion for nearly two blissful years, my brother, Robert James, made his grand entrance on January twenty-seventh, 1957. After plotting deviously to do away with this bratty little upstart for a few months or so, going so far as to suggest cutting him up into small pieces with carrots and potatoes and then eating him, I resolved that having Bobby around wasn't such a bad idea after all. He might prove to be an interesting family pet. Of course, after he learned to talk, the curious creature became even more appealing, and we bonded firmly and lovingly, secure in our love for one another and sharing everything.

Bobby and I looked more like twins than siblings who were nearly two years apart in age. Although I had been born with an unruly shock of black hair and he with whitish blond, it pretty much evened out in several years to light brown for both of us. I was small for my age, so by the time he was three and I five, we were of equal height. Add to this the fact that both of us possessed identical facial expressions and our paternal grandmother dressed us in matching homemade outfits and you had the formula for the twin theory.

I suppose it should have irked me that people thought we were the same age, as children always struggle to appear older and more mature, but it really wasn't a concern at all. The truth is, I never actually thought about it that way. I was pleased that I looked so much like Bobby, for even as a small child, I felt inferior to him.

Not only that, but I vividly recall being tormented by severe bouts of anxiety, which had no basis in reality. It seemed as though something horrific was about to happen and that there was nothing I could do to stop it. These panic attacks manifested themselves as dark phobias and would haunt me throughout my childhood. The worst period was during my seventh year, when I'd awaken with a cry of terror late at night, certain that I smelled smoke and that the house was on fire.

My long-suffering parents would have to take me from room to room until the entire place was searched thoroughly before I calmed down enough to return to my bed. Petrified of fire with its savage, destructive flames that had the potential to reduce an entire forest to smoking embers in a matter of days, I couldn't even bring myself to watch it on television from the safe haven of the living room couch.

I suppose the other disturbing feature which defined those early years in the sterile, suburban netherworld was my bizarre introduction into the tepid world of self-abuse. I remember the day it all began as clearly as if it were last week.

One summer afternoon in 1959 Bobby and I sat playing idly in the living room as our mother dutifully ironed nearby. Mom had warned us repeatedly not to touch or go anywhere near the iron when it was turned on, as it had the potential to burn quite severely.

Mom left the room briefly to put a few crisply-ironed garments away. I found my curious blue eyes turning onto the forbidden object of fascination as it sat perched atop the ironing board, seeming to smirk at me.

"It can't be all that hot," I thought mischievously, moving toward it stealthily. I felt my pulse quicken and watched Bobby out of the corner of my eye as he continued playing with his plastic trucks.

Suddenly, as if I were watching something detached from my body, my hand darted toward the iron. Before I even realized it, felt my right index and middle finger pressed into the scorching, hot metal object.

After a brief pause, the savage pain assailed me like something inhuman. I bit down hard on my tongue to keep from screaming and forced the injured hand into a tight fist, just as Mom returned, smiling amiably. Her face fell a little as she must have seen a slightly contorted look around my mouth. "She can't suspect!" I thought, panicking. "She'll be really mad at me."

"Janie, is something wrong?" Her voice sliced into my pain. I could no longer hold back the sobs that were turning me inside out. They burst from the depths of my gut and shook every fibre as hot tears splashed onto the carpet. Bobby looked up, startled.

"What on earth is the matter with you?" Mom's voice rose an octave or so. I knew I had to think of something fast, or she'd know the awful truth, that I'd disobeyed her.

"Bobby hit me with his fire engine." The bold-faced lie popped out of my mouth before I'd consciously formulated it. I was very much afraid of Mom's anger, which could be quite spectacular at times.

Bobby's eyes opened wide with surprise and disbelief. "No I didn't. No I didn't, mommy!" Our exasperated mother then promptly sent the poor little guy to his room, never suspecting that her daughter would be falsely accusing him of a crime he didn't commit.

I then slunk dejectedly off to my room and crouched on my bed, rocking rhythmically back and forth and hitting my head against the wall in an effort to cope with the brutal agony.

Then, after about twenty minutes or so, I noticed something that could only be described as oddly positive about the pain. Although it was startling and relentless, it served a somewhat beneficial purpose: It distracted me from the constant, dull ache that was ever-present. It wasn't really a hurt, but more of a sadness.

At that young age, I had no way of knowing that it was depression and psychological turmoil. I only knew that it felt bad and the burnt fingertips got me liberated from it for awhile. Thus began a harrowing journey into self-induced torture that would go on for the next thirty-six years. I was four years old.

\* \* \* \* \* \* \* \* \* \* \*

Nursery school was benign and pleasant, but kindergarten proved to be another matter altogether. Our class was virtually held captive by a rather demented, totalitarian harpy whose massive girth was matched by an equally colossal mouth that roared. She behaved like some kind of all-controlling maniac who obviously got her jollies by striking fear into the hearts of five-year-olds.

In her defense, I'll state that she was probably an extremely unhappy and sick person who should never have been allowed to continue teaching. However, in those days, that kind of thing was not unusual. I really don't think people like that are in teaching positions today for that length of time, what with all the investigations into incidents of child abuse. But this was the early 1960's. She likely should have been on medication, or even hospitalized.

She would play all sorts of head games with us, picking favourites to lavish praise upon and despising others, myself included. This certainly didn't do a hell of a lot for my self-esteem, when the woman would hold up a picture I'd drawn of a houseboat and sneer mockingly, "Look, class, Jane did a picture of a house in the water. Jane's retarded, you know. She doesn't know that a house belongs on dry land." Some of the kids had laughed, but more out of nervousness than anything malicious toward me. We were all afraid of her, even the children she liked, for they feared she'd suddenly turn vicious.

How I survived that nightmare, I don't really know. I was overwhelmingly relieved when the last day of school arrived, as if the weight of the world had been lifted from my bony shoulders. Freedom from slavery and oppression at last!

Bobby desperately wanted to go to school too and sort of got his wish. While I was in Kindergarten Hell, he appeared on Miss Dorothy's Romper Room. The poor little guy was so nervous and confused with the garish lights and cameras that he got hopelessly befuddled. From then onward, he was given the rather demoralizing label of "Pokey" on the air, no less.

I don't think that Bobby was carried away with rapture over his television debut. It amazes me that the show is still going strong today, thirty-five years later. There's just no accounting for the gullibility of the public, I guess.

Both of us fared much better the following year, when Bobby entered nursery school and I left Kensal Park Public School for grade one at Woodland Heights. The school was only a half-mile up on Springbank Drive. It was small, but pleasant, and I made some good friends, most notably a girl named Darlene D. who walked with me to school every day.

I had a wonderful teacher and took delight in reading and learning. The only down side to the year was the school bully, Sally, who took delight in beating me up and stealing my recess snacks every day. I despised this pug-faced little brat, but resigned myself to getting pummelled regularly and relinquishing my cookies. Some things in life, I figured, were simply to be accepted. It was a philosophy with which I was to get extremely well acquainted over the years.

This was to be our family's last year in London for awhile, for our father got a teaching position at Dalhousie University in Halifax, Nova Scotia for September of 1962. We made plans, therefore, to head for the East coast early in June, after school ended for the year.

I don't remember feeling particularly bad about the proposed move, exactly, except for the somewhat dismal fact that we'd be leaving our grandparents. We didn't see our paternal grandparents that often, as they lived in Waterloo and our parents didn't own a car to travel there, so we only visited a couple of times a year. It was another matter with Grandma and Grandpa Colerick.

Bobby and I loved visiting them in their great, comfortable, kid-proof house at 619 Talbot Street. Nearly every weekend, we'd pack our little suitcases and truck on over to spend a couple of days while our parents worked.

Grandma was loving and strong-minded, and sometimes didn't agree with the way Mom and Dad were raising us, figuring that Dad was far too lenient. Yes, Bobby and I were the unfortunate products of that idiotic Dr. Spock and his twisted methods of child-rearing. These advocated permissiveness, permissiveness, and more permissiveness. Kids don't want that at all, in actual fact. They want discipline to offer the warm security that they are loved and cared about.

Grandpa Colerick was a dear soul. We adored him, climbing all over this big, affectionate man who looked so much like Walt Disney that some people had to look twice. He reciprocated our adoration ten-fold, lavishing sloppy, wet kisses on us and giving us toys, candy and other little trinkets, for no reason other than to make us feel truly welcome.

Mom had always been very close to her father, and had had to live in fear for his safety for four years when Grandpa went overseas in 1941 to man an anti-aircraft vessel during World War II. When he left, Mom was fourteen and upon his triumphant return, she had been an eighteen-year-old young woman. It must have been terrible for them to be separated like that, in such life-threatening circumstances.

Edward Henry Colerick was a man who had an indefatigable sense of humour, and had more jokes than there are holes in the Albert Hall. I know that's what got him through traumatic events like his brother's death, at thirty-four from Hodgkin's Disease, the Depression, when all their furniture and belongings were repossessed, that awful war, and bouts with unemployment. He just refused to think of himself as having any major problems and if they ever proved to be overwhelming, he'd just recall other events in his life that had been even worse.

He had a voracious appetite for food, classical music and a tremendous affection for his family. I loved that man passionately, with his enthusiastic bear hugs and that bottomless pit of a heart. What I wouldn't give to have both him and Grandma living with us today, happy and healthy.

I know I would have been in even more dire straits if it hadn't been for Grandma and Grandpa in those early days of my childhood. I had this nagging sense of dread a great deal of the time and didn't really feel wanted by our parents However, I knew that I could retreat to the haven of 619 Talbot Street and everything would be okay.

Now we were going to be fifteen hundred miles away from this paradise on earth and Bobby and I would be on our own for the first time since we were born.

# Chapter Two

# The Maritime Years

When our family moved to Halifax in June of 1962, we weren't exactly greeted with a plush, red welcoming carpet by the neighbourhood children on Abbott Drive. They resented us moving into the Shaw's home and "taking over", so Bobby and I stuck close together for quite awhile.

Ron and Freida pummelled us verbally with talk of how great and flawless our predecessors had been and sneered at our efforts to win their trust and affection. The O'Hara's lived next door, a pleasant, outgoing couple with three children, David, Daryl and Donna. Donna was a year my senior, a skinny, grinning kid with a spectacular splash of freckles and a penchant for mischief. She took pity on me one afternoon as I sat glumly with Bob on her swing set and she blithely offered me a cookie.

"Not unless my brother can have one too", I replied, fixing her with my steady gaze. This caused Donna to erupt in peals of laughter. She never forgot that and it impressed her no end that the two of us were so close.

As the summer wore on, Bob met another boy his age, named George, a short, cuddly, precocious kid who lived up the street. He, thankfully, didn't know the Shaw children. When my brother began to spend more time with George, I grew rather sad and despondent I was glad when September arrived and we made our way to St. Andrew's Public School for our first day of class. I was in grade two, and had a motherly, grey-haired teacher named Mrs. Hillis. I liked her immediately, as she responded favourably to my eagerness to learn and express myself.

The other kids seemed to approve of my presence and several of the boys took a shy interest in me. Harry, who looked like a cross between Ernie from My Three Sons and Jerry Lewis in The Nutty Professor. He joked incessantly and I couldn't help noticing how tight he wore his pants. There was nothing sexually precocious in my interest, just amusement that he was such an amazing extrovert and treated me like a close, personal buddy.

I was somewhat shy, but slowly, Harry drew me out of my shell. Davie was short and stocky, with a blond brushcut and a self-deprecating manner, and he could usually be seen hanging around with Harry. They were dubbed "Heckle and Jeckle" and the girls in our class would run screaming and hollering when the duo approached them with water pistols firing wildly.

Beatrice had a ribald, savvy nature and even had the nerve to tell the teacher off on occasion. She was cute, vivacious, with sparkling green eyes and large dimples. Her mother dressed her like a little Kewpie doll. Beatrice teased me for working hard and doing everything I was told.

Charlene was as quiet and introverted as Beatrice was forward and bold. She was pretty, rather plump, with large, sombre eyes. She rarely took part in our extracurricular activities, but I liked her. Since my seat was right in front of hers, we talked together a great deal.

The rest of the class was pleasant and non-threatening, and after several weeks, I relaxed completely in the stimulating atmosphere. I really got into my studies, particularly English.

Bob was in kindergarten and resigned himself to it after awhile. Luckily, he had George, so the two of them walked to and from school together.

I seemed to have gotten over my anxiety about the house being on fire, for at seven I was far too old to go running to Mommy and Daddy everytime I felt nervous or tense.

My first boyfriend in Halifax turned out to be smiling, affable Petey, a devotee of Hockey Night in Canada, Coca Cola, and Red Skelton. He did wonderful Red Skelton impersonations, and watched the comedian's show every week without fail to pick up new tips.

We goofed around a great deal and were occasionally told by Mrs. Hillis to "settle down". He had a cleft in his chin like Kirk Douglas and a mass of dark, wavy hair, and we huddled together on the playground at recess and kissed one another on the cheek.

One cold, winter day, Petey came rushing into the classroom from outside, gasping and crying. He'd run all the way to school and gotten too much frigid air in his young lungs. I was really worried about him and whimpered as the teacher tried to calm him down. That stayed with me for the next thirty-three years, because I despised seeing someone I cared about suffering, even then.

As the year drew to a close, I grew extremely fearful with apprehension, for it was announced that our grade three teacher would be the dreaded Miss Killiam. Killiam looked like Eleanor Roosevelt, only much uglier, with a nasty, ferocious sneer and a reputation for giving pupils the strap.

This was a thick, leather thong with a red stripe down the centre and was used to whack a child's palm until it turned red, swollen and bloody. Corporal punishment was quite legal in those days, in Halifax, anyway, and parents reluctantly put their loved ones in the care and disciplinary action of adults who really should have known better.

I remember going to bed every night that summer and praying desperately to God to let me have Mrs. Hillis again for a teacher in grade three. My prayers went unanswered, though, for in September of 1963, I stepped into the classroom and looked upon the tall, hunched, scowly woman who would be my tormentor for nearly ten months.

We were all terrified of Miss Killiam and watched in stupefied horror as crying, pleading pupils were dragged out in the hall to be viciously strapped into submission. They'd return, tear-stained, red-faced and holding their damaged, pathetic hands while ol' Fergie snarled, "That'll teach ya! Now sit down and behave yourselves!"

One morning, my dear Petey got it, and it nearly tore me up inside to hear his frightful moaning and sobbing out in the echoing corridor. I hated that creature and fantasized that she got hit by a truck on the way to school.

I suffered a great many nightmares that year and at eight years of age felt suddenly very old and jaded. I became withdrawn, escaping into my schoolwork and refusing to communicate with my parents. Then, on November twenty-second, President John F. Kennedy was assassinated in Dallas. I returned home after school to see both Mom and Dad in the living room, shaking their heads in disbelief.

It had just been announced on the television that a very special, peaceloving man had died from gunshot wounds to the head. I saw the funeral played out in front of me, with little John John saluting his father's flag-shrouded coffin. I suddenly felt as though I was being swallowed up by a choking chasm of despair.

What kind of world were we growing up in?

I met a small, delicate red-headed girl that year, named Joan. She was a loving, compassionate child, but there was something intensely melancholy about her. I noticed that Killiam was unusually kind and gentle to her, and we all marvelled at the way it seemed that Joan could seemingly do no wrong. She was sick a great deal and missed many days of school. Sometimes she'd put her head down on her desk, too weak to hold it upright.

One morning, I arrived at the playground to hear a bunch of older girls singing, in loud, raucous tones, "She loves you Ya, Ya, Ya" and wondered what the heck was going on. Joan ran up to me, brimming over with excitement and enthusiasm. "Did you see Ed Sullivan last night?! They had this rock and roll band on called the Beatles! They looked really weird, with this long hair and they were jumping around like crazy!"

"No, we're not allowed to stay up that late", I answered, regretting that I'd missed something intriguing. Joan really took to the Beatles Her parents bought her tons of Beatles paraphernalia, including 45's, posters and little dolls in the group's likeness. Paul McCartney was her favourite and she dreamed of marrying him one day.

I went home to her small, dilapidated townhouse on Reddon Avenue and wondered how such a poverty-stricken family could afford to lavish expensive gifts upon their daughter. Then I began to put the pieces of the puzzle together.

My suspicions were confirmed one day when Joan got sick in class and had to be sent home. She missed attending my birthday party, something she had been greatly anticipating. Her family then suddenly packed up and moved far away without a trace or word of farewell.

Then I knew the awful truth: Joan, so kind and sympathetic to everyone else, had probably been dying of some dreaded disease. That was why Killiam was nice to her, her family gave her everything her heart desired and why they'd mysteriously vanished. I felt very sad, and wished that it had been me who had died and not my dear friend.

I hung around with a tall, gawky classmate named Mary Ann, who emulated everything I said and did. Instead of making me feel good, this extremely annoyed me.

Then my heart was sent into spasms when tall, dark and

devastatingly handsome Alan took an interest in me and we began to "go steady". Alan was Jewish and his parents were absolutely horrified to learn that their son was seeing a "little shiksa". His mother phoned Mom and implored her to discourage me from getting so close to him, but mom thought that this was ludicrous. She just told her, in exasperated tones, "But they're just children!" and decided to ignore the whole matter.

Alan scared the hell out of me one day when he said, "Look up at the sky. See those clouds? That's a sign that the world's going to end tonight." I believed him, and after I went to bed, I hugged my parents so tightly that they reacted with, "Why, what's going on with you this evening?"

"Nothing", I replied, not wanting to alarm them and went into Bob's room to kiss my dear brother farewell. I was sadly resigned, because, after all, Alan knew everything and if he said it was the end of the world then it must surely be.

I don't recall ever feeling so filled with joy and relief I was the next day when I awoke to the yellow sunshine pouring into my bedroom. "Thank you, God!" I screamed, "Thank you for sparing all of us!"

I never actually got the strap in grade three, but Killiam psychologically tormented me a great deal, using fear and apprehension that knew no bounds. One day, I drew a picture of her, a ridiculous caricature, with "Killer Killiam the Monster" scrawled underneath. When I passed it to one of my classmates, she saw me out of the corner of her eye and snatched the yellow piece of paper out of my clenched fist.

"What's this!?" she fumed, shaking her meaty finger in my reddening face. "Is this supposed to be funny, young lady? You will stay in after school and get the punishment that's coming to you."

I knew what the punishment would be, and it made me feel sick. Running home from school at noon, I begged mom to let me stay there for the rest of the day. She thought that I would only be made to write lines on the blackboard, but I knew better. I spent the afternoon in sheer agony, waiting for the dastardly deed to be meted out to me at three thirty.

Well, she didn't give me the strap, or any other punishment for that matter. She just told me never to make drawings like that again or I'd really "get it for sure". That's how she controlled me, by making threats and causing me to recoil in fear.

Something happened to me that year, despite the Beatles diversion of the spring, something strange and terrifying. All of a sudden, I didn't feel like a child anymore and I definitely didn't feel safe. I never would again.

Grade four was a marked improvement, with a pleasant-natured, attractive teacher named Miss Franklin and a solid, rewarding friendship with a pretty, long-haired classmate named Pamela. I'd met Pammy two years before, when she called for me at our house to "come out and play". Then, I didn't see her again until 1964.

We had a lot of fun together. She introduced me to her two brothers and sister, Dennis, Norma and adorable, curly-haired Nick. Her parents were extremely strict, but I couldn't help noticing how much her father looked like actor David Hedison, from the television series, "Voyage To the Bottom of the Sea". It was one of our favourite shows.

I had a wild crush on Hedison and Pammy teased me mercilessly, saying that I had too vivid an imagination and that he was "way too old" for me. I wrote a lot of short stories that year, something I'd been doing for several years, and Miss Franklin would sometimes read them aloud to the rest of the class. This both thrilled and embarrassed me and I would sit with my head buried in my arms, waiting for her to finish.

Bob had gotten very close to George, who excelled in school and spoke like a miniature adult. I was a little jealous of their friendship, for I still wanted my brother all to myself.

In the meantime, our family went for many Sunday outings to places like Point Pleasant Park, Peggy's Cove and Cape Breton's Cabot Trail. Dad cooked hamburgers and hotdogs on a Coleman stove. He and mom loved watching us playing happily on the beach, in the woods and clambering over the smooth, white rocks at Peggy's Cove lighthouse.

In the summer of 1964, we rented a cottage at Montague on Prince Edward Island. We had a wonderful time, swimming, rafting, playing in a big treehouse and visiting Anne of Green Gables home. One afternoon, Bob got badly stung by a disgruntled jellyfish that he accidently stepped on while pulling our raft in the ocean. He screamed in agony while Mom picked off the bloodsucking red strips from his pale, thin leg. I felt so sorry for him and couldn't help wondering why he'd gotten attacked and not me.

Our family was happiest and closest during these summers and I cherish them a great deal. Mom and Dad seemed happier and more relaxed with one another when we were in Nova Scotia. They spent Saturday nights entertaining friends, going to movies with the McCluskies and square dancing. Mom often wonders wistfully what would have happened to all of us if we'd stayed in Halifax, but I always respond that none of us have any way of predicting that.

We had a series of friendly, playful babysitters during those six years, beginning with a thirteen-year-old girl named Ginger back in 1962. She loved to play "fox and the chickens" with us and let us stay up really late watching movies like "The Courtship of Eddie's Father" on television. She used to echo Carolyn's remark of "You and your brother are so close" and told us about her large family of eight brothers and sisters.

One summer, when both our parents were working, we had two sisters come in to take care of us, Ruth and Mandy.
Ruth was thin, quiet and shy, while sister Mandy was robust, freckled and outgoing. We loved them both, and after the Monkees burst on the scene in 1966, they'd bring the band's albums over for us to enjoy.

Bob and I were both quite enamoured of the Monkees, more so than the Beatles and watched their series faithfully every week. Mickey Dolenz was my favourite, so I abandoned David Hedison for the grinning, goofy and extraordinarily cute rock and roll drummer.

Music had gradually become a mainstay of my life, even more so than Bob's, who generally followed me in whatever direction my tastes took me. I enjoyed the Mamas and the Papas, Bob Dylan, Simon and Garfunkel and the Everly Brothers, although I wouldn't get heavily involved with the latters' work until 1970.

The Nashes, friends and colleagues of Dad's, had a daughter my age named Leslie. She got me interested in Joan Baez. Leslie looked a lot like the dreamy, revolutionary Baez herself, with long, thick brown hair parted in the middle and a wide-open, steady gaze.

I liked her, but thought that Mom grew to favour her over me. She would speak of how polite Leslie was and "such a good girl to eat all her vegetables". I was shaping up to be an extremely insecure kid, with a deplorable self-image.

Grade five brought a new teacher, Mrs. McDonald, a sentimental, grey-haired woman who seemed to have a great many health problems. She missed a lot of time and would often be forced to sit down during her lessons and hold her head in her hands without speaking. She would sometimes get quite silly, making loud jokes about my midi blouse, saying I looked like Popeye and giggling like one of us kids.

In retrospect, I believe that poor Mrs. McDonald suffered from some sort of mental illness, alternating between giddy highs and sadly-reflective lows. It would be another twelve years before I would encounter many Mrs. McDonalds in the psychiatric hospitals.

I was still going steady with Alan, but was getting more intensely involved with my schoolwork in an effort to escape a growing sense of sadness that was overtaking me, step by step. I didn't know where this was coming from, but Pammy noticed my mood changes and did her best to try to jostle me out of them. I told her I always wanted to be a little boy, not from any desire other than the one born of feeling that my brother was more deeply loved than I.

I didn't like wearing dresses and fidgeted nervously while Mom outfitted me as if I was some kind of plastic Barbie doll. She loved to take me shopping at the "Tots to Teens" store and preferred the hideous colour pink to any other. I thought I looked intensely ugly and that she was trying to camouflage my physical shortcomings with crinolines, frills, buttons and bows. It would be a truly glorious day, I thought to myself, when I could choose my own clothes and wear corduroy pants like Bob if I desired.

Pammy was taller than I, and somewhat slimmer. I wasn't overweight, but as I approached the age of twelve and the onset of puberty, I got a little chunky. In 1967, I gave up candy and gum for Lent and felt very virtuous when I saw my brother, Pammy, and my other friends chomping on chocolate bars, licorice and black balls. Maybe I'd look more like the svelte, willowy Pammy by Easter. The stage was being set for many future years of eating disorders.

When I was in grade six, I developed an all-consuming, mad passion for the circus. It all began when I saw pictures of a ten-year-old Mickey Dolenz dressed as television's "Circus Boy", a popular series in the 1950's. After my attention was zapped into the world of sawdust, clowns, wild animals and Big Top barkers, I became obsessed. My bedroom walls were festooned with circus posters, I drew bright, colourful pictures of painted clown faces and strongmen and began to write furiously about children who ran away to join the Greatest Show on Earth.

I wrote my first novel at twelve, a three hundred-page epic about circus life at the turn of the century. I'd read all of the Enid Blyton books on the circus, as well as an intriguing work of Noel Streetfield's entitled "Come to the Circus". It was about two orphaned children who are adopted by a travelling troupe. I wanted to write as well as Streetfield and must confess as to practically plagiarizing parts of her book, not word for word exactly, but certainly employing similar ideas and plot structures. The book took four months to complete and I'd sit up in bed until three AM many nights, writing away furiously and hoping that I'd be published before I reached my teens.

A year before, I sent a hand-written television play to the CBC, based on their 1965-66 series entitled,"Mystery Maker". It was about a little boy named Zoltan McNamera who lived in an underground cavern, orphaned years before and afraid to show himself to the world.

I got an encouraging letter from someone at the CBC network named Robert Gibbons who said, among other things, that I had "an amazing talent for an eleven-year-old" and that I should be patient and "someday everything would click and fall into place". I hoarded this letter possessively, refusing to show it to my parents.

I'm not sure why I did this, other than perhaps I figured that they'd laugh at me. I was very secretive about my writing and my life in general for that matter. I don't think I ever showed them any of my childhood work and I don't believe that they were aware of how hard I was flogging away at it.

I'd started taking piano lessons at age seven. By the age of twelve, I entered a music festival, placing second. The name of the piece was "Grandmother's Waltz". Though I felt invigorated by the applause, it was highly unnerving and I brimmed over with stagefright.

That year, I won a set of Britannica Junior Encyclopedia by writing an essay on marching bands for our newspaper. I'd been fitted with braces the previous year and refused to smile with my mouth open when they photographed me. I felt that they made me look absolutely frightening. Then, after winning a certificate from Jack and Jill magazine for finishing a story and having it published, I jokingly remarked to Pammy that I hoped I hadn't "peaked at twelve" and that it would be all downhill from that point on.

I was at my best while writing, for it gave me a high that nothing else could. I relished the idea of rushing home from school, shutting myself in my room and making up stories until it was time to do my homework. I still have some of them and smile at the innocence and naivete I held onto in those days.

Pammy and I both excelled academically in grade six and were told we'd be entering the Major Work Class at Westmount Public School at the beginning of junior high. We were pleased, but somewhat apprehensive at acquiring such an advanced workload.

Both sets of grandparents visited us in Halifax several times and we made a few trips back to London for a couple of Christmases. We travelled by train and loved the idea of sleeping and eating while clicking rapidly along on endless steel tracks. It was a long journey, but we were happy to see those beloved people and be thoroughly overcome with welcome and love.

Grade seven proved to be a jolting example of culture shock of the extreme academic kind for Pammy and me. After being the top students at St. Andrew's, we were starting to fall behind at Westmount early on in the year.

Our classmates were truly frightening, with their incredible poise, intelligence and verbal cuity, particularly a sharp-witted, charismatic girl named Glenda. She seemed more like a world-wise, strikingly-mature adult than a twelve-year-old child and possessed an amazing vocabulary. That girl never received anything lower than an A in any subject, so Pammy and I resigned ourselves to being the "token dummies".

Both of us were excruciatingly shy and with all these articulate, brilliant eggheads surrounding us every day, it was hard to feel very good about ourselves.

Pammy, in particular, really crawled into herself that year and would stammer and stutter painfully whenever she was asked to stand up and recite anything. It was as though something in her head had clicked off and she couldn't access any thoughts or ideas lying buried inside. I found things a little easier, but even so, it became quite obvious that we were not going to be stellar students.

Pammy's difficulties stemmed from a particularly trying home life, where she was thwarted rudely by her parents everytime she tried to assert herself and become more autonomous or independent. Her father didn't want to see his little girl growing up at all and kept her in line with verbal abuse and nasty threats.

I hated the way they made her cry and forced her to behave like a whimpering little puppy in their presence. Pammy had recently acquired a new baby sister, Elizabeth, and was made to stay home and babysit a great deal. I figured that either That girl's parents would have to loosen their chokehold on their daughter, or she would drastically rebel one day.

When I was eleven and Bob nine, we got an adorable little white and brownish kitten, which we called Taffy. We'd befriended the firemen down the street. When their large female gave birth to five tiny ones, we carried one home, held it up with big, pleading eyes and cooed in unison, "Can we keep it? Please?" Our parents relented, even though Dad was allergic to cats.

Taffy became the best thing to happen to me. He had six toes on each paw, which gave him an endearingly awkward look, and followed Bob and I around everywhere. I dearly loved that cat, and lavished him with treats and tiny gifts. Many nights, I'd cuddle Taffy next to me in bed and feel invigorated by his steady, strong purring. I even wrote a short story about him called simply, "My True Love".

Taffy sat curled up on my bed and watched me pouring over my major work studies. One story in a collection of short fiction was entitled "All Summer in a Day", by Ray Bradbury and it really got to me. It was about a society on a faraway planet that had lived in the dismal shadow of constant rainfall for many years. One day, the people learned that the sun would finally emerge for a scant twenty-four-hour period and one little girl in particular was absolutely elated. Then, she got trapped in dark building underground and ended up missing the whole event. That sad tale spoke to me in ways that no other piece of literature ever had, for in some respects I felt like that poor little child, being deprived of the life-giving light of hope all her life and then somehow missing her big chance.

That year, we were introduced to the big, bad world and its many ills. They included the Vietnam war, the growing drug problem and the gradual disillusionment of youth for the society in which it was forced to exist. Pammy and I were morbidly fasci-

nated by these traumatic events, which we couldn't really comprehend and grew despondent that our brothers might one day have to
go over to be viciously killed.

Even our music seemed to be acquiring a cynical, bitter edge,
one that alternately repulsed and intrigued us. Drug-infused rock
from artists like Jimi Hendrix and the Who were permeating the
airwaves in 1967, urging youth to forego our parents' misguided
ideals and develop a world of "love and happiness through experience and acid".

None of the kids in our class had experimented with drugs
before their thirteenth birthdays. We were too paralyzed with fear
to indulge. Besides, the schoolwork was so difficult that we needed
to be at full thinking capacity if we wanted to make it to grade eight.
I didn't like the way my life was developing. I found myself
constantly battling a feeling of malaise, fighting to keep my head
above water and look for something meaningful on which to grasp.
Did everyone else feel my growing disenchantment for life?

I was afraid to tell my parents how much I hated school, or
that I feared I wouldn't pass. Teachers in the past had stated on my
report cards that I was an exceptional student, but seemed to have
some difficulties concentrating. They didn't know what to make of
this, since there didn't seem to be anything wrong with me. The
truth was, I hid a lot from Mom and Dad and kept my negativity
deeply submerged. It would not fully show itself to their shocked
and bewildered eyes for another two years.

Miss Jefferson was our homeroom teacher, a flighty, pink-
cheeked blonde who had the potential to really lose it when she got
angry. The rest of the time she was sweet and smiling and assured
some of us that we would be "great leaders someday". The other
teachers were alright, I suppose, in a nondescript kind of way, but
demanded a lot from us.

Once, I stayed up all night to furiously devour four novels
before a big test the next morning. I'd left all my reading until the
last minute, a habit into which I was quickly sliding. By six AM, I
knew that I'd never complete The Jungle Book by seven thirty.
"I'm going to flunk for sure," I thought unhappily, wondering if
Pammy got her studying done.

As it turned out, I knew enough to pass the difficult test, but
unfortunately, I didn't learn from my mistakes. I ended up writing a
big term paper for science the night before as well and refused to

look at the grade when it was handed back to me. Some things are better left unknown, I reasoned.

Final exams were simply dreadful and I panicked during the geography one, blanking out for an hour and having to leave three essay questions incomplete. For one thing, I'd been totally rattled two months before when Martin Luther King, Jr. was cruelly assassinated on April fourth, 1968 and thought the world was finally losing its collective mind." Who'd want to kill a peacemaker?" I asked Pammy, staring at photos of the slain
civil rights leader.

"Lots of people", she replied solemnly. "I think we're going to have to grow up real fast from now on." She was right, for, two months later, Senator Robert F. Kennedy was killed in Los Angeles. I was particularly devastated by this senseless act of violence, since I'd grown quite enamoured of the charismatic politician and was following his Presidential campaign closely. I came downstairs on the morning of June fifth to find Mom and Dad standing in front of the radio, looking tense and unhappy.

"Hey, what's wrong?" I asked, wondering at the long faces.

"Bobby Kennedy's been shot," Dad replied angrily and I felt my knees buckle under me.

"What?! Why? What the hell's going on?" I prayed all day that he would recover and watched with a feeling of sickness in my gut as the scene in the Ambassador Hotel was played out on the television at school all day.

"Now I know there's no hope for this world we're living in," I whispered to Pammy, "I can't see growing up in a place where good people keep getting blown away like this." When Kennedy died, just like his brother five years before, I suffered my first really deep depression and wouldn't emerge for a very long time.

Bob and I were informed that we'd be returning to London to live at the end of the month, as Dad had a new teaching position at The University of Western Ontario. We sat together on our last night in Halifax, watching Family Affair on our old black and white television, while cartons and suitcases lay strewn about us in the living room.

Buffy asked her Uncle Bill, "Do you know what it feels like to move away?" Bob turned to me and said sadly, "We know what it feels like, don't we?" I hugged him close and knew that, whatever happened, we'd face it together.

# Chapter Three

# 1968-1971:

# No Love-In For Our Family

It was difficult saying good-bye to what had been our reasonably happy home for seven years. When Pammy walked away from me for the last time, I had trouble choking back the tears.

Taffy did not weather the ride in the airplane's baggage department well, for he panicked wildly and tore off all his claws trying to escape the carrier. When we retrieved the frightened, trembling feline, his eyes were wide saucers and his ragged claws lay at the bottom of the case. I held the poor little animal in my arms, and promised him that nothing bad like that would ever happen to him again.

We moved to a small, plain-looking townhouse in a subdivision called Berkshire Village. Bob and I were not at all impressed with its red brick starkness. Oh yeah, I couldn't call him Bob anymore, for he decided that when we moved to London, he would use his middle name from then onward and be called "Jim" after his dad and Star Trek's "Jim Kirk".

So, Jim and I tried to settle down for the remainder of the summer in a veritable suburban wasteland that offered no breathtaking Maritime scenery and was totally bereft of any other companions.

We made our way one afternoon to the Berkshire Club, a beige, brick building that contained both an indoor and an outdoor pool, games room, tennis courts and a "teen room" where you could hang out and smoke, if you were between the ages of thirteen and nineteen.

We stuck together during those first few months, refusing to admit that we were terrified of being out of our element and facing a brave new world that did not bode terribly friendly to outsiders.

Mom went with us to the outdoor pool in the afternoons and we had a measure of fun diving, swimming and pretending she was the Great Whale and we were helpless, frightened minnows. It was the last time the three of us had any jolly, reckless good times for many years to come.

Although I was thirteen, I looked closer to eleven and was treated like a snotty-nosed brat by other neighbourhood kids. I had long, straight hair parted in the middle, as was the style of the day and was somewhat attractive but babyish with my round face and innocent, non-expressive eyes. Jim had started to let his hair grow longer and he looked rather cool, so he presented a more appealing, trendy image than I did.

However, the other children treated him badly, telling him that he had a "fairy face" and that he shouldn't be hanging around with his sister all the time. This caused him a great deal of unhappiness and propelled him to change his image after school began in September.

I found myself back at Woodland Heights Public School, where I'd attended grade one seven years before. It had changed a lot, having expanded somewhat and was full of hip, tough-talking kids, who smoked and used the "f" word with no sense of remorse.

My grade eight class was enormous, with over forty students and they, quite frankly, scared the daylights out of my severely over-protected heart. Pat was the quintessential hippie, a big, brazen girl with scraggly long hair, wild clothes and a penchant for doing drugs and making out with any guy who would look sideways at her.

I couldn't believe that a thirteen-year-old could live like that and recoiled from her instantly, fearing she would pressure me to drop acid or smoke dope in the washroom. The rest of the females in my class were basically cut from the same flower-strewn cloth. I decided that I would be very lonely and isolated that year.

The guys weren't much of an improvement. Tony, a dark, handsome boy, looked oddly dissipated for a young kid and refused to do his homework or follow orders. He snickered at Mr. Harrison, our homeroom teacher and called him a "stupid jerk" behind his back.

Paul, although appearing much the "wholesome jock type", was guilty by association in my books because he hung with Tony all the time. The only guy I found marginally palatable was a good-looking, beaming youngster named Shelby, who was of Dutch descent and seemed like a diligent, hard-working student.

During the first week of classes, Mr. Harrison instructed us to write the cliched, "How I Spent My Summer Vacation" essay and was quite impressed with mine. It was a serious, somewhat mournful dissertation upon the perils of moving to a different province and finding it hard to cope.

"You have a great deal of talent, not to mention the ability to make me feel," he told me, eyes smiling through his thick glasses. "Keep it up. You're going to be a real asset to this class".

That cheered me somewhat, but didn't compensate for the dismal sensation I had that told me that I was in for a lot of unpleasantness that term.

Fortunately, I met a soulmate a couple of weeks later in the form of large-eyed, quiet and rather pretty Karen, a pretty, long-haired twelve-year-old who'd just moved with her family from Belle River, a small resort town just outside of Windsor.

Karen and I hit it off right away, and we'd go over to her family's townhouse every afternoon following school to watch "Dark Shadows" with older sister Sheila and drink several cups of tea with plenty of milk. We despaired over the rampant sexual exploits of our classmates and the wild consumption of illicit drugs that was going on all around us. I desperately needed some stability in my life and Karen's family provided it.

Sheila, at sixteen, was pretty, vivacious and had a raucous, outgoing personality and a strong desire to be an actress. She had been totally captivated by show business as a child and loved to imitate movie start like Elizabeth Taylor and Zsa Zsa Gabor. I liked her a lot and she approved of my amateurish singing talents, which I'd developed alone in my room over the years. She taped me crooning songs like "Tammy" and "Blowing In the Wind" into her recorder.

Karen and I talked about the Monkees, Star Trek (which I liked and she said she would try to) and wondered about the future of humanity. Her parents were very close, a warm, loving couple who played games in the evenings with Glen, Cathy and eight-year-old sister Beverly and instilled strong Christian values in their children. I really missed that sense of family unity and admitted to Karen that I feared Jim and I were drifting apart there in Berkshire

Hell.

In truth, we were. Jim had gotten in with a bunch of neighbourhood toughs, like Kirk, Jason, Rory, Lennie and Reggie. The latter was a real juvenile delinquent, getting arrested periodically for breaking and entering. He is currently doing time in prison. They'd all get together at the Berkshire Club and plan out their various ways of defying authority.

Jim was happy to have finally been accepted and really needed the sense of belonging and oneness that those boys offered him with their loyalty and friendship. But I despised them and they figured I was the "loser sister", worthy of supreme contempt and ridicule.

These kids had no form of discipline or stability at home. Their parents were all divorced and they ran wild in the streets, devoid of any purpose or direction. Even my brother's music began to reflect his new, hardened lifestyle. He abandoned the fresh, innocent exuberance of The Monkees in favour of Black Sabbath, Jimi Hendrix and The Who. I refused to listen to those records and lost myself in Simon and Garfunkel and Joan Baez. We were at a stand-off point, toe-to-toe, and ultimately, he rejected me completely.

Meanwhile, our parents were having their own problems. Mom wanted to work and was dissatisfied in the small, plain townhouse environment. I felt sorry for her to a degree, but was too wrapped up in my own misery to offer any comfort.

Dad was happy enough paying only two hundred dollars per month rent and said the place was "just fine". But he got to escape to the university every day, while the three of us were stuck in this suburban ghetto.

I lost myself in Star Trek and music and spent all my free time with Karen. We were the social outcasts at school and were laughed and snickered at as we walked by. Jim's friends remarked to him, "How can you possibly be related to her?" and he felt obligated to giggle in agreement.

He was torn between loyalty to his sister and the compelling pull of peer pressure. It was 1968, after all and the world was on the brink of Something Really Powerful and Earth Shattering. Childhood trappings had to be shed for the brave new shining armour and I was completely unwilling to yield to it.

Karen and I moved in our solitary sphere, eschewing cultural pressures and demands and holding fast to our past securities, as well as the remnants of happier days. Maybe the world was moving closer to a torrential maelstrom, but we would grasp tightly to the elements of the past, no matter what.

School was unbearable and we were despised for our hard work and ambitious undertakings. If a project was graded a possible five points, we achieved six for our added efforts. The other kids dubbed us total losers, worthy of the utmost contempt.

But we persisted in being "browners", feeling that if we couldn't be popular, we'd at least be academic success stories. I found my studies terribly boring and easy after the Major Work Class and had to do extra reading to keep my brain cells alive and functioning.

By my fourteenth birthday, I was starting to feel very depressed, not having fully recovered from Bobby Kennedy's assassination. I needed something to grasp hold of to keep from drowning.

I discovered Cliff Robertson's Oscar-winning film, "Charly" and spent hours each day after school sitting alone in a darkened theatre, watching it over and over. Since I looked less than twelve, I got in for children's fare and so it would only cost me fifty cents to see it twice each afternoon.

In total, I saw it sixteen times, enthraled by the poignant, brilliant performance of a frustrated, mentally retarded man who got a ground-breaking operation to alert him to the world of intelligence and insight.

Then, in early June of 1969, I learned that Cliff Robertson would be appearing at the Capitol Theatre in Halifax for the premiere of his next film, "Too Late the Hero". Karen, Sheila and I decided we'd phone him there and talk to him. I adored Robertson, even though he was old enough to be my father and desperately wanted to tell him how much I loved "Charly". We spent the next five hours glued to the phone, after calling the theatre long distance and leaving a message for the actor.

He actually called back at eleven thirty PM after Mom, Dad and Jim urged us to "give it up." I talked to Robertson for about five minutes, sounding like the frantic, gasping teenybopper that I was. It made my day and I still think of it and smile, wondering why the hell a famous, Academy Award-winning actor wanted to talk to a silly fourteen-year-old girl miles away. That's just the kind of guy he was.

The next day, I had to read one of my compositions entitled, "The Blood-Curdling Death of Eb Slaughter", complete with Southern drawl, to the entire school. I was quite unhinged by the experience. Everyone liked it, but I didn't appreciate being on display like that. Mr. Harrison insisted, since it was the last day of school and he wanted to "show off" my writing talent. I was, nonetheless, very happy to see the end of that ego-deflating grade eight class and my less-than-illustrious public school career.

Karen and I spent the summer together, listened to a lot of music and I amassed quite a collection of 45's. She was a wonderful kid, so giving and warm, and accepted me with all my bizarre idiosyncracies.

Jim ran wild with his delinquent buddies and we barely spoke to one another. We just weren't travelling in the same dimensions anymore, and I missed the closeness we once shared.

I started high school that fall at Westminster Secondary School, and was quite befuddled by the vast number of students teeming in the halls. Sheila was in grade twelve and knew the ropes, so she guided Karen and me through the first harrowing days.

Then I got the ghastly news that Karen's family would be returning to Belle River at the end of September. I cringed at the thought of spending the year devoid of their friendship and support. As their car drove away on a dark, autumn night, I cried for hours, knowing that I was alone in a frightening sea of hungry sharks. What was I going to do now?

Grade nine proved to be somewhat better than grade eight, but just barely. Luckily, I met two friendly girls, Meike and Jackie, who offered me companionship and a buffer against the ravages of high school life.

Meike was of Dutch descent, a short, stocky, dark-haired girl with thick-lensed glasses and a wide-open smile. She was as insecure as I, afraid to plunge into the deep waters of sexual and drug experiences and preferring to hold onto the remains of a cherished childhood. So was Jackie, fair-haired, gap-toothed and gangly, who loved to laugh and make fun of the world and its inhabitants. If it weren't for these girls, I never would have survived the year intact.

The classes weren't difficult, in fact the work was pretty

simple and boring, but I welcomed the chance to develop some extracurricular friendships. Like Melody, Meike had extremely strict parents, who held onto her with a tight rein and made certain she did all her chores, homework and didn't stray too far away. Jackie folks were more relaxed and had a warm, close-knit quality that seemed to be lacking in my own homelife.

We all avoided the "harder" kids, and gravitated toward the more studious, simple-visioned ones. That was quite reassuring. There were too many scary things going on in the world for us to fully comprehend and digest, so we listened to our Simon and Garfunkel albums, drank tea and avoided temptations to smoke or try drugs.

Then Jackie became friendly with a hip, world-wise student named Wanda. and started to feel that Meike and I were "hopelessly passe". I didn't like Wanda and voiced my negative opinions to Jackie. She thought that I was being too harsh and judgmental, so I began to avoid her and stuck with Meike.

The other kids in our classes were truly a mixed bag. Cheryl, whose father was a well-known judge, felt I was a "lost cause" and ridiculed me openly. Rufus, a tall, skinny kid with big feet who came from Pakistan, proved to be the "class clown", joking constantly to offset his feelings of insecurity. All of them seemed bored and restless and adverse to studying. I felt I should work hard and make something of my empty life, so I buried myself in my schoolwork for the rest of the term.

I did well on my final exams and looked forward to grade ten, figuring that I had only four more years and then I could join CUSO (Canadian University Students Overseas) and teach English to people in the Philippines.

This was my big, altruistic goal and I picked the Philippines because it was far, far away. Cliff Robertson had gone there to film "Too Late the Hero" as well and that added to the allure. I existed in a dream world back then, totally apart from the reality of my situation. I longed for blissful escape and thought the faraway land in the South Pacific would take me far away from everything that was bothering me.

That summer, I went to visit Karen in Belle River, spending two weeks in a wonderful idyll on the shores of Lake St. Clair with a happy, loving family. When I returned, all hell broke loose.

I suddenly became aware that our family was a totally mal-functioning and miserable one. I sat in the middle of the living room, crying bitterly, hitting my fists on the floor and screaming, "I can't stand it here! There's no love in this family! You're nothing like the Karen's parents! You don't sit together in the evenings and play games with us! You don't love Jim and me! I don't want to live like this anymore!!"

Mom and Dad were extremely shaken and upset and tried to reason with their distraught teenage daughter. "What do you want us to do for you?" Mom asked as I sobbed uncontrollably.

"I don't know! I just don't know! But I'm so unhappy! I want things to be the way they were in Halifax!"

Dad couldn't handle any of this emotional stuff, so he left the room. Mom tried valiantly to calm me down, asking me over and over what could she do to make me happy?

But I just didn't know. I was painfully aware that my life was a total mess and felt that I wanted to die. Later, I took a kitchen knife and nicked my wrist, the first time I'd deliberately hurt myself. I watched the small droplets of blood dot the white enamel of the bathroom sink and thought to myself, "I wish I had the guts to really slice myself up bad."

But I didn't. Instead, I started pulling out all my eyelashes, until finally, they had all disappeared. I looked like one of those old-fashioned China dolls and Mom later grew alarmed at this obvious act of self-mutilation. She felt completely helpless as her unhappy daughter wandered about in her prison of despair and loneliness.

Grade ten didn't prove to be much of an improvement. I impulsively got my thick, long hair cut very short one day, so short that it looked as if I was in some sort of army recruiting camp. Mom wasn't particularly pleased about this, but I just didn't care any-more how I looked or what image I portrayed to a world that had obviously spurned me.

My homeroom teacher was a grinning, optimistic man who embodied the radical mien of the 1970's and applauded the students in the U.S. who rebelled against the Vietnam War and got them-selves arrested. I liked Mr. Stevens. but felt he thought me to be a hapless loser, so I didn't talk to him much.

There was one girl in my homeroom, Shelley, a chirpy, attractive redhead, who embodied everything I wasn't. She was popular, outgoing and had an amazing wardrobe. I found myself staring at her in an effort to emulate her ingratiating sense of cool. I couldn't, however, with my shorn hair and dowdy clothes.

I gained a lot of weight that year, eating out of a sense of emptiness. I despised my semi-corpulent appearance. All the other girls seemed so slim and attractive and here I was, a blimpy, ugly cow who couldn't even relate to my own brother.

I hated myself and sunk further into my despair. I never really reached overweight status, but I was fifteen pounds heavier than I'd been in grade nine and felt huge. The more miserable I was, the more I stuffed myself with junk food. Dad began to give me disparaging looks out of the corner of his eye.

Jim was thoroughly disgusted with me and ignored me whenever I entered the room. His friends, particularly Kirk, taunted me repeatedly and said I was "really gross".

I met Beverly that year, a plump, retiring girl with the innate ability to articulate well despite continuous catcalls from the other students. I admired her guts and began hanging around with her quite a lot. We both managed to lose ten pounds over a two-month period and the other kids remarked that we were "looking good".

I went to a slumber party with a casual acquaintance and Meike was there, cheery as ever. We listened to Three Dog Night albums and drank wine, and bemoaned the fact that we didn't have boyfriends. The year before, I got involved with another grade nine student, Kevin, who asked me pointedly, "Do you ball?" and I'd run quickly away from him, fearful of any intimate contact. It was just too soon and I wasn't ready to relinquish my childhood innocence just yet.

I had a pretty good time at the party, even though I didn't feel as though I truly belonged there. For one thing, these kids were all more popular than I was and for another, I felt as though I had to play a role while I was there and not let my own dumb personality shine through it all.

In the summer of 1970, I had gotten absolutely hooked on the Everly Brothers, after watching their summer replacement show for Johnny Cash. I was certain that one day, I would marry Phil. I loved the harmonies, which I'd been introduced to by one of our former babysitters in 1962 and yearned for my past uncomplicated life. I loved the Everlys' show, and watched it religiously, even joining their fan club, Everly Brothers International. I got personal mail from president Martial F. Bekkers in Rotterdam, Holland, and felt a sense of oneness with this remarkable duo.

So, when I entered grade ten, I was looked at somewhat oddly for my affection for a singing act that was fully esconsed in the 1950's and early 1960's and was urged to get into the more current artists.

I refused, feeling that my heart belonged in that more uncomplicated, purer time period. I bought dozens of their albums and wrapped myself in the delicious music for many hours. It was my way of rebelling against the turbulent world of the early 1970's, and nobody was going to take it away from me.

So I made it through grade ten as a true enigma: A displaced child who refused to grow up and enter a new, frightening decade, one that was heralded in with the four student shootings at Kent State University in 1970. I despised the world in which I was living and the way it was affecting everyone. There had to be an effective way of staving it off.

Lizzie became the person to most aggressively avoid. She embodied everything that scared and appalled me. She was a known drug user, hated her parents' authority, and, worst of all, my brother thought she was positively "in the groove", whereas I was most assuredly not.

When I found out we were moving to Westmount, to a posh home in those evil suburbs near Berkshire, I balked. It was 1970 and I just didn't want to live close to Lizzie, whose home was a mere block away.

It was a very comfortable house, something Mom really wanted, but I hated it. Worst of all, my dear cat died in this white brick place. It was September of 1970, after I'd just begun grade ten. He got bladder disease, so severe that the poor little guy sat for hours, crying in his kitty litter while he tried in vain to go. Finally, we couldn't let Taffy suffer anymore so he was put to sleep.

When Mom came home and told me, I collapsed with grief, sobbing and feeling that my life was over. She cried with me, knowing how much that cat meant to me. He just couldn't take the stress of moving from Halifax, and it cut short his precious life.

Later I played the Everly Brothers' "Let It Be Me" and when they sang the plaintive line, "So never leave me lonely", I despaired that I had been left extraordinarily lonely with the death of my beloved pet. It was the end of an era, an era of carefree abandon that we had left behind in the Maritimes two years before.

So when we were settled in Westmount, I grew fearful that Lizzie would try to coerce me to take drugs. I strenuously avoided her, while Jim couldn't understand why I was being such a stodgy stick-in-the-mud. The poor girl was desperately unhappy herself, with all kinds of family problems, but I didn't see it at the time. I was just so certain that she was "the enemy". Lizzie was, however, simply a victim, like myself, and was only using different means to escape her pain. I hope that life is better for her now.

I don't know how I got through that year, but by 1971 I felt battle-worn and exhausted from holding back the angry troops and staying clear from a brother who seemed to hate everything I stood for. I'd done well academically, but not so favourably in the social arena.

Meike really liked me, but felt I was lapsing too frequently into an emotional abyss that she couldn't reach. Beverly had made other friends, although she still looked out for me, thinking that I was on a self-destructive downward spiral. I knew that I would either have to take some drastic measures to halt that process, or fall deeper into the pit. As it turned out, the latter was to be the grim reality.

**Chapter Four**

# The Shadow Girl

By the time my sixteenth birthday came around, the maladaptive high school behaviour had begun to take a particularly ominous turn. Always somewhat obsessive about body size and weight, such as comparing myself constantly to other girls and feeling massive beside them, I decided that I would finally do something about it. Thus began my initiation into the wonderful world of dieting, a place that would nearly be my eventual mausoleum six months later.

Society was still very much, in 1971, reeling giddily from the impact of Twiggymania. As the fashion industry gained more and more influence over young girls and women in Western civilization, it became increasingly necessary for us to resemble stick figures. My role model was Susan Dey, one of the stars of the Partridge family, a youth-oriented television show that was a megahit in the early seventies, thanks to teen heartthrob David Cassidy.

I yearned desperately to look like the lissome Laurie Partridge, beautiful, poised, and most importantly, impossibly thin. I read in 16 Magazine, the teenage Bible of entertainment rags, that Dey had once been somewhat plump. Her mother had then insisted that she go on a strict regimen of lean meats, plenty of fruits and vegetables, and absolutely no fats or sugars. "So that's how she did it", I marvelled, vowing to follow this perfect physical specimen's example and pare at least twenty pounds from my hideously obese (or so I imagined) frame. I was heavily steeped in teenage negativism concerning my sense of self-worth.

Though I wasn't actually overweight, and never had been, I was what my father termed "chunky" (a word I grew to despise). I knew at a very young age that my father preferred skinny women, and one of the things that had attracted him to my mother was the fact that when they met, she had had only one hundred twelve pounds on her five-foot eight inch frame.

As a doleful adolescent who desperately craved Daddy's affection, I wondered then that if I was really thin, he'd pay more attention to me. That's how young girls' minds work; I was nothing unique. At five foot three and one hundred ten pounds, I was certainly not Twiggy material, and thus I set about to transform myself into a sylph-like vision of loveliness. Nothing, I vowed, summing up every fibre of stubbornness in my tortured teenage soul, would stop me from achieving this stellar goal.

Mimicking Susan Dey, I immediately cut out anything with any fat or sugar content. These included all desserts, sugar in my tea and on cereal, and butter on vegetables. Of course, all snacking was forbidden. It was not as difficult as I thought it would be; in fact, denying myself treats and fattening foods felt sublimely virtuous and hunger pangs were something with which I was to feel familiar and happy. It felt good to be in discomfort, and so my self-abuse manifested itself in hunger and craving. Again, I'd stumbled upon something to take a bit of the sting out of my emotional swarm of insipid hornets.

To my extreme joy, I lost three pounds that first week, and knew that my chunkiness would soon be a fading memory. I relinquished my invitation to our Latin teacher, Mrs. Wright's end of the year dinner for all of us at her place, because she would be serving spaghetti and that was verboten. I'd recently cut out starches as well, which meant any form of pasta. I simply told her I had other plans for that Saturday.

My mother was getting a bit suspicious of my eating habits, wondering why I refused all desserts and was starting to pick at my meals, but I appeased her by saying I was "eating healthier" and replacing artery-choking sweets with fruit. That must have appealed to the nurse in her, so she stopped questioning me.

Another strong motivating force for my stringent dieting was Meike and her drastic weight loss on the Stillman Water Diet. Appalled that she'd stuffed herself with Maple Buds and accumulated far too many pounds of blubber, Meike, along with her mother, took up this rather unbalanced regimen with a vengeance. They ate a cup of oatmeal with Sucaryl for breakfast, a hard boiled egg for lunch, a small broiled hamburger pattie for supper, plus eight glasses of water per day.

Tired of being called "Aunt Jemima" by mean neighbourhood kids, she possessed an iron-willed determination. Within six weeks

Meike lost twenty-five pounds and was actually on the skinny side. Ecstatic, she went out and bought a new wardrobe of flashy, mod clothes and suddenly found herself exceedingly popular.

I bubbled over with jealousy, as the girl was now thinner than I, and I felt absolutely enormous beside her. So, by the time school ended for the summer, I'd lost seven pounds and knew that I could adequately compete with "show-off Meike".

Early in July, I visited Karen in Belle River. Although I had my customary wonderful time swimming, water skiing and spending long summer evenings playing board games with her ever-tight family, something bizarre was starting to happen. My dieting began to show signs of becoming obsessive. Since Mom was over a hundred miles away, I figured that I could easily get away with eating as little as possible. After all, my weight loss had slowed down ands it was necessary to cut back even further if I was going to achieve my goal.

I decided to eat only half of what the others did, sticking to my guns about avoiding all sugars, fats and starches on top of that. The result was that I ingested very little and began to suffer some ills effects of denying myself to such an extent. I started feeling weak and dizzy and found that I was starting to think about food a lot more as it took on an increasingly prominent place in my daily meditation.

I mentally calculated the number of calories in everything that went into my mouth, something that would eventually make me a virtual slave to numbers. Fearing that my figures might be wrong, I invested in a brand name calorie counter which told the numbers of every supermarket product from Cool Whip to frozen entrees.

I carried this valuable volume everywhere and memorized it for hours at a time. I played little numbers games, like saving up a day's calories in order to splurge on a slice of pizza, for instancc. I would only allow myself to consume six hundred calories a day and my mind ached with fatigue as I constantly calculated and plotted.

Karen began to voice some concern for my health and asked, "Aren't you getting a bit carried away with all this dieting stuff?" This happened one night after I'd picked at supper and opted instead for a dish of sugarless jello.

"What do you mean?" I snapped defensively, not wanting any intruders in my world of denial. "I'm just being careful. Maybe

I want to look more like you and less like a jersey cow. Okay?"

Karen shook her head and fell silent, knowing from past experience that when I took that unpleasant tone, it was best leave matters alone. Karen despised arguing and raised voices.

I remained in Belle River an extra week, as I wished to make up to my friend for my recent moodiness and also to continue my strict dieting away from Mom's prying eyes.

Swimming began to lose its relaxing, fun aspect and became a means to burn more calories. Thus the exercising rituals began during that extra week at Karen's. I decided that when I returned home, I'd swim every day at the Woodcrest Community Pool for at least an hour a day. Biking would be a good idea as well.

Upon my arrival back in London, Mom seemed distant and preoccupied. This usually meant that she was having difficulties with Dad or Jim, perhaps both. One evening, she broke away from her own dark thoughts long enough to mention that my arms looked thinner. However, she then quickly added that it was probably because of my tan. I agreed, sighing inwardly with relief and changed the subject.

No-one could find out about my increasingly complicated dieting rituals, especially Mom, who could be given to theatrical outbursts. I never felt further apart from my family as I did that summer, as for the first time I was being secretive and even lying to achieve my goal of slim perfection. Something about it gave me an odd feeling of exhilaration.

As more of my time was invested in calculating calories and exercising, less was devoted to keeping my room tidy. For the first time, it began to appear quite dishevelled. Always a neat-freak, I now left dirty clothes strewn all over the floor and let my waste basket overflow with papers and garbage. Worst of all, I felt no twinge of guilt for such blatant slovenliness. It just didn't seem important anymore.

Luckily, I was to travel by plane to Barrington, Rhode Island early in August to spend a couple of weeks with Aunt Elizabeth and Uncle Ray. I knew then, with perverse glee, that I could get away with murder as far as dieting and exercise went. I hadn't stepped on the scale for awhile, as it depressed me when the numbers weren't low enough. Even so, I knew that I wanted to lose more weight, or at least not gain any back. That was absolutely imperative, for I thought that this would happen if I didn't practically starve myself.

When I reached Barrington, a horrifying transformation began to take place. I was no longer controlling the diet; it was slowly and cruelly manipulating me. It wasn't a matter of choice anymore, but one of urgent necessity. A new, disturbing element was added to the bizarre mixture: Fear. It propelled my dwindling body into wild spasms of exercise to such an alarming extent that my physical movements became forced and exaggerated.

Each morning, I'd get on my cousin Jimmy's bike, accompanied by Aunt Elizabeth on her own vehicle and peddle ferociously. I searched out steep hills and worked up lathers of sweat as I steeled myself against the enemies of fatigue and aching muscles. "God, I'm not working hard enough!" I despaired, grasping the handlebars in white-knuckled panic. I was barely aware of my aunt struggling to keep up the frenetic pace that I had set.

This free-floating fear became my constant companion and would not loosen its grip on my heart for months. I was still fat, unspeakably so and those despised pounds were not going to disappear unless I worked out religiously to the point of near-paralysis.

I began to ignore my body's pitiful signals to slow down, as if switches labelled "Fatigue" and "Hunger" were permanently turned to the off position. These distressing feelings were created only to keep me obese and had no relevance in my world anymore. They were simply cruel obstacles designed for deceitful purposes.

Accompanying the manic exercise routines was an increase in social isolation. My communication skills had never been a strong suit. So, as the ritualistic activities enveloped more and more of my life, my relationship with my cousin, Susan, faded into oblivion.

Susan, nearly two years my senior, was a bubbly, intense and extremely outgoing teenager. She was blessed with a winning personality and a healthy dose of self-esteem. Sue had graduated high school that spring, where she'd been surrounded by copious close friends and had thoroughly enjoyed herself and her overwhelming popularity. Susan possessed an easy, infectious laugh, was perkily cute, loving and had embraced a multitude of extracurricular activities. These included gymnastics, in which she excelled.

I'd recall ruminating that this girl was my polar opposite in every conceivable way. I twitched with envy at Susan's innate ability to care strongly about each and every individual that entered her universe with effortless abandon and wide-eyed acceptance. She was a tiny, fine-boned girl who could eat anything and everything she wanted without gaining an ounce. Yes, I thought dismally, my cousin had it all. It seemed inconceivable to me that we shared many of the same genes.

Sue hassled me frequently about my paltry eating habits, telling me of her friend, Marcia, who starved herself to the point of emaciation, becoming quite sick in the process. I countered with an abrupt, "I'm not like that. Don't compare me to your friends".

After graduation, Sue had studied to become an X-ray technician. She was currently employed at Miriam Hospital, working at something she loved and garnering a new set of friends. I accompanied her many days to work, dressed in one of her uniforms and easily blended in with the medical atmosphere. I watched, with reluctant admiration as she took X-rays of a wide variety of patients, exuding confidence. My bubbly cousin kibbutzed with them before telling them firmly, "Don't breathe," then zapped them with radiation.

I didn't particularly like the look, smell and sounds of the hospital, for they caused fingers of quivering uneasiness to run haphazardly up and down my spine. I trudged throughout this green-walled, crowded facility, behind my energy-buoyed cousin for eight interminable hours a day, feeling as though my joints were composed of gelatinous material and my muscles were shot full of Novocaine. Weakness and dramatic periods of dizziness overcame me more frequently as the days progressed, but I staunchly refused to relent.

My diet now consisted of a glass of orange juice for breakfast, a container of non-fat yogurt for lunch and a bullion cube and small serving of custard for supper. I adhered to this regimen faithfully, adding an hour of swimming per day along with the three hours of cycling.

The pounds loosened their grip on my frame and disintegrated into delicious oblivion by the middle of August. I discovered with morbid fascination that I weighed only ninety pounds and it seemed as though I had achieved my goal. The months of hunger and exhaustion had not been in vain.

My joy was shortlived, however, as I quickly became obsessed with that now-familiar fear once more. I can't let myself gain any of it back! I must keep up my strict dieting and exercising without any lapses or I'll balloon out to one hundred ten again. That would be a fate worse than death!

Much to my aunt, uncle and cousins' chagrin, I kept my food intake very low and forced the strenuous work-outs, even as I resembled, as Susan said, "a tiny bird curled up in a little ball".

Happily, I shopped for new clothes, revelling in the sight of a now-svelte body in garments I'd never had the guts to wear before. "Laurie Partridge, eat your heart out," I smirked, admiring this unrecognizable thinness of mine in a department store mirror. "Wait'll I get back to school. Nobody will recognize me."

The only drawback to this newfound paradise was the constant and all-enveloping tiredness that muffled my excitement and unabashed gloating. Getting out of bed in the morning became more difficult. As I lay there on my side, knee bones rubbing against each other with reassuring sharp friction, I fought the intense desire to vegetate for the rest of the day. But of course, that was forbidden. There was so much to do to keep those evil calories from conspiring to transform me back into an unsightly mountain of shivering flesh.

Both Susan and Aunt Elizabeth coerced me to eat more, both obviously concerned that I was becoming sick and suffering from malnutrition. I made them promise not to mention anything to Mom, but they must have felt torn and confused. All they knew for certain was that I was retreating further and further into a self-destructive world and that even I was incapable of stopping the process.

What stuck most firmly in my mind about that transitional summer in Rhode Island was the way in which I became less aware of what was going on around me. My senses turned in on themselves and the outside world faded into a dissolving memory. Many years later, as the process recurred, I would refer to it as "encompassing myself in my own concentration camp."And what was my crime? Being a chunky kid in a society that worshipped and paid homage to the sylph.

*    *    *    *    *    *    *    *    *

I spent all of August with the Holtzes and upon my return to London in early fall, everyone went absolutely bananas. My family freaked when they caught a glimpse of what used to be their daughter, sister and granddaughter and they all wondered what I had done to myself. After putting her arm around me and feeling nothing but bones, my semi-hysterical mother hauled me onto the bathroom scales and was mortified to see that the number read only eighty-seven pounds.

I smiled inwardly, even as I was given a crass ultimatum: "Eat or you're going into the hospital." Hospital? I flinched at the mere thought of such a horrifying notion. Surely they were issuing empty threats, designed simply to scare the hell out of me.

School was about to begin and I revelled in the anticipation of dazzling my contemporaries with my new look. However, I felt somewhat uneasy about being able to keep up the kind of energy-charged pace that grade eleven would require along with my exercise routine. I was now struggling to do the swimming and cycling, as my muscles seemed to be being gnawed on by invisible, hungry beasts and my blood thinned by camphor. Surely the simple act of refusing food wasn't producing all this agony?

My head swam in little ripples of undulating seasick waves, blurring my vision and muffling my ears and produced a constant humming that made it difficult to decipher what people were saying. I fought the craving for constant sleep, and made the unpleasant discovery that I was unable to concentrate on anything that I tried to read. What was I going to do with a difficult subject like physics?

Shoving all those distasteful thoughts out of my head on the first day of school, I decided to bask in the attention I was getting for having lost twenty-five pounds. Reaction varied from blatant jealousy ("Geez, how did you do it? That's fantastic!") to the left-handed compliment ("You sure look better than you used to.")

Beverly was the sole voice of reason, although I didn't appreciate it at the time. "Good God, Jane. What the hell did you do to yourself?!"

I brushed my friend's concern off like invisible particles of dandruff from an expensive new suit. These disparaging comments were not going to dampen my glorious moment in the sun.

That moment was short-lived, however. Even though I'd initially made a positive impression on my classmates, I felt no more a part of their exclusive world than I had at one hundred ten pounds. As a matter of fact, it now seemed as though I was encased in some kind of isolation bubble, peering out at everyone from an antiseptic, untouchable realm that forbade any interacting or mingling.

Locked in my prison of denial and forced physical activity, I had no energy or thought processes left over for anything or anyone else. And what was more, I seemed to be condemned here forever, continually being punished for the crime of striving for perfection in an imperfect world. Saunders Secondary School, in the fall of 1971, could and would not appreciate what I'd endured to get where I was at that time.

It didn't know what it had cost me to try to mix in and become indistinguishable from the students who swished and swaggered so effortlessly through the halls, exchanging meaningful glances with one another and wearing the close-fitting garb of the divinely inherited.

I still sat alone in the cafeteria at lunchtime, chewing morosely on my egg white and watching them enjoying the fruits of popularity and inherent coolness, all long-haired, mini-skirted and bell-bottomed non-conforming teenage chic. Damn them, damn them all.

I made ambitious plans to try out for the cheerleading team, something I'd always wanted but deemed unthinkable, as well as the volleyball and basketball teams. I was under the mistaken impression that thinness rendered one virtually infallible and capable of astounding feats of daring and social occupancy of the shrineof the upper echelon.

Now, at a sleek and glamour-gilded eighty-five pounds, I could even compete with Sandy, and the other kids would then speak her name and mine in the same staccato breath. Then that smug, egotistical Jason would be all slack-jawed and oggle-eyed over me too. Sarah was a former hefty-weight who lost an amazing number of excess pounds the year before and emerged surprisingly sensual and crackling with the vibrant vivacity of Popularity Personified.

She was thus transformed from a shy, reclusive butt of numerous and cruel fat jokes to the object of every post-pubescent boy's fantasies. Suave, cocky Jason practically bronzed her discarded sugarless bubble gum in his embarrassing efforts to win her affections. Well, now I was thinner than Sarah, so logically I should now shine as "The Number One Girl Who Had It All and Worked Damned Hard To Get It".

Reality came thundering down upon me like heavy, dislodged boulders and crushed any hopes for high school utopia in a dustcloud of sad finality. I failed miserably at cheerleading, volleyball and basketball, as my movements were all misdirected, spastic energy and lacking any precision and muscular coordination.

My chief objective was burning calories and in my obsessive, narrow-fielded vision, I lost sight of the real purpose of these sports: namely, teamwork and the pleasures of being together with other kids. My habits of the past several months had rendered me even more socially isolated than ever, and completely incapable of enjoying anyone's company.

It all smacked of bitter irony: I had lost all the weight in order to gain acceptance by my peers, but something about the methods I'd employed were unhealthy and repugnant. Nobody wanted to be around a sick person, I thought darkly. A sick person---could that be possible? Was there something wrong with me after all, as my family claimed as they wrung their collective hands and bemoaned my appalling transformation?

As September wore on and the days shortened, I began to notice how incredibly cold I was all the time. It penetrated every cell, cramping my wasted muscles and making my teeth chatter. I would walk stiffly about with my body tensed against the discomfort, clamping my jaws and rubbing clammy skin to erase some of the numbing goosebumps.

To my surprise, I saw that I was beginning to grow fine hair, like soft duck down all over my body. I reassured myself that nature was seeing to it that I didn't freeze to death. For some reason, the sight didn't repulse or frighten me, but was oddly comforting and pleasurable.

My bouts of exercising had become sporadic lately and ceased altogether toward the middle of the month. I was just too weak, tired and drained to do more than drag myself to and from school. Upon my arrival home, I'd collapse into our black leather lazyboy chair and remain motionless until bedtime.

I became less and less aware of the clamour and chaos all around me. My parents dragged me onto the scales every few days, despairing as my weight plunged further and further to critical levels. Mom implored me to eat, wailing that I was going to die if I persisted in starving myself, and Dad became moody, distant and grim. He was secretly very frightened but outwardly uncommunicative.

Jim reacted with fourteen-year-old disgust and revulsion, taunting me that my hands looked skeletal and that I was acting "really weird." I knew he cared, though, even with his negative comments. But teenage boys don't come out and say that to their sister. It was one of the unwritten rules of adolescence.

Studying became futile. I could no longer comprehend anything I was reading and went about my classes in a semi-somnambulistic state. I remember sitting in class, but not really feeling as though I was there. I would feel my bones digging into the hard seats and be overwhelmed with the cold and was too weak to push a pen across the page.

Karen came to town for the Western Fair, as always, and I recall struggling to keep up with her. I begged to stay in the Progress Building where it was warmer and was overwhelmed by the permeating aromas of corndogs, caramel corn and fries that wafted about everywhere.

My hunger had past the point of voracious and had reached a level I'd never experienced before. It was all-encompassing, a distressing, yet comfortingly familiar companion. It assured me that I was being "good" and not giving in to the powerful desire to eat.

The best way to describe it was to say that it was comparable to having a metal prong stuck deep into your leg. Although you knew that it would be a wonderful rush of relief to remove it, you would no longer be aware that you could feel pain. Pain assured you that you were alive and a part of the world, and thus, starvation meant that you were empty and thin.

Karen was terribly worried as she saw me shrinking before her very eyes, my clothes hanging limply as if there was nobody inside them. I talked little to her, not fully aware of her presence and too overcome with exhaustion to carry on any kind of a conversation. She must have feared for my life then, as everyone did. I told her that everything was fine, that I would eat when I got back home. "All the food here is full of fat," I objected.

Throughout this disquieting period of my life, I never thought of myself as suffering from anorexia nervosa until just before I was hospitalized in October. Even as my weight plummeted to seventy-five pounds, most of my hair fell out in large handfuls, the calves of my legs swelled enormously from the edema of starvation and my teeth got alarmingly loose, I maintained stubbornly that I was not Fiona in any way, shape or form.

Fiona was the daughter of John and Sally Gerard, who were colleagues of Dad's and friends of the family for many years. Mom has a photo of Fiona and me as little children at Port Stanley, and I'd spent time with her off and on for most of my life in London, both before and after Halifax.

After Fiona returned from boarding school several years before, her parents were distressed to see that she was absolutely emaciated and refused to eat. She was later diagnosed with anorexia nervosa and I looked at my friend with morbid fascination as all her bones protruded out of her baggy clothes. She seemed oblivious to the way she looked.

By 1971, Fiona was still critically anorexic and had spent a lot of time in the hospital. Evidently she'd been very unhappy at boarding school and had kept to herself most of the time. She was unusually bright and a quiet, kind-hearted girl, and I truly felt sorry for her. But certainly my problem was not anorexia; it couldn't possibly be.

I was completely unaware of how I looked to others and imagined myself to be much heavier than the spindly Fiona. Perhaps I had a lot of problems, but she was really sick. Mom had taken me to various physicians since my return home, including our pediatrician, Dr. Stewart. I gave him a concocted fairly tale about having stomach pains and he swallowed it, ordering Gravol and telling me to "try to eat something. You really should weigh more at your age."

One of the few fond memories I have of this time was of my father taking me clothes shopping. He'd never done this before, and I noticed that since I had lost all the weight, we'd grown closer. My convoluted thinking resulted in assuming that this was because I looked so much more attractive, but the poor guy was worried sick about his little girl.

Perhaps he wanted to spend time with me while I was still alive, for I got the impression that everyone was becoming resigned to my starvation routine. My family had recently ceased begging me to eat and let me sit glumly at the table staring at my untouched plate.

My last day of school for awhile was the stuff of which melodramas are made. I fainted during French class and our teacher

frantically sent me to the school nurse. My mom was then called at
work to come and get me. Miss Connaught told me that I desperately needed help after I sheepishly apologized for causing a commotion during her class.

Since both my parents worked during the day, I was sent over
to Grandma and Grandpa's from that day on, ostensibly so someone could keep a watchful eye on me. It had been decided that I
would be admitted to St. Joseph's Hospital, as my problem had
escalated to the point where my life was in danger.

Secretly, I was relieved. I hated feeling so lousy all the time,
not being able to attend classes and lying at 619 Talbot Street in a
semi-vegetative state for hours. I had developed a keen interest in
cooking after returning from the states and spent hours concocting
meals for the rest of the family.

I was to learn that this was one of the symptoms of anorexia,
but at the time I thought it was the answer to my nagging hunger. I
could enjoy all of the aspects of eating without actually putting a
morsel into my own mouth.

Every morning, I cooked scrambled eggs for Grandpa, drawing in the aroma like a dehydrated sailor sucking up fresh water. It
gave me an exhilarating sensation of well-being. As I sat watching
my grandfather enthusiastically eating my finished product, my
soul was extremely gratified.

The days began to dissolve monotonously into one another.
During the day, I allowed myself the coveted reward of consuming
a whole digestive biscuit, taking over an hour to let every morsel
dissolve on my tongue. Then, to get rid of the calories lurking in my
body, I'd drag myself outside and walked with slow-motion heaviness down Central Avenue to Richmond Street and back. It took
over forty minutes to do the two-block distance and I nearly collapsed every time.

Poor Grandma and Grandpa, having to watch this horror
show for eight hours a day and wondering how much longer I'd
live. I was so inwardly focused that I never thought of their sorrow
and worry, only that I had to adhere to my daily routine. It was the
epitome of all-encompassing self-absorption. I was sick, selfish
and oblivious to my family's agony.

Finally, a bed opened up at St. Joe's and I was admitted
under the care of Dr. Gerald Tevaarwerk. He was a jolly, easy-
going European physician to whom I instantly took a liking. He

asked me some fundamental questions, then spent a lot of time discussing my dietary habits.

Finally, after examining me and writing for a few minutes in his chart, he looked level-eyed at me and said, "You know that you are suffering from anorexia nervosa."

At this point, I was neither shocked nor indignant, only relieved that matters were now out of my inept hands and securely ensconced in those of a thoughtful professional. "Yeah, I guess so. This wasn't supposed to happen."

Dr. Tevaarwerk smiled comfortingly and put a large, warm hand on my withered one. "We're going to help you here. Don't worry. You're going to be alright." For the first time since this whole nightmare began, I thought that perhaps there was some hope for me after all.

\* \* \* \* \* \* \* \* \*

I was put on a behaviour modification program to regain some of the lost weight, a method with which I was to become very familiar over the years and grow to despise. Back in 1971, anorexia nervosa was not the well-known and highly-publicized phenomenon that it is today. Little was documented about the disorder and treatments were basically experimental and awkward. I was the sole sufferer in our school's four hundred populace and it was very unusual that I was well-acquainted with another anorexic, poor Lucy.

It was ironic that I emulated Susan Dey and put her on the pedestal of the artistically and visually exalted, because it was later brought forth that she, too, had been anorexic at the same time that I was. Yes, the modern Western World was going to hell in a handcart, accompanied by the sweet strains of David Cassidy's youthful voice.

I grew quickly tired of the behaviour modification routine. I was supposed to eat something at each meal in order to receive any privileges. My first privilege was to be able to get out of bed for an hour a day, even though it was an effort just to roll over. Fear once again reared its repulsive head and symbolically wired my jaws shut.

I couldn't eat that disgusting Special K they gave me, which would undoubtedly put great rolls of ugly, yellowish flab on my body and crush the beautiful thinness out of it. Eating was wrong; it felt insidiously evil, it was a sign of weakness and I hated it. Surely something could be worked out with Dr. Tevaarwerk to get me out of that prison-like hospital without relinquishing my hard-earned skinny body. I had gone through so much unspeakable agony and torment to achieve it. This just wasn't fair!

For a week, I lay in that semi-private room, staring vacantly at the television and feeling too weak and tired to move a muscle. My consciousness rolled in on itself, old songs by the Everly Brothers wafted into my ears and ignited enticing memories of happier, healthier days. I was dying.

I'm not sure what zapped me back into the realm of the living and gave me that  initial push to fumble out of the suffocating chasm and breathe with renewed vigour. It was probably my family's prayers and their frequent visits to my bedside, forcing me to see that death was not acceptable at the age of sixteen. Or perhaps it was my intrinsically stubborn nature that awoke from the spell of psychological suicide and decided that it still had things to accomplish before my time came.

Whatever the catalyst, I lost no more weight after that. I even took a few mouthfuls of food the next day, something I hadn't done in many weeks.

My recovery progressed fairly rapidly after that and within six weeks I was able to go home for a few hours. The road was not bereft of a vast number of potholes, however. There were only certain foods that I would allow myself, like unbuttered spinach, raw carrots and celery, uncreamed cottage cheese and digestive cookies. Everything else was forbidden.

A dietician was sent up to work with me and for a long time I was unresponsive to her suggestions to try different foods. "You people are just trying  to make me fat!" I snapped, dismissing her with a cold stare and defiantly folded arms.

Dr. Tevaarwerk wanted me to be weighed twice a week and with each minimal gain came a step closer to freedom. I fought him all the way, protesting vehemently when I gained a few ounces and secretly rejoicing when I lost, even if it meant giving up some privileges. I was confused, angry and desperate, feeling stabs of guilt whenever I ate and waves of comforting virtue when I refused. For awhile, it seemed as if I'd never make any lasting progress, for any gained weight was immediately lost again.

But eventually, I tired of the hospital routine and longed to go back to school. I was very much afraid of failing grade eleven and having to repeat the year. This began to take precedence over my desire to be ultra-skinny.

My first overnight pass was a truly bizarre experience. When I entered my bedroom for the first time in two months, it was as though I hadn't been there for years. From the time I'd returned from Rhode Island I'd been only partially aware of my surroundings and thus, everything had a feeling of unreality about it.

Now, much better and well-nourished for the first time in six months, it was as if I'd awakened from a coma. I sat on my bed, revelling in the familiarity and realizing how homesick I'd been. Everything was going to be alright, just as Dr. Tevaarwerk had assured me. I would soon be coming home to a normal life.

I told my doctor that I did not want to weigh more than ninety pounds, so he calculated that I would be able to eat fourteen hundred calories per day to maintain that.

I returned to school in November, on a day that was dusted by the first snowfall of the season. Dad would drive me there and back to the hospital in the evening and I was extraordinarily nervous about jumping back into the fray after such a lengthy and mysterious absence. I weighed eighty pounds and still looked very gaunt and frail I had hollow cheeks, thin hair and bones protruding from my stylish clothes, which Dad had helped me pick out.

I felt alienated and set apart from my classmates. The atmosphere at school was so vibrant and colourful compared to the muffled colourlessness of St. Joseph's Hospital. Moving between the two realms proved to require more sophisticated adaptive skills than I possessed. On top of all that, I'd fallen staggeringly behind in my studies.

I decided to drop both physics and Spanish, as I could make up the credits in grade twelve. I already had an extra one for that year anyway and aside from that, I couldn't grasp the fundamentals of physics at the best of times, let alone after missing two months of it.

Reactions to my health crisis were mixed. Teachers thought I was suffering from some life-threatening illness until they learned otherwise and treated me with awkward over-protectiveness. The students, on the other hand, figured I was strung out on Speed, thus achieving such a scrawny body. I must confess that I didn't find

this assumption too distasteful. At least it gave me a certain element
of coolness and 1970's chic that had never been associated with me
before.

Readjusting was difficult, as I was still very wrapped up in
the anorexic experience and obsessing about food and calories. Not
only that, but I had been living a lie for months, claiming that I'd
lost my appetite and thus had been unable to eat for so long. The
truth was that I had been riddled with jolting hunger pangs the
entire time, fighting the constant desire to stuff food into my sali-
vating mouth.

There just didn't seem to be another way to explain why I
couldn't eat; the whole experience was so bizarre. How could I tell
everyone that I was simply too terrified to eat anything for fear of
becoming fat? It didn't make sense and would have produced anger
and frustration from all concerned. So I lived this brazen lie, secure
in the knowledge that anorexia was something about which little
was known or written.

I had a difficult time at school at first. I felt as though I was in
a thick, isolated bubble, watching the other kids from a distance as
they arrived at Saunders each day from their homes. They were
living out their academic lives with spontaneity and rampant energy
of normal, healthy teenagers and were generally unfettered by life
and death concerns.

How could I ever attain that level of carefree abandon again?
There was nothing typical about my situation, having my home at
the hospital, being monitored as I ate, weighed frequently to keep
privileges and looking like a starving Biafran with large tufts of hair
missing. How could this have happened to me?

For the first time, I thought about how chillingly similar I
was to Fiona. She'd always appeared as a kind of sideshow freak to
me, untouchable, mysterious, and frightening. Now I was the embodiment of these elements. In my relentless quest for popularity
and chic, glamorous sleekness, I had achieved the antithesis and all
my suffering had been counterproductive.

I ate only enough to maintain my weight at eighty pounds,
holding fast to the deceitful notion that I had no appetite whatso-
ever. My math teacher tutored me after school in Trigonometry, but
I found it very difficult to grasp.

English, with the personable and charismatic Brian Kellow,
involved a great deal of catch-up reading but was manageable.

French and geography presented little challenge that I wasn't able to meet. That left physical education, much desired for the exercise involvement. Academically-speaking, anyway, my situation didn't appear dismal and hopeless. Perhaps I wouldn't flunk grade eleven after all.

I hung around primarily with Paula Harmon, whom I'd gotten to know a bit the year before. She shared my desire for slimness. She wasn't anorexic, but monitored her eating carefully and was quite skinny, priding herself on being able to wear the same clothes she had since grade eight.

Paula was small-boned, with a round, cherubic face, wire-rimmed glasses and large, serious eyes that reflected a rather sombre nature. She was bright, articulate and we bonded quickly and with a fierce intensity. It felt good to have a friend who wasn't consumed with seething hormones and addled with psychedelia and hard rock.

My life had settled into a sense of relative calm, for awhile anyway. Although I still felt like a freak and had trouble concentration, the raging fears, so prominent in my thoughts for so long, had abated. Then came the fateful Day of the Dad's Oatmeal Cookie.

I had been released from the hospital after maintaining my weight for a month. One afternoon, shortly after returning home in early December, I sat down at the kitchen table to do some studying. As I opened my math text, my eyes fell idly upon a box of cookies on the counter and I found myself unable to pull my gaze from it. I had loved those cookies at one time and would think nothing of eating four of them at a sitting. "Despicable fat slob!" I spat at myself for pausing to lust over junk food. Those days were long gone.

My mind suddenly began calculating calories and energy expenditure. I had walked two miles home from school, so surely I could eat one cookie at one hundred calories a shot and still have a hundred to spare. My hands shook as I extracted the forbidden treat from its cellophane wrapping. My heartbeat thundered heavily in my ears and seemed to strain to escape a taut ribcage. I lifted the hard, brown biscuit to dry, trembling lips.

Then, in a single, rapid motion, I bit off a tiny piece and turned it over and over on my tongue. Sucking on it until it was nothing but a mass of pulpy, sugary sweet pap, I squeezed my eyes shut tightly and swallowed hard. The clock on the kitchen wall hammered  the cloistered silence away and I felt as though I had succeeded in committing a diabolical crime.

A hole had been torn in the dam of resistance and great torrents of water came bursting forth. I devoured the rest of the cookie greedily, chewing just enough to be able to swallow it without choking.

Then, all too quickly, the morsels were gone and I sat there amid a little pile of crumbs and wanted more. My appetite, long dormant and  lying in wait like a panting tigress, leapt from its hiding place and demanded to be fed. Pushing all negative thoughts aside, I reached for another cookie and ate it, faster and more savagely than the last. I kept this motion going until, ten minutes later, the entire box was gone.

"Oh God, no!!" I gasped in strangulated horror as my stomach stretched with more food than it had seen in many months. "What have I done?!" Panic wove its spidery legs around each nerve of my body and propelled me off the chair. Then I launched into a frenetic frenzy of physical activity, running blindly up and down stairs, flailing my arms to burn more calories and clamping my teeth down on my tongue to keep from screaming.

I had to get rid of that disgusting mass of sugar and fat that sprawled from one cnd of my stomach to the other, creating blubber with each passing second which would gather with laughing conspiracy on my bones.

I'd never experienced such unbridled anxiety and as the sweat burst out of my pores. My legs felt like soft sticks of gum as I refused to stop moving until I literally collapsed in a twisted pile in the bare hallway.

Then, as quickly as the panic attack had hit me, it abated, leaving me with a curiously warm sensation of grudging acceptance. Sure, I'd eaten far too much just then, but that was only because I'd denied myself for so long. It was the initial reintroduction into the world of eating, a brief, passing phase that would not show itself again.

Now I could eat normally, fourteen hundred calories a day and reach my goal of ninety pounds naturally and comfortably. I would announce to my family that night that my appetite had returned and all would be well. The nightmare was over.

But it had only just begun. Shortly after the feeling of well-being had settled upon my family and me, my love-hate relationship with food and eating took a disturbing turn. I became deluded, somehow, into thinking that I could eat whatever I wanted in unlimited quantities as long as I kept physically active.

I could consume three substantial meals a day, plus countless snacks, treats and calorie-laden concoctions, if I traded off the locust-like eating with rapid walking, numerous sit-ups and push-ups. I even made a valiant stab at jockdom by joining the track team.

This was a beneficial move, for it got me actively involved with other students and provided a focus for my ambitious spurts of energy. Everyday after school, I ran circuits in the halls, totalling over five miles each day, then practised racing, followed by muscle-strengthening exercises. Being light worked to my advantage, so I became one of our coach's favourite athletes.

I even began developing some friendships through the track team, but was so focused on calorie-burning as opposed to team-work that these relationships didn't ever really go anywhere. It was an extremely egocentric and all-encompassing world I occupied and I was incapable of breaking away from it.

By Christmas, I weighed eighty-five pounds and was taken aback by the sobering reality that I had only a five-pound margin before hitting the red-letter ninety-pound mark. I'd been eating with reckless abandon, so delirious about being able to fill my face to its capacity and escape the ravaging hunger pangs that had become my enemy.

I remember how hunger had crossed the border from over-whelming to simply normal and regular sensations of needing food. It had caused surges of fluttering panic as I was forced, by my greedy masticating, to abandon my "security blanket" of feeling deservedly starved and thus thin and empty enough to be accept-able.

Losing that gauge left me awash in negative emotions of shame, guilt and self-loathing. I began to feel fat again, as I had at one hundred ten pounds, and bemoaned my lost skinny virtuousness. What was happening to me? Why was I relinquishing my perfect body for the love and pursuit of food, the enemy? It would make me ugly again, and no longer the centre of my father's attention.

For whatever else the anorexia had accomplished, it had gotten me noticed at last and had somehow united my parents in a common cause: Saving daughter Jane from herself. Even Jim was less hostile to me and some of his friends even stopped to talk to me in the halls now. This whole experience certainly had not been entirely bad.

One afternoon, feeling positively hungry and gluttonous, I engaged in a feeding frenzy that included such formerly banned delicacies as ice cream, frozen Cool Whip, scooped right out of the container, Pop Tarts, English Muffins with jam and canned rice pudding.

I ate rapidly and thoughtlessly, shutting out all notions of what those calories would do to me, in favour of continuing the lusty affair between my taste buds and the decadent, nutritionally-bereft goodies. By the time my parents returned from work, I must have ingested over ten thousand calories and was in a state of utter chaos.

They found me racing up and down the stairs and watched as I kept up an impossible pace for over an hour. Then I sat on the livingroom floor and engaged in sit-ups until I thought I would vomit. Tears streamed down my face the entire time and my body was racked with broken sobs.

This became an all-too-familiar scene at our house: Bingeing and manic directionless exercise, accompanied by hysteria and crying jags. It must have been difficult to watch and my father, understandably, grew short-tempered and impatient. He could not understand why I was eating so much, given that I only wanted to weigh ninety pounds and it was causing me so much pain to consume food as such an accelerated pace.

I didn't understand it either at the time, but in retrospect I believe that my body was simply fighting to regain all of the weight that I'd lost. It was not natural for me to weigh much under one hundred ten pounds. Craving so much food, and such high-calorie food at that, was old Mother Nature's way of looking out for herself.

I nervously stepped on the scale the next day and shuddered as it registered eighty-six pounds. I was almost at my maximum. That was it, I thought firmly. I just won't eat a thing for three days to compensate for that disgusting binge. This brought a barrage of protests from Dad, who had gotten weary of the whole anorexic set-up and finally lost his temper at my juvenile behaviour.

It infuriated him that I was so wantonly self-destructive and that even though I'd "gotten my appetite back" I was no closer to recovering from my food obsessions than I ever was. It was saddening, exasperating and made him feel helpless and ineffective. He and Mom were forced to sit back and watch me drowning in misery and self-abusive activities. Where would it all end?

Christmas came and went, punctuated with a heated argument between Dad and me about eating. He told me that I was afraid to grow up and act my age, and that I should go with the fourteen-year-olds like Jim as that's how old I looked and behaved. I sulked on the couch, arms folded defensively across my chest and scowled at the in the inescapable fact that he was right.

In the New Year, a psychiatrist was summoned to help me. His name was Wendell Haim, a long-haired, bearded hippie who came to the house, sat cross-legged on the floor of the family room. He then told us that the whole family was sick, not just me. He said he wanted to treat the four of us.

I thought Dr.Haim was crazier than I was and was opposed to this kind of communal family therapy stuff. Jim was also adamantly against any "stupid shrink picking away" at his head. For once I agreed with him, for after all, I was the one with the problem and because of it, everyone was suffering.

Dad said something to me around that time that hurt me deeply and caused even more feelings of guilt and self hatred to well up in my heart. After one of my emotional scenes, where I ran about the house screaming and crying my head off following a binge, he said sharply, "Now look. This nonsense has gone on long enough. There are three other people in this house and I'll be damned if one member is going to ruin everybody's lives! You'll either get help or you'll be asked to leave".

A thick, salty lump had risen in my throat, threatening to choke off my air. I couldn't believe my ears. I was being told that if I didn't get better, I'd be kicked out and banished from
my home for destroying everyone. What could I do to stop this insanity?

I agreed to see Dr. Haim, who was the embodiment of the quintessential crazy shrink, making even his nuttiest patients appear sane. Although I believe that his heart was in the right place and that he was basically a good person, L. felt that all my problems stemmed from the fact that I desperately craved love and affection from a dominant male personality. Since he thought my father was a poor provider, he took it upon himself to be a "surrogate one".

With his unruly, curly hair, affable grin and khaki clothes, this man was the eccentric/rebel/misunderstood-but-conscientious/male role model that he imagined that an affection-starved sixteen-year-old woman/child needed and craved.

Thus he went about trying to "win me over" with a heartfelt poem written for and about me entitled "The Chrysalis" that made me feel exalted and special. He conducted our sessions over at his pad that he shared with his live-in girlfriend.

Who knows how long this strange little cerebral affair would have continued, but it came to an abrupt end one afternoon. I remember it vividly, as if it happened only last week.

I was sitting in my usual place in his den, firmly ensconced in a brown beanbag chair while James Taylor droned away on the stereo. I'd lost touch with my faithful companion of music during my anorexic months and it felt warm and reassuring to experience it again. I was as relaxed as I was capable of being then and waited for Dr. Haim to return from the kitchen, where he was talking to his girlfriend.

He came in shortly, bringing me a cup of herbal tea, then lit some incense and sat down beside me on the hardwood floor. There was even a door of beads and a Woodstock poster on the wall. I was tempted to ask him if he took in American draft dodgers, but decided against it. It wasn't my nature to be a smartass back then, although my mind worked that way at times.

We sat quietly for a few minutes and listened to the music. I breathed in the musk aroma of the incense and felt somewhat awkward at the extended "Pinter pause". Just then, Haim leaned over and started brushing a strand of hair from my eyes. I moved back,thinking that he was behaving inappropriately for a therapist. The next thing I knew, this hippie shrink was all over me, pressing his thin, unkempt body on top of me and whispering in my ear, "Just relax. Everything's okay."

Well, I didn't appreciate these clumsy advances, even if he somehow believed that being deflowered would help me tremen-dously and make me feel wanted and loved. I rolled over quickly and struggled to my feet, exclaiming breathlessly, "I want to go home now. Take me home, please."

That was the last of my sessions with "Dr. Love". I told my parents that the rest was going to have to be up to me and that I no longer needed therapy. I felt embarrassed, humiliated and betrayed.

How could a man who wrote such insightful and sensitive poetry be such a lech?

Oddly enough, I began to improve after that incident. My eating levelled out somewhat and became more evenly balanced with my workouts for the track team. I even participated in several track meets, never placing anywhere near first, but running the 880 with an acceptable amount of aplomb.

I stopped weighing myself regularly after hitting eighty-six pounds and far surpassed the ninety-pound mark by the end of that school year. Weight, calories and numbers faded from prominence in my life and my old interests of academe, music, writing, art and piano took the forefront again. The panicky urgency of burning off calories was abandoned in favour of more cerebral pursuits, and thus I reclaimed my life.

I'm not sure what caused this transformation, but I think it was becoming fed up with the superficiality and emptiness of chasing a thin body. My mind craved other stimulation besides that singular and narcissistic one. Besides, I greatly feared losing the love and support of my family.

Dad's threat had struck fear into my heart, and I knew I would relinquish anything to remain at home with him, Mom and Jim. Maybe it took this negative, life-threatening experience to make me appreciate what I had and what I could have squandered.

By that summer, I was back up to one hundred five pounds and though I would have chosen less weight, I knew that it was simply not meant to be. What was more, I had erroneously thought that weighing ninety pounds would cause my father to love me more, when in actuality it nearly alienated him for good. It was an invaluable lesson to learn and I had learned it the hard way.

Unfortunately, it would take twenty-three more years before that would eventually sink into my thick, stubborn skull.

I would be plagued by at least five more life-threatening episodes of anorexia, along with bulimia, until the age of forty. I hope that now, as I write this, that this devastating illness will never lunge viciously at me again. It just takes too much and leaves you with nothing but broken dreams and spent spirits.

## Chapter Five

# Sustaining In the Psychedelic Vacuum

There was a short period of relative calm after the anorexic experience, before the next onslaught of obsessive activity tore our frazzled family apart. And once more, I was the eye of this destructive hurricane.

By grade twelve, I was settled enough emotionally to return to intensive studying. I felt that I had to compensate for just squeaking through grade eleven by the skin of my ass. Relations with my family had returned to old, familiar patterns: Dad was reclusive, introverted and retreated into his work, spending more and more time away from home.

Mom escaped into her morning movies, classical music and reading in an effort to push away feelings of inadequacy and loneliness. Jim ran wild with the pack of Westmount wolves, thumbing his nose at authority and school. We all moved in our own separate orbits, never touching each other, never connecting or conversing together in any meaningful way. We were all living under the same roof, but we weren't living together at all.

I looked, as always, to music for comfort and serenity. The Everly Brothers wrapped their soulful, serenading harmonies around my pain and soothed me into blissful numbness. I lost myself in the pages of their international fan club newsletter each month. I lived vicariously through the eyes and hearts of two insightful and endearing siblings from Kentucky whose influence spanned the entire spectrum of rock music.

I amassed an impressive collection of albums and played them for hours at a time, losing myself in a bygone era of ducktails and drive-in movies. It wasn't my time, but a recent nostalgia wave sent ripples of the 1950's lifestyle as it crashed over the battle-weary, prematurely jaded time period of the early 1970's.

I remember wishing fervently that Time would magically begin a period of reversal to a more freshly-scrubbed and musically pure state. I knew, realistically, that this was futile dreaming.

It was as if molten lava had been poured over the Everly Brothers' domain. It was forever preserved in fossils that were merely objects of curiosity and ridicule by a society awash in the sexual revolution, the Vietnam war, and unchecked, maniacal drug-consumption.

As I'd stubbornly refused, at age twelve, to conform to the late 60's mod dress code, I immersed myself, in 1972 in a form of rock and roll that had become hackneyed and outdated. When Don and Phil Everly sang about young, untouched love, bird dogs, being the eternal fool and living in a blissful, endless youth in the rolling foothills of Kentucky during the 1940's, I was able to temporarily shut out the ominously disturbing present. Even when these brothers sang about drugs (as they did with their cover of Mary Jane) it was somehow quite innocuous and safe.

They allowed me to cling ferociously to my virginal childhood and escape the storms that whipped about my world, buffeting it upon the rocks of sexual permissiveness. In short, I was extremely reluctant to let go of my treasured past, even though it had not been a particularly blissful one.

I attended a highly-anticipated Everly Brothers show at the Seaway Beverly Hills Hotel in Toronto on March seventeenth, 1973 with my mom, Aunt Jean and Uncle Lin. While there, I met Julie, a regular contributor to the fan club magazine. She was notorious for following the brothers during their tours with a tape recorder and getting interviews with them, no small feat, since they were very particular about their relationship to the press.

I instinctively knew who the woman was even before she introduced herself and she seemed pleased at this. I had written a letter to the editor of the Globe and Mail complaining about the sad lack of any coverage of the Everlys' week-long stint at the hotel. I discovered through Pat that Don and Phil had seen it.

Naturally, my teenage heart fluttered wildly and practically went into spasms after the guys signed a glossy photo of themselves with "To Jane, Thank You" scrawled across it. Just prior to this, my mother had grasped Don by the arm as he and Phil walked by us in the lobby, and told him,"My daughter has some pictures of you that she drew".

I had planned on approaching them after learning that they would leave the stage and exit through the hotel's gift shop, but after seeing my heroes at such close range, I'd frozen into an immobile chunk of dried wood.

Musicians had meant so much to me over the years and this was the first time I'd ever been fortunate enough to meet any. I was so overcome with emotion that I nearly threw up right there in that fancy hotel lobby.

Afterward, Julie and I sat together in the coffee shop and talked for several hours about our love for the Everlys and their music. She was older, about twenty-five and was a somewhat plump, curly-haired woman. She had pleasant, round face and rather old-fashioned glasses.

I admired her straightforwardness and common sense; she was also fortunate to occupy a place on the outer fringes of the musicians' lives, but was careful not to exalt the position into something it wasn't. She respected them, particularly Don, and never overstepped her boundaries and tried to needle her way into either of their personal lives.

I was in awe of her maturity and in what she had achieved in her relatively short life. Julie was an accomplished journalist and had set ambitious career goals for herself. I felt honoured that this woman would want to spend any time with a sheltered, immature seventeen-year-old. Perhaps I wasn't such a total loser after all.

I talked to Julie by phone a few times after that night and we exchanged addresses. The two of us kept in touch for awhile, but suffered a bit of a rift after the fateful day that the Everlys played Knott's Berry Farm in July of that year. It signified the end of an era, for on that sunny summer afternoon, Don and Phil split up onstage, thus dissolving the entity that was the professional and private Everly Brothers. The two of them would barely speak to one another for the next ten years.

I had planned on travelling alone to Ottawa that August to see them, but of course, the rest of their tour was cancelled. Julie became irritated with me because I still used Everly Brothers' stickers on my envelopes. She thought it highly inappropriate and was a grim reminder of the past, from which we were all supposed to be extricating ourselves.

But what destroyed our friendship completely was something insidious that overtook me at Christmas of 1973. I succumbed to drugs, after having consciously avoided the frightening spectre for the past five years. It had not been planned in any way. I was in my last year of high school, doing exceptionally well academically, but practically devoid of friendships.

Meike was still with her rather unsavoury crowd and Beverly had it firmly planted in her mind that I simply had too many problems and needed to "straighten out". It wasn't that she disliked me, but she was anxious to get into a good university in the fall and decided that her schoolwork should take precedence over looking after a confused pal. I really had to agree with her. Leslie distanced herself from me as well and I was very lonely.

I suppose if there was anything about my life that really disturbed me at this time, it was a growing sense of confusion about my sexuality. As I found myself on the threshold of adulthood, I deliberated over the sad fact that, at eighteen, I was still a virgin, and had no particular desire to change that status.

I was acutely aware that many of my contemporaries were sexually active and had been for several years, but the idea of engaging in awkward, panting sweats with some overeager, horny, adolescent boy left much to be desired.

I seriously questioned whether or not there was something wrong with me. I'd never even masturbated; in fact, I didn't even know how, since I'd surreptitiously avoided reading anything about sex, equating it with something vile and disgusting.

The sexual revolution that surged and seethed all around me was cause of much agitation and fretting. I longed for the more innocent, abstinent days of the 1950's and wished that I had been born twenty years earlier.

I couldn't understand why I felt so hopelessly out of step with the morals and practises of my generation or why I'd been such a staunch non-conformist from the age of twelve. What was I so afraid of? Why had I never traversed through that "boy crazy" phase and become reoccupied with seeking out boyfriends and back seat gropings in the dark? Was I some kind of aberration? Or worse, could I be gay?

This unsettling question preyed on my mind constantly throughout grade 13. It wasn't as though I had ever been attracted to women; after all, my mind had been constantly obsessed with male rock stars for many years, not to mention television and movie stars like James Darren, Warren Beatty, Paul Newman, and Jon Voight.

However, in all my many fantasies with them, the sexual component never entered once. What did was something that I'd always known to be pretty bizarre and extremely abnormal.

From the age of four, I'd lie in bed at night, spinning my own "mini movies" in the hushed privacy of my own personal bedroom theatre. The scenarios were all strikingly similar: The "hero", for example, David Hedison in his role as Captain Lee Crane on Voyage to the Bottom of the Sea, would be steeped heavily in some kind of life-and-death crisis.

He'd either be severely wounded, badly hurt or gravely ill with some traumatic, multi-symptom disease. Using my trusted imagination to the maximum, I'd put the hapless guy through long, agonizing sessions of delirium, excruciating pain and soaring fevers. Either that, or he'd be racked with pain, moaning pathetically while people milled about, trying to administer to him.

Finally, after a substantial chunk of time had elapsed, he'd slowly recover, until finally, all traces of the illness or injury had disappeared.

From age four onward, I deliberated upon why I wove those elaborate soap opera-like scenes, and figured that I must be pretty twisted. I never divulged my "passive crimes" to anyone, for fear of being branded "sick" or "cruel". I would often force myself to stay awake until three AM, totally absorbed in the deliciously warm and tingling sensation that my imagination produced in my body.

I now know that this pleasant feeling was the equivalent of an orgasm, and i suppose that can adequately explain why I never got into masturbation as a kid.

It wasn't the actual pain and suffering I put my heroes through that caused the heated rush for me all those many years, but rather the effect that they had upon those around them. In virtually all of my fantasies, loved ones surrounded the sick or wounded one, wringing their hands in despair, crying and losing themselves in worry and regret that they hadn't appreciated the stricken person more when he was well.

It doesn't take a student of Sigmund Freud to conclude that what my heart and soul craved was love and acceptance. I was vicariously living through the person lying ill, soaking up thirstily the attention and devotion that radiated from everyone who thought, regretfully, that it might be too late to make amends.

But then why did I always use males, and why males the I

had a wild crush on? Well, that could be explained by some elementary dimestore psychology: Although I didn't become aware of my motives until 1992, I learned that it stemmed from a lifelong belief that my parents loved my brother more, just as Tommy Smothers had always lamented to brother Dick in their famous stand-up routine.

So intense was my conviction that I'd really wanted to be a boy and searched for a reflection of myself in all the boys and men of the media that I adored. I don't know common this phenomenon is, but there are probably a great many children, teens and young adults who look to music, television and movie stars to fill a void in themselves and by living through them, they can feel wanted and loved themselves.

Most kids develop an affinity for famous, glamour-gilded personalities, but only a certain percentage become truly obsessed. I was one of those. It's just recently that I've begun to live completely as my own person and not as the embodiment and reflection of someone else who I think I wish to be.

At eighteen, I knew none of the psychological ramifications of my fantasies, only that they occupied a substantial amount of my conscious thoughts. And, coupled with my lack of sexual interest, I really began to wonder if they stemmed from an intense dislike of guys. Maybe it was time I forced myself to become more socially interactive with my peers and not live so much of my time in a dream world.

This rather uneasy decision coincided with that fateful Christmas Eve, which would lead to a head-on collision with heterosexual sex and mind-altering drugs. These elements would literally rock the foundation of my isolated existence.

Dad, Mom, Jim and I were over at our Aunt Louise's home for her yearly, seasonal bash. The house was jam-packed with people milling about, jostling and bumping into one another. I remember looking about frantically for some relatively quiet and secluded corner which would offer a brief respite from the vocal chaos.

I spotted David sitting by himself on the living room couch, looking as if he'd like to be anywhere else but where he actually was. He was the eighteen-year-old brother of my cousin Joanie's friend Tina . David was a reasonably attractive, long-haired kid with thick-lensed glasses and a slight overbite.

I'd met him a year ago, shortly after he'd arrived in Canada from Holland, and was excruciatingly shy  because he knew very little English. I sat down beside him and we talked for awhile. His English had greatly improved, and he'd lost the bashful, self-consciousness completely. He'd planned on attending the midnight Christmas Eve service at St. Paul's Cathedral and asked me if I wanted to come along. Eager to escape the congested party, I readily agreed.

On the way to St. Paul's, David told me he'd acquired his own apartment, and now had "tons of friends". He talked rapidly, never making eye contact, and I sensed that there was something odd about him. We met up with two of his friends at the church. They were a strikingly attractive guy with long, jet-black hair named Lane and his female friend, Eleanor, a pretty blonde with an open, straightforward manner.

After the service, Eleanor offered to have us all over at her family's house. When we got there, my eyes were dramatically opened to the lifestyle that David had adapted during the past year. As the four of us sat cross-legged on the floor of Eleanor's bedroom, listening to Yes as it reverberated from her boyfriend, Gerry's speakers. Lane then took a small plastic bag out of his jacket pocket. I could see that it was full of pot and the red flags instantly shot up in my head. "Oh, God, they're all a bunch of druggies!" I thought with a shiver of panic. "I gotta get the hell out of here".

I stood up shakily and turned to David. "Can we go back to my Aunt's now?"

He smiled reassuringly at me. "In a few minutes. Just relax, Jane. Ever tried this stuff before?"

I shook my head violently, while Lane and Eleanor smiled and rolled their eyes. "Don't get all uptight", Eleanor murmured, snuggling closer to Lane, "It's not going to hurt you or anything."

Against my better judgement, I sat back down, eager not to appear out of it and childish. Although I was very much afraid of drugs, I felt a twinge of curiosity. Was it really all that dangerous? I wondered. Could smoking pot one time make me a filthy addict, eventually shoving needles into my veins?

I decided to shuck off the outer layer of fear and embrace what had become commonplace in the suburbs of Canada and the U.S. With that initial, hesitant toke on a thick, crudely rolled joint, I crossed over into a world that would nearly consume me with its decadence, depravity and despair.

As I recall, the marijuana had no effect on me initially. But after smoking for several weeks I noticed that it produced a rather comforting sensation of well-being and cosiness, as if I was tightly wrapped in a down comforter.

My cerebrum became insulated in a muffling fibreglass, effectively protecting it from incessant prodding of too much stimulation from the outside world. In short, I liked it, and thanks to David, who knew several pushers in the area, I was kept amply supplied in my new and deliciously forbidden habit.

Of course, being very much the amateur, having started into drugs at a comparatively late age, I wasn't too adept at hiding it from my parents. Consequently, they became quite distressed upon returning home one night and smelling pot smoke in my room (I foolishly thought that smoking at an open window would prevent its odour from being detected).

Well, all hell broke loose, and I could detect the extreme disillusionment in their frightened eyes as they struggled with the reality of having a kid on drugs to deal with. Although I was angered at their accusations that I was some sort of sewer-dwelling addict, I couldn't help but smirk inwardly with the smug satisfaction of seeing them squirm.

Over the past couple of years, I'd grown very angry and hostile toward my parents, particularly Mom. I didn't really understand it, but sometimes I felt that I despised her, and wanted her to stay out of my life completely.

It was strange that she infuriated me that much. With what I knew about Dad, he should have been the enemy. A year earlier, he had confided in me about his girlfriend, Sally Smith. Showing me a photograph of a pretty young brunette and telling me that he had gotten to know her very well over the past several months, I realized that his marriage to Mom was over. I should have hated what he was doing, having an illicit affair behind her back, but instead I felt sorry for him.

If my Mother had shown him more love, kindness and understanding, he wouldn't have to go searching for those qualities in another woman. Can you believe that? But like most teenage girls, I thought that Daddy could do no wrong. Dad obviously told me all this to help assuage some of his guilt, and perhaps because he figured that I'd react the way I did. I don't know for certain and we never discussed it.

My drug involvement just caused the rift between Mom and I to widen even further and I deeply resented her interfering in my life. It was none of her business. It wasn't as though I was pressuring her to use marijuana after all.

What the hell was the matter with her? I figured that if she concerned herself even half as much with her marriage as she did with my extracurricular activities, then her husband wouldn't be fooling around on her. It seemed to give me just cause to feel smugly superior and self-righteous. I was a real gem of a daughter, wasn't I?

My life spiralled downward soon after that introduction to seductive psychedelia. I quickly tired of pot and was curious about other illicit drugs, such as mescaline and LSD. It was extremely easy to get anything my adventurous little heart desired, as David and his friends had an abundant supply of everything. It was an exciting, rivetting new world that I had stumbled upon and like an eager explorer, I wanted to experience everything firsthand.

Knowing it was wrong and having been well-educated in the perils of drug addiction, I nonetheless took furtive pleasure in thumbing my nose at the Establishmentarian notions of what was right. I enjoyed the wild thrill that spun me in its tightening web.

I wasn't too happy about the way some of them made me feel, however, or the manner by which they caused these huge gaps in my consciousness. Mescaline was particularly bad for the latter. Once I took some just before a Slade concert at Centennial Hall and ended up missing the entire show. I sat down with a group of my new friends. The next thing I knew, the band was leaving the stage amid cheering and wild applause. I turned to Wayne, with whom I'd gone to the concert and asked why Slade had only performed one song.

"They were onstage for over two hours," Wayne had replied, looking at me as if I had live snakes sprouting out of the top of my head. "Where have you been?"

I had then spent the next half hour looking for my purse under the seat, completely lost in a drugged fog, while Wayne became quite exasperated. I decided that I had taken too much mescaline that time, so from that point on, I halved the dose and reached a satisfactory compromise between being too stoned and too based in reality. I used it at school, at home, and particularly with the gang.

Drifting away completely from Beverly and my identity as a serious, conscientious student, I embraced my inner-city compatriots, with their flamboyant clothes, gutter lingo, hard-edged cynicism and anti-social stance. Finally, I belonged somewhere, with what I thought to be the "popular kids". It was exhilarating, ego-stroking and, most of all, the drug culture itself assuaged my nagging problems and feelings of worthlessness.

Many kids used drugs for these reasons and it hasn't changed much in twenty years. Now you hear about high school and university students taking stuff that's extremely impure and hideously mutated. Drugs aren't as "safe" as they were in the 1970's, and it's frightening to think of what they'll be like in another two decades.

Purple microdot was a somewhat tame form of acid that became my personal favourite. I liked it because it caused just enough sensory distortion to allow me to feel lightheaded without totally abandoning a foundation in solid reality. Objects would swirl silently, entertaining my battle-weary eyes and distracting my mind from anything around me that I figured I couldn't handle.

In class, I became an expert at appearing "normal" while secretly experiencing spectacular mental fireworks. It was not uncommon to hear things, to smell strong essences from all kinds of normally odourless objects. Often it would feel as though something was running damp, tiny fingers over my skin. It was strangely reassuring, even though I felt shivers of fear when I'd look up from my book to discover that nobody was anywhere near me.

Food tasted different, like unexpectedly registering the flavour of marshmallows after taking a mouthful of spaghetti. It was as though all five senses were transmitting the wrong information by getting their frequencies confused. This altered state of existence became familiar after several months, and it was essential to remain in it.

This was a blissful distraction from the way I experienced life in the "real" world. I figured that as long as I was getting signals crossed, I could coexist in the world I'd rejected by slipping into a safe pocket whenever I chose.

David invited me to a party at his place one Saturday night, where I'd spent a great deal of time with Wayne. We talked for many hours, with our hands wrapped tightly together, and I could sense that he was very attracted to me. Wayne was my age but looked about sixteen, with long, shaggy red hair, large green eyes and a wide, vacant grin.

Small and wraithlike, he'd sit for hours on the floor, hunched over like a half-starved sparrow, while rocking mindlessly back and forth. He dressed in dirty, ragged jeans, and faded, worn flannel, and he could have fitted right in with the media's cliched impression of today's "alternative look". I was never all that enamoured with Wayne, but I really wanted a boyfriend, and he was more than willing to fill in for one. I didn't even like him all that much, for he had a mindless, semi-moronic giggle and talked constantly about the virtues of being "totally blasted" on chemicals.

Wayne and I began a heated period of intense dating from that night on, meeting at David's, where he rented a room, then getting stoned and wandering aimlessly around the downtown area. We never did much, preferring to explode our brain cells and revel in the effects of experiencing London's core at night with city lights dipping and strobing.

After we tired of this, Wayne and I would return to his place, where we'd make out on a threadbare couch amid empty bottles, discarded roaches and filth. I knew my mother would despise this apartment and that made it somewhat attractive despite the squaller.

I noticed that there was a pair of disapproving eyes watching me as I went through my various motions of furtive affection with my new boyfriend. Stewart, a rather heavy-set, puffy-faced blond who had a penchant for using the hard stuff (heroin was his drug of choice) had been attracted to me a few months earlier, when the two of us saw a film about Pink Floyd together.

We'd held hands throughout the movie, and later had gone back to David's, where he'd persuaded me to kiss him. Drugs had lessened my inhibitions substantially, for I would never have done anything like that straight and after that, Stewart seemed to think that we were going together. I had simply been flattered that someone had thought I was sexy and responded favourably to the compliment.

With my long, straight hair parted squarely in the middle, smallish figure and clear skin, I wasn't bad looking, but still suffered from my old, familiar "mouse mentality".

A short while later, I'd met Wayne and since I never considered myself to be going with Stewart didn't think I needed to break anything off, or terminate any relationship with this "poppy seed

Casanova". Stewart apparently thought differently and I was shortly to me miscrably made aware of this on what was to be the worst night of my life so far.

I formed an uneasy alliance with the other kids of this warped inner circle. There was Keith, a skinny, ravaged young man with an omnipresent black top hat and whose vapid grin revealed two missing teeth and a penchant for infesting vast quantities of a potent form of acid known as Black Death. You couldn't get much of a sensible conversation out of the Acid King, but he had a good and compassionate heart. Keith was one of the few who didn't ultimately turn on me.

Paul, tow-headed, stocky and with a bit of a nasty streak when he was stoned, didn't really like me much, but tolerated my presence because he was tight with Wayne. He was volatile and unpredictable and I steered clear of him whenever possible.

Eleanor, the girl I met on Christmas Eve, became close friends with Maryanne, a pudgy, tousled-haired seventeen-year-old with striking features and ultra-tight clothes. Eleanor ultimately left home to move in with David and Wayne, whereupon Maryanne took her the streetwalker's route and the two of them earned money for drugs by sleeping around for profit.

You'd think that I would have clued into the reality that perhaps these kids weren't particularly well-adjusted and happy, but I was too blinded by all the crap I was swallowing, snorting and smoking to notice, or care for that matter. All I was concerned with was the undeniable fact that I was affiliated with a bunch of cool teenagers for the first time in my life and I was going to enjoy it to the hilt.

I finally met the notorious Bruce, Eleanor's boyfriend, around March of 1974. During his absence, he'd cleaned up his act and was repulsed and disgusted by Janet's drug use, prostitution and motley friends. He broke up with her after she got busted for possession, and latched on to a virginal fifteen-year-old innocent, who would later succumb to the very substances he'd grown to hate.

One night, Bruce, Wayne, David and I were sitting on the floor, steeped in Elton John's "Goodbye Yellow Brick Road" and reefer. (Bruce convinced himself soon after his return to London that pot wasn't really dope, so it was okay). I had reached the stage in my less-than-illustrious chemical career where I was desperate to stay high all the time.

Life had become unbearable, with my parent's marital problems, their constant harrassmentof my friends and lifestyle, growing difficulties with my schoolwork, guilt about shoplifting (to get the kinds of clothes that I wanted) and the pervasive feeling of emptiness that gripped me whenever the drug haze cleared. That was to be avoided at all cost, for it needled the message into my head that I was wasting my life away and heading for total self-annihilation.

One morning, I snorted some powder before school, a substance I knew nothing about, not even its name. I was so heavily stoned that I felt that my brain was suffocating and that I was being slowly paralyzed from the inside out. My muscles weren't getting the right messages and refused to move without a lot of spastic jerkiness. It was truly frightening, and as the feeling worsened, my eyes blurred alarmingly and my tongue seemed to swell up and fill my entire mouth.

Fumbling and stumbling down the corridor, with my ears clogged and muffling all sounds that pummelled me from the outside, I staggered into the English teachers' lounge and fell in a heap at Mr. Kellow's feet.

Well, he helped me over to a couch and talked to me for over an hour, realizing I was wasted and fearful that my life was washing down the drain. When I straightened out enough to return to class, I began to question my unhealthy habits.

So as the four of us sat smoking, I told Bruce that I was a bit frightened at the way the chemicals made me feel at times, but that, overall, the bad was worth the tremendous good. I'd try anything, even going so far as to claim that I'd shoot heroin if it wasn't so addictive.

"Clean up your act, chick", Bruce exclaimed, shaking his head, "You're going to destroy yourself one of these days. I've seen it happen too many times. That's why I quit drugs. It ain't worth the shit you go through. Believe me. Get out while you still can."

I didn't listen to him then, and instead of heeding my own conscience, I decided to take the Big Existential Plunge and do a hit of Windowpane, a very powerful acid that was infamous for its wild hallucinogenic qualities. I was somewhat reluctant, but Wayne had promised to look after me. I left our house early for the

evening, and fought the urge to turn around before boarding the bus
to Wayne's.

People had really flipped out on Windowpane, never to return to sanity. The psychiatric wing of Victoria Hospital, the leg-
endary seventh floor, was inhabited almost exclusively by burned-
out acid freaks. What if that happened to me?

But by this time, I'd numbed my better judgement with
countless hits of mescaline, Purple Microdot and a host of other
substances I didn't even know the proper names of. Common sense
had become blurred with the constant exposure of my senses to
mind-bending chemicals. Windowpane was simply the next logical
step.

Wayne thought it best that I took only half a hit, so we spilt it.
I mellowed quickly, feeling a rush of adrenaline with the realization
that there was  no turning back now. We settled on our favourite
dumpy couch and put the Steve Miller Band's "Joker" album on the
stereo. I hated that record and still cannot bring myself to listen to
the title track when it's played on the radio today.

My musical tastes had radically altered since immersing myself in the drug world. I had abandoned the Everly Brothers and
embraced the harder, more streetwise Canadian band The Guess
Who. I'd seen them perform in concert the summer before in
Windsor and had been mesmerized by the electrifyingly charismatic presence of lead singer Burton Cummings.

With his wild mop of curly, black hair, well-built lumberjack
body, packed with dynamic, raw energy, he literally dominated the
stage. Sweat flew from his head as he pounded fiercely on his
piano, spitting, growling and stretching elastic-like vocal chords to
their soaring limit.

I fell into instant lust as my long-dormant sexuality began to
poke it's hesitant way out of its cryogenic state. This rock and roll
sex machine grabbed hold of my post-pubescent senses and ripped
the lid off my bland, sublime little universe.

So when I'd written to Julie and told her about the Guess
Who, and later, about my drug dalliances, she became quite dis-
gusted with me. She had then  promptly ended our correspondence.
I was haughtily indignant, feeling she was being cold and unfair, so
I put her letters and my Everly albums in mothballs. It was time that
I grew up anyway, I figured.

I knew that Burton Cummings used drugs liberally and his

band's songs were a drastic departure from the innocent ideals of
Don and Phil Everly. After I'd been hanging out with the druggies,
I began buying albums like Uriah Heap's "Demons and Wizards",
and Deep Purple's "Burn". For Christmas that year, Jim gave me
Pink Floyd's "Dark Side of the Moon" and I borrowed his "Paranoid" album by Black Sabbath. These records don't have a hell of a
lot in common with "Wake Up, Little Susie" and "Bird Dog".

Anyway, as I sat with Wayne, listening to the wholesome
strains of "Some people call me the Space Cowboy, some call me
the Gangster of Love",I noticed that a poster on the back of the door
had begun to swirl and swarm, seeming to breathe and pulsate to
the beat of the music. Paul, sitting nearby, grinned at me and said
knowingly, "Chick, you are so stoned."

After that, my cerebrum erupted, and I lost control of my
emotions. Without knowing how, I ended up crouched on the floor,
with my face suddenly soaked with tears. I could hear wild, uncontrollable sobbing, which seemed to be coming from a far corner of
the room. Then I realized that it was me who was crying so
hysterically.

I felt a choking, strangling sensation, then heard a voice
speaking in guttural, flat tones into my left ear. The words tore into
my eardrum, and I could feel hot, thick blood gurgling from it and
running down the side of my face.

Oh God, I'm wounded! I'm  going to die, I thought, terror
clutching my chest and gripping onto my ribcage. Then, I knew
with a sensation of pure horror that I had somehow  crossed over
into a vast, dead wasteland where I'd mever again see my family. I
would thus be forever condemned to walk with the dead. It was a
punishment for betraying my parents and defying their authority
and their love.

"No! This can't be happening! I've got to get out of here!"
These frightened words leapt out of my mouth and rolled across the
floor, disappearing under a bookcase. I was shouting, screaming in
mental agony as I watched my life circling down a huge, gaping
drain. I was powerless to stop it. "Why? Why? Why is this happening to me!? Why won't you let me see my family? I'm sorry I let
them down! Please! I want my mother! I need them! Don't you
understand?!"

Wayne, David and Paul grew angry at this point, totally
repulsed  at this mama's girl who refused to grow up and assert her

independence. We spent the next few hours locked in this macabre one-act play of damnation, as I grew more and more desperate and they even more resentful of my behaviour.

Wayne tried to get me to listen to James Taylor albums in order to calm down. It was futile; I was completely unhinged in a classic case of drug-induced paranoiac psychosis. Nobody knew what to do with me in such a maniacal, out-of-control state.

They decided to shame me out of it, taunting me and shouting, "Get out of here then, you whining little baby! Go home to your precious family and shut the fuck up!"

My panic escalated into unleashed, raving hysteria as I screamed and wailed, pulling my hair out at the roots and looking wildly about. I saw my three so-called friends there in the room with me one minute, then mysteriously vanished the next.

I suppose this theatrical display lasted about four hours, after which the worst of the drug's effects wore off. I was left in a semi-vegetative, exhausted state, wandering about from room to room and mumbling incoherently.

Paul smirked as I stood in my hollowed-out sludge pile of a spent body and pushed me aside roughly. "You're disgusting, Jane. Acting like a fucking lunatic in front of us, freaking out from a little hit of acid. If that's the real you, then we don't want you here."

Wayne was quick to come to my defense. "Shut up, asshole. She couldn't handle it. Some people flip out on Windowpane. It happens."

I wrapped my arms tightly around my shivering frame and decided to see if Jim was home. It was long past midnight and the last bus had left Dundas and Richmond for Westmount over an hour ago. Hopefully, our parents were still out, or had retired for the night and were safely asleep.

Luckily, Jim was at home and picked me up. I said little to him on the drive home, only that I had done some heavy acid and was feeling pretty shaky. He told me to be careful, because a friend of his had gone on a trip and never returned.

Now, surely that negative experience was enough to put a lid on my anti-social, sociopathic lifestyle, but no, it took an even more gruesome incident to do that.

It was a week before my nineteenth birthday. For several months, Wayne had been pressuring me to sleep with him, and I had adamantly refused. I was fearful of sex and not particularly attracted to him in that intimate way. Though some definite stirrings had been aroused by some of the music I was exposed to and the guys who performed it with lusty abandon, I had no desire to lose my virginity to Wayne or any other boy for that matter.

Again, that persistent, nagging question gnawed at my psyche: Was there something wrong with me? After all, every other couple in our circle was sexually active and spoke glowingly about it. Joe told me repeatedly that "If you don't have sex with me, our relationship's gonna die", and finally I felt pressured enough to go on the Pill.

Then, on April fifteenth, 1974, the two of us were sitting on his bed, actively engaged in our customary necking session, while he periodically pleaded with me to do it with him.

I began to sense that he was somewhat more firmly insistent on this particular night and I knew that I had set myself up for certain disaster. I had told my father that I would be out all night. He thought that I was going to sleep with Wayne, but in actuality, I was just testing him, secretly hoping he'd put his foot down and forbid me to go.

I found out that my parents had spent many sleepless nights debating about whether or not they should not allow me to hang out with the "grass gang". Mom was sick with worry, but Dad assured her that if he laid down the law, I'd run away and disappear from their lives forever. So the consensus was to be permissive.

Jim and I had always craved discipline, as we'd be certain of our parents' love if they'd shed their lenient parenthood crap and give us some hard-stooled rules to live by. But the Big, Progressive Theory of Parenting in the 1970's was to let kids do as they pleased, loosen the ties and open the door to disaster by refusing to set limits and guidelines. Mom and Dad were only doing what they believed in their hearts to be the right thing, but it was so very, very wrong for my brother and me, and all children.

So when Dad didn't stop me from spending the night at Waynes, I felt that he really didn't love me. He wanted me out of his life and messed up on drugs, casual sex and wanton self-destructiveness.

While Wayne was kissing me, he suddenly shoved his hands down my pants and grabbed me hard. I reacted with surprised anger, yanking my face away from his and yelling at him to stop it. Instead, he leaned forward, pulling me down on the mattress and pressing his chest against me with such force that I was unable to breathe.

"Relax. It's no big deal. You want it just as bad as I do. Don't make me force this."

I knew that I would have to go through with it, even though I felt sick at the prospect and was absolutely terrified. The others were all out in the living room, a scant few yards away, and I couldn't let them witness another spectacle of a half-crazed immature brat crying for Mommy.

"Okay, just get it over with", I thought dismally, lying still on the dilapidated mattress as Wayne ripped my clothes off. In all fairness to him, he really believed that there was nothing wrong with what he was doing, that he was simply helping me to enter the Wide Wonderful World of Sexual Gratification. Besides, at eighteen, he was at the height of his sexual peak and so it was a pretty big deal to him.

What I remember most vividly about my first time was that it hurt like hell. As Wayne entered me, it seemed as though this huge log had been rammed into my body, splitting it in half. Without going into a lot of graphic detail about the whole event, it's sufficient to say that I spent the whole time sobbing for him to stop while he went at me for what seemed an hour or more.

When it was over, I couldn't bear to look at him and rolled over on my side, facing the wall, curled up into a fetal position. Later, after Wayne fell asleep, I put on my clothes and walked with pained difficulty out of the bedroom and out into the bright, crowded and noisy living room to get a cigarette. I'd taken up smoking soon after meeting my new friends, an activity I'd sworn years before I'd never engage in. Right now, I really needed a nicotine fix after that nightmarish encounter with Wayne's penis.

Stewart was sitting over in the corner, and when he saw me, the stoned fellow sneered, "Fucking slut". I wanted to die. After everyone had left and David had gone to bed, I lay on the couch and listened to the radio all night, unable to sleep and still hurting both physically and emotionally from the events of the evening.

At around four AM, "Cathy's Clown", by the Everly Brothers, a song I'd once played over and over, came on and I broke down in tears at my lost innocence and the death of my childhood dreams. My little brother had been on drugs since age eleven, my dad had a girlfriend, and I was totally fucked up on acid and mescaline. Not only that, I'd just lost my virginity to a man I didn't even love.

I collected myself as the Everlys' harmonies washed over my stinging  body and vowed that when I walked out of that broken-down house on Blecher Street in a few hours, I'd never return. My birthday was fast approaching and so was my graduation from high school. It was time to grow up, shed the imperfections of my misspent youth and move on. If I continued at this rate, I would not Reach adulthood, or if I did, I'd be reduced by drugs to a giggling, drooling idiot. If my family wasn't going to stop me, then I had to put the brakes on.

So I did. I never saw any of those kids again. David eventu-ally married and had a child with Down Syndrome, which was actually not caused from David's chemical abuse. Stewart  died several years later of a heroin overdose.  I shudder to think about what happened to Wayne, but I feel even more sorry for his chil-dren if he was foolish enough to reproduce. Wayne had been a drug user for many years before I met him and studiously avoided being straight. Maybe he cleaned up his act eventually and achieved some measure of happiness. I hope so. Nobody deserves to be con-demned like that forever.

I'm not proud of anything I did that year and there will always be a part of me that wonders if my life in the years to come would have turned out any better if it not for those chemicals. But that's a question that no-one can really answer.

# Chapter Six

# Strawberry Fields (Not) Forever: Love Proves Fruitless In the Summer of 1974

I ended up missing the prom because Frederick, the fellow who'd asked me, had the unfortunate reputation of being Dork Personified and I figured there was enough against me already. So he went alone, met a pretty, outgoing girl and had a wonderful time, while I sat home and listened to Guess Who albums. It was a fitting end to a totally miserable and vacuous high school experience.

The only positive thing about it was winning the award for Highest Standing in Grade thirteen English. I still have it in a cardboard box, somewhere along with my framed photograph of the Everly Brothers and a certificate that stated that I'd been published in Jack and Jill magazine, as well as the ones signifying that I'd graduated from one grade to another in piano. Well, the past nineteen years hadn't been a total loss, I figured.

Summer jobs were hard to come by that year, so I ended up working at a strawberry farm in Lambeth. I slaved my butt off for paltry wages and having to walk six miles home every night after bending over for eight hours and picking strawberries for sixty cents a quart.

However, the experience wasn't entirely negative, for I met some pretty amazing kids who helped me re-emerge from the shell I'd retreated into after the drug experiences. I actually had some fun for the first time in years.

Not only that, but I fell in love, in a big way, with twenty-five-year-old Charles, son of the family who owned the farm. He looked a great deal like a young Anthony Newly, with that same sly grin and pixyish face. I was attracted to him from the beginning, as he showed me considerable kindness and gave me all sorts of wonderful compliments that I yearned for at every possible opportunity. I wasn't used to this and for a man six years my senior to show such interest, when he could have had his pick of more sophisticated women, I was privileged to be able to turn his head.

We talked endlessly for hours, about our future plans, relationships, music and anything else that popped into our minds. He was studying to be a chiropractor and I let him practise on me. Charles had an expert, confident touch and commented on my well-developed lower back muscles, which were the result of doing many backbends over the years.

I had decided to attend York University in Toronto in the fall, a school specializing in the Fine Arts, English and the Humanities. I'd been accepted at the University of Toronto and the University of Western Ontario, but chose York because U. of T. was far too large and UWO was in London. I desperately wanted to leave home and live in residence.

Our love affair blossomed into some serious physical contact that began with the back massages and progressed to include a lot of making out in Charles' car. We'd go to drive-ins and pay little attention to the movie, so lost were we in deep kissing, groping and wrapping our arms tightly around each other. I discovered that I really liked this, probably because I had such strong romantic feelings for this mature, fascinating and easy-on-the-ego fellow who I secretly felt I didn't deserve.

Once I felt comfortable enough with Charles, I told him about my past experiences with anorexia, psychiatrists, and the drug sessions of the past year. I even showed him where I'd cut a cross in my right wrist with a razor blade at seventeen.

That had been quite frightening at the time, and unquestionably twisted. I was babysitting for one of the lifeguards at our community pool. He had two young boys, and trusted me with them, as he knew that I'd done a lot of babysitting and enjoyed it.

Later that night, as I sat on the couch listening to "Sour Suite", a melancholy song by the Guess Who, about the negative side of being a famous rock star and how empty it was, despite the adulation , I began to feel very depressed.

As I lost myself in Cummings' plaintive vocals, that familiar nagging ache which plagued me periodically and seemed to have no cause to be doing so. It was inescapable, a kind of pain that wouldn't go away, no matter what position I shifted to, which record I was playing, who was with me at the time, or what time of day or night it was. Depression is all-consuming, relentless and takes no prisoners. It doesn't care if you're halfway through your teens and have your whole life ahead of you. I'd felt that way at four, when I burnt myself on the iron.

Suddenly, the memory of that afternoon flashed into my thickening head. I'd somehow felt better after the immediate pain assaulted me. I couldn't explain it then and still was unable to, but maybe if I hurt myself again, I could get a welcome respite from the inner anguish.

Without hesitating, I went into the medicine cabinet of the family's bathroom and searched it frantically for something sharp. Just then, my gaze alighted upon a package of Wilkinson Sword razor blades. Of course, I thought with a strange sensation of exhilaration and exuberance. Fumbling with the package, I took out a blade and sat down on the tiled floor, then rolled up my right sleeve. I'll just make a few little nicks, just enough to draw some blood. I remembered accidentally cut my finger as a small child and not being the least upset by the sight of blood. Then there was that incident when I was fourteen and made some small deliberate cuts on my wrist. There was nothing to it.

I shut my eyes tight and cut in a forceful, downward motion, from the top of my wrist, lengthwise, an inch and a half long. Then, upon opening my eyes, I was overcome with guilt and remorse, seeing the cut gap widely and angrily and revealing veins and this repulsive yellowish substance.

For some reason, a picture of Jesus flashed into my mind, and I took this to mean that I should ask for forgiveness. Finding it difficult to pray with blood pouring all over my arm and painting the black linoleum, I quickly cut again, horizontally this time, so that I'd carved a cross into my wrist.

I recall feeling very ill at this point and searched wildly in the cabinet for bandages while blood splattered the sink and counter in a macabre crimson pattern. I managed to find a box of gauze and wrapped it repeatedly around my wounded arm, then secured it with adhesive tape. Then I hastily wiped up the mess and threw the used blade in the garbage, fearful that the parents would return and see my gruesome evidence. Mentally, I felt better, less distraught, as I let the pain sink into me in a warm release.

I felt secure enough in my relationship with Charles to tell him all this and after I finished he sat, silent and wide-eyed, fumbling with his car keys and shaking his head slowly.

Finally, I lit a cigarette and remarked, half-jokingly, "Well, do you think I'm a real whack-o?"

Charles forced a smile. "Um, well, you gotta admit, it's a pretty awful thing to do to yourself. Were you trying to commit suicide?"

I shook my head. "No, not at all. I just wanted a release from the other kind of pain. The cutting did that for awhile anyway. But I'll never do it again, I promise. Please don't hate me, Charles."

He cautiously put his arm around my shoulders. "Hey, I don't hate you. But all this stuff you told me about your past, the drugs and the shrinks and starving yourself.....well, it's kind of difficult to absorb all at once."

My heart sank. I'd punched a hole in our idyllic union, thanks to my stupid big mouth. I knew that things would never be the same again.

I was right. Charles began to see another girl, named Annie, even as he was still dating me. He told me this and I tried to be mature and philosophical about it. He said that she didn't smoke, had never used drugs, and was very innocent. I thought I was going to puke from the sugar overdose.

Although I knew about Annie, I still held out a wispy hope that Charles would tire of her colourlessness and stop seeing her. But, since I hated myself and had a very poor self-image, I knew she was infinitely more appealing than a fucked-up ex-druggie, ex-anorexic nutcase who deliberately slashed herself.

One morning, upon awakening, I knew in my heart that Charles was going to finally break off our relationship and see Annie exclusively. The reality of it seeped into my bones and settled there, and I rode to the farm ready to face the death march.

As soon as I saw Charles, I crumbled and dissolved into an emotional slag-heap. Unable to work, or barely function, for that matter, I stayed in the bunkhouse while Charles' younger brother put an eight-track tape, Paul McCartney's "Band On the Run", in a portable player. I lay there on the floor listening to it over and over for the next eight hours or so.

I couldn't move, and these pathetic, muffled sobs racked my body the entire time. I wished someone would come in and put a shotgun blast through my miserable head. I despised Charles for his shallowness, but I hated myself more. My life was a useless mess of mistakes, pain, self-loathing, and self-destructive battlegrounds.

Well, this self-pity jag lasted for about a week, after which I collected myself and prepared to make the one hundred twenty-mile trek to Toronto the Good for a brand new start at York University. Maybe I'd put a monkey wrench in my love affair with Charles, but I was not yet out of my teens and there was a big, exciting, uncharted world out there to be explored. Maybe I could leave the gross imperfect past behind and achieve success and happiness elsewhere.

I saw the Guess Who in Windsor again at the end of the summer with Karen, and even got to meet Burton Cummings after giving him some pictures of the band that I'd sketched. He was very nice to us, even complimentary. It was a positive way to end my early youthful years.

However, I still cannot listen to "Band On the Run" without feeling this uncomfortable, remorseful little twinge

**Chapter Seven**

# "The Ivory Towers Are Crumbling All Around Me": My Freshman Year At York

I drove up to the campus from London with Mom and Dad, and it was a very stressful journey. Dad was cloaked in his customary silence, and Mom's sombre demeanour indicated that she was quite upset that her little girl was leaving home. Earlier that afternoon, I'd heard her crying in her room and couldn't help feeling sorry for her. Now she'd really be alone. The two of us had overcome our animosity toward one another and had achieved some measure of peace and harmony and now I would no longer be living with her.

In all likelihood, I'd fall in love at school, get married and start a family of my own. Well, she still had Jim, and now that he'd settled down somewhat and abandoned many of his "jungle buddies", the kid was actually becoming an ally to her as her marriage to our father quickly unravelled in the fall of 1974.

Finally, after what seemed an eternity, I spotted the university campus. It looked as though it could have been square in the middle of Siberia and the drab, monotonous starkness made me shudder inwardly. I discovered later that York University had been designed and constructed in 1965, in grim preparation for student riots which were igniting American campuses and threatened to creep northward.

One of the buildings had been erected as an actual fortress with a high stone wall, which could be manned with heavily-armed guards, guns ostensibly aimed at disruptive students. It was slate-grey, ominous and loomed out of the flat, barren surroundings, standing like some hideous relic of the Medieval era. This was where I was to spend the next four years of my life?

I turned to look at Mom, but she was busy trying to figure out ourbearings. "You're in Founders Residence. Let's see if there's someone we can ask for directions."

I returned my gaze to the desolate campus wasteland, with one building that cast tall, ebony smoke-stacks into the overcast sky and giving it the appearance of an industrial town.

There weren't many buildings in 1974. I've heard that the university is absolutely massive now, two decades later, but I haven't seen it since 1978. They were spaced far apart and were all decidedly unattractive. Western's campus, in comparison, was paradise-on-earth, with its stately, beige-brick edifices and lush, fertile grounds. I secretly wondered if I'd made a big mistake opting for this shuddering wilderness. I ruminated with bitter irony that York was predominantly Jewish, which made the striking similarity to a concentration camp utterly obscene.

I quickly forgot about the campus' ugliness upon reaching Founders Residence. It was a rather attractive brick building with a courtyard containing trees, believe it or not, and the rooms' windows cranked open sideways to take in the pleasant view. It looked like something out of Percy Bysshe Shelley's times and I knew I could tolerate the rest of the place if my living quarters were this capable of supporting life.

After helping me to unpack, Mom and Dad left, somewhat reluctantly. I felt a sharp jab of homesickness as I hugged my Mother tightly and promised to phone collect every Sunday night. Dad mumbled, "Good luck", but I could see that he was secretly proud of me for making it this far, after so much trouble in the past several years. I took comfort in the knowledge that I'd be home for Thanksgiving, only five weeks away.

After they'd left, I looked around at my living quarters and wondered how I could make them even more comfortable and familiar. It was a double room, for I'd decided that, in my freshman year, I would be more easily integrated into the residence society if I had a roommate.

Our beds were standard institutional singles and we each had a desk, large bookshelves, a heavy wooden chair and a plastic-cushioned, lounging type seat. There were fluorescent lights above the desks and a garish overhead one, which didn't do the room any justice. In short, it was a very typical dormitory room; nice, but in drastic need of some creative decorating.

I wondered about my roommate. She'd obviously already

arrived, because there were two duffel bags, a large knapsack, countless cardboard boxes of clothes and an acoustic guitar strewn about. The guitar caught my attention and I pictured a hippie type, free spirited musician, with peasant blouses, sandals and love beads, looking frail, ivory-toned, with long, wavy hair.

So much for assumptions: Just then, a rather chubby, plain-looking girl entered, with shoulder-length flaxen hair and an open, ingratiating smile. She was dressed in ordinary jeans and a decid-edly unhippie-like sweater. "Hi, I'm Wanda. Nice to meet you."

"Hi, my name's Jane. I guess you're stuck with me for the semester. I like your guitar."

"Thanks. My boyfriend Ike gave it to me. I don't play that great or anything, but it helps me relax. God, I miss that guy already. He's going to Lakehead University in Thunder Bay. We've never been apart like this before."

Poor Wanda. She cried every night for weeks, and there wasn't much I could say or do to cheer her up. But I liked her. She was honest, affectionate and turned out to be a damned hard worker.

Since we were both English majors, we spent a great deal of time talking about our courses, and discussing our favourite au-thors, books, etc. Both of us enjoyed writing as well, and though we weren't certain what we would end up doing after graduation, we knew that some type of writing would be involved. I was thinking about doing my graduate work at Carlton University in Ottawa in journalism.

I'd kept a diary for the past three years and had brought it with me. It chronicalled my experiences with anorexia nervosa, drugs and my dismay over our family problems. I held onto this document for three more years, then got rid of it in 1977. It was just too painful a reminder of terrible times in my life, and thought that if I threw it out, I was denouncing the past and assuring myself that it would never repeat itself.

I met a fascinating assortment of kids during those first weeks at Founders, people to whom I was to grow extremely close over the next few years. Felicity was a gregarious, buxom blonde with a rabid Mickey Mouse fetish. She had a Mickey Mouse phone, comforter, pillow, sheets, stuffed animals, mouse ears, Mickey Mouse sweatshirts, notepads, pens, pencils, and everything imagin-able. Walking into her room was tantamount to landing in a Disney Never-never Land of rodent adulation.

I was impressed that anyone would be so totally devoted to a cartoon character. Felicity was admittedly at York to study for her "MRS": That is, to find a prospective husband and then get the hell out. She ultimately succeeded, by the way, after meeting an affable, good-natured boy at our college pub and instantly beginning a whirlwind courtship.

Sylvia was younger, at seventeen, but had the maturity and poise of someone twenty or more. She was slightly pudgy, with large breasts, and hated the way they turned her into some plastic sex object. Sylvia was pretty, intelligent and well-bred and had a caustic wit and drop-dead sarcasm that drove the guys nuts. We got along very well from the start and I was impressed that she had spent her childhood in Kenya.

Brad looked a bit like Dustin Hoffman and had a quirky, semi-innocent quality about him. He was embodied with a great deal of common sense and had a streak of compassion a mile long. Gill and I both became instantly infatuated with his little-boy-lost sensuality.

Devon was the "resident clown", a goofy, Nutty Professor-esque kid with slightly buck teeth, geeky glasses and a haircut that belonged in some radical-cum-chic underground movie. I liked Devon for his brash humour and unconventional personality traits, but never grew particularly close to him. He was too off-the wall and therefore somewhat intimidating.

Kenny was a kind-hearted, mild-mannered "gosh-darn-golly" guy who could have been played by Ron Howard and who many girls befriended for his honesty and intelligence. However they didn't become romantically linked to him because they thought he was too tame and milk-fed.

Sidney was dubbed "Founders' Queer" for obvious reasons. I despised the way people ridiculed this tall, sleekly svelte young man with a gorgeous mane of light brown hair and these volup-tuously full lips. But Sidney was much more than just a pretty face; he was the quintessential modern scholastic tragic anti-hero, perse-cuted, yet bravely rising above the scorn and hatred by implement-ing his quiet, innate belief that "people are basically not all that bad a trip". I really liked this guy and so did Laura, and it wouldn't be long before the three of us bonded fast and hard, buffeting one another against the pain that would visit all of us.

And of course, I can't forget the famous team of Patrick and

Adam. These two complete polar opposites were tossed together as roommates and the result was nothing short of comic genius. Patrick was a sheltered, virginal, desperately shy boy, who looked like Beaver Cleaver with his chubby, cherubic face and klutzy mannerisms.

Adam was the arrogant, egotistical son of a television newscaster who wanted to follow in Daddy's footsteps. He reminded me of Ted Baxter from the Mary Tyler Moore Show. He thought he was God's gift to the female population and set about trying to bed each and every girl of Founders A House. You can imagine the inane results of pairing up these tow. Pat was positively repulsed by Adam's vulgarity and blatant sexism and Adam thought Patrick to be a hopeless, hapless mama's boy.

Mark was one of the many Jewish students at Founders, and was an extremely intense, studious and self-sufficient young man who knew, at nineteen, that he was capable of dealing with a serious marital relationship. He had wed Reva when he started university so the two of them lived in the married students' residence. Alan would become very important to me later on.

I left the two most significant members of Founders, as far as my life was concerned anyway, to the end of these descriptions, because they had the most effect on me; one beneficially and the other, quite detrimentally. Courtney was a study in vast complexity, mixed with a liberal dash of unabashed charisma and I never encountered anyone like her before. She was tiny, with short-cropped, very blonde hair, gigantic blue eyes that bored right into your cerebral cortex and a substantial, animated mouth that was rarely still.

Courtney was Dutch, complete with a pretty heavy accent and she had the ability to wrap her vocal chords around English syntax, vernacular and idiosyncracies and mangle the hell out of them. The result was an endearing, truly original language, spoken with sincerity and open-faced straightforwardness. She was no slinger of bull, and if you didn't like the directness, well, that was just too damn bad.

She'd had a difficult time growing up, the product of strict, authoritarian parents with a hard set of rules and no margin for human error. Alice left home at fourteen, and was "adopted" by a loving landlady who made sure she attended school. It became necessary for her to get a job at sixteen, so she became a competent waitress at a restaurant called the Crock and Block.

This serious, single-minded survivor knew at an early age that she wanted to study psychology at university and earned every penny of the tuition herself. She depended upon no-one and was a person unto herself, shunning close, personal ties and preferring to appear strong and independent.

However, there remained within Courtney that lost little girl who'd felt essentially unloved by her parents and who had been sexually abused by her eleven-year-old cousin at age five. Loneliness and depression would overtake her at times as she grew older and she realized that if she was to achieve a measure of happiness, it would be entirely up to her.

She began her studies at York in September of 1973 and had a difficult time in residence. She was unable to develop emotional relationships with the other students and lost herself in her studies. Courtney distinguished herself by becoming a fiercely diligent student and demonstrating a substantial amount of dignity.

When I met her, she was entering her sophmore year and was twenty-one years old, at least two years older than the rest of us. Some of the residents disliked her at first as she referred to us as "kids" and they took great offense to that.

"She thinks she's so damned superior", one girl snorted after Courtney breezed out of the common room one evening. "I'm no kid, for crying out loud."

I really liked her, for she had a certain worldliness and was stamped with the vestiges of experience, unlike most of us who'd always lived at home and were fresh out of high school. Not only that, but she was kindhearted, offering to buy me a coffee that first day and asking if I wanted to listen to her Leonard Cohen records.

This girl's room was a sight to behold. It was nearly completely camouflaged with a wide variety of lush, green plants, such as split-leaf philodendrons, spider plants and some species I'd never seen before. She had strung a large, heavy fish net across the ceiling and had antique lanterns hung everywhere. Posters on the wall ran the gamut from studiously arty to inspirational poetry by Kahlil Gibran. I was utterly diminished when I set foot in this junglescape.

That was Courtney: Creative ambition and very unique. What she lacked in social grace and the finer points of etiquette, she made up for with aplomb.

Courtney had been arduously pursued during her freshman year by a flamboyant male student who resided in Founders' co-ed dormitory. His name was Simon and he was something to behold. Simon had rebelled ferociously against the shaggy-headed, hippie threads of the times by cutting his dark hair very short and dressing exclusively in tailored business suits and black "pickle-stabbers".

This ultra-conservative mien was offset, however, by his manic consumption of alcohol and exceedingly extroverted personality. He was French-Canadian, and when intoxicated, would speak in a quasi-Francophone dialect, throwing expletives like "Tabarnac" around to show that he was truly bilingual.

He had a crude sense of humour and made the most aggravating sexist comments and jokes that I'd ever been privy to. My first reaction upon meeting him was "what an asshole."

Simon had evidently fallen hopelessly in love with the then long-haired Courtney, admiring her freshness and introverted shyness, but she thwarted all of his awkward advances. Still, the two of them would sit for hours, night after night in her elaborate bedroom, discussing philosophy, life's meaning, the ravages and pitfalls of life in the 1070's, and the future.

For it seemed that Simon possessed an alter ego to balance out the drunken clown with the obscene leer and penchant for dirty jokes: He was also extraordinarily compassionate, with a heart of gold, a boy who desperately needed to help people and guide them through life's battlegrounds. In his own way, Simon was every bit as complex and enigmatic as Courtney.

But the romance never blossomed. Courtney found it difficult to maintain relationships of any kind and though she genuinely liked Simon and appreciated his kindness, she recoiled at the notion of "going with" him.

So that was the Founders gang of 1974, at least the students I encountered during "frosh week", a five-day initiation program into the finer social points of being a properly decadent university student. I enjoyed the festivities, even our exposure to a strip club (upon Simon's suggestion) and by the time classes began, I knew that I was really going to like my stay in the Ivory Towers of Toronto.

\*　　\*　　\*　　\*　　\*　　\*　　\*　　\*　　\*

Academically speaking, my freshman year at York proved to be exciting and challenging, although I was not terribly enamoured with my Natural Sciences course (which involved the anatomy of the steam engine) I loved my English and Humanities ones. The latter was entitled "Illusion and Reality" and dealt with these properties in intricate detail.

We studied everything from R.D. Laing's "Sanity, Madness and the Family" to "The Tales of Hoffman", Offenbach's famous opera. Films were shown to us, like "The Cabinet of Dr. Caligari" and we learned all about epistemology and the philosophies of Descartes and Sartre.

With Professor Schneider and tutorial leader Bob MacMillan (who looked like a young but ravaged Albert Einstein, complete with droopy mustache) we delved into the fascinating theories of Carl Jung and seriously questioned what constituted an illusion and what proved that something was indeed real.

I loved thinking in such a uniquely abstract way and excelled in this course, spurred on by the contagious enthusiasm of MacMillan and the quiet intensity of Mr. Schneider.

My sociology selection was entitled "Women and Society" and explored the past and present roles of women, placing a large emphasis on the Women's Liberation Movement, which was in high gear at the time. One of our professors was Esther Greenglass, a renowned writer and speaker for women's issues. I was excited to be among such fertile, ground-breaking minds.

I also took Canadian literature and Romantic literature, and embraced them for exposing me to the works of Leonard Cohen and William Blake. Academe was expanding my mind in ways that I'd never dreamt possible and certainly more effectively than drugs ever had.

Our residence had parties nearly every weekend, involving the copious consumption of alcohol, dancing and talking for hours about music, sex, relationships and politics. We were revelling in the heady feeling of being away from home for the first time and "cutting loose". I dated quite a lot, but didn't particularly want a serious relationship. I was too busy having fun.

When I went home at Thanksgiving, I was happily stunned to find that Jim was now treating me with affection and respect. I guess he admired the fact that I was living alone in the Big City, where nights sprang to life in a wild, splashy circus of wonderment and I was no longer the pathetic loser. I felt the tremendous strain between our parents then, as if something was about to explode in a spectacular, fiery airburst and this was the silent countdown to Armageddon. I was relieved when it was time to return to York.

I met a wholesome-looking, pleasant-natured boy named Ben before Christmas, who was a Seneca College student. We began a fairly intensive relationship. I didn't fall in love with him, for I deemed Ben to be far too boring. He fell all over me and mooned those big, brown eyes of his at me constantly. I liked a little more friction, some sense of a challenge. Ben was simply too damned easy and convenient.

Mom adored him, though. He came home with me one weekend, bringing flowers for her and candy for me. "He's wonderful!" she enthused, hoping that she'd have him for a son-in-law someday. She still speaks wistfully of him to this day, twenty-one years later.

After Christmas, things started to fray a little around the edges. Eager to excel in my studies, but desirous of a healthy, energetic social life, I began to become extremely fatigued. I allowed myself only five hours of sleep a night and this semi-deprivation began to take its toll after a few weeks.

One afternoon, as I practically nodded off in my sociology lecture, a girl I knew casually, named Amber, leaned over and smiled, saying softly, "I used to have that problem, falling asleep in class all the time."

I looked at her. She was a pleasant-looking girl with thick, long hair parted squarely in the middle and a sly, ironic grin. I sat up straighter, somewhat taken aback that my sleepiness was that obvious. "Yeah?"

Amber put her hand over her mouth and whispered, "I get these pills from my doctor. They're great. I can stay up all night and never get tired.

I looked scornfully at her. "What? You mean Speed? I don't do that shit anymore."

Amber shook her head vehemently. "No, no, not beans. It's called Ritalin. They give it to hyperactive kids to settle them down, but it has the opposite effect on a normal person. They're perfectly safe and legal. Wanna try one?" I was suspicious but desperate. She procured a bottle and took out a little blue pill. "Swallow it with your coffee. Takes about twenty minutes to work."

Foolishly, I took her advice and within twenty-five minutes or so, I felt a jolt of adrenaline as my nervous system switched on to auxiliary power. As the lecture ended, I felt suddenly confident that I could get through the next class at full capacity. "Hey, thanks", I remarked gratefully. "So do I just go to a doctor and ask for this Ritalin?"

"Yup. I can get mine to take you on if you'd like. He's really cool."

Well, that was the beginning of what was to be a horrific ordeal with a drug that should certainly have been illegal for anyone, but particularly vulnerable and weary university students. I was to discover that Ritalin is highly addictive and promotes all kinds of psychological problems, intensifies depression and contributes to anxiety and panic attacks. So my drug use did not end with my nineteenth birthday after all. For someone with a one hundred forty-eight I.Q., I was ridiculously stupid.

Ritalin was only the start of a steady downward spiral that would continue for the next two years. I had a great deal of difficulty with interpersonal relationships once the initial joy of connecting with the other students in residence wore off.

First came my utter devastation upon learning that Brad had chosen Wanda over me. He'd gone out with both of us for a period of time, and I secretly hoped that I would be the "lucky one", even though Wanda seemed somehow more settled, even-tempered and emotionally stable.

I had begun to behave a bit erratically, probably due to the Ritalin, and in an effort to calm my jangling nerves I had started drinking more frequently at our college pub, The Cock and Bull. I'd often consume at least four rye and ginger ales per night. I'd never been much of a drinker in the past, but I was beginning to enjoy the warm fuzziness that the alcohol produced. There were always students from the residence willing to spend evenings at the pub so I never lacked for company.

After Brad and Wanda began going out together, I sunk into a deep well of self-loathing and regret. I remember well the night that I discovered I had been unceremoniously dumped. Under the impression that our resident Casanova was going to take both Wanda and me to an on-campus movie, I dissolved into a puddle of misery when Brad announced that he only planned on taking Wanda.

After my initial outcry, which resembled the death scream of a mortally wounded hyena, I was totally inappropriate and immature. I followed them to the movie and sobbed loudly all through it. Poor Brad felt terrible, and in my anguish I thought that he deserved to squirm for being such a selfish, unreasonably and extremely cruel prick. Wanda chose to ignore the entire scene.

Finally, halfway through "Young Frankenstein", I felt a gentle, firm hand on my shoulder. Turning, I looked into the compassionate brown eyes of Mark. Unknown to me at the time, he was having marital problems with Reva and I suppose he felt a desperate need to reach out. Like Simon, Mark lived to help people in need, for it eased his own pain and pushed his problems into a further recess of his mind.

The two of us left the theatre and spent the next hour talking. Well, I basically cried and he murmured to me that whatever was bothering me, it would pass with time, I'd smile again and regain my previous joie de vivre.

I didn't tell him why I was so upset, for he was a close friend of Brad's and I really didn't want to put Mark in the middle of a very messy situation. He was to find out later, but thankfully didn't hold my childish behaviour against me. It would be another year before this remarkable, kind-spirited young man would leave his wife and desire a relationship with me.

I suppose I reacted so violently because, only six months previously, Charles had done exactly the same thing and it brought that sensation of self-recrimination flooding back.

Wanda had known why I was so upset and avoided much contact with me afterward. This was pretty awkward since we were roommates, so I began spending more time in the adjoining college's coffee house, which was adjacent to Founders. Word was getting around the residence that I was unusually unstable and emotionally overwrought, and I aroused some morbid curiosity as well as some revulsion.

Some of the students had seen the cross-shaped scar on my wrist, when my wide bracelet covering it slipped occasionally, and rumours circulated that I had been seriously into drugs in high school and had suffered a measure of brain damage.

The resident don, a butchy but pleasant young woman who was in charge of the girls of A House, took me aside one night and blatantly asked me if I had been selling any chemicals to any of the students. I was indignant, and replied that I had never been a dealer and would never stoop to that repulsive lifestyle. She then drilled me about my past experiences, and even wanted to look at my arms to examine them for tracks. I despised her for branding me a junkie with no morals or principles.

What was happening to me, and why was I being persecuted for doing what so many teenagers of the 1970's had done? Of course, she didn't know about the Ritalin, which was now getting completely out of hand.

I had gone from ingesting thirty milligrams per day to over a hundred twenty and still felt a desperate craving for more just to function normally. Amber had assured me that this drug was not addicting, and when I reminded her she replied casually, "Don't be a douche. I wouldn't get you into anything dangerous."

One girl I had begun hanging with was a pretty, fragile, raven-haired student named Charlotte. She was engaged to an older man named Will, and talked endlessly about him and her impending wedding.

Sylvia grew weary of this chatter very quickly, but I liked her enthusiastic nature and admired her popularity with the other kids.

She and Wanda became tight and after Wanda forgave my emotional bloodbath, the three of us would gather in Charlotte's single room, playing Olivia Newton-John albums and talking about the future.

In my characteristic, self-deprecating manner, I would tell Charlotte that she wouldn't like me so much if she knew me. She would laugh uproariously and wave her hand in a gesture of playful protest. "Don't be silly. Of course I would."

Well, this friendship would soon bite the proverbial dust, as one night my jealously of Wanda and her relationship with Brad erupted into a war of angry words. Wanda was hurt and felt crushed by the weight of my accusations, and later, feeling remorseful, I wrote her a note asking for forgiveness and explaining my hosility.

The message got misconstrued somehow, and Wanda took it as further nastiness on my part. She fled from our room, crying brokenly and told me that she didn't wish anything more to do with me.

Charlotte despised me from that moment on and wouldn't even speak to me for the rest of the year. She would only shoot furious glances in my direction.

One afternoon, I tried to explain that I hadn't meant to say anything offensive in the note, that it was supposed to speak positively of Wanda, and somehow made matters even worse. Frustrated and bewildered, I ultimately exploded at her and spat out, "Fine. You want to be a bitch about all this? Well, I don't think Brad likes you at all. He feels sorry for you because you have no backbone, no sense of dignity. You just throw yourself at him."

Suddenly, Brad stormed in and besieged me with a "conscience speech" that left me totally defeated and stinging with remorse.

He said that he had tried to be fair with me, that he and a lot of the others were aware that I had "problems", but that I was basically a very nasty and vindictive human being.

Before leaving the room, Brad turned to me and said rather regretfully, "You know, Jane, you choose to be this way. You dump on people then expect them to feel sorry for you because you've had a hard life. Well, I think you need to grow up and realize that the world doesn't owe you."

I was inconsolable, crumbled on the floor, buried my head in my hands and rocked back and forth for the next hour. My universe was falling on top of me and I was drowning in despair.

Courtney stuck by me, however, sympathetic to my pitiful cause, and assured me that as my life stabilized, people would come around and forgive my transgressions. Sidney was loyal to me, as was Sylvia, and mentioned that most of those kids were "immature little brats", and therefore I wasn't missing out on anything worthwhile as far as earning their friendship was concerned.

So I began to avoid most of the Founders residents, and stayed with people who accepted me. They were somewhat different and off-centre as well: Courtney with her rather austere lifestyle and problematic past, Sylvia with her precociousness and strong sense of style, and Sidney with his homosexuality.

Courtney and I would talk into the wee hours, guzzling strong coffee and submerging ourselves in Neil Diamond's "Hot August Night" and Gallegher and Lyle. She, like myself, had no desire to become romantically entangled with anyone, as it would illicit far too much pain.

Sylvia and I worked with David as he gave out flyers for the "Gay Alliance", York's homosexual and lesbian society, and I admired the fierce loyalty that Sidney felt for his cause. There was rampant homophobia on university campuses in the mid-1970's, and Laura and I were often branded "gay" for our affiliation to the Alliance. Neither of us cared; Sylvia because she wasn't the least bit concerned with image or labels, and myself for a completely different reason.

One night, Sidney and I were sitting on the floor of his room, drinking wine and listening to music as usual, when I brought up the issue which had been weighing on my mind for a very long time. Still very much confused about my sexuality, even though I had been attracted to boys, I had begun to feel a great deal of resentment and hostility toward the male of the species. Never having developed a very satisfying relationship with my father, I wondered if that could be the reason for this.

Sidney had looked at me intently and asked what exactly I had meant by that. "Well, I used to think that maybe I was, well, um, you know, gay like you. Then I thought, no, I've just had a lot of bizarre relationships with guys, nothing that's ever been particularly satisfying or lasting. Now I have all this anger toward men. And I look at someone like Rhoda, that friend of yours, with her delicate features and her gentle personality, and I get kind of, well, turned on by her. What the hell's going on with me?"

Sidney leaned forward and put his hand on my shoulder in a gesture of comfort and reassurance. "It sounds as if you might be bisexual."

I thought for a minute and then replied slowly, "Yeah, that kind of makes some sense. How does a person know that sort of thing?

"You expose yourself to other women who feel the same way. I have a friend, Geraldine, who lives in the graduate residence. She's a lesbian, and she should probably talk to you. Are you ready?"

I was a bit hesitant, but agreed, and met Geraldine several nights later. I was surprised that she looked nothing like my preconceived notions of how a lesbian should appear. She was attractive, vibrant and very feminine.

We talked for an hour or so, and she suggested that I go to a gay bar that she knew of in the west end of the city. Geraldine had two gay friends who frequented the place and told me that she could arrange to have them escort me.

I surprised myself at how easily I accepted all of this information and was willing to follow the advice of a stranger. I suppose curiosity was a part of it and an intense desire to feel as though I belonged somewhere, and had a sense of identity.

I met Geraldine's friends downtown, where they picked me up in a red Volkswagen. I was somewhat taken aback at the driver's appearance, for she had ruggedly masculine features and wasn't the least bit attractive. Her partner was softer looking, less the stereotypical "butch".

They took me to a rather run-down building on a darkened, secluded backstreet. I was met at the front door by a woman with two Dobermans and guessed that they were there to guard the place against unwelcome intruders.

I bought a screwdriver and settled down at a table with Jill and Darlene, looking at the dimly-lit surroundings as people milled about, talking, laughing and dancing to Minnie Ripperton coming from the loudspeakers.

Jill, the tall, mannish girl, turned to Darlene and muttered discouragingly, "Well, I have my choice of a fat one, a fat one, or a fat one."

There did seem to be an inordinate disproportion of overweight women there, but I noticed some strikingly attractive ones sitting off to the side of the room. I felt a bit ill-at-ease as my eye caught sight of women looking at me and smiling coyly. This was a new experience, and it felt somewhat awkward. Was it a mistake to come here?

Just then a three-girl singing group took the dance floor and lip-synced to the Supreme's "Stop! In the Name of Love". They called themselves, "Diana Gleam and Her Impossible Dreams" and they certainly had plenty of charisma and unbridled energy. I enjoyed the performance, and after the trio left the floor and ran past the table, "Diana" pinched mc on the butt.

"Lucky you", said Jill, "she thinks you're sexy." The idea didn't bother me; in fact, I felt complimented with a positive rush that even Brad hadn't ever produced. Perhaps David had been correct in his assessment of my sexuality.

Darlene taught me how to slow dance. "It's not like it is with a guy", she said smiling, There was an extra beat, not the rocking on either foot as I was accustomed.

I got picked up that night, by a sweet-faced, plump and soft-spoken girl named Bobbie. She had come to the place with a girlfriend, but left her there for me. It was a very awkward situation, because I didn't want to rebuff her attentions, but at the same time, I hated the thought of breaking a couple up. I was very much afraid of offending someone and causing trouble. I knew I was there as a kind of experiment and felt like an imposter. I wished that I hadn't gone.

It was my shyness more than any kind of reluctance to explore the possiblity of a sexual relationship with another woman. As Bobbie's car pulled up to the residence, I paused before getting out. "Um, thanks for the ride."

To my dismay, she began to cry quietly. "Hey, what's the matter?" Sitting back down, I realized that I couldn't just leave her like that.

She choked back the tears and replied brokenly, "Are you just going to leave me here like this? I thought you liked me. I left Gloria back there and everything. Did I get my signals crossed?"

I felt terrible. Something had told me that Bobbie misunderstood me when I agreed to let her drive me home. But it was late, and I had been growing uneasy being so far from the campus and surrounded by strangers.

"Bobbie, I didn't mean to give you the wrong idea. I've never been out with a girl before. I'm sort of new at this. I just need a little time to get used to it."

She seemed to brighten up a little after that. We sat and talked for an hour or so, and I ended up promising her that I'd call in a few days. But I never did. My conscience, formed from many years of a fairly religious upbringing, as well as a hefty dose of moral hypocrisy, dictated that it was wrong to love someone of the same sex. It would only bring shame and retribution upon me and my family.

Bobbie did kiss me, though, and it felt rather pleasant, not threatening or aggressive, as it often did with guys. So that was my exposure to the homosexual lifestyle as I prepared to leave my teenage years behind. I don't regret that night, although I felt terribly guilty and ashamed for years afterward.

Ironically, rumours began to circulate at Founders that Courtney and I were involved romantically. This was based on the fact that we were seen together a lot, and because neither of us had boyfriends.

The rumours intensified after Wanda and Courtney traded rooms, leaving Wanda in a single and Courtney paired with me.

Both of us pretended that the tongue-wagging didn't bother us, but, in reality, it upset our peace of mind greatly.

Shortly after my night at the gay bar, Simon began to come on to me with single-minded intensity, but I rebuffed his advances. His childishness and drinking turned me off, and besides, I wasn't even remotely interested in him romantically. He was the butt of most of the residence jokes and was laughed at behind his back for his clothes, haircut and crude humour. I was thoroughly embarrassed to be seen with him.

One night, I'd had too much to drink and didn't walk away when Simon planted an energetic, wet kiss on my unsuspecting lips. He was delighted and murmured, "Where have you been all this time?"

After that, I spent a great deal of time talking with him, somewhat relieved to be semi-involved in a straight relationship. Nothing sexual happened during this period of time; not that he didn't desire it, but I was insistent that we remain celibate. Sex just didn't appeal to me at all  and I wasn't particularly attracted to Simon physically, even though he was quite good-looking in a cherubic, "Peck's-bad-boy-touched-with-sweetness" kind of way; sort of a Pre-Raphaelite innocence brushed with a stroke of decadence.

I told Simon all about my past, emphasizing the fact that I'd had a difficult life and had "really suffered". He was very empathetic and hugged me close to him, assuring me that he understood why I sometimes lashed out at people and denounced the unfortunate events that had robbed me of a happy and carefree childhood.

I played on Simon's sincere desire to be an amateur psychotherapist, revelling in the attention he paid to my angst, and wallowing in self-pity in an effort to gain his sympathy. It worked, and before long he devoted all of his spare time and energy trying to "fix me" and counselled me for hours at a time. He urged me to talk about things that were bothering me and offering broad shoulders to sob on. This probably would have continued indefinitely, except for the terrible night that changed both of us forever and tore our relationship to pieces.

When I arrived at Simon's room in F House, my instinct was to leave right away, as it was obvious that he was quite intoxicated. He'd drunk one half of a bottle of Vodka and was acting extremely childish and undesirable. I was wearing a short, pale blue mini-dress and he commented upon how sexy I looked.

"Simon, you shouldn't drink so much," I said disapprovingly, sitting down beside him on the bed. That was a fatal mistake.

What happened next was that this normally kind, considerate and decent boy tried to force himself on me, his inhibitions loosened by the alcohol. As he leapt on top of me and started to pull my dress off, my memory flashed back suddenly to a year before when Wayne had done the same thing.

"God, what am I going to do?" I despaired, panic welling up in my throat. I had a brilliant idea, or so I thought. I'd pretend to go into a frozen trance, and then Simon would stop.

It was actually a very mean thing to do, for when I stiffened my body and stared straight ahead, motionless in my pretend freak-out, poor Simon was overcome with remorse, fear and regret.

He quickly got off me and sat at his desk, and I can only imagine what desolate thoughts consumed him for the next five minutes while I continued to lie there like a dazed zombie. It was the bitter and melodramatic end of our union, for after that, Simon grew to despise me. He was grimly reminded of his shameful behaviour everytime he looked at me and remembered how he'd caused me to react in such a frightening way.

He took refuge in the arms of another girl, Amanda, who lived off-campus Richmond Hill and could not even bear to meet my gaze. I wanted him back so badly, with a ferocity that knew no bounds of reason.

One night, our residence held one of its infamous "Purple Jesus" parties. It was named for an extremely potent alcoholic concoction that consisted of ninety proof alcohol and grape Kool-Aid.

Simon was the bartender, and stood behind a row of wooden tables upon which were placed bottles of beer and wine for those who couldn't stomach the Purple Jesus. Courtney and I attended, against my better judgement.

Sylvia, Sidney and Rhoda weren't going to be there and I had no other friends left at Founders. Everyone had heard about my hellish night with Simon, and dismissed me as a total flake with no redeeming qualities or graces. Wanda and Darlene still hated me, and even Adam thought it best not to pursue me arduously anymore.

I set out that night to get as plastered as I possibly could and pretty much succeeded before too long. One did not have to drink too many paper cups of that colourful substance to become intoxicated to the point of being rendered comatose, so by ten o'clock I was staggering all over the room.

I couldn't take my eyes off Simon as he poured drinks and chatted amicably with the other kids. I had become obsessed with winning back his love and affection and had even resorted at times to pleading with him to take me back. It was obvious that Simon wanted nothing more to do with me. I was crushed, my spirit pounded into the rock-hard ground of defeat.

Finally, I couldn't take it anymore. I stumbled over to the bar and stood facing Simon, weaving back and forth in a drunken stupor and feeling very dizzy. I opened my mouth and shouted in a slurred voice, without really thinking, "So tell me, Simon, why the hell did you ever go out with me in the first place?"

It was a line right out of a tacky B-movie, not any words rooted in real conversation. He looked steadily and grimly into my bloodshot eyes and replied, "Because you've got a great body."

I exploded into rage at this ludicrous, sexist statement. Without hesitating, I picked up a magnum of white wine from the table and poured it over Simon's head, leering and snickering as I did so.

I emptied the entire bottle, then stood and waited for his reaction. There wasn't one. Simon remained motionless and said nothing, which infuriated me all the more. Bursting into tears, I shouted, "You fucking bastard!" and went running out of the suddenly quiet lounge, heading unsteadily for my room. It seemed as though my world was collapsing all around my ears.

I got safely inside my sanctuary and fell on the bed, sobs racking my body. This was a new level of misery and self-hatred, and I felt an overwhelming desire to rip up my arms with a razor blade.

Jumping off the bed, I fumbled around the darkened room, looking for something sharp. Suddenly, I heard a soft rapping, and turned to see a young man standing in the doorway.

I recognized him as eighteen-year-old Jeff, a blond, blue-eyed F House resident who usually kept to himself and was painfully shy. He sat down with me on the floor and tried to comfort me, saying that Simon wasn't worth all my grief and that he certainly didn't deserve anyone like me.

I told him that he was full of it, but secretly it felt reassuring to hear such kind words from a relative stranger. Jeff and I became fast friends. Although he was really attracted to me, I felt nothing even remotely romantic as far as he was concerned. He was to become very discouraged and despondent over my lack of enthusiasm, but pursued me for the next year or so.

Things continued to disintegrate after the fateful Purple Jesus party. Courtney told me repeatedly that I shouldn't keep going after Simon and pleading for him to take me back. She said it would only cause the chasm between us to widen even more, but I refused to take her advice and kept up the shameful behaviour.

I continued to abuse Ritalin, going for several days at a time without sleeping and becoming more and more erratic. My drinking increased even more and I went for long periods without eating. I began to lose weight and my skin took on an unhealthy, sallow appearance. My friends were very concerned. Finally Sidney suggested that I move in with him for a week or so to escape the miserable atmosphere at Founders.

He had gotten an apartment several months before and loved the solitude and peace of mind that it brought him. I took him up on his offer, and gratefully abandoned A House for seven days of lengthy, soul-searching talks. We eased each other through the pains of being out-of-step misfits in a decidedly close-minded and exceedingly judgmental society.

It was during this period that I grudgingly accepted that I was "different", after fighting the urge to cover myself in symbolic ashes and sackcloth for many years. I did not really want to become absorbed and assimilated into a world which spat out everything and everyone with which or with whom it did not comprehend or identify. Those were the things that our generation accused our parents of doing, after all. I wanted to believe that I was far more idealistic and progressive than that.

I continued attending my classes from Sidney's and made a concerted effort to study diligently. Final exams were less than six weeks away and I wanted to maintain my A average. Scholastic achievement was very important to me then. Dad was uncharacteristically proud of me for an essay I'd written for Humanities and this meant more to me than he would ever know. I was determined to show him that I wasn't stuck in that confused, emotionally distraught phase forever.

I discovered that Courtney had achieved a substantial amount of respect from the other residents at Founders. Upon returning, I talked with the brash and egomanical Adam, who paused long enough in his persistent flirting to say that I didn't have to worry anymore about everyone thinking that Courtney and I were lovers.

"They wondered at first, when you two moved in together and all, but then realized that wasn't the case, since Courtney is highly regarded around here. They still think you're pretty weird, but everyone likes her. Thought you might want to know that."

"Uh, thanks, Adam", I responded flatly, that creeping sense of inferiority assailing my nervous system again, "but if you think you're going to worm your way into my pants with that kind of talk, you can just forget it." I left him standing in his undershirt and track pants, with his mouth agape in an expression of annoyance.

It was difficult having a friend like Courtney, who was held in so much higher esteem than myself and I began to suffer even more intense bouts of depression. They left me emotionally and physically drained, and, of course, popping Ritalin constantly only aggravated my negative moods.

That crazy doctor of Amber's would write me prescriptions whenever I wanted, for over two hundred pills at a time and never questioned my vast consumption of them. He was obviously one of those notorious "Dr. Feelgoods" who make their fortunes by creating as many druggies as they can.

The drug robbed me of my appetite as well and I feared becoming anorexic again. My parents were embroiled in their own problems, so I don't think that they noticed how much I was declining during that period. I didn't go home often and talked little of my life at York. How could I let them know that I felt as though I was being sucked under a giant wave of water and was absolutely powerless to stop myself from drowning?

I followed Simon around like a little lost puppy, taking extreme delight when he stopped to talk to me or toss a bone of attention in my direction. Most of the time, however, he glowered darkly at me and snapped, "Go away, Jane. I don't want to have anything to do with you. Just leave me alone. God, I am trying to get something going with Lorna and it's so damned hard when you're on my ass constantly."

If I had any vestiges of self-esteem left at all, they quickly vanished after those bone-chilling statements from the man I loved so desperately. He became the focal point of all my waking thoughts, and I ruminated obsessively about the manner in which he had cruelly deserted me.

I should have hated what he had done, forcing himself upon me while in an alcoholic haze, but instead I blamed myself for wearing such a provocative dress that evening. I had obviously asked for it.

Jeff grew weary of my all-consuming passion for Simon, and ultimately cooled off his advances considerably. "I can't compete with a god", he told me sadly one night and walked out the door. We still remained good friends, but he must have realized that he was out of the running as far as being my boyfriend was concerned.

As for Ben, who thought the sun rose and set upon me for some unexplained reason, well, he got unceremoniously ousted from my life after wanting to spend the night. He felt that our relationship, if there indeed was one, needed to progress beyond the hand-holding stage. I wasn't sexually attracted to him and told him that I was not about to engage in sex just to please him. "I did that the first time, over a year ago and lived to regret it. I won't repeat the mistake."

Poor Ben couldn't understand why I dangled him idly on a chain and refused to commit either physically or emotionally. He figured he had always tried so hard to be the Perfect Gentleman and give me anything I wanted. I felt very sad about this entire situation and tearfully waved him farewell. It was difficult being so driven toward the wrong man while the right one stood right under my nose.

I wanted to tell him that there was no challenge with our relationship, that everything fell into place far too smoothly and that I was bored and fidgety. But I realized that my thinking was not only rather warped, but exceedingly immature, so I simply refused to see him again.

Ben would have made an excellent husband, for he was hard-working, conscientious, very kind, considerate and generous. However there seemed to be a big part of me that needed to be treated as poorly and unfairly as I treated myself and that I simply craved a man who would abuse the hell out of me. I didn't recognize any of this at the time and wouldn't piece this disquieting picture together for another eighteen years or so.

As the school year began to wind down, relationships and personal dynamics in Founders residence solidified and gelled.

Matthew became a parody of himself, a dirty old man in training, who produced guffaws and snickers from all the girls he tried frantically to make his conquests. Poor innocent Patrick was totally distraught at having such a rude and promiscuous roommate that he began to suffer emotionally.

He hid from the world most of the time, terrified of interpersonal contact and isolated himself. I felt sorry for him and spent time with the poor kid in an attempt to make him feel more comfortable around girls. He continued to quake in his brown Oxfords and refused to meet my gaze most of the time.

Sylvia and Sidney grew very close and I twinged with jealousy. She had recently put herself on a strict diet to lose twenty pounds, little knowing that it would lead her into extremely treacherous waters.

Sidney, deeply respected her sense of haute couture, her cultural background, superior intellect and open frankness and I wondered if he possessed any romantic feelings for her. They just connected so well, and it wasn't unheard of for gay people to be attracted to the opposite sex.

Mark and Reva's attempts at a reconciliation failed miserably and they separated for good. Mark and I remained close, but I discouraged any kind of relationship with him, realizing he was on the rebound.

Wanda and Brad's relationship intensified tremendously, as she abandoned poor Ike up at Lakehead University and pulled out all the emotional stops with this quiet, unassuming English major who had so effectively put me in my place a couple of months before.

He later apologized profusely, stammering that he had been unnecessarily nasty and unfair. I had simply smiled and replied, "No, Brad, I had it coming. I screwed up with Wanda and Darlene, and they'll hate me forever. Don't feel bad."

Devon and Kenny became good buddies, Kenny playing straight man to Devon's inane antics. I still found Devon hard to take, but his sidekick was admirable for his sincerity and humility.

Rhoda, dreamy-eyed, wistful, idealistic and with an artistic heart of pure gold dust, gravitated toward a young seventeen-year-old student, Billy, and grew resentful as Sidney showed a definite interest in him. Rhoda was unhappy that Sidney was trying to foist his lifestyle on an inexperienced boy, and this would cause a rift between the two of them which would continue into the next year.

Courtney studied hard and seemed to be experiencing some difficulties of her own in dealing with her past. She became involved with the Cock and Bull's manager, Roland, toward the end of March, and this would become somewhat sordid over the summer.

He was kind of a rough-hewn playboy type, roguishly handsome and with a trademark leer. I never liked him very much. He thought of me as a hopelessly mixed-up kid and dismissed me as too much trouble and thus I was safe from any of his advances. Courtney was vulnerable to this kind of young man and fell helplessly into his clutches. I thought it best not to interfere, though, as Courtney would undoubtedly resent me for it. She was obviously crazy about him.

There were other students at Founders whom I knew casually. One of these was Beth, a pretty, somewhat shy girl who referred to herself as a "classic Jewish Princess" because she wanted guys to treat her like someone special. I told her that all women want that, and that it certainly wasn't anything to get down on herself for.

Thelma was a rather irksome young woman with a goofy, early-Lucille Ball flamboyance, whose favourite song was "Philadelphia Freedom" by Elton John. She belted it out at every opportunity. Other than that, she was pleasant and friendly, but I didn't get very close to her.

I met Kelli late in the academic year and liked her immediately. We wouldn't become friends until September of 1975, but I admired her caustic wit, wary intelligence and carefree attitude about the world in general and residence in particular. "Ten years from now, this whole university trip will be a rapidly fading memory, so don't make such a big deal about everything."
Well said, Kelli.

There were many others, all interesting in their own way, some dedicated to their school work, others enamoured with the social scene, but all individuals with definite ideas about and plans for the future. We were all thrown together in this comparatively small building for eight months out of the year, to achieve, learn and grow. We should have been making the most of our opportunities, but not many of us did.

Final exams were challenging, but upon completion, I knew that I had done extremely well, except for Natural Sciences. I didn't care for the course, and only scored a "B", but managed to hold onto an "A" average for my freshman year at York University.

So even though I was physically and emotionally wasted by the end of April 1975, I had accomplished what I had set out to do academically. Of course, the next two years were another story.

**Chapter Eight**

# Staring Into the Abyss: My Second Year In Founders Residence

After a summer of working as a lifeguard at the McMaster Community Pool with sixteen-year-old Fawn and twenty-year-old "Vera the Maneater" (a vibrant, red-headed firecracker who boasted that she'd bedded a half-dozen guys in two months) I returned somewhat reluctantly to York's desolate, brown campus. Still, it was a tremendous relief to get away from my parents' constant battling, with Mom hurling insults and accusations about Dad's suspicious whereabouts and Dad storming angrily out the door. I didn't know how poor Jim tolerated living there all year and my heart broke for the poor kid. He stayed away most of the time, safe in the hands of his school chums.

Fortunately, I'd managed to kick my Ritalin habit, as I wasn't about to look after the safety of sixty or so kids at a crowded public pool while stoned on dope, legal or not. The idea repulsed me, so I tossed the remainder of my prescription down the toilet and bid a hasty good-riddance to those little blue pieces of misery and slavery.

Withdrawal had been horrendous, with severe muscle cramps, nausea, headaches, wild chills, the classic symptoms of denying your body what it craves. I felt like absolute crap for about a week and mumbled to my curious mother about having a touch of the flu. She didn't question it, for I truly looked sick.

It took longer to overcome the psychological dependency. I'd looked upon Ritalin as my private little "well-being factory". After swallowing one, I'd anxiously wait for that electrifying little kick that would jump-start a sagging pleasure meter and cause me to feel able to cope with whatever I needed to. I loved those fleeting moments of euphoria and the feeling of empowerment that it fuelled me with. Denying it to myself produced a deadening despair that I couldn't shake loose.

I cried a great deal that summer, sometimes at work and occasionally Fawn or Vera would catch me and grow concerned. I just told them that my parents were expecting to get divorced and they understood immediately. Vera had gone through the same ordeal with her mother and father two years before.

One afternoon, I did a wild and crazy thing in an effort to snap out of my doldrums and create a new, flashy image. I bleached my hair nearly white. It was only meant to be blonde, but I'd been using that tacky "Sun-In" spray for a month and it had stripped all the colour out of my hair shafts. I loved it but my family wasn't nearly as enthusiastic. Grandma tried to make light of it by saying that I looked like Nikki Newman from "The Young and the Restless". Nobody else was amused, however.

While at home, I lost myself in my music, playing Buffy Saint-Marie's self-titled album for hours at a time, along with Paul Simon, Patti Smith's "Horses" and, of course, the Everly Brothers and the Guess Who. I had eclectic tastes and gravitated toward artists who were true originals and defined their type of rock. I never wanted to restrict myself to any one form of popular music, for that limits a person far too much and robs one of enjoying and appreciating a variety of artistic expression. Music had always been my primary drug, a powerful ether against pain and loneliness. However, in the near future, it would begin to turn on me as well and become an instrument of my self-destruction.

I had a single room at Founders in the fall of 1975 and upon arriving early in September, I discovered that many of the old students had returned. There was also a large group of new ones, fresh, eager, somewhat apprehensive faces that were blithely ignorant of what university and residence life were truly all about.

Ruby and Martha were high school friends from South Porcupine, a small Northern town near Timmins, Ontario. Ruby was nicknamed the "Polish Princess", due to her undying loyalty to her family background. She reminded me for all the world of Shirley Temple, with her mass of curly, fair hair, coy grin and trademark dimples. This comparison was not lost on Ruby, however and she even plastered a poster of the pint-sized film star on her door. She struck me as utterly scatterbrained, a fun-loving, hard-partying chick who too centre stage whenever possible and just exuded charismatic charm and effervescence.

As I got to know her better, though, I found Ruby to be extremely serious-minded, conscientious, very loyal and ambitious, with her own set of personal demons. All the superficial extravagance was an effective cover for a particularly intense and complex young woman.

Her friend Martha was attractive but somewhat overweight and seemed pleasant enough, even with her tendency to complain a fair amount. She hung very close with Ruby at first, and spent a lot of time in their room studying.

Lizzie looked like a young Joan Baez and was equally as politically-minded and progressive in her thinking as the visionary singer. She was smart, articulate, delicately pretty and loved music, art, and modern dance. She went to a lot of student films and had a creative flair for them herself. She was certainly one of the more interesting of the new breed of A House residents.

Ingrid was a quiet, rather eccentric art student and I didn't get to know her until later on in the year. She didn't mix much with the others, and rarely came out of her room.

Martial had recently moved from Holland and was extraordinarily shy and withdrawn. I first met him in the common room where he was sitting alone and staring glumly at the floor. He was blond, blue-eyed, with an infectious smile and a glimmer of wildness on the inside of a demur shell. I knew that we would get along well.

Velvet, like many of us, had long, straight hair parted in the middle and the largest, saddest eyes I'd ever seen. Her brother had been a freshman the year before, but I hadn't known him. She was very mousy and retiring, but seemed friendly. She followed Courtney around most of the time like an adoring younger sister.

Brandi was this tiny, hobbit-like human dynamo with jet-black hair, wide-eyed enthusiasm and the most extroverted presonality I'd ever encountered. She was from Buffalo, spoke with a really pronounced American accent and chatted like a magpie on Speed. It was hard to fathom that this was the flesh-and-blood sister of the ultra-introverted Weaver, a boy I'd heard about the year before but never seen, as he only left his room to go to class.

George (nicknamed Georgio) was older than the rest of us, and, at twenty-six, had a bushy, reddish beard, long, stringy, oily hair and sloppy lumberjack shirts, as well as thick-rimmed glasses that looked like the bottoms of pop bottles. He was certainly not much of a sex symbol. Georgio was rather rude, obnoxious and had a dirty mouth. I thought him to be nothing short of repulsive.

And then there was the amazingly handsome (to me anyway), verbally-gifted and outrageously funny Burton, a boy with whom I fell immediately in lust as he stood before me with a shaggy mane of thick, wavy hair, dark, penetrating eyes and a tall, lanky body. He dressed casually, in jeans and flannel shirts, with well-worn Adidas and a lumpy, oversize jacket. Burton would have been right at home in the wild woods of the Northland, frying fish over a campfire and imitating the mating call of the Canadian moose.

I was drawn to his macho magnetism and softened by this quirky, artistic edge he tempered it with. His sense of humour was tasteful, not disgusting like that of Simon or Georgio and he was careful not to tread on anyone's ego. I thought that any girl who won his heart would be set for life.

Alanna was only seventeen and somewhat intimidated by the broad-minded lifestyle buzzing all around her. She looked very young, like a grade ten student and kept asking me if everyone slept around here. I assured her that it was simply a vicious rumour, that A House was really a convent in disguise.

I made a concerted effort to keep myself on the "straight and narrow" that year, avoiding all drugs of any description and prescription, drinking less, sleeping and eating regularly, as well as side-stepping the pitfalls of interpersonal relationships. I'd decided that I would no longer pursue Simon with a vengeance and if I did manage to become involved with a guy, there would be no repeat of that awful night when Simon jumped my bones and I flipped out on him.

I was glad that nobody except Sidney knew that I had gone to a gay bar and resolved not to go anywhere like that again. I still felt guilty and ashamed and wished that I had been turned off by the experience. If I was totally straight, then I should have been, right? And what if my parents ever found out?

My classes certainly proved to be a mixed bag of delights.

My major was definitely English, with a minor in Philosophy. I had chosen two English courses, two third-year Philosophy ones and a third-year Humanities course entitled, "Iconography". Unfortunately, I had to go to Professor Schneider and drop out of it, though, because I hadn't done the required summer reading which had involved over fifty text books. It had just seemed too overwhelming, so I gave up on it in June. He was disappointed in me, and said I shouldn't have made a commitment I couldn't keep. I felt remorseful and instead picked a political science course. It concerned the psychological profiles of political figures and was taught by Paul Roazen, who's book, "Brother Animal" dealt with Sigmund Freud, so I knew it would be a fascinating experience.

The philosophy courses were extremely difficult, probably because they were at a third-year level. One dealt with existentialism and the other was the philosophy of Freud. I became totally overwhelmed very early on and the deeper I submerged myself into the bleak principals of existential thought, the more it fed my ever-growing depression.

So the stage was being set for another bad fall, academically this time. I hoped that my instincts were wrong and I would gain a stronger foothold later on in the term.

Socially speaking, the situation was close to ideal. Although I still ached for Simon, and cringed everytime I caught sight of him with Amanda, I was happy that the dashing Burton was paying a great deal of attention to me.

I didn't realize at first that Ruby liked him too and I guess he was "playing the field" in September and early October and not willing to have to make a choice between us.

Our residence parties were as rambunctious and alcohol-soaked as ever, with Ruby captivating everyone's attention as the giddy, wild and totally uninhibited exhibitionist. She somehow always remained conscious long after everyone else had either passed out or gone off to bed.

A bunch of us would frequent the Cock and Bull regularly. I'd start drinking draft instead of liquor, mainly because it was cheaper and didn't produce as unpleasant a hangover the next day. We danced there a lot and of course the last song of the evening that got everyone up slow-dancing rapturously and closely was Led Zeppelin's "Stairway To Heaven". I wonder for how many student pregnancies that emotional bath of a tune was responsible?

One night, I became totally captivated by a song I hadn't heard before, called "Crime Of the Century" by a British band known as Supertramp. I bought the album and was immediately drawn into the insidious, psychological messages and warped, dismal sentiments expressed in the record's songs. One in particular, "Hide In Your Shell" could have been written for me, about me, and a tremendous wave of sadness doused my parched consciousness.

I took refuge in Supertramp's music, collecting other albums like "Crisis? What Crisis?" and "Even In the Quietest Moments". All of them were a welcome respite from the glut of empty, mindless disco garbage that assaulted the airwaves in the mid-1970's. I call this period of "music" simply "Malignant Discoma" and even wrote a poem about how much I despised it. Unfortunately, the Cock and Bull was not immune to this cancerous outgrowth of rock music, so I deliberately refused to dance to any disco tunes. Needless to say, I sat on my ass a lot that year.

Slowly and insidiously, Supertramp's world, a murky maelstrom of dashed hope, mental anguish and terminal illness of the human spirit, began to become my domain and I'd sit for hours alone in my room, enveloped in it.

I could not understand why I was so depressed all the time. I decided that it had a lot to do with the fact that our parents were splitting up and that shortly our family would join the burgeoning suburb of broken homes.

That Thanksgiving weekend was nothing short of devastating for our family, as Mom screamed vehemently at Dad that he had betrayed her, that he had another woman and that she hated him for it.

I sat on the stairs with Jim, silently listening to the War of the Wanklins, which promised to take no prisoners.

"Get out!" she finally screamed from the bowels of the kitchen, and as she lunged at Dad she finally lost it completely. "Get out you Goddamned bastard! I never want to see you again !!" He immediately vacated the premises and poor Mom collapsed on the floor, sobbing pitifully.

I was thoroughly disgusted with her behaviour, however, feeling she was acting terribly childish and with no shred of dignity. Jim looked solemnly at me and said quietly, "That's her life she's watching going down the drain."

That kid could be so profoundly wise and kind-spirited and I smiled at his insight and thoughtfulness. "Yeah, you're right. What the hell is she going to do now?"

That was the end of their marriage. Dad moved out, with only his rocking chair and the clothes on his back, and moved into a highrise nearby in Westmount. Mom became extremely depressed and was to come to rely on Jim for emotional support. I beat a hasty retreat back to York, true to form for me, and stayed there for most of the year.

A group of us went to Oktoberfest in Kitchener just after Thanksgiving and had a great time dancing the polka and getting absolutely hammered on Carlsburg beer. I spent the entire night with Burton and was certain that he had chosen me to be his girlfriend. I felt a twinge of sympathy for Ruby, but let it pass as quickly as it came.

After the Christmas holidays, which are best forgotten, Dad drove me back to Toronto. I said little to him, but wanted to express how much I missed him and that I wished he could reconcile with Mom.

As we stood in my room to say good-bye, Hagood Hardy's "The homecoming" began playing on the radio. I embraced my father tightly, tears bursting out of my eyes and choking my throat with heavy sobs. It was so incredibly sad, this death of our family and with it the accompanying soundtrack of this plaintive tune. Everytime I hear it, my mind turns backward to that night long ago when I longed for my Daddy to come home again.

I had no centre base anymore and I began to vacillate at school. Classes were difficult, even more so because I was finding it increasingly hard to concentrate. This had never been a problem before and I found it most distressing. I'd read the same paragraph repeatedly, instantly forgetting its contents, then grow frustrated and angry with my apparent stupidity.

What was happening? Why couldn't I grasp the fundamentals of empiricism, or the thought processes of Keirkegaard? Words would blur out of focus and run together in a swarm of black marks on an undulating page. This was crazy; I wasn't doing acid or mescaline. Why wouldn't my thickened brain register those words and translate them into some kind of meaning?

I returned to my old habits of excessive drinking at the Cock and Bull. I took comfort in the pub's darkened, intimate atmosphere, a safe, cocooned haven against the barrages of academe.

Courtney, who'd been waitressing there for a year, pulled a few strings and got me a job as well, as I was getting into dire straits financially. It was stressful, particularly during peak hours and I made a great many mistakes taking drink orders and making change. Still, the tips were gratifying and people seemed to take my errors in stride. I worked twenty hours a week, including Friday nights, which necessitated sleeping fewer hours in order to cram in study time. Still, I managed to keep my social life in full bloom, taking advantage of my newfound friends, particularly Burton.

We only made love once. It was an awkward, amateurish event, after which I feared that I had become pregnant. I'd recently gone off the Pill, as it was causing some distasteful fluid retention in my legs and hadn't used any kind of contraception prior to intercourse. Fortunately, I got my period three weeks later, but not after twenty-one days of pure hell, wondering what I would do if I had to leave school and give birth out of wedlock.

My mother had always pounded into my head that the Absolute Worst Thing I could do would be to bear an illegitimate child. I often thought that even committing suicide would be less devastating for our family than that, although I was to find out that this was not the case.

Mom herself had been a "love child" and I imagine that Grandma had been quite blown away by the whole thing and put the fear of the Lord into her daughter's heart about repeating the incident in her own life.

It turned out that my relationship with Burton was merely a fantasy on my part. He had enjoyed my company, the sex, and genuinely liked me, but it seemed that he had been in love with Alanna all along.

This came as quite a rude shock to both myself and Ruby, but evidently, Rob was intensely attracted to Alanna's virginal sweetness and youthful naivete. However, she rebuffed his advances and the poor guy was left on his own.

I was very upset and felt the pain clear into my hair follicles. I had been dumped, in favour of a better, more wholesome girl, just as I had by Charles and Simon. I must be some kind of repulsive freak, I thought. I truly hated myself.

I turned to the pub's bartender, an amicable, shaggy-haired twenty-five-year-old named Brian, who had never attended university and had no desire to. He was upfront, friendly and had a wide, ingratiating grin that attracted me immediately. He'd broken up with long-time steady, Esther., and I secretly hoped that he would turn to me for comfort and solace.

We got along extremely well, but Brian did not seem to be terribly enamoured with my blatant fawning and eagerness to praise him whenever the opportunity presented itself. I persisted, however, because I desperately wanted a boyfriend and craved a sense of intimacy with a guy who would accept me as I was.

Then came my unfortunate eye incident, which was to cause me untold trauma and leave some pretty substantial emotional scars. I had been wearing soft contact lenses for nearly two years, deciding at nineteen that I wasn't going to wear unsightly glasses anymore and look the part of the quintessential nerd when I entered university.

By late 1975, I required a new left lens, as it had gotten an opaque film on it, so I went to the optometrist in the campus mall to be fitted. Evidently, the lens was too tight and ended up wrinkling the cornea. I knew that something was wrong when I began to see colourful rainbows around lights and when I visited my opthamologist in London, he told me that the condition might be permanent.

I was devastated. What if I ended up going blind? Any kind of light caused a great deal of discomfort, so I wore a black eye patch over the eye, and suffered the humiliation of being called "Moshe" for Israeli leader Moshe Dayan, by insensitive students on campus.

My depressive episodes intensified as I felt more like a sideshow attraction than ever. An extremely arrogant, but sinfully good-looking student named Clark, looked at me working in the Cock and Bull with my whitish-blonde hair, black eye patch and funky clothes and deadpanned, "Hey, Halloween was last month." He smirked and shook his head, adding that my bids for attention were getting a bit wearing.

Clark had a mean streak two miles long. He knew he was gorgeous, and loved to play nasty head games with the female students. He was brilliant, but used his intelligence to skewer people emotionally, first drawing adoring young women into his minefield and then standing back and laughing while they stepped upon his instruments of destruction and writhed in tepid agony.

I believe that Clark was a true misogynist, for he was very kind and compassionate to the guys, especially Martial, whom he spent a great deal of time consoling. Martial wanted a girlfriend desperately, but seemed to come up empty-handed regularly.

For weeks, I despaired over my wounded eye, fearing it would never recover. I pictured it swelling up under the patch and dropping out of its socket, leaving me with this bright, red hole and frightening people with it unintentionally.

My friends assured me that it would get better and said that the patch was really chic and gave me an intriguing personality that set me apart from the "mainstream".

In time, the eye did recover and I decided not to sue the optometrist, but simply put the whole nightmare behind me. I couldn't wear contacts for a year afterward, however, and was forced to geek status by donning very untrendy glasses. I removed them frequently and squinted a great deal, bumping into people and looking very foolish in an effort to preserve my appearance. Ah yes, "all is vanity......"

\*    \*    \*    \*    \*    \*    \*    \*    \*

One night, I stayed up until nearly four AM talking to the quirky and darkly-shrouded Ingrid, the first occasion I had to really get to know her. I discovered that she had been diagnosed with manic depressive psychosis. It was a condition I'd read about in the past but didn't know any sufferers of it firsthand until now. She was supposed to take a large amount of something called Lithium Carbonate every day to keep her mood swings levelled out. Evidently, Ingrid had the tendency to plunge into deep, horrific ravines of anguish, as well as soar to giddy, hysterical heights, but she decided that her medication was useless and refused to take it anymore.

I didn't think this was particularly wise, since I'd noticed how reclusive and low she'd been all year. Now she chatted away non-stop, waving her hands spasmodically and laughing uproariously about nothing.

Ingrid told me later that she'd been confined to a mental hospital in her hometown and had despised it. They had put her on a drug called Mellaril, which caused her to gain sixty pounds and feel sluggish and doped up all the time.

I was morbidly fascinated, never having met a mental patient before, although one of Jim's friends had been on the adolescent ward of the London Psychiatric Hospital.

I liked this fragile, round-faced girl with the gap between her front teeth and pronounced dimple on her chin. I felt strangely drawn to her tragic past and emotional instability.

With all her problems, Ingrid had accomplished a great deal in her eighteen years of life. She'd worked as a journalist on her high school paper and had interviewed many up-and-coming rock performers, because of her dogged determination and refusal to stumble over obstacles.

In her senior year, she scored a prime interview with Elton John and even showed me the lengthy, fascinating piece, beaming with pride and enthusing about how incredibly gracious and cool the musician had been to her. I was quite impressed and admired her ambitious undertaking, despite being plagued by illness.

We became fast friends after that night, even though Courtney warned me that Ingrid had "a lot of problems". I thought this was rather insensitive of her, and chose to ignore the statement.

As the weeks went by, Ingrid's moods became extremely erratic and she would alternately laugh and cry for no apparent reason. I suggested to her that she take her Lithium, but she merely scoffed at me and said it was "poison".

We listened to records a lot, drinking coffee in the Cock and Bull and plotted my strategies where nabbing Brian was concerned. Ingrid thought that he and I would be the "perfect couple", even though it was evident that he was still hung up on Esther and talked about her wistfully.

Courtney decided to break off her uneasy relationship with Clark, who treated her poorly and started seeing an English student named Bob, who looked and sounded for all the world like Pierce Brosnan. It seems as though York University was chock full of celebrity look-alikes as I reminisce about it now.

Ian was an unusually thoughtful and pleasant young man, who excelled on the rugby team and obviously adored Courtney. I was pleased that she'd abandoned the roguish Clark in favour of a man who would treat her with the respect she deserved. Still, it would be another year before she and Ian were officially a couple.

So, with all of the social interaction with other students, and my waitress job, I was temporarily distracted from my personal problems, at least for awhile. I hadn't gone blind in my left eye, as I'd feared, and my courses were becoming a bit less overwhelming and complicated. Perhaps the year would be preferable to the previous one.

Then I got another set of traumatic components to deal with and I was once more plunged into a cataclysmic maelstrom. It began with a love letter that I passionately penned to Brian, speaking of my undying devotion and that I would do anything to be his soulmate. I thought he would appreciate it and that this would let him know that I was serious in my intentions to become romantically entangled with him.

He reacted extremely negatively, exploding in anger at me after work one night and sneering sarcastically that he most assuredly didn't feel that way about me and how the fucking hell could I mess with his head like that?

I was dumbstruck, feeling as though he'd plunged a hot poker through my gut. I burst into tears, pleading with him to stop yelling at me and that I had only intended to make him feel good.

I suppose he felt threatened by my love for him and hadn't suspected that I felt that way. I was not particularly adept at handling relationships and had misjudged his affection and friendliness toward me.

I had desired Brian so profoundly because I secretly knew that I couldn't have him and it was that age-old "thrill of the chase" that attracted me so intensely. I was aware of his deep-rooted feelings for Esther, but decided to play a game with myself, challenging my ability to lure him away from her.

He must have known this, even if I didn't at the time, and it infuriated him that I was confusing him and setting up road blocks for my own selfish purposes.

At that point of my life, I saw this as another example of being rejected for another, more worthy opponent and I became more depressed than ever after Brian's outburst.

Ingrid suggested that I see a doctor for some medication for these depressive episodes which were causing me to sleep all day and avoid classes and work at the pub. I had been seeing this physician downtown for a few months, having heard about him through Lizzie and he'd prescribed Librium for my problems with concentration. I'd been taking it faithfully and the drug gave me a mild sensation of well-being, but caused a great deal of unwanted sleepiness and dulling of the senses.

Ingrid told me that Librium was bad for me, so my doctor prescribed an antidepressant called Anafranil. I was told it would take a few weeks to work, but that after that time my depression would lift considerably.

I didn't tell my family about the Librium or the Anafranil. I figured they had enough stress without knowing their daughter and sister was a headcase.

A week after starting the medication, I sat in my room alone, listening to "Crime of the Century" and drinking from my mickey of scotch. I'd been consuming a great deal of liquor lately and kept a supply in my desk drawer at all times. Draft just didn't do it for me; it was like guzzling water.

Between the angst-ridden episodes and the excessive quantities of the alcohol, I sunk into a despair that was more profound and agonizing than ever. Suddenly, like a page quickly turning, I saw the writing clearly and boldly before me: "I want to die. Oh, God, I don't want to live like this."

Impulsively, I reached for my bottle of Librium and, in a kind of strange trance, I emptied it all over the bed, letting the pills pelt the spread in a shower of death. Scooping up a handful, I quickly stuffed them into my mouth and swallowed them with a large gulp of scotch.

Just then, my bedroom door flew open and Courtney stood there, her mouth gaping open and an expression of horror in her eyes. "Oh my God! What have you done?!"

I hadn't locked my door and apparently I had told Courtney that I would meet her at the pub for coffee a half hour earlier. When I didn't show up, she got a bit worried and decided to investigate.

I was furious at the rude intrusion of my privacy and from being interrupted so abruptly. "Get the hell out of here!" I screamed, throwing the empty bottle across the room in a fit of rage. "It's none of your Goddamned business what I'm doing!"

Courtney then proceeded to try to discover how much of the medication I had taken. I refused to tell her anything, yelling obscenities at her and calling her a self-righteous little bitch.

She burst into tears, sobbing that I had drastically changed over the past few weeks, that I obviously despised her and everyone, but most of all myself. She was desperately afraid for me and hated the way I flaunted my problems and treated her with emotional sadism.

Then, as I stared at my so-called friend in disbelief, I saw her turn for the door. "I'm calling your father," she announced, "so don't try to stop me. It's about time he knew what's going on with his fucked up daughter."

She made good on her threat and two hours later, Dad arrived, having driven from London in record time. I had passed out by this time, so he sat with me for the next seven hours, while I slept. I'm sure he must have wondered what the hell was going on with me.

When I groggily awoke, with the world's worst hang-over, he took me to Howard Johnson's for lunch. I hadn't been eating much of anything for weeks, but suddenly felt voraciously hungry. We didn't talk much during the meal, but I assured him that I had made a very stupid error in judgement and that it wouldn't happen again.

Dad had always found it difficult to talk about personal issues, particularly with his loved ones, but I think he was convinced that I had simply had far too much to drink and became confused. I told him that I would stop drinking and throw out the rest of my Librium.

Still, after that night, nothing was the same again. The antidepressants were ineffective, but I continued to take them in the vain hope that they would magically take hold of my sagging mood and inflate it like a balloon.

I confided to Paul Roazen that I took Anafranil and that I was having some emotional problems. He told me to talk to a professional, so I contacted a psychologist who was well known on campus. He turned out to be another lecherous shrink who told me all I needed was a good fuck. I told him off and never returned, feeling that the entire profession was nothing but a sick joke.

I began to grow increasingly angry, erupting at the residence and accusing people of being cruel and unfair to me. I was the poor, downtrodden victim and only Ingrid understood and cared about me.

Courtney turned away from me, and so did Sidney. Sylvia had lost a great deal of weight and was quickly becoming anorexic and after she rejected my offers to help her, I left her to fend for herself.

Sidney was disillusioned, feeling I'd grown hard and judge-mental, so he spent more time with Sylvia and Billy. Rhoda kept to herself and I stayed away from Ruby, Martha, Lizzie and Alanna. I felt that they were too "happy" and "carefree" and couldn't possibly identify with anyone having difficulties. In other words, I was doing some pretty heavy wallowing in the self-pity quagmire.

Ingrid began to slide into her own depressive swamp, crying endlessly in her room and turning to a lesbian friend for comfort. She didn't want a sexual relationship with her, but needed some stability. I was unable to provide any for her at that time.

I dropped my Philosophy courses early in March, fearing I'd fail the final exams, so I had only three left instead of the required five for second year. I vowed to make them up during the summer and decided to concentrate on the English and Political Science ones, which were manageable.

Alone and craving companionship and affection, I turned to Simon again, who still wanted nothing to do with me and rejected all my advances. Amanda had moved to A House, after problems at home became too much for her. I had to bump into her frequently and see her with my ex every single day, which really hurt.

One night, I managed to get him to talk to me in his room, but the conversation soon turned ugly and volatile when I brought up the subject of Amanda. "I talked to her the other day", I said, secretly enjoying watching Simon squirm uncomfortably. "We were discussing you and what you did to me. She didn't know about that night. Imagine that. You just happened to forget to tell her, didn't you?"

Simon lost it upon hearing this. "Why are you talking to Lorna, you bitch? Listen, you drag her into this and I'll have your hide." He was livid, bursting with rage.

I felt completely defeated at this outburst and hurt that he despised me so much. I ran from the room crying bitterly, wishing I had a gun to blow my brains out. Why was my life so awful? Whatever had I done to deserve this kind of treatment? Was I some kind of mutated creature that had to be shunned and hated by everyone?

I gave up on Simon for good after that, knowing that he would never come back to me and that Lorna meant the world to him. I felt as though a metal vice was crushing my ribcage and my lifeblood was draining out of every orifice.

I didn't do very well academically that year, achieving only a "B" average and feeling dissatisfied with my essays, tests and exams. By the end of the semester, I knew that if I didn't smarten up and apply myself in third year, I might not graduate in 1978.

I couldn't imagine the degradation and humiliation of failing university. Then what would become of my life? I'd end up waitressing in a bar until I retired, and of course, no decent guy would marry me, since I was such a loser. Maybe suicide would ultimately be my destination after all, and the next time, I vowed, as I rode home to London on the train for the summer, I'd make certain that nobody barged in on me.

# Chapter Nine

# *Lakeshore*

The summer of 1976 was spent waitressing in a seedy, sleazy hotel called Ye Olde City Hall, but I enjoyed it nonetheless, bar brawls, blood, broken glass and all. The other waitresses were friendly and I achieved a certain amount of social success there. My bosses were pleasant, fair-minded and overlooked a lot of my mistakes. We made about thirty bucks a night in tips, as it was a very busy place, and this made up for having to mop up puddles of blood occasionally.

My emotional problems abated somewhat, although the nagging depression that caused me to want to sleep most of the day hung on like a damp fog.

When the fall descended, I felt semi-confident that I'd do much better academically and socially than the previous year. Of course, I'd promised myself that last time.

I was back in residence again, having decided not to rent an apartment off-campus. I should have, because most students found that dorm life was pretty much intolerable after a couple of years, but I thought I could handle it. Besides, it was better to have a large group of people around all the time than be isolated in a highrise.

Courtney lived in a huge, ultra-modern complex near the campus called University City. She'd moved in with Bob, after they overcame their personal difficulties over the summer. He was good for her, I thought, stable and considerate.

I became close friends with Ruby and Lizzie that year, as they, like myself, were serious, intense and wanted to effect positive changes in the world after they graduated. Ruby wanted to be a lawyer and was majoring in history. She worked slavishly, as did Lizzie, a psychology major. I took their lead and began the semester studying very hard.

I was enrolled in two English courses, two Humanities ones and a film course, having abandoned Philosophy as a minor and deciding upon Humanities. My thinking seemed to be more in tuned with that form of reasoning anyway. I hadn't made up my two dropped courses from second year, but figured I would before graduation. There still seemed to be plenty of time. 1978 still appeared a long way off. I'd be twenty-three then, practically middle-aged.

I discovered that Brian and Esther were back together. Brian approached me one night and was extraordinarily kind and gentle to me. He said he didn't really burn my love letter, as he claimed he did the year before in a fit of rage and that I meant a lot to him. Suddenly, it was safe now, since he was betrothed to another. I smiled and wished him happiness, secretly pining for him still.

Simon and Amanda were hot and heavy, although she had confided to me recently that she thought he was getting "weirder and weirder". I didn't think she should be slagging him behind his back if she was supposedly in love with the guy, but I said nothing.

I also became tight with Kelli, who'd recently been unceremoniously dumped by her longtime boyfriend, Howard. She cried for weeks in her room afterward, but eventually recovered enough to regain her previously cheerful disposition. During her mourning period, she lost an incredible amount of weight and looked amazingly trim. I barely recognized her, except for her distinctive buck teeth and granny glasses.

Kelli was wonderful, funny, extremely intelligent, hilariously sarcastic, with a very sensible head on her slim shoulders. She had heard rumours that I had tried to kill myself the year before and assured me that I would "live to regret it" if I repeated the performance.

She cared about me a lot, but didn't want me dissolving into a pile of self-pity dust. "You're too smart for that crap," she sniffed. "Look around you at all the dummies in this school who'll never amount to anything. You'll go places, girl. Just keep your head together."

I had a dear English professor named Derek Cohen, whom I learned to respect highly. I did a tutorial on "Madame Bovary" and he was impressed at the firm grasp I had on the character's tortured psyche. I think he knew I was experiencing some emotional difficulties and was very kind and sweet to me.

Professor Evans was another matter. He taught one of my Humanities courses  on Shakespeare and decided early on that I wasn't a particularly gifted student. He didn't like any of my essays and whenever I'd comment during his tutorials, he'd either ignore me or disagree with whatever I said. He chose favourites as well, and made it quite obvious who those fortunate students, all female, were.

The other two professors were pleasant, though, particularly Professor Ewen, a proper Englishman whom I'd had in first year teaching the Romantic Literature course. He was curiously eccentric and absolutely adored William Blake and instilled a love in me for this insightful poet that remains today. Ewen looked like a cross between Donald Pleasance and Ray Milland, thus bringing two more screen luminary look-alikes into the York University environment.

The film professor was a rather strict but kind-hearted middle-aged man whose name escapes me, but he taught us to appreciate the American cinema, past and present. I first learned to love screenwriting during this period in my life.

Even with the compassion and enthusiasm of Professors Cohen and Ewen, my depression persisted and was aggravated by some paralyzing anxiety attacks that made it nearly impossible for me to attend some of my classes. I'd suddenly become gripped with fear that something terrible was about to happen, even though there was no logical explanation for the sensation. I'd feel as though I was suffocating and that my heart was fluttering wildly against my chest wall, banging around in a chaotic fashion. These panic attacks lasted for several minutes and during that time I wouldn't budge, fearful that I would start flailing about like a madwoman. After it was over, I was left feeling exhausted and drained.

I started taking Librium again, which seemed to be effective in curbing the attacks, and enabled me to attend my lectures and tutorials. However, the drug caused excessive drowsiness and several times I nodded off in class. This didn't go over big with some of my professors and tutorial leaders and they recommended that I do my sleeping at night instead of partying.

As the Christmas season neared, I knew that I wasn't going to do well scholastically that year at all, since I was unable to concentrate and my courses all seemed to require far too much reading. Unread books piled up on my desk, my room fell into a state of pure squalor and I became too lethargic to either study or tidy up. My face broke out in a rude case of acne as I was too depressed to shower regularly. I even slept in my clothes and wouldn't change them for days at a time. I lived on coffee and cigarettes, foregoing nutrition for a jolt of caffeine and nicotine.

My friends were getting quite concerned about me and made valiant attempts to get me to seek professional help. I refused, telling them that I had tried talking to people and they were crazier than I was.

I sifted languidly through the days, barely aware of my surroundings. I was consumed with thoughts of death, felt constantly nauseated and achy and had no energy for even talking to anyone.

Kelli gave me some space, as did Lizzie, but Ruby persisted in trying to straighten me out. She told me that she had suffered periods of depression in high school and they had nearly destroyed her.

I didn't go home often, as Mom was still very despondent over the dissolution of her marriage, and I felt I couldn't tell her about my problems. I hid at York, lying to her and assuring her that everything was "just fine". I didn't see much of Dad or Jim, and rarely visited my grandparents, who must have known something was wrong with me.

I began to lose touch with reality during the Christmas break and stayed in my bedroom at home in London. I just lay on my bed, feeling that I was being visited my mysterious aliens who would occasionally whisper to me in low, guttural voices. I couldn't make out any distinct words, but I got the impression that I was being comforted by something or someone who was mysteriously hovering above and reading my mind.

For some reason, I thought all of this was perfectly normal and accepted the voices as elements who were there to get me through my hideous nightmare.

When classes resumed in early January of 1977, I didn't even go through the motions of being an active university student anymore. I abandoned my tutorials, except for Derek Cohen's and only occasionally attended my lectures.

My grades slipped drastically, due in part to this benign neglect, and also because the essays I did manage to rattle off were poorly thought out and badly constructed. I'd taken pride in my schoolwork in the past, but now it was unimportant and extraneous, with no meaning and little intrinsic value. As I slid down the drain academically, any sense of security I might have clung to in the past dissolved completely.

Then came the fateful accusation of plagiarism by Professor Evans that pushed me violently over the edge. It was a paper about Shakespeare's philosophical outlook upon love and relationships. Although it was not a very good essay, I spent more time on it than I had on any other during the month of January.

When I got it back, Evans had scrawled a horrific "F" across the bottom in bold, red ink and wrote that I had obviously stolen my ideas and concepts from a published source.

I felt terrible, never having failed anything in my life before and I bristled at the accusation of plagiarism. I most definitely hadn't stolen anything, so in a black fit of pique, I wrote Hill a long letter. It stated, among other things, that he needed to quote my supposed sources before giving me a failing grade.

I never gave him the message, though, for the night before, my life changed forever and was rudely swept out of my control and far from the university campus.

I sat in my cluttered, filthy room, listening to Cat Stevens' "Sad Lisa" over and over. Simon had once told me that it was a hauntingly appropriate song for me and my troubled life. As I sat on an unmade bed, drinking Johnny Walker scotch, my eyes filled with tears.

Suddenly, frighteningly, a strange, sinister voice began taunting me from my left stereo speaker. I had been experiencing a lot of these auditory phenomena lately but none of the voices had sounded negative before. It was a male voice, low and evil-sounding, and began chanting repeatedly, in a throaty, flat tone, "You know what you have to do. Punishment is in order".

I had bought a package of razor blades the day before, feeling the need to mutilate myself. It had been preying on my mind for weeks, the urge to cut and experience the sensation of warm blood spurting from the wound and running everywhere.

Still, I fought this compulsion daily, knowing instinctively that if I began slashing I would be unable to stop. Now, as the frightening voice assailed me, I remembered the blades and allowed my gaze to light upon the desk drawer where they were safely tucked away.

The voice repeated its command, louder this time, with more insistence and anger. I knew that the time had arrived to go a step further than simply cut for self-abusive purposes.

Feeling numb and wooden, I got off the bed, walked over to my desk and opened the drawer. The packaged of blades beamed up at me as if to say, "We knew you'd come for us".

Fumbling with the cardboard covering, I extricated one of the objects of destruction and sat back down on the bed. The voice nagged at me, overpowering Cat Stevens' plaintive vocals. The time was ripe for death; it would come as a blessed release from my mental torment and the overwhelming malaise that had gripped me for so long now.

Raising the blade, I slashed across my left wrist, not realizing that you have to cut vertically to inflict a mortal wound.

Just then a voice rang out from the other side of the door. "Hey, Jane! Could you please turn your stereo down? It's awful loud." It was Ruby.

I was afraid to move, fearing the nasty voice in the speaker would be furious if I became distracted. The music stayed at its present volume and the obviously exasperated Ruby rapped again and shouted over the music, "Jane, I'm not trying to be a bitch, but could you please just turn the volume down? I'm trying to study. Hello? Is everything okay in there?"

The next few minutes are very fuzzy; I can't recall how Ruby figured that something was wrong, but she evidently got the resident don and insisted that she use her master key to gain entry into my room.

I remember the don becoming alarmed at what I had done and trying to talk to me. I was deathly afraid of my mysterious voices and said little. She took me to the emergency room at York-Finch Hospital where I was sewn up and drilled by a young male intern for over an hour.

He asked me if I was attempting suicide, but I refused to answer and hoped that I would be allowed to leave as soon as possible. The intern decided that I should be admitted to the hospital's psychiatric wing for observation. "You'll only be here for twenty-four hours or so," he assured me when I expressed my distaste for hospitals. "Don't worry, you were probably just crying out for help. I don't think you're in too serious trouble".

I didn't tell him about the voices I'd been experiencing, because I knew that would get me committed for sure. However, as an orderly took me upstairs to the psychiatric floor, I couldn't help feeling a strong desire to get some help for a problem which had gone careening out of control during the past few months. Perhaps I should come clean and tell the doctors everything and then I could get over the nightmare that was stealing my life, inch by inch.

It was very late, so when I arrived at the floor, everyone was in bed and the unit was shrouded in darkness. I crawled into an institutional bed in a quiet, semi-private room and lay there for the next few hours, huddled in a fetal position and shaking with the fear of the unknown. The voices had ceased for the time being and I fervently hoped they would never show themselves to me again.

Should I tell them about those voices? What would happen to me if I did? I was already doing poorly in my classes, so I couldn't afford to miss any time from school. Did Ruby and Lizzie know where I was?

I drifted off into an uneasy sleep, painfully aware of the throbbing in my wounded wrist. God, I'm a bona fide nutcase now, I thought ruefully, and I'm surrounded by a whole bunch of others. I hope my family doesn't find out about this.

The next morning, I was awakened by a relentlessly chipper, cheerful nurse and instructed to go for pills and breakfast in the lounge.

I walked out into a bright, pink-walled room full of patients sitting about, some staring off into space, others engaged in conversation with one another. I sat by myself in a far corner, not wishing to mingle with any of these people and most definitely not feeling as though I had anything in common with them, particularly the corpulent, middle-aged man nearby who was drooling and sitting still and immobile.

I was handed a small paper cup with my Anafranil and wondered how the hell they knew that I was taking this medication. Breakfast was inedible, some sort of pasty-looking hot cereal and dry toast. I drank the juice and coffee, then made a concerted effort not to overhear any of the patients' conversations. That was impossible, because this cheerful, perky blonde woman with a thick Scottish brogue began chatting about a place called "The Lakeshore" and expressed extreme relief that she wasn't in that "terrible place".

I assumed she was referring to a psychiatric hospital, one which sounded more like Dachau or Auschwitz than an institution for helping people get over various mental infirmities. From the sound of it, I shared her sense of gratitude about being at York-

Finch.

Later that day, after lying on my bed and staring at the tiles on the ceiling, the voices began again, accusing me of wimping out on my suicide plans and damning me severely. The same throaty tone, this time emanating from the fluorescent light over the bed, began to instruct me to find another sharp object and repeat my actions of the previous night. This time there was to be no slipping up.

Terror-stricken, I decided to spill my guts to the psychiatrist who called me into his office soon after to see that I was stable enough to leave. I stammered in frightened tones that I had been hearing voices for several months and that they were telling me to destroy myself. Fear of their hostility was overriding my discomfort at being confined in hospital and I sighed with relief when the doctor spoke kindly and gently to me. He said that they would certainly be able to help me there.

The psychiatrist gave me a white pill and said, "This will help you with the voices", then instructed me to return to my room and rest.

I don't remember calling my parents and telling them that I had been admitted to the hospital, but I'm pretty sure they found out about it soon afterward. I had no idea how long I'd be at York-Finch, but I knew that it was not a long-term facility. Ifelt comfortable and secure in the knowledge that this medication I had been given would solve all my problems and return me to my previous self. Life would be worth living again and I wouldn't be a failure, having to drop out of York and push drinks to leering customers for the rest of my days.

The next morning, I was assaulted with vicious words from my demons. That now-familiar voice accused me vituperatively of being a shameful coward for betraying him and uncovering his presence. I was instructed to steal a China cup from my breakfast tray and break it in the sink, after which I was to cut my throat with a piece of it. I knew that I had no choice, that if I didn't kill myself, this tormentor would. I thus followed his instructions and hid in the bathroom to accomplish my sad mission.

I was not to have any privacy, however. They had moved me into an observation room with another girl named Lucy, who was being watched twenty-four hours a day. I guess they figured I was a measure of risk and decided that a nurse should sit with me constantly.

So when I entered the bathroom, a nurse followed me and stood there quietly as I took the cup from my robe. She hadn't seen me remove it from the tray. "Give me the cup, please."

I ignored her and without hesitating, smashed the cup on the edge of the sink, and grasped a large, sharp chunk of it in my hand.

Suddenly, my "guard" yelled for assistance, and leapt on top of me, twisting my arm behind my back and shoving her knee on top of my wildly kicking legs.

Then there was a whole throng of attendants piling onto me. I fought valiantly, screaming and struggling to hold onto my piece of China. Then someone wrestled it out of my clenched fist and I was being lifted from the floor and onto the bed.

To my horror, I was placed in some kind of canvas harness and it was secured tightly to the bed while I heard one of the nurses say to another, "She's psychotic; I know that look."

Then I felt a sharp stab in my left hip and realized that they must have given me a shot of some kind of tranquillizer. It took three doses of Thorazine to calm me down sufficiently, because after the first I overheard that I would be sent to Lakeshore Psychiatric Hospital.

Remembering what I'd overheard about that terrible place, I screamed in protest. "She doesn't want to go, I guess", someone said, "Well, I've got news for her. She can't behave like this here."

Later, I was prepared for transport to the dreaded purgatory. After the ambulance attendant had placed me on a stretcher I fumbled in a drugged haze for the phone to call Ruby and tell her where I was going. I told her I broke a cup, and she responded that it was no big deal. She didn't know all the details and after the receiver dropped from my limp hand, everything went spiralling into a black void.

\*   \*   \*   \*   \*   \*   \*   \*   \*   \*   \*   \*   \*

"I think she's finally coming around," I heard a female voice say from somewhere off in the distance. "Yeah, you're right, it's about time." Opening my eyes, I felt my thickened head spin wildly. My mouth seemed to be stuffed with cotton and every muscle in my body ached. As my vision cleared, I looked into the face of a young black woman.

"Hi",she said, smiling with open friendliness. "You know you've been out of it for three days. Welcome to Lakeshore. I'm Paula, and this is Debbie". She pointed to a large, obese woman of about twenty who chirped, "Hi, want to get the hell out of bed?"

I nodded, a wave of nausea washing through me. "Yeah. What is this place anyway?" I noticed that I was in a large room with garish yellow walls and two long rows of narrow beds. Old, worn curtains separated each bed and there were small tables beside them. It looked like something out of a World War II movie about an army infirmary. I wasn't particularly impressed.

There were about twenty patients in the room, all women of various ages, sizes and races. Suddenly a young, pixy-faced girl rushed over to me and exclaimed, "Hey, you cut your wrist? Let's see."

Her name was Susan and I was to later discover that she had been in and out of the place many times. She was married and had two young children, and had great difficulty coping with her life.

I reluctantly showed her my bandaged wrist, then made an effort to stand up. I felt as though I'd been whacked over the head with a tree trunk, but after a few minutes, the drugged sensation abated somewhat and I managed to walk a few steps across this dismal-looking room.

I learned that two of my university friends had been to visit me for the past three days while I was "out to lunch" and had tried several times to get me out of bed. Evidently I collapsed on the floor everytime and had to be lifted back onto the mattress by staff members.

The two friends had been Ruby and Lizzie and it turned out that they were extremely faithful about visiting me, coming every day for many miles across the city to offer comfort and support. I was very grateful but felt that they were wasting a great deal of their free time with someone like me, who had gotten herself into that mess in the first place.

I discovered that Lakeshore Psychiatric Hospital was made up of cottages, small, one-storey wooden buildings strewn over a wooded area on the shores of Lake Ontario. I was in Cottage B, an admitting building and apparently the best one of the bunch to be confined in, according to Debbie. She said you had the ability to acquire privileges, including weekend passes.

These privileges had to be earned, however and the ward was

locked at all times. The nurses at Cottage B were pleasant enough, and dressed in street clothes. In the beginning, I felt that the negative rumours I'd been privy to at York-Finch were
totally erroneous. I figured that I probably wouldn't be there that long and that the patients weren't something repulsive and people to walk in fear of at all.

My voices had stopped during my first week there and within several days I earned the privilege of wearing my clothes instead of pyjamas.

Paula and Debbie became my buddies and although they obviously had some emotional difficulties, they were kind, helpful and good company when I felt isolated from my previous "outside life". Debbie's depression, she reasoned, stemmed from the fact that she had gained ninety pounds in the past year on her medication. She figured that if she got down to her previous weight, her troubles would evaporate. I wasn't too certain because her moods seemed to yo-yo with great alarm, shooting to euphoric heights and plummeting to dismal lows.

Paula was quiet, a sullen girl who perked up occasionally but spent a lot of time sitting on her bed with her head lowered. I felt sorry for her, but she only seemed to feel comfortable confiding in Debbie. So I let it be.

Susan got released in a few days, but returned less than twelve hours later with a bandaged wrist. It turned out that she would mimic everything that I did and after noting that I had cut myself, she followed suit. I was a bit irked, but kept my feelings to myself. Besides, I felt sorry for this poor girl, who obviously was not happy in her role as wife and mother in the suburbs of Toronto.

Josie was a very troubled sixteen-year-old who acted out frequently and couldn't maintain her privilege level because she would have alarming screaming fits and pound her fists on the floor. She behaved more like an eight-year-old than a teenager, and I grew impatient with her obvious bids for attention. She followed me around, which I found most annoying and I would snap at her to "get lost" on many occasions. None of the other patients liked her, with the exception of twenty-one-year-old Denise.

Denise lived with a brutish father who routinely abused her sexually, and the poor girl took her anger and revulsion out on herself, slashing her arms, savagely with razor blades. When I met her, they were bandaged from elbow to wrist.

She was delicately pretty, with light blonde hair, pale blue eyes and an ethereal quality that made her father's ugly actions even more atrocious and terrible. I talked to Denise a great deal, but she would speak about her dad with pretend banality, with an off-hand, casual attitude, as if the abuse didn't bother her at all. Her thin, pathetic arms betrayed her, however.

Gloria was a middle-aged widow who yearned to be with her departed husband and in a mood of black despair, she stabbed herself forty times in the gut with a carving knife. This tiny, intense woman spoke calmly and matter-of-factly about how she'd lost most of her liver because of the suicide attempt and was disappointed that the doctors at Lakeshore didn't believe her when she assured them that she felt fine and was capable of
returning home.

I didn't buy it either and I knew that if Gloria was released, she'd make certain that her next attempt on her life would be successful. The thought gave me chills.

Megan was a peculiar young woman who appeared to have the entire Cottage B staff wrapped around her pinkie. I couldn't determine what was wrong with her, but she was sent to a general hospital for a week and returned bed-ridden and attached to an I.V.

Nurses milled about her and she took full advantage of her situation by issuing orders and whining profusely at every opportunity. Debbie said she must be very ill or the staff wouldn't put up with her antics. She looked like a female Harpo Marx, but unlike the famous comedy brother, Megan was never silent.

I resented the attention she received and the manner in which she could do no wrong in the eyes of the ward authorities. The rest of us were kept on a very tight leash and told to keep our mouths shut most of the time.

I welcomed visits from my university friends, thus maintaining a link to a previous life, one of freedom and relative normality. Lizzie and Ruby listened patiently while I glumly regaled them with tales of woe from mental hospital hell. After a week had elapsed, I fell into an awkward sort of routine, rising at seven in the morning, showering, milling into the communal dining room for meals, then trooping to occupational therapy, a kind of kindergarten for adults. Here, we fiddled around with lumps of clay, worked with tiny, ceramic tiles and learned how to do macrame.

Mom visited every weekend, but I don't have much recollection of this, since my psychiatrist, Dr. Baines, put me on a series of extremely potent major tranquilizers from day one of my "incarceration".

Dr. Baines was a personable, red-headed woman, looking nothing like my concept of a "shrink",but rather, more like somebody's mother, or perhaps a high school math teacher. She spent a great deal of time with me, asking me about my voices and the depression which had overwhelmed me for so many years.

I was put on Mellaril, which made me stagger and drool, looking the part of the stereotypical mental patient. The dose was gradually increased so that I noticed the voices getting fainter and less frequent, but unfortunately, the drug gave me symptoms of tardif dyskonesia.

These included making uncontrollable movements with my mouth and tongue and touching my hand unconsciously to my lips. I didn't realize that I was doing this, but my mother told me much later that it was very obvious when she saw me at Lakeshore. She grew increasingly distressed at how Mellaril was submerging my personality and spontaneity under a river of drugged stagnation.

I remembered what Ingrid had said about the drug: That it had caused her considerable weight gain. Fearful of this, I cut down drastically on my eating and would only consume five hundred calories a day in an effort to stave off obesity, something I feared more than insanity.

I began to notice that I was losing touch with my senses and didn't trust them anymore. I panicked when I felt myself drifting off into a great open pool of nothingness and in a desperate attempt to feel something, anything, I began burning the backs of my hands with the lit embers of my cigarettes.I would crouch in the bathroom stall and press the burning end against my skin until my nostrils were overwhelmed by the odour of burning flesh. I'd repeat the action until there were several swollen welts looking defiantly at me. The pain was reassuring and also fed my craving for self-abuse.

It wasn't long before I was discovered and my cigarettes were immediately confiscated. That didn't stop me, however, for I would beg, borrow, or steal other patients' cigarettes and sneak off for my bizarre, frightening ritual.

It bothered me a great deal that I wasn't able to experience that kind of intense pain that the burning should rightly have produced. It was a dull, weak kind of discomfort, but burns were supposed to be the worst kind of agony. I desperately wanted to distract myself from the emotional wasteland I wandered in.

As the weeks progressed, I took on the role of the hapless guinea pig, as Dr. Baines tried one drug after another in an effort to cut through the mental confusion and sense of hopelessness that enveloped me.

A great deal of my four-month period at Lakeshore is a miasmic blur, for I was almost completely out of touch with reality. I walked about, going through the motions of everyday activities, but not realizing that I was doing them. My single-minded purpose was to get myself to feel that I was really alive and not in some separate, frightening universe, damned forever and cruelly under the spell of my mysterious voices, which returned often to torment me.

I was run through a history of psychological tests, such as the popular inkblot one and asked hundreds of questions over a period of about two weeks or so. There seemed to be some definite contradictions, because even though I heard voices and seemed depressed and flat, I wasn't experiencing delusions or convoluted thinking.

I wasn't given a diagnosis there, but rather, I was treated symptomatically and believed to be seriously ill. One night, I broke the bulb from the nurses' reading lamp and tried to slash my wrist with it, feeling unusually self-destructive.

The staff were extremely upset with me and made plans to send me to the infamous and dreaded S.O.U. I was sick with fear and revulsion, for this acronym stood for Special Observation Unit and was a ward right out of "The Snakepit". Here, all the patients' beds were in the centre of a square room, surrounded by iron bars.

On the other side, a large group of nurses and attendants watched constantly as people writhed, moaned, tore out their hair, made attempts to strangle and hit one another and rolled about on their beds in various contortions of mental agony.

My heart sank at the thought of being submitted to this hellhole and I pleaded with the nurses and Dr. Baines to be given another chance. Fortunately for me, the S.O.U. was full and by the time a bed became available, I had greatly improved and didn't have to be sent there at all. But it had been a close call.

I was tested on a vast number of antidepressants, such as Elavil, Ludiomil and one of the M.A.O. inhibitors. None of them seemed terribly effective, but finally Elavil was chosen because I experienced fewer side effects with it.

Mellaril was continued, along with a potent antipsychotic drug called Stelazine, which was supposed to be very effective in controlling auditory hallucinations. It worked well, but the side effects were somewhat distressing. It caused excessive restlessness and I couldn't find a comfortable position, either sitting, standing or lying down without rocking continually. I felt as though I had to move some part of my body at all times.

I hated this; it was worse than Speed and gave me a quirky, itchy feeling in my chest. I should have been given Cogentin or Dissipal for the side effects, but wasn't for some reason. The voices many have been under control with the Stelazine, but physically I was in extreme discomfort.

It wasn't long before copycat Susan began burning her hands with cigarettes and lost her privileges for a week. Then she stopped eating and drinking for six days and ended up sick and bedridden. My heart went out to her and I couldn't see then how very much alike we were.

Debbie got released after putting herself on a diet and losing twenty pounds. She was more relaxed and happy but I still thought there was more to her problem than the weight issue.

Paula took a mouthful of bleach one afternoon but spit it out at Debbie's urging. She was sent to another, more strict ward and I never saw her again. I sometimes wonder what became of this sad-eyed young woman who sat for hours in silence, locked in her solitary prison of despair.

Denise went home to that bastard of a father and cut herself some more after he forced himself on her again. She came back, and was told that she would be hospitalized for four more months. She swore bitterly at her doctor and promised to go AWOL. I thought it was grossly unfair that she was the one to be locked up all the time.

Gloria grew despondent and was sent to the long-term cottage, much to her distress. They informed her that she'd be in for another year at least.

I got to know some of the male patients at O.T. during our group therapy sessions. One was named Todd and I was immediately attracted to his little-boy-lost quality and ethereal beauty. He was nineteen and had been admitted so that he could get off drugs and put his shattered life back together. He was earnest and sincere, but a bit too idealistic and unrealistic about the
world and his situation. He thought that he could just turn his back on

his unhealthy past after spending a few weeks getting the chemicals out of his system, but it didn't really work out that way for most people, I'd discovered.

Other young people in our group told him that there was more to changing his life than that and he would need to establish new friendships and dissolve old ones, leaving them behind in a cloud of Angel Dust. I knew from my own drug experiences that this was absolutely essential.

I liked Todd, perhaps too much and wanted him to feel the same way about me. However, he was attracted to a serious, mournful-eyed teenager named Camilla, who'd overdosed at her home and felt very shaky about moving on with her life. Again, I was being overlooked for a more preferable, beautiful girl and it hurt.

Ken was about forty-five and developed a gigantic crush on me for some reason, though he was old enough to be my father. I treated him poorly, I'm ashamed to say, and made fun of his attempts to win my affection. Gloria comforted Ken and told me not to be so cruel and heartless.

Susan began to eat voraciously after her fast and gained a substantial amount of weight. I was losing and by April was down to ninety-nine pounds, something that made me feel quite good about myself. I had no appetite and was subsisting on vegetables, coffee and as many cigarettes as the staff would dole out to me.

There was a coffee house on the hospital grounds called the Moorehouse. It was designed in a nautical fashion, with portholes, lanterns and large fishing nets strung across the ceiling, similar to Courtney's room in residence. We sat there in the early evening, drinking coffee, smoking and listening to music being pumped from two speakers.

It was there that I met Rick, an energetic, dynamic twenty-seven-year-old whose winning personality compensated for extremely unattractive features, including a mouth with very few teeth. Everyone liked Rick for his quick wit, constant joking and considerate habits toward others and I found myself drawn to this man who seemed desperate for love and affection.

We began to go out together, even though common sense dictated to me that he was not the best choice for a boyfriend. He had been a prisoner, was a chronic schizophrenic and probably would always be strongly tied to the psychiatric community.

Still, I was lonely, far from home and away from all my friends, and Norm made me feel special, important and he told me that I was the best thing that ever happened to him.

I wouldn't let him kiss me, though. There was something about those missing teeth that put me off and I'm not proud to say that I was somewhat repulsed by his homeliness. Thinking back, I was being a terrible snob, very superficial and not very kind. I had let myself become far too conditioned to the popular concept of the "ideal man": Tall, dark and handsome. They were the only attributes that Rick lacked.

Besides Ruby and Lizzie, other residents that visited me at Lakeshore were Sylvia, who brought me a copy of "Gone With the Wind" that I still have in my bookcase, Sidney, who murmured, "Get the hell out of this place," when he caught sight of Josie acting out, a boy named Rudy, who'd danced with me at the Cock and Bull and admired my "small, firm breasts", and Alice, who didn't come as often as I would have liked because it really disturbed her to see me like that, so drugged and blunted out of the real world.

I secretly wished that Simon would drop by, but he never did. I don't blame him; he likely didn't want to encourage me or perhaps he found mental hospitals too repulsive and frightening.I couldn't be transferred to the London Psychiatric Hospital because Dr. Baines didn't want to take any chances, but fortunately I was visited nearly every day by Aunt Elizabeth, who lived fairly nearby in Orangeville. She'd moved there with Uncle Ray the year before and was very lonely and isolated in that small town.

She made the trip by car faithfully to spend hours with her messed up niece in the loony bin. Thank God for Aunt Elizabeth, for she kept me rooted in my family life, as well as the outside world. She brought me presents, books and other treats, and talked to me as she always had, with none of the hesitant awkwardness with which others reacted to me.

I found out much later that the poor woman would sit in her car for a half hour or so after trying to make conversation with a drugged-out sick person whom she dearly loved and cry bitterly. My illness was extremely hard on my family.

My cousin John Avey came as well, bringing me a wise book called "Hope For the Flowers" about overcoming depression. He was well-acquainted with it himself, having suffered a severe bout of despair when his father died.

One of the patients, a seemingly tough young woman named

Katie, would dissolve in tears whenever she spoke of her little boy, Josh. She had him at the age of seventeen and had fought to keep him, feeling that the kid would love and never leave her, as his father had done.

Katie carried a picture of Josh with her at all times, which showed a sad-eyed little tyke in a large bathtub, looking lost and alienated. I admired the woman's fierce devotion to her child and was drawn to her indomitable spirit and the way she thumbed her nose at some of the nurses who rebuked her. We kept up a correspondence upon leaving Lakeshore, but she soon dropped from sight. I sometimes wonder what became of this rough-hewn, tattooed lady with the heart of gold.

I sat by a small radio in the common room a great deal and was keenly aware of the songs that were popular during that period of time. Whenever I hear "Rich Girl" by Hall and Oates, Manfred Mann's "Blinded By the Light", or "Dancing Queen" by ABBA, I am hustled abruptly back to that dilapidated psychiatric facility of 1977.

Lakeshore was closed down several years later, probably because the Health Department condemned the unclean conditions and run-down buildings. It was eventually used in the filming
of the television series, "Night Heat". I flinched as I watched people running about inside the underground tunnels, where I had been brought, semi-conscious on a stretcher that first night, feeling that this was a frightening concentration camp and I was here to be punished and abused.

Finally, after four months, Dr. Baines figured that I was stable enough to be released. She left me on Mellaril, Stelazine and Elavil, with nothing for the unpleasant side effects and suggested that I contact the LPH for outpatient counselling.

I had stopped burning my hands, which by now were entirely covered in red, puss-filled sores and was no longer plagued by sinister voices and strong urges to break objects, then cut myself on broken pieces. The only reason for this so-called "transformation" was that the large dose of medication had produced an overwhelming feeling of apathy.

They dulled my senses to such an extent that I was completely incapable of any spontaneous activity or thoughts. "Drugged into submission" was the way I would later describe the early spring of 1977. I celebrated my twenty-second birthday as a rather pathetic casualty of the "psychiatric machine" of the period.

My parents were relieved that I was being released and would be returning to London. I had to drop out of school and one weekend in January, Dad and Jim had gone to Founders residence to pack up everything in my room.

There was a definite air of finality to this, and I knew, with a feeling of regret, that I would never set foot on York's campus again. My life had ground to a halt with the bleak foray into the psychiatric world. Was there to be a "picking up of the pieces" of life? I was quite pessimistic at that point.

Grandma and Grandpa had been terribly worried about me and felt regret that they hadn't been able to see me at Lakeshore. They couldn't comprehend what had happened to their dearly-loved granddaughter but treated me no differently when I came home. I was extremely grateful for their adamant refusal to act as though they had to walk on eggshells with a "sick person" in their midst. I was still their "little Janie", perfection personified. They didn't see any warts or defects and never would.

Mom and I took a much-needed vacation to Daytona Beach in Florida, early in May. While there, I suffered a very bad sunburn from the Mellaril. I wished that they had told me at the hospital that this drug increases the effects of the sun's ultraviolet rays dramatically.

Although we had a great time at Disney World, making two separate trips into the land of make believe, I had begun to lapse into anorexic mode again, obsessing about food and calories. I managed to lose five pounds during the week we were there. Mom was not particularly pleased that I was so inordinately concerned with size and weight and it put a slight damper on an otherwise carefree excursion.

Still, Florida was a positive way to ease back into the world after a third of a year in a strange, hypnotic and unquestionably frightening no-man's land. Little did I know, but I had not seen the last of this unnatural lifestyle; rather, Lakeshore was just the beginning.

# Chapter Ten

# *Landslide*

My freedom came to an abrupt halt early in June, when I turned what was supposed to be a week-long stay at the London Psychiatric Hospital into a five-month ordeal.

I had arrived on P1, an admitting ward, in this odd-shaped, red-brick building, which certainly was not designed for practicality. It was extremely long and narrow, with a hallway stretching a quarter mile and separating the north section from the south.

At each end, the building splayed off into four tentacle-like parts, each two stories high, and they comprised the sixteen wards of the hospital. The five-floor office portion of the LPH was halfway between the north and the south ends and I couldn't help thinking, as I trudged the entire length of the hall toward the patients' canteen, that whoever was hired as the edifice's architect must have been on mushrooms when he or she laid out the floor plans.

The ward itself was made up of a large, spacious dayroom, with one wall constructed entirely of windows. Two rows of tacky, turquoise plastic chairs faced one another, with equally unattractive tables at either end, containing large, metal ashtrays that looked like ugly hubcaps, as well as torn magazines.

A bulletin board near the big, glass-encased nurses' station contained personal hygiene tips and a lengthy list of ward rules. I was underwhelmed by the "Cuckoo's Nest" ambiance and secretly wondered when the dictatorial nurse Ratched would appear and make all our lives miserable.

After putting my clothes away in a small, wooden cupboard in a room I was to share with three other patients, I took an uneasy seat in the dayroom and tried, without much success, not to stare at the other people scattered about.

One young fellow, with a mass of thick, dark hair and a rumpled white shirt paced up and down, alternately chainsmoking and hugging himself tightly. I averted my gaze, and let it light upon instead a chubby, moon-faced girl who glanced in my direction when she felt me looking at her.

"Hi", she said with a distinct lack of emotion in her voice. "I'm Bonnie. Is this your first time?"

I nodded hesitantly, wondering if this young woman had been elected as the welcoming committee. "Yeah, I'm only here for a med change." I already knew some of the institutional lingo, having picked it up at Lakeshore. "It's only for a few days or so. How about you?"

Bonnie set her mouth in a grim line, then replied slowly, "Been here before, several times, so I kind of know the ropes. Here goes: First, don't bum stuff here, not money, cigarettes, matches or anything. Second: Do what the staff tells you, and don't make an ass of yourself arguing with them. And third: Never play games. It'll get you in shit and they'll keep you in here longer. Get it?"

I pretended to fully comprehend and accept Bonnie's "Golden Rules of Hospital Etiquette". "Got it". I stood up and retrieved an ashtray from the end table, sensing that this chick was on some sort of power trip and I was supposed to go to her if I ran into any difficulties.

Well, maybe she was sort of obnoxious, but I needed some kind of guidance in this place. Despite having been exposed to this lifestyle at Lakeshore, I was a little wary of the LPH, for it had the reputation of being tough and impenetrable.

The head nurse's name was Mrs. Davis, a small, somewhat hyperactive middle-aged woman who seemed pleasant enough, as long as nobody crossed her.

The other nurses, registered nurses, assistants (RNA's) and psychiatric nursing assistants (PNA's) were a veritable mixed bag. Jerry, a PNA who reminded me of a physical education instructor I'd had in public school, was cheerful and non-threatening.

Toni was a thin, blonde and incredibly intense RNA of about thirty who possessed a great deal of compassion, but would tolerate no nonsense on the part of any of us.

Jessie was a fortyish, plump, observant RNA who had amazingly sharp eyes and didn't miss a thing. I liked her right away, for I sensed that she put our dignity and self-respect above the rules and rigid ward standards.

Harry, a lanky, buzz-clipped PNA of about fifty possessed sharp features and a tongue to match, but could be soft-hearted on rare occasions. I just found him to be a bit too sanctimonious for my tastes.

Rose was delightful, a chubby, curly-haired RNA who loved Stephen King's books, rock music and befriended some of us, turning a blind eye to any minor infringements of the rules she may have caught sight of in an effort to be fair-minded. She was genuine about it, because I'm sure she felt some of the hospital policies were not in the patients' best interests.

Jeannie was a large, red-headed RN who usually doled out the medication in the mornings and afternoons, and who was to eventually treat me with a lot of hostility. She would often accuse some of us of "playing games", a phrase I was to learn to despise.

The rest were alright, but they didn't make much of an impression on me those first few days. They did make certain, however, that we, the patients, realized that they, the staff, were in charge and capable of revoking privileges if we didn't "tow the line" and keep our wisecracks to ourselves.

There were a lot more RNA's and PNA's than registered nurses on all the wards of the LPH, probably because they required less training and were instructed in bedside care specifically. The same is true in psychiatric hospitals today, with only a few RN's on each ward to pour medication and do the administrative duties.

The patients on P1 ranged from burned-out druggies to paranoid schizophrenics and covered all the symptomatic bases from clinical depression to severe anxiety disorder. I'd been around the community long enough to be able to put a label on just about everyone, and I hated this quasi-analytical, terribly dehumanizing quality of mine.

But it was the only way I could cope with being surrounded by people who otherwise scared the hell out of me, with their erratic outbursts, psychedelic drug-tripping in the washrooms, sudden, sometimes violent attacks upon the staff and verbal abuse toward the nurses and each other.

For those first five days on P1, I was exposed to all of these unsavoury elements. Instead of steeling myself against it and working to get released as soon as possible, I quickly succumbed to the antisocial milieu and joined the "crazy club".

Looking at that period of my life from a 1995 perspective, I am trying to determine why I crumbled so dramatically near the end of that week, when I could have just done my short sentence and left. I can only conclude that I felt that I had more there with the psychiatric in-patient community than with my previous life on the outside.

After all, I was no longer an undergraduate at York University, working toward an Honours degree in English and humanities. There was no place to go in the fall and I'd severed contacts with everyone at A and F Houses.

The mental patients at Lakeshore had taken the place of my academic friends. They had filled a gaping void, offering me companionship and a buffer against loneliness and social isolation.

Upon my release from the hospital in Toronto, I vacillated, having no sense of identity anymore and no discernible, mapped-out future. There was only a series of hazy question marks and a world devoid of other human beings who shared similar interests.

Then, when I arrived at the LPH, the aimless wandering ceased. I was back in familiar territory, complete with a strange kind of purpose: Living life as a mental patient and grasping hold of the goal of being the most messed-up, needy mental patient on the ward.

I wish that I had insisted on returning to school in the fall of 1977, if not at York, then at UWO. Then I know that I could have left the Lakeshore experience behind me. But then, that could just have been wishful dreaming, or an attempt to lay blame for another eighteen years of emotional agony.

Well, whatever my motives were, I didn't walk out of the LPH after my psychiatrist, Dr. Goode, made plans to change my medication. Instead, I stopped eating and tossed myself into another anorexic storm. Lapp had decided to take me off the Mellaril and Stelazine, and try me on a drug called Modicate, which was given intramuscularly once a week. This was another antipsychotic and was supposed to be quite effective for people with auditory hallucinations, mental confusion and behaviour difficulties.

I had become agitated during my first few days on P1, and experienced a strong urge to harm myself. I had not been hearing voices, but wanted to electrocute myself by putting a metal knife into a light socket. I was wandering around in a fog and not entirely sure what was happening around me; only that I wanted to feel something that would "jolt" me back into a sense of feeling.

Not only that, but I wanted the staff to know how unhappy I was and felt they were not paying enough attention to my suffering. I suppose, then, that my proposed action was a rather immature bid for attention, something I'm pretty ashamed to admit.

In a last-ditch attempt to shake the nurses into recognizing that I wasn't some sort of "goldbricker", I told Bonnie what I wanted to do and she informed Dr. Goode. He then proposed that I remain in hospital for two months and try to get my behaviour problems under control.

Then I stopped eating because I longed for the nostalgic days when I was sixteen and deliciously thin. I felt grossly obese, even though I weighed only ninety-eight pounds and vowed that I would lose at least twenty more and be "perfect".

I despised myself during that time, for I thought of myself as an "imposter" for hiding out in a hospital and acting more crazy than I actually was, simply because I felt I had no other identity.

This intense self-loathing caused me to appear swollen and hideous to my own senses. I would lie in bed and run my hands over my body, touching great, shuddering rolls of flab where, in reality, there were only bones. I wanted to take a sharp object and hack the imaginary adipose tissue from my frame, exposing beauty and virtue. Then, perhaps, the tremendous guilt would disappear, or at least lessen in intensity.

I drank coffee for breakfast, tea for lunch and supper, and two cans of diet cola during the day. That was it; no juice, milk, or anything with the potential for any calories to be lurking inside.

The staff didn't say anything at first, probably figuring it was more attention-seeking crap. But after a few weeks, some of them began to remark on my bizarre diet and urged me to eat at least a piece of toast.

My parents were furiousat me for staying in at the LPH long after my lock-up period had expired. They didn't want to believe that I could still be sick, so they assumed that I was deliberately staying in there to punish them.

Mom visited frequently but Dad didn't stop by very often, and when he did, hc was pissed off and irritated. I don't blame him, since I had been given no definite diagnosis at Lakeshore. I was obviously just screwing around, making him feel guilty and remorseful.

After denying myself food for several weeks, I grew extremely weak and tired. I was losing a lot of weight, and Dr. Goode, in his frustration, had pawned me off on another psychiatrist, the flamboyant and inimitable Dr. Braun. This lady was something else indeed. Somewhat chubby, her ample figure was accentuated by tight-fitting blouses and extremely short skirts. She was about forty-five, with long, blonde hair tied tightly in a topknot and she walked with great rapidity on spiked heels.

On top of all this, the woman spoke in a thick European accent with a pungent air of authority ("You vill do vat I say!") Still, with all the overpowering aspects to her, Dr. Braun could be cheery and ingratiating if she chose to.

Evidently, Braun had a lot of experience in dealing with patients suffering from eating disorders. She informed me during our first visit that I would be weighed daily and if I continued to lose she would implement strict measures.

I took her threats lightly and persisted in my self-imposed starvation. My days consisted of struggling to awaken in the morning, crawling weakly out of bed and sitting in the dayroom, puffing on cigarettes and drinking black coffee. I attended O.T. but felt as though I was working in a trance and drifted in and out of this seasick sensation constantly. I always found myself fighting the urge to lie down on the floor to sleep.

I'd forgotten how horrible it felt to deprive myself of nutrients. I was voraciously hungry, longing for a bite of an apple or even a swallow of milk. My hair began to thin out and my teeth seemed to be getting loose.

My world shrivelled and I avoided other patients, feeling too overcome with fatigue to engage in any conversations. Unlike the last anorexic episode, I didn't exercise at all, feeling too sick and dizzy to even walk very far without stopping to bend over and pause for a minute or two.

I figured that this was happening because I was six years older now and my body less able to adapt to the neglect. Part of it was the Modicate, with its sedating qualities, but that didn't occur to me at the time. I hated myself for being weak and faltering. Once, I even took a small bite of an oatmeal cookie, and immediately made myself vomit it up. I couldn't afford that kind of slip again. It was too dangerous.

My father despaired over my illness, wondering why the

anorexia was rearing its repulsive head once more in our lives. He felt helpless to change my hell-bent path to self-obliteration and it caused him to feel very depressed.

I didn't care how my family felt. I was so completely self-absorbed that I was only concerned with my own twisted sense of beauty and demented ideas about what should make up a successful young life in the late 1970's.

I lost a pound a day for the next two weeks, much to the staff's dismay and finally Braun put her stilletoed foot down. I was to be confined to bed until I gained two kilograms. I now weighed seventy-nine pounds and was emaciated.

I spent two long, barely-tolerable months trapped in the observation room, across from the nurses' station. I was determined not to gain an ounce, even though a long-suffering dietician visited daily and planned out a twelve hundred-calorie menu for me. I figured out, quite joyously, that I could eat exactly half of this menu and maintain my weight, so I did that.

It was nirvana: I could eat a substantial amount of food and stay thin! The down side was having to remain in bed, reading endlessly to occupy my mind and losing whatever muscle tone I had left. I got bedsores and went for days without a bath, while my hair was almost dripping with grease and I became caked with filth.

Jessie, my favourite RNA, took me under her wing and insisted that I be bathed regularly, despite Braun's carved-in-stone regulations about total bedrest. She also spent many hours attempting to get me to try different foods, like peanut butter, and reading me articles about anorexia and how it could be fatal. She showed me a section from Reader's Digest about a fifteen-year-old girl named Stephanie who literally starved herself to death, but I was unmoved.

I was allowed no visitors for over two months. This should have distressed me, but I was too caught up in playing games with food, revelling in the nurses' attempts to get me to eat and playing the part of the total asshole to let it get to me too much.

I became cut off from the world completely as my universe shrunk to a small hospital room, a bed and six hundred calories a day. Food became the centre of my solar system and the planets circling within it were my personal attendants, giving me more attention than I had ever experienced.

I liked it; so what if I couldn't get out of bed, if I could only see a small square of blue sky from my window and I'd read the same books and magazines at least three times each? This was still a very safe and comfortable environment in which I was snuggled.

Dr. Braun became very impatient with me, telling me I'd spend the rest of my life in this non-existence if I didn't smarten up. She knew that my perceptions were awry, but I was unable to change them. I would have to see the error of my ways myself.

Finally, through no effort of mine, the scale showed I had gained the two kilograms. After spending the summer in bed, I was allowed to get up and move into the dayroom.

After that, something changed in my head, as if a switch had been magically turned on. I was once again among the other patients, receiving visitors and no longer focused solely on food, calories and my own foolish emotional needs. Although I dreaded gaining weight and becoming obese, I was tired of being as "sickie". Somehow, there had to be more to my life than this hospital.

The staff had grown weary of my attention-seeking and chided me for taking their time away from the other patients. I was told that no other patient on P1 had claimed so much of their time and energy as I had and that I should feel very ashamed of myself.

In truth, I did, and as the weight began to come on again and I was allowed off the ward for short periods, I vowed to make drastic changes for the better and have people like me again. I hated being the nagging thorn in so many sides and wept bitterly far into the night that I could have let myself slide into such a state of degradation.

I started to become better acquainted with some of the other patients. Jewel was obviously mentally challenged, a fortyish woman whose medication slurred her speech and caused her to stagger and weave, often bumping into walls as well as other people. She was intensely attached to Mrs. Davis and behaved as though she was the head nurse's daughter, always seeking advice and approval.

I got along well with Jewel, for she had an aura of untouched innocence. She suffered emotional problems along with the retardation and that made it impossible for her to live on her own. She got a kick out of doing odd jobs around the ward, like delivering HS snacks to the patients.

Dorothy looked a lot like a young Katharine Hepburn and was unusually bright, but unfortunately suffered from severe delusions. She'd be sitting in the dayroom watching television, and suddenly would begin moaning and shouting, believing that people had descended upon her and were planning on doing her harm.

Ron was about forty-five, a big, husky guy with a blond brushcut and a ruddy complexion splashed with large, purplish veins. He was an alcoholic and was on P1 in a last-ditch attempt to get off the bottle.

Peter was the young man I'd seen pacing on my first day on the ward. He had told us in group therapy that he'd been sniffing glue since the age of twelve and was trying to develop the other side of his brain to compensate for the section which had been destroyed by the chemicals.

He was quiet, intense and intelligent and I felt quite drawn to his tragic demeanour. We went out together for awhile, but I broke it off when he became increasingly irrational and unstrung emotionally. Peter's still an inpatient in the LPH today and I encountered him when I returned there in the early 1990's.

There were thirty-six of us on that ward, equally divided between men and women and the majority were in their early to mid-twenties. Admitting wards usually contained a great many young people, because they were in their early stages of their illnesses, and had not spent much, if any, time in hospital before. Schizophrenia and manic depressive disorder usually first appear between the ages of eighteen and twenty-five.

Eve Ann was a pretty but overweight twenty-year-old who suffered extreme highs and lows and was later diagnosed as manic depressive. When I first met her, she was in a state of complete euphoria and spoke in loud, brash tones. During my next admission to P1, she was the complete opposite, sullen and quiet, with her head bowed, and would frequently burst into tears. She'd also stopped eating and had lost a great deal of weight.

A lot of the younger patients who I'd assumed were admitted because of drug problems were actually mentally ill and had used chemicals to cope with distressing symptoms. I felt like a terrible imposter, overcome with guilt that I didn't have a bona fide disorder and was simply some kind of despicable faker. It made me hate myself even more.

Dr. Braun made certain that my weight didn't slip and refused to let me use laxatives or do much exercising, two things I really craved. When I reached ninety pounds, I was told that I was to weigh a minimum of one hundred and five before I could be released and that I had to maintain it consistently or be hastily readmitted.

My parents were pleased that I was eating normally again, even if I did express remorse everytime I gained a pound. Dr. Braun took me off Modicate, which she deemed ineffective and put me on another intramuscular drug, Imap, which was supposed to "give me some energy" and ease my depression, as well as control the voices.

Nobody ever argued that I wasn't depressed and this was said to be the root of all my difficulties. The voices could not be explained by the medical profession and I think that everyone thought that I was pretending to hear them. Still, Braun put me back on Stelazine, plus an antidepressant called Ludiomil. After suffering that insidious restlessness from the Stelazine, she prescribed a drug called Dissipal, for side effects.

When I was released from P1 in November of 1977, I weighed one hundred and two pounds, had maintained it for two weeks, my depression had greatly diminished and I felt emotionally capable of handling myself on the outside. I didn't feel the need for constant attention anymore, as my family had begun to take a more active role in my life and I was happy to move in with Mom to her new apartment in a downtown apartment complex called London Towers.

She'd sold our rambling house on Village Green Avenue in Westmount, after meeting a man named Keith Samlu at her new found singles club, "A Club For the Previously Married", an organization she still belongs to today. Keith was a big, friendly, jovial guy with a hearty, infectious laugh as well as a big love of food, fine wine, romantic evenings, and my Mom.

He was Jewish, and therefore, unlikely to marry a Gentile, and was eight years her junior, but neither of them cared. They needed each other, and developed a strong, tight bond that greatly helped my mother through my years of problems.

I settled in fairly comfortably with Mom in this rather spectacular apartment, with an indoor pool and exercise room, but an extraordinarily tacky purple and red lobby. Whoever designed it must surely have been colour blind.

So our family truly had something to celebrate that Christmas: It was Jim's second year at Western and he was finally applying himself academically, Dad was easing into a new life with his longtime steady, Mom had a new outlook and was pulling herself out of her own sepulcrous despair and I felt, for the first time in years, that I was triumphantly on the road to recovery.

I announced to everyone, including my very relieved grand-parents, that there would be no more illness, hospitalization, and that, soon, I would make up the second year courses I needed and perhaps return to university in the fall of 1978. There was a new life on the horizon and I was determined that I would find something purposeful to do with my future.

In January of 1978, I enrolled in a second-year children's literature course, or "kiddie lit" as it was affectionately called. UWO didn't hold the same fascination or allure as York, but I resolved to make the best of the change and apply myself diligently.

However, it didn't take long before my exalted plans began to fall apart. Studying was extremely difficult and with the heavy doses of medication, my head felt sluggish and thick. When I amassed the books that I had to read I was dismayed at the vast numbers. "I'll never get through these!" I moaned dismally, but figured I'd better at least give my work an honest try.

I suffered my first major disappointment after writing a children's story about the circus and receiving a lukewarm grade. I had thought it was well thought-out and cleverly constructed, but my professor deemed it "sloppy and cliched".

I had to travel to the LPH twice a week for appointments with an out-patient psychiatrist and get my medication from the ward. As I sat on P1 one afternoon, waiting to speak to Lois, I felt a twinge of longing to be a patient again. Shaking my head vigor-ously, I fought this terrible sensation. Why was I so drawn to this place? I wondered, looking around at the same patients I had lived with for five months.

As the days progressed, my studies faltered and I wished to be back in an environment that was comforting, familiar and pre-dictable. I had become institutionalized over the past year and had somehow convinced myself that I could not function in the outside world.

Within another week, I was back in, having told my doctor that I felt suicidal. My mom brought my suitcase full of clothes, and I was overcome with relief at being released from my terrifying university world. School just wasn't for me anymore, I figured.

But Dr. Braun had other plans for me. She insisted that I study for eight hours a day and instructed the staff to make sure that

I did so. My books were all delivered to my room and I was told to read them, one by one, ostensibly absorbing every detail and concentrating steadily with only a break for lunch.

I couldn't retain anything that I read during that time. Words flew in and out of my consciousness, as my heavily-
medicated brain refused to take in any meaning from the written words. I began to doze frequently and would be jostled awake by staff members who shouted, "Hey, none of that! You're to study, not sleep, young lady."

It was agonizing trying to keep my eyes open and constantly fight the overwhelming, paralyzing fatigue. I lay on my stomach, head propped up in my hands while I vacantly turned pages, forgetting what I'd read the second I got to the next paragraph.

Dr. Braun decided to keep me on the same medication, but increased the dose of Imap from one milligram per week to two. This helped me to concentrate better but the hefty doses of Stelazine and the Ludiomil were extremely stupefying.

I wrote a test for the course while in the hospital, sequestered in Mrs. Davis' office, and did surprisingly well. Still, I took no comfort in this admission and when I was released six weeks later, I breathed a heavy sigh of relief. Now I could take a welcome respite from studying eight hours a day.

I don't have a clear memory of the next several months, due to the high doses of medication causing a substantial amount of confusion and general apathy. I do recall dropping out from the course temporarily, then achieving a deferred standing and writing the final exam in August rather than April.

My final grade in Children's Literature 203 was a fairly healthy B, thus giving me sufficient confidence to enroll in five third year courses that September. That was to be an extremely poor decision.

Jim could not resist a bit of gloating that he had "caught up" with me academically and that I was now attending UWO with him on "his turf", so to speak.

I shouldn't have taken five courses, including a very challenging one in third year French. This meant reading several thick and complex novels in French, as well as speaking it fluently in the laboratories and writing all of our essays in the language.

My professor thought that I was stupid and lazy. She told me that she was utterly amazed that I had made it to university when all

I could respond with was a monosyllabic "yeah" or "no", with an occasional "I know" thrown in for variety.

The heavy doses definitely caused this apparent "semi-retardation" and I should have told all of my professors about them. However, fear of being labelled "crazy" and "weird" kept me silent, so they grew impatient and frustrated with my lack of animation and poor verbal skills.

I also took three English courses and a film one on the American Cinema, which involved watching movies like "Citizen Kane" and "On the Waterfront" repeatedly each Tuesday night from seven until ten PM, then dissecting them extensively.

Unable to concentrate and simply drifting from one class to another without learning anything substantial, I began to long for my old, close-knit friendships at York. It became a mission to develop and maintain a series of intense, meaningful relationships with UWO students in my various classes, so I began to latch on to people who I deemed "potential Courtneys, Rubys, Lizzies or Sidneys".

As September wore on, I got to know two female students fairly well: Bonnie, a twenty-six-year-old film student with short, poker, straight hair and a solemn, yet charismatic face, and Lynne, twenty-two, who literally vibrated with energy and enthusiasm.

She took on the role of the well-balanced, industrious student par excellence and possessed a distinctively cheerful mien with an affinity for fun and frivolity. I met her in one of my English courses on Beowolf, and this bubbly, extroverted girl was the perfect foil for my stodgy, thick-headed persona.

Bonnie boarded in a small basement apartment on Victoria Street, near Western. Often, she'd envite me over to listen to Todd Rundgren albums and drink herbal tea. She seemed to appreciate my reluctance to participate in our film tutorials as I told her I was painfully shy, but she assured me that our enigmatic professor, Mr. Gedalof, whom she really liked, would draw me out eventually.

As the weeks progressed, I told Bonnie that I had left school in January of 1977 and was making another stab at third year, finding out that it was certainly not easy to leap back into the fray. I left out the part about the mental hospitals.

She appeared to be quite understanding and compassionate about my situation and said that she herself had left school for three years in order to work and earn money for tuition, which was increasing alarmingly in the late 1970's.

Bonnie assured me that a student definitely had a healthier appreciation and outlook on academe after a lengthy absence and that I would grow to be as passionate about learning as she was. But I had my doubts.

Lynne was a pleasant distraction from those depressive moods that had begun to prey on my mind again. She believed that I was far too serious and should take time to burst out of my uptight casing and get more of a charge out of life. Underneath the bravado, she was a somewhat sad young woman who was living away from home for the first time and found it lonely and somewhat threatening.

I continued to do poorly in my courses and finally was forced to go to a French tutor for rudimentary lessons to augment my professor's teaching. This failed miserably, as I simply could not think coherently, so incased in "Imap isolation" was any fragment of a thinking, cognitive brain.

Early in October, I took a trip to Toronto to visit my old Founders buddies. Ruby and Lizzie had gotten an apartment off-campus in University City, where Courtney still resided with Bob. They had all become quite chummy with Shirley, a formerly self-conscious, bespeckled first year student who gained a considerable amount of confidence and assertiveness after becoming chief bartender at the Cock and Bull.

Now Shirley tossed orders and expletives about with reckless abandon and didn't seem to care much for my peculiar eccentricities anymore, as to what she had once professed. I felt very uncomfortable, being with everyone again after the Lakeshore and LPH experiences. I thought I no longer could re-establish myself as an integral part of the Founders subculture. I stayed with Courtney and Bob, but they seemed to feel awkward in my presence, and even Courtney was often at a loss for words as far as I was concerned.

I attended a loud, congested party at one of Shirley's friend's houses and was somewhat taken aback when Simon showed up, alone and looking a bit morose. I walked up to him, my heart pounding wildly, and said with a sad smile, "You know, I always loved you. I still do."

He said nothing, just stared at me for a moment and walked away. He was evidently still going out with Amanda, but she had not wanted to attend this party. I felt like a fool, heavily laced with shame and regret.

I was supposed to stay in Toronto for three days, but left after only two. I just didn't belong there anymore, for too many events had transpired in my life. It just was not possible to pick up a life when I'd left nearly a year before and have everything resume as it once was. Life didn't work that way and I knew that I would never see any of those people again. I didn't, as a matter of fact.

Back at Western, I slid into an opaque sea of choking mud. I had more-or-less given up trying to study or retain anything that I read. Evenings were spent sitting like a week-old vegetable in front of the television, soaking up Movies of the Week and tasteless sitcoms.

Even daytime fare enveloped my attention and I became an ardent fan of "The Price is Right". Classes began to fall by the wayside, and I now wondered why I had so completely lost interest in university, when I had wanted to return so badly.

I received a sixty-four per cent in an essay on film noire, and didn't even flinch. My French professor informed me that I was failing her course and that I'd better start applying myself, but I shrugged with practised non-chalance. Nothing intested me; I put in time, wasting my days, with no future plans and no desire to accomplish anything except make it to bedtime.

Finally, in November, I made the uneasy decision to quit school. There just didn't seem to be a point in flogging a dead horse, or postponing the inevitable. Dad, however, was quite unhappy about my plans and expressed a lot of negative emotion. I cried and made some tearful attempts to explain to him how difficult it was to concentrate. I told him why I couldn't expect to pass any of my courses, which were incomprehensible to me.

I believe now that he was simply exasperated that my emotional problems were so persistent and that I had been far too impulsive and unrealistic by enrolling in five full-time courses instead of two or three. He felt that I was extremely self-defeating and feared that I would get nowhere with my life if I didn't "get it together".

Devastated, I felt trapped, forced to continue in what had become an agonizing ordeal. I despised what I had evolved into: A useless, vegetative blob that might as well be non-existent. Self-loathing strode to the forefront once again, a now-familiar entity that totally captivated my consciousness.

There was only one choice left to me. On Thursday morning of November sixteenth, I sat alone at home and played Burton Cummings solo albums over and over, trying desperately to lose myself in the words and music of a happier, more settled time in my life.

Then, I realized with a deadening sense of dread that I had to die, that there would never be any happiness anymore for me. I felt calm, even oddly comforted, as this decision cleared into sharp focus and was accompanied by a sensation of security.

I trudged into the kitchen, took my bottles of Stelazine, Ludiomil and Dissipal from the counter and smiled when I realized that there was a month's supply of each there.

Swallowing a lot of pills is difficult, for your gag reflexes go crazy and you have to constantly fight the urge to vomit. I took great handfuls, stuffing them into my mouth as though I was starving and they were life-giving morsels. I flinched slightly at the bitter irony, and gulped several glasses of water to wash down these tiny instruments of destruction.

Within minutes, the bottles were empty and I returned to the living room, lying down gently on the plush, velvet couch while Cummings' vocals lulled me out of my lingering apprehension. After awhile, my head began to feel heavy and full. As a peculiar humming voice assailed my ears I saw the image of my mother flash before my eyes.

God, what am I doing? I despaired, but didn't move. I dimly recollect dialling my out-patient psychiatrist's number and mumbling to her that I'd taken "some pills".

She immediately called for an ambulance and two anxious attendants arrived, strapping me onto a stretcher and speeding all three of us to Victoria Hospital.

Well, I guess my doctor had contacted Mom, because she was at the emergency department when I arrived. I couldn't see anything, but was able to hear her asking me in frantic tones why I had taken the overdose.

The next thing I knew, I was awakening to the sight of my family standing around, smiling uneasily. It was a couple of days later. While I was unconscious, I nearly died and a team of doctors worked diligently to save my life.

I'd taken a great deal of medication and had to have my

stomach pumped, as well as being flushed out with fluids. Like most overdose patients, my face and body swelled dramatically. With the tubes and wires protruding everywhere, as well as my sallow complexion, I was not, as Dad was to say later, "a beautiful sight to behold."

Mom told me several weeks afterward that Jim had put his head on my chest and cried when I was unconscious and this caused me untold grief and regret. I thought I must have been the world's most selfish, God-forsaken piece of shit that ever walked the earth. I spat inwardly at myself, deliberating on what I had put my family through.

I stayed at the hospital's psychiatric wing for the weekend, then was transferred to the LPH, something that made me very unhappy. I had preferred the more humane, comfortable atmosphere of the general hospital and pleaded with the doctors to let me stay. However, policy dictated that if you had been a patient at the "Highbury Hilton" before, you could never be sent someplace else. It was like the Eagles song, "Hotel California": "You can check out, but you can never leave."

When I arrived back on P1, I was greeted by Angela, whom I'd met the last time I was in and to whom I had grown close. Theresa suffered from a debilitating form of schizophrenia and had tried to kill herself at least ten times. She almost succeeded the most recent time when she attempted to hang herself. She was very pretty, with long, thick fair hair and gigantic blue eyes, and I felt the great amount of pain she was in constantly. She was only twenty-two, but had lived a lifetime already, and not a happy one.

Peter was still there, along with a personable patient named Freddie, who paid a lot of attention to me. I didn't mind, however, because he was unusually attractive and articulate.

My roommate was a tall, skinny young woman of twenty-five with large glasses, very short hair and prided herself on being a vegetarian. Her name was Lisa and I immediately liked her. She appeared somewhat withdrawn, though and was put on close nursing observation (CNO) because of her urges to hurt herself.

I had a sinking feeling that I would be in for quite awhile, as my suicide attempt was treated as a very serious matter, even though I'd called someone and had subsequently been rescued from myself.

I felt very low for the first several weeks, having caused so much grief for my family and further screwing up my life. There didn't seem to be much hope left for any kind of bright and productive future. For the first time, I seriously wondered if I would spend the rest of my life moving in and out of this institution.

I grew so alarmingly depressed, sitting for days in a chair and staring emptily at the floor, that Dr. Braun recommended shock treatments. I hadn't been given ECT (Electroconvulsive Therapy) since the days in Lakeshore and wasn't too keen on being submitted to anymore of this seemingly barbaric form of treatment.

I had been so out-of-it at Lakeshore that I barely recalled the ECT, only had memories of being terrified of the anesthetic that was administered my a needle in the vein of my hand. The nurse would prick me and then say "Off to sleep you go," whereupon everything would go black and quiet after I began counting backward from a hundred.

After the treatment, I would feel disoriented and sluggish and would unconsciously drool from the corner of my mouth for several hours. Most likely some of my forgetfulness at that hospital was due to being zapped twenty times in seven weeks.

Braun insisted that I wouldn't get well unless I had the ECT, so I reluctantly agreed to take twenty more shocks to the grey matter, still frightened of the needle prick.

However, after receiving seven, I experienced a grand mal seizure, just prior to the treatment and so they were wisely discontinued. It wasn't the first seizure I had had. The first time I was admitted to the LPH, I was sitting with my mother in the dayroom when I lost consciousness and began convulsing wildly and spasmodically on the floor.

I have no recollection of this and got no warning or "aura" preceding it, but was placed on Dilantin shortly afterward. It was determined that I suffered from epilepsy, after being given an EEG and CAT scan.

Mom is certain that the convulsions were caused by the mega-doses of anti-psychotic medication I was given in both Lakeshore and the LPH. I agree with her, for grand mal seizures are a possible side effect of too high a dose of neuroleptic drugs and I still take medication for this drug-induced epilepsy today.

My depression worsened, and by January of 1979, Dr. Braun was becoming frustrated. Not only was my condition refusing to budge, but I had been caught "playing games" with Lisa.

The two of us were on SOR (Special Observation Routine), which involved having a nurse, RNA or PNA within arm's length at all times. We were placed on SOR due to the severity of our depression and fear for our safety. One night, as we sat at a small table in the dayroom eating supper, Lisa grabbed a China teacup from her tray.

I met her steady gaze, but said nothing to the nurse. As Lisa quickly put the cup in the pocket of her housecoat, I knew that she wanted to break it later and cut her wrist, as she'd expressed a strong desire to do for the past several days.

Later that evening, Lisa, the same nurse and I were in our room, getting prepared for bed. Laura, the nurse, was a pleasant and friendly young woman who spent a lot of time fixing our hair and counselling us to get our heads back together and live the carefree, happy life of two people in their early twenties.

We had to retire at ten, one and a half hours earlier than the other patients, because of being on SOR. Sue had placed the stolen cup under her pillow. She obviously forgot that, because suddenly she lifted it in the air for a split second, long enough the expose the "weapon".

"What's the cup doing there?" demanded Laura, her perkiness suddenly dissolving. I knew that Lisa was in trouble now and I squirmed uncomfortably as the guilty party stammered and mumbled incoherently.

"So that's what you two were up to earlier!" the angry nurse exclaimed, looking first at Sue and then at me. "I saw you making eye contact. You planned this together! Well, I think you both need to do a little time in seclusion."

Seclusion involved two small, square rooms where a patient was locked for hours, even days at a time and slept on a mattress without sheets or a pillow, or anything with which he or she could hurt themselves.

It was supposedly a drastic last resort to ensure that a disturbed person is completely safe and has "time away" from the rest of the ward, but it was usually very unpleasant and traumatic for the unfortunate patient involved. I'd never been locked up in one of those rooms before and wasn't looking forward to it.

Lisa was put in one room, but since the other was already occupied, I stayed on a bed in the runway outside the seclusion doors. It was a small, cramped area encased in shatter-proof plexiglass and could also be locked from the outside.

A nurse from a neighbouring ward came in to stay with us. She sat outside Sue's locked door at the foot of my bed.

I felt terrible, having participated in this theatrical activity. I knew that I could have been partially responsible for someone harming themselves, perhaps severely and I didn't like the way that made me feel about myself.

I had no difficulty hurting myself, but I really didn't want any part of doing it to nother. Besides, I despised the reputation I was getting on P1: That of an attention-seeking, whining time-waster, who just needed to get off her pathetic ass and straighten herself out. The staff didn't like me much, and Dr. Braun was beginning to wonder if being in the hospital was doing me more harm than good.

But I desperately wanted to stay there, being looked after and watched for twenty-four hours a day. I enjoyed the thought of relative strangers worrying about me, of being peculiarly respected by the other patients because I was "so disturbed" and needed to be on the special observation for such long periods.

I didn't like it whenever the SOR was lifted, for then I felt that nobody cared about me and that I could just go off and harm myself in the shower stall without being stopped. Then they'd all be sorry. I'd go to the nurses and tell them that I wanted to kill myself, that I couldn't stand feeling so terrible all the time.

The next thing I knew, there would be somebody sitting beside me, following me to the bathroom and feeding my pathetic neuroses. Then they'd become distracted from patients who needed the staff's attention more.

That's how I dealt with my depression and feelings of inadequacy. I'm quite ashamed of all of it now; in fact, I look back to those P1 admissions and cringe at my behaviour. I deserved everything that was coming to me, to a point anyway.

Lisa really was mentally ill, however. She'd spent six months on the seventh floor of Victoria Hospital where they tested, drugged, shocked her and pumped her full of sodium pentothal in an effort to determine what caused her long periods of listlessness and blunted affect.

Sometimes she'd sit in the dayroom and go into a complete trance and would have to be fed and clothed. Finally,
she was diagnosed with catatonic schizophrenia.

Angela seemed to be somewhat better but experienced delu-

sions about the government persecuting her. Personally, I don't
think this belief was particularly crazy, given that the U.S. was only
a year away from electing Ronald Reagan as President.

I discovered that Freddie, whom I liked a lot and wanted to
go out with, had stabbed his girlfriend and was awaiting trial for
assault. Needless to say, I rebuffed anymore of his advances.

One young RN, Tess, befriended me before Christmas and I
was drawn to her compassion and insight to my difficulties. She
was very tiny, weighing only ninety-eight pounds and had experienced some problems with eating in the past. She had read about
the anorexic episode of the previous year in my chart and we had
long, intensive discussions about the subject.

Then, at Christmas, something terrifying and inexplicable
began to happen to me. I began to experience some bizarre symptoms with my eyes. All of a sudden, for no particular reason, I'd
feel my eyeballs rolling to the side and my gaze would be drawn to
the edge of my field of vision.

This was quite disconcerting, as I would be incapable of
looking straight ahead again for several minutes. Not only that, but
it would seem as though my mind and vocal chords were paralyzed,
and I couldn't communicate any of this verbally until the forced
sideways glances stopped.

It's still difficult to describe this frightening process and
when I tried to walk forward, I would not be able to see where I was
going. There seemed to be no rationale for this and I was afraid to
divulge these experiences to the staff for fear they'd think I was
making another bid for attention.

I had to spend Christmas in the hospital, regrettably, because
I had only recently gotten off SOR, so the staff had a little party for
those of us who couldn't go home for the holidays.

Suddenly, as I was being handed my gift, my eyes drifted
completely over to the side, and Tess noticed it. "What are you
doing?" she asked, surprised and a little irked.

I tried to explain to her how it was uncontrollable, but she
thought it was attention-seeking behaviour, as I'd feared. "Is this an
act?" she asked accusingly.

After that, things got much worse. The episodes increased
and became more severe, lasting for longer periods of time and
disrupting some of the other patients, who got spooked by the
"spastic eyeballs".

By January, I'd grown accustomed to being ridiculed and punished for these "staring spells", as I labelled them. Some of the patients voiced their disappointment and couldn't understand why I was doing such a repulsive thing.

I became more despondent and spent a lot of time lying on my bed, trying to escape into sleep and forget about all my troubles.

One afternoon in early February, Lisa learned that she was being sent to the Behaviour Modification Ward at the opposite end of the building. I was stunned, wondering why this poor girl was being punished because she was ill.

The Behaviour Modification unit, on ward H2, had the reputation for being extremely strict, horrifying and comparable to a Nazi concentration camp. We'd all heard the frightening rumours about patients being starved, worked half to death for a few paltry privileges and treated sadistically by a cruel and vicious staff.

Lisa was petrified but went willingly, knowing that she had no choice because she was an involuntary patient. Back in the late 1970's, before the Mental Health Act was instated, patients could be certified, or committed, for a whole host of reasons. Doctors could force someone to stay against his or her will by saying, for example, that the person was "dangerous to his or herself", even if there wasn't a lot of evidence to confirm that.

Certifying a patient wasn't wantonly abused by the psychiatric community, of course, but there was a wide margin for human error. Some people were involuntary even if they weren't dangerous to themselves or others. The Mental Health Act cleaned this up quite a bit.

I visited Lisa a month later, along with Patricia, another patient we'd both befriended, and heard about the controversial ward firsthand. Lisa told us that they'd had no privileges upon arriving on H2, and had to hook a rug in order to earn six cigarettes a day. She wasn't a smoker, so didn't receive much of a reward for her labour. There was a strict routine each day, including jogging around the halls in the morning, exercises twice a day, no off-ward privileges except a half hour per day in the patients' canteen, and no weekend passes at all. If your rug wasn't done in time, you got no rewards until it was.

Lisa told Patricia and I that she had hated the routine at first, but had resigned herself to it. If all went well and you didn't break any of the many ward rules, you could be transferred to the more lenient ward, G2, after three weeks. It didn't sound too awful, but I was extremely thankful, nonetheless, that I wasn't there. That was about to change, however.

I vacillated on P1 for the next two months and between the depression, the staring spells, having no privileges and spending a significant amount of time on SOR, I began to go even further downhill. Still, I felt safe and secure in the hospital, and was very much aware of my identity as a troubled mental patient. I even had a mission: Don't make a huge effort to get well, because this was better and more fulfilling than a vacant life on the outside with no future, and little chance for happiness.

I was just beginning to get weekend passes in April when Dr. Braun blew me away with the horrific news that I was going to Behaviour Modification.

She'd been making threats during the past six weeks but I didn't take them seriously. One Friday afternoon, as I made plans to go home for the weekend, Tess came marching into my room.

"Jane, you're being transferred to H2. Get your things packed up now."  I felt as though I'd been ripped in half with a sharp metal meat cleaver. I protested vehemently and burst into tears. "No! No! You can't send me there! Please don't send me to H2!! I'm begging you!!"

I struggled ferociously while three male PNA's wrestled me into a wheelchair and tied me securely. Tess was disgusted with my childishness. I screamed that I wanted out "Right now!" but she responded, "No. You're certified. You're not going anywhere."

I felt betrayed by the one nurse who'd been so kind to me and as she wheeled me, kicking, moaning and screeching, out of P1 and into the elevator, I saw any shred of hope that I may have had wafting away in the winds of sinister change.

I might as well be dead, I deliberated, continuing to writhe and kick spasmodically. Whatever did I do to deserve this night-mare?

## Chapter Eleven

# Auschwitz in the L.P.H.: The Death of Hope

The first thing I noticed about H2, aside from the ominous locked door, were these terrible, ugly blue walls. They literally set my teeth on edge, and as I was hastily wheeled onto the ward, I felt as though they were closing in and choking the spirit out of me.

A short, stocky man approached and told me that I would be put in one of the seclusion rooms until i calmed down. I tried to tell him that I was feeling better now and that it wasn't necessary to lock me up, but he insisted.

Alone in that room, clad only in a drafty hospital gown with not even a sheet on the cold, cement floor. I cried bitterly. Desperately wanting my mother to comfort me and transport me away from this horror and desolation, I wondered if anyone would call and tell her that I wouldn't be coming home for the weekend.

I wasn't released from seclusion until much later on in the evening. I cautiously walked out into the crowded dayroom where patients sat watching television, reading, talking to one another and sitting at tables with large, square objects in front of them.

These were the infamous rugs, in various stages of progress, and I quickly turned my eyes away from them. I couldn't bring myself to be associated with the B. Mod routine so soon after being dumped here.

I spotted Lisa across the room, talking to another patient, and couldn't help wondering why she hadn't been transferred to G2. After all, she'd been here for over two months.

I didn't talk to anyone, so I sat alone in a far corner, hugging my knees against my chest in an effort to quell the trembling that gripped my body. I was terrified of this ward and the infamous atmosphere. On top of that, those damned blue walls gave me the creeps.

The next day, I was allowed visitors, so Mom arrived, looking very sad and bewildered. I tried to explain to her that I didn't need to be on this awful ward and that I would do everything in my power to get the hell off as soon as possible. It was one thing to be safe and secure on the familiar P1, but quite another to suffer untold humiliation in this dreaded prison.

The head nurse, Mrs. Samuels, sat me down later that day in her office and explained the ward's policies to me, running down the list of the rules, regulations, as well as what was acceptable behaviour and what was not. Things that were not tolerated and punished by a loss of privileges for twenty-four hours were: Swearing, hoarding candy or gum, lying, being late for meals, missing jogging in the morning, sleeping in, and a host of others that I've since forgotten. Punishable by having to go back and start the process over again were things like, hitting another patient or the staff, self-abuse, and going AWOL (running away from the hospital).

The Behaviour Modification Program was started by a two-man team from the U.S., Dr. Freeman, a psychiatrist, and Mr. Walters, a social worker. They figured that the patients with so-called "behaviour problems," which could accompany mental illness or be even "cured" by a strict program using the "reward and punishment" theory.

It sounded an awful lot like a combination of Pavlov's dog and Nazi war criminals' experiments in the death camps during World War II and I will never believe that this kind of treatment does anything but promote fear and hatred, as well as foster feelings of loathing in the patients.

I began working on my rug the date after Mrs. Samuels' introductory lesson, on my twenty-fourth birthday. Instead of attending a party in my honour, receiving presents and getting toasted with pink champagne, I sat and poked inch-long pieces of wool into a canvas full of holes, stopping only for meals, bedtime, and the jogging and exercise sessions.

The staff on the ward were decidedly questionable. Dave, the man who had placed me in seclusion, was a bit of a smartass, issuing orders and commands and then sitting back to watch us all squirm. He had an undistinguishable accent and a ruddy, blistering complexion, which reminded me of a hard-drinking captain of a fishing schooner.

Sally was a short, squat, matronly RNA of about forty-five, who spoke with a high, somewhat gratingly nasal voice and wasted no time in reminding me how she'd warned me on P1 that I would soon be transferred to H2. She said this with a self-satisfied smirk. Sally was certain that she had all of us figured out early on, and pronounced me a "shameful goldbricker."

Phyllis was the most promising of the entire crew, with her quiet, dignified manner, despite an obvious harelip and cleft palate. I'm sure that she felt more compassionately drawn to us because of suffering alienation and endless torment as a youngster, and therefore knew only too well what it was like to be different.

Gina was a young, twenty-five-year-old woman with a substantial athletic prowess and saw to it that we always engaged in our two twenty-minute per day exercise religiously. Since she was close to my age, I was somewhat drawn to her, even though she made certain that the dividing line was clearly drawn between patients and staff.

Eric had a distinctive mean streak and from the beginning took perverse pleasure in lording discipline and harsh restraint over us. He was the first staff member to leap into an altercation between two or more patients and would manhandle some of us extremely roughly. He had sharp, piercing features and a burly, hairy frame, which lent a curiously bestial look to the man. I disliked him from the outset.

However, the worst male PNA by far had to be the ruddy, white-haired Gerald S., who not only shared Eric's sadistic streak, but took great delight in taunting and jeering at us. if he took a particular dislike to someone, as he often did, old Gerald would dig and chip away at his or her already wavery confidence until the poor soul was reduced to tears.

It was painfully obvious to me that this ward of the hospital attracted, for the most part, a specific personality type: Those who got a charge and an adrenaline rush, from exacting control, as well as punishing anyone who didn't immediately buckle under their authority. Even the kinder staff members were not immune to this behaviour altogether, although it would be unfair to claim that all were completely vicious and cruel.

Still, as I am recounting the story of my time spent as a virtual prisoner of H2, I get the old, familiar sense of dread and all of that sixteen-year-old despair and hopelessness rushes back like a gigantic tidal wave. Perhaps I can forgive to a degree, but I shall never be able to forget.

The rest of the nurses, RNA's and PNA's melted into a large unsettling juggernaut, one to be avoided, or out-run, whenever possible. These people held all of the power and they revelled in it. One had to be a particular type of person to work on the Behaviour Modification Unit, one that could effectively strip off the vestiges of conscience. The staff that hung in there, many for years, did so with grand aplomb.

Occasionally there would appear a "new kid on the block," a greenhorned staff member who would grow appalled at the way the patients were treated, especially in the neighbourhood of verbal and psychological abuse. They'd be privy to people getting beaten up for talking back, forced to live for days on liquid nutrition because their rugs weren't being hooked fast enough, and shoved into seclusion, often for the crime of being emotionally and mentally ill.

Finally, after several weeks, the green-complexioned staff members would sicken at the sights, grow despondent about being one of the "bad guys" and then would subsequently disappear, never to be seen again. It got to the point where we could spot a "staffer with a conscience," and we'd twinge with regret, knowing that he or she wouldn't be around for very long. And they never were.

I met a curious assortment of fellow patients there, such as Stanley whose gregarious forwardness and wickedly ribald sense of humour were absolutely overwhelming. He rushed about the ward like a young man overdosing on Speed and craving a release for his explosive energy. Thin and blond, with wide, blue eyes that seemed perpetually startled by sudden headlights, Stanley paced frenetically up and down, waving his spindly arms and alternately laughing maniacally and sputtering words like an ailing engine. There were no lapses of silence, no sitting, resting or quiet intervals in which the poor fellow could catch a breath; just endless, noisy movement.

Not only that, but he was evidently quite attracted to me from the outset and began an intensive period of ardent pursuit, some- thing which didn't exactly bowl me over with pleasure or joy. Add to this Stanley's annoying habit of employing little pet names like "darling" and "doll" and you have a most disquieting picture of a very sick and misguided twenty-four-year-old.

Rita was only fourteen, a tough-talking, feisty girl who would have been very attractive if not for her constant sullenness and that suspicious cast in her light blue eyes. Rita had spent most of her young life being shipped from one foster home to another, and evidently, none were even marginally acceptable. She had been physically and sexually abused, as well as used as a household maid, chief cook and bottle washer. like most of the teenagers I would encounter on H2, Rita was not mentally ill, only reacting to harshly unfair treatment by people who really should have known better. Anyone would have a behaviour problem under those conditions and here she was locked up in a hospital being punished.

Sandi, fifteen, was a wisp of a girl, with feathery, yellow hair and a face that appeared carved from delicate porcelain. Like Rita, her home life was deplorable, but she preferred it to the rigours of B. Mod. The two girls hung out together, frequently incurring punishment for going AWOL and watching as their childhoods slipped quickly down a rust-encrusted drain. I felt very sorry for them and the others who got transferred from the LPH's adolescent units to a place hideously inappropriate for patients that age.

Roberta was a quiet nineteen-year-old who had an affinity for punk rock, a mass of blonde curls and eyes like a light summer sky. she was slightly overweight, speaking wistfully of her days as an anorexic in 1977, and liked me until all my craziness spun hopelessly out of control. I wouldn't get to know Roberta well until 1990, when we lived in the same group home, but in 1979, she slowly began to harbour a great deal of resentment toward me.

Fred was a middle-aged man with a penchant for the young women, myself included, but there was a lot more to it than this awkward gesture toward lechery. Fred was severely troubled, feeling responsible for his young son, Jeremy's hearing impairment, and slashed away at imagined demons in his tortured mind. I found myself growing close to this gentle, soft-spoken man, and knew that his bids for female attention were cries for comfort and affection. I was to have a very strange and provocative encounter with him later on that year.

Among this first batch of people that I shared my living space with on H2 were Shane, a hip, savvy, twenty-two-year-old who bragged superfluously of his wanton drug use and took great delight in discussing my experiences with Ritalin.

This was one of his pet substances, and he believed that there was no greater aspiration in life than to do as much of the stimulant as was humanly possible without destroying your nervous system. Shane liked to live life on the proverbial "razor's edge" and I must confess to being somewhat enamoured of his cool confidence and brash, roguish grin. He had dark, somewhat unorthodox good looks, a curious combination of young Tyrone Power and prematurely dissipated Robert Mitchum.

Shane fancied a cheery, air-brushed snippet of a girl named Rhonda, who had this idealized, over-simplified view of life, including the inherent belief that the B. Mod. Unit was this exalted "good" place, whose primary purpose was to "help and guide poor, uninspired souls through the rigours of life." Where she got this idea is beyond me, but good old Rhonda, steeped in the philosophy of hippiedom and this bewildering "love everyone and share your needles with a friend" even wrote a "thank you" note to the staff when she left.

Beverly was another of the adolescents, a sexually precocious fourteen-year-old with jet black hair, ebony eyes and a "come hither" pout. At first, I found her to be both too outrageous and obnoxious for words, but as the months progressed, I began to realize that her seemingly out-of-control hormones were simply a substitute for parental love and nurturing. I remember one afternoon catching the tiny, slender Beverly crying bitterly in the music room as she listened to Sister Sledge's "We Are Family." I found out later that her neglectful father had refused to visit her on her birthday, one more example of a long list of snubs from the man.

I met Patricia soon after arriving on H2. She was a thirty-eight-year-old mother of two teenage boys, slightly overweight with large, expressive eyes that exuded a sombre vagueness. Her pale face was splashed with freckles, and wore her straight black hair cut very short. Patricia cried a lot and worried about her family. The staff, thinking her to be too heavy, put her on the infamous eight hundred-calorie diet, and whenever Patricia would cheat, someone would ride her relentlessly.

The poor woman would get so famished at times that she'd sneak uneaten food from other patients' trays and Dave, among others, would taunt, rebuke and chide her mercilessly until she removed the forbidden morsels from her mouth and put them back. I felt sorry for her, for Patricia was forced to take on the role of the ward scapegoat. I became her ally and passed her my food under the table.

Geri waved her pretty blonde trappings like an alluring banner, affecting the personality of a sexy airhead. She was aware of the male attention she elicited and revelled in the spotlight emitting from the male patients and staff members' shining eyes. I found her vacuous tittering annoying, her voracious acid-gobbling pathetic, but couldn't help be grudgingly admiring of her unabashed honesty.

It was as if she looked into the mirror one day and said, "Well, Geri, you've got a face, a body, not much else. Make the most of it, deal with it, and if drugs take some of life's sting away for awhile, go for it." She suffered from hallucinations, which I figured were a symptom of all the mind-exploding substances she ingested, and was put on a hefty dose of Stelazine anyway.

There were many other characters coming and going during that year and eight months on H2, and i remember most of them. They became my only human contacts, since I was basically cut off from my family and friends, and even though most of them eventually turned on me, I really needed them.

After a few weeks of relative calm, my life became suitable fodder for a first-class psychological melodrama of epic proportions. I had nearly completed my three-week program and was soon to move on to the more relaxed and liberal setting of G2. Then one morning, I felt a powerful urge to injure myself, feeling that during the past nineteen days or so I'd grown fond of the strict discipline and the security of this repetitive routine on the ward.

It seemed hard to believe that in that short time I'd get institutionalized, but I had a strange sense of identity and purpose with the ritualistic atmosphere, the six cigarettes a day which were doled out to us and the nightly sojourn to the canteen for pool games.

It was a way of determining that I was a part of something stable and longstanding. Even if it wasn't the university world or the society of residence, it proved a bit of a substitute. I hadn't been on the ward long enough to see the sinister and really negative side to it yet.

What I did see, I liked for its feeling of community and routine. Now the time was approaching to be transferred to another unknown habitat and I huddled in a whimpering little ball. I made the decision to stop this frightening inevitability from occurring.

Taking a bobbypin that I'd gotten from a patient in the canteen the previous evening, I scraped the tips back and forth across the brick wall in the washroom until they became sharpened to fine points.

Then, I rolled up my left sleeve and dug my makeshift weapon up and down my forearm until it left long, bloody tracks on it. The sight of the superficial damage caused me to smile inwardly. "This'll get me in deep shit," I thought, secretly repulsed by what I was doing, but at the same time feeling justified and oddly noble about it.

Later, after my arm was completely raw and unsightly, I rolled the sleeve back down, flushed the bobbypin down the toilet and walked back into the dayroom. Patients sat about waiting for O.T. to be announced, some slumping in their chairs morosely while others chatted in clusters.

I sat with Joe, who had recently arrived and wasn't cheerfully anticipating the rug hooking procedure. Just then, Mrs. Samuels called me into the nurses' conference room to take my blood pressure again. It had been checked the previous morning and had registered rather high, at twenty-five over ninety-nine.

Of course, when my shirt was rolled up, my handiwork was uncovered. "That's a minus, Jane," she said solemnly, examining the bloodied gouges and getting up to call in one of the RNA's. "No privileges, no visitors for at least two weeks."

Suddenly, I felt nauseated and weak, realizing that there was no way out of the consequences of my hasty, foolish actions. Another damned rug to bend over for hours a day, no cigarettes, trips to the canteen, and worst of all, no visits from my mom. I realized that this hadn't been such a great idea after all.

I was stripped and searched thoroughly, all my clothes were locked up, and I was told that this kind of self-abusive behaviour would not be tolerated.

Sally, true to form, sneered and said tartly, "Well, this is certainly no surprise. Don't you ever give up?"

I resigned myself to the rug hooking and to watching the other patients going off the ward to O.T., the canteen and into the pool room with their visitors. But with all the unpleasantness came the satisfaction of knowing that I'd be spending at least another month on H2.

By the time my second rug was finished, this time using recycled wool, I was very lonely for my mom. I craved a bit of freedom, along with a few token privileges and those wonderful six cigarettes a day. All around me, uneasy interpersonal relationships were developing, then dissolving, as the teenagers formed into adolescent cliques, only to symbolically tear at one another's throats several days later.

Angela appeared one day on the ward after being transferred from P1 by Dr. Braun, and befriended Geri. I felt sorry that Angela had been abandoned by the same doctor who'd done the same thing to me five weeks earlier. She smiled sadly and said with a shrug, "Who cares anyway?"

Then, one day, before my "sentence" was up and I was getting prepared for relative freedom on H2 again, something terrible happened. I was sitting in the dayroom watching television, when my eyes were suddenly pulled off to the side and I felt as though every nerve in my body was being tied into tight little knots. I don't know how else to describe it, other than as an extreme overwhelming agitation that exploded into choking, frenetic activity.

I lurched forward in my chair and fell, writhing and twisting onto the floor. It was the uncontrollable twitching of someone having a grand mal seizure, but I was fully conscious. My face smacked hard on the floor, but I didn't flinch, as I was so caught up in being too full of spastic energy and having no proper way to release it.

I became aware of short, gasping moans coming from my mouth, and just then I noticed several bodies hovering over me and calling out, "What are you doing? Get up, for God's sake and start acting like a human being!"

Someone grabbed my arm while another yelled out for assistance. "Let's get her into seclusion. She can't be acting out like this in front of the other patients."

I felt terrible, wanting so desperately to stop all the movement and the noise but unable to. Something's possessing me from the inside, I thought in horror, as I began to drool out of the side of my mouth.

A nervous giggling began sweeping across the dayroom, amid comments like "She's acting so weird! Like a maniac or something. Get her the hell out of here."

Eric and Stephen, another PNA, hoisted me roughly off the floor and twisted my arms behind my back. then I was dragged, struggling violently and screaming over and over, "Help me please! Please somebody make this stop!"

"We'll help you alright, into seclusion for a day or two until you can learn to behave yourself."

While I flailed my arms like a demented windmill, a nurse stripped my clothes off and tied a hospital gown on tightly. I was then shoved into that dismal, square isolation room where the heavy metal door clanged shut with ominous finality.

Then Sally stood at the tiny window in the door and watched as I ran around the room in circles, muttering incoherently and beginning to hit my head against the walls. My heart felt as though it would project itself out of my chest, or else explode in a spray of crimson before bouncing onto the cold floor.

My eyes were still forced in that unnatural position, off to the side, and they ached tremendously. All the adrenaline in my glands seemed to have swelled and overflowed into every pore, causing systems overload and producing enough nervous energy to power a twin-engine jet into hyperspace.

Finally, after what seemed an eternity, the nightmare ended and I collapsed on the floor, while Sally continued looking on and shaking her head slowly. "What is happening to me?" I gasped inwardly, pressing my cheekbone into the cement and allowing my heartbeat to return to its normal rhythm. Something insidious and unspeakable had taken hold of me and was not going to loosen its awful grip for the next year and a half.

The stage had been set for my psychological undoing and the floodgates were opened wide for unchecked abuse by the staff of the Behaviour Modification "Extermination of Dignity" camp.

My psychiatrist on the ward was Dr. Harrington, and Mr. Walters was my social worker. The team met with Mrs. Samuels and the ward staff every Wednesday morning to discuss their patients and decide if and when one of us would move to G2. Along with that, medication levels were talked about, as well as privilege levels, and only on this occasion were any new ones added for any of us.

After we were talked about, each of us was taken into the conference where we'd be besieged with a series of questions, starting with how we were feeling and moving on to more specific details.

Harrington was a large, balding man who reminded me of General Patton. He was from South Africa and spoke with a strong British accent, and actually wasn't a bad sort, just somewhat ignorant about what a bad system behaviour modification really was. I'm sure that he truly believed that Dr. Freeman and Mr. Walters had stumbled upon a beneficial concept by bringing the theories of B.F. Skinner into the psychiatric hospital arena and was simply unable to grasp the eventual erosion of the patients' sense of hope and autonomy.

The first Wednesday conference I took part in, following my incident with those "staring spells," consisted of Mr. Walters grilling me about my so-called reasons for "acting out" in such a disturbing manner.

Mr. Walters was a short, fair-haired man of forty-three, with wire-rimmed glasses and a pronounced limp. I'm not sure whether he had suffered with polio as a child or had a prosthetic leg, but he seemed to have great difficulty moving around and carried a cane at all times.

He spoke in a high, raspy voice, not unlike John Fiedler, the actor who played one of Bob Newhart's patients on his television series about a laconical psychologist. He fixed me with a hard, steady gaze, as if he figured that he'd miss something if he even looked away for a brief moment.

"The nurses seem to think that you did it for attention," he said quietly. Then he added, "Do you wish to enlighten us?"

I didn't know how to respond to this. obviously, everyone had made up their minds that my episode was merely a put-on, so anything I said to the contrary would either be ignored or refuted. I stared at the floor and muttered slowly, "Mr. Walters, I don't understand what's going on. I couldn't stop it from happening. it was like I was being controlled by something. I can't explain it. I...."

"Jane, we don't want to see anymore of this kind of behaviour. First you scratch up your arm and get a minus. Then you act out in the dayroom and have to be placed in seclusion, where you hit your head against the walls. We believe you can control these outbursts, and strongly advise you to do so."

Then Dr. Harrington piped up, "You're going to do another rug and go through the program again. And this time we expect all of this negative behaviour to cease."

I left the room feeling frustrated and extremely unhappy. I could only hope that it would never happen again and that I could simply go through another three weeks on H2 and get over to G2 where I'd be safe from all this.

This was not to be, however. Several days after my encounter with Harrington, Mr. Walters and the nursing staff, another episode occurred, this time in the dining room at suppertime. I had just sat down with my tray and was deciding whether or not to eat any of it. I'd been feeling rather fat lately, figuring that one hundred eight pounds was far too heavy and that a twenty-pound loss would be beneficial, as well as offer me much needed security.

Reaching for my coffee cup, I suddenly felt a surge of electrical hysteria rattling and searing every nerve ending in my system. I fell sideways off the chair and onto the tiled floor at several patients' feet. My eyes had jerked sideways as well and strained to maintain some kind of peripheral vision and i began to utter loud, guttural moans as my left arm and leg pummelled my chair in a quick and persistent rhythm.

I couldn't stop this activity, anymore than it would have been possible to cease breathing and before long, i felt a number of hands closing over my upper arms and ankles. "Okay, let's go to seclusion. You obviously can't behave appropriately here. Stop thrashing around like a wild animal!"

I couldn't determine who was speaking, or how many staff members had been summoned to forcibly remove me from the dining room, but it didn't take very long before I was hustled through the dayroom and down the darkened, depressing corridor to that awful seclusion room.

What followed there was another session of frenetic running about, strangled yells and repetitive head-banging. An hour or so later, I crumbled to the floor, exhausted and terror-stricken.

This became an established pattern. I'd awaken in the morning feeling rational, sound and calm and by mid-afternoon, the sessions would hit with the forces of a megaton nuclear bomb and shatter the daylights out of my world.

I was allowed no visitors from that point on and all hope of earning privileges was revoked. These spells occurred up to six times a day and always necessitated being placed in seclusion.

Dr. Harrington took me off Stelazine and Imap and gave me a

heavy dose of Haldol, another potent antipsychotic drug. This made matters even worse. For now, along with the other symptoms, I endured the intense discomfort and trauma of my head being forced backward so that I was staring blankly at the ceiling. Often my eyes would roll backward instead of sideways, and instead of realizing that these could be side effects from the Haldol, I was chided and yelled at for "putting on an act".

I remember walking down the outside railing in the dayroom and feeling as though invisible hands were clutching at my head and jerking it far back. It was extremely painful and just then Dave approached and said with a disgusted leer, "That's about all we're gonna stand from you, young lady. You must really love that seclusion room. Come on, that's where you're headed."

I was inconsolable, as the staff stripped my clothes off and shoved me into that sickeningly familiar solitary box. "I can't help it! You've got to believe me! Please don't put me in here! Can I talk to Dr. Harrington?"

"Oh, we're supposed to cater to you now? Let you see the doctor on your command? I don't think so. Maybe you should spend a few days in here, until you decide to stop all this crap."

Dave took great pleasure in wielding his power and swaggering clout like some Napoleonic dictator. I despised him. I was learning to hate everyone on B. Mod. for refusing to listen to me and labelling me a fake instead of doing something to release me from this hideous prison I was fettered within.

I spent Christmas Day in seclusion and my family was denied visitation rights. Mom, Dad, Jim and our grandparents had a miserable holiday as they were agonizingly aware of my absence, and they weren't even allowed to give me my presents.

Karen and her folks travelled all the way from Belle River and the staff wouldn't even let them see me for half an hour. Her mother left religious pamphlets for me, which one of the nurses tore up. My life was spiralling into the sewer, and after Sally shoved my Christmas dinner into my confined quarters, I was in such an out-of-control state of hysteria that my face fell squarely into the instant mashed potatoes. Merry Christmas to me.

Early in the New Year, Harrington the Warden took me off Haldol and decided to give Nozinan a try. It was similar to Chlorpromazine, but with fewer side effects. He started me on fifty milligrams a day and worked up to two hundred and for a couple of weeks, my symptoms decreased markedly.

I felt more like my old self again and revelled in the joy of being able to sit still for hours at a time with out the staring spells ripping into my equilibrium.

The other patients had developed a strong animosity toward me over the past months. They felt that I was acting out on purpose, probably because the staff told them so and they lashed out with a great deal of verbal abuse.

Lisa said that she was extremely disappointed in me, thinking that I had been a good head on P1, but now I was quite despicable. She refused to talk to me and would shoot disparaging looks my way when I entered the room. I tried fervently to explain that I couldn't help myself, but she merely scoffed and moved to the furthest corner of the dayroom.

Rita, Sandi and Beverly laughed at me, calling me "the freak" as they surreptitiously avoided me. Harriet, one of the other teenage patients of East Indian descent who had tried to kill herself by swallowing methyl alcohol, grew quite hostile, and like Lisa, wouldn't talk to me at all after awhile.

"You know what you're doing alright", was the last sentence she uttered to me. I was despondent beyond belief, for all my buddies were metamorphosizing into enemies.

Probably my most vocal adversary was Roberta. She approached me late one evening, after the women from the Lutheran church had visited, singing songs with us and offering refreshments afterward. They came on the first Tuesday of the month and we all welcomed them heartily, as they treated us like regular people and overlooked our psychiatric infirmities.

This time they were forced to see H2 for what it was: A bona fide loony bin. After twelve days of feeling and acting very rationally and normally, I flipped out again with a vengeance and had to be escorted from the dayroom, flailing, screaming and pounding my head on the floor.

"How could you carry on like that in front of those Lutheran ladies?" Roberta asked angrily, hissing the words as she spoke them. "I hate the way you're acting. It's fucking embarrassing and sickening. You just do it for attention. There's not a damn thing wrong with you and you know it. There are really sick people here, and you make a mockery of all them. I'm ashamed to be on the same ward as you. I think you're full of shit and you know what else? You're never, never going to get out of here."

There were no words to describe how terrible I felt. I was totally, completely, chillingly alone. My family was off in the nebulous netherworlds of the outside, the staff couldn't, or wouldn't help me and now my fellow inmates hated my guts.

One morning I sat in the bathtub, feeling anxious and ill-at-ease and thought that life was never going to get any better. I've somehow been condemned to this nightmarish existence for the rest of my life. I was not yet twenty-five and life, as I had once experienced it, had ceased to exist. I slid further down in the tub until the waterline was even with my nose. I could just slide under the water now and end the torment. Life was worse than any hell I might encounter following the sin of suicide. "Lord help me," I murmured. "forgive me for copping out like this."

But before my head was submerged, Sally came bustling into the bathroom and yanked it out of the water, grasping my long hair and crying out in exasperated tones, "Alright. I guess you can't even take a bath unsupervised, can you?"

That guaranteed me another session in seclusion, where the wild flailing and shouting returned in full force. I ran about in frantic circles, bashing the back of my head against the wall until the pain was so excruciating that I passed out.

A great pocket of fluid formed around the outside of my skull, and I was hipped off to Victoria Hospital for X-rays to determine whether or not I suffered any head trauma. While I was there, I entertained thoughts of escaping, of running home to the safety and solace of my family and far away from the unspeakable horrors of H. But of course that was only a silly pipedream, because Carol went with me and refused to leave my side until a van returned us to the L.P.H.

There was no serious damage inflicted by the persistent banging, other than perhaps a few hairline fractures that would heal with time. However, to ensure that no more injuries were sustained, by hands were tied behind my back and a hockey helmet strapped onto my head during my sessions in seclusion. It was very difficult and uncomfortable to sleep this way, but I had no choice. Because of the restraints, all my meals had to be fed to me by a staff member.

Due to the incessant activity, I burned a great deal of calories and was losing weight rapidly. I didn't care, though, and eating

wasn't exactly a top priority, so it became the mission of the staff to try and force food into me. i couldn't understand why they were so concerned with my physical well-
being, while not giving a damn about my emotional state, so I wasn't terribly co-operative. This attitude was not exactly in my best interests, for it simply gave them more evidence to support their theory that I was playing a lot of games with them.

I did manage to get over to G2 once, though, but it was a short-lived moment of victory. For three weeks I managed to function surprisingly well, early in February of 1980. I still had episodes of my eyes veering off to the side, but the maniacal activity and head-banging subsided when Harrington reduced the dose of Nozinan from two hundred milligrams to one hundred. He didn't see any relationship between the reduction in medication and my more relaxed demeanour, but I was beginning to wonder if there was a connection.

I was extremely elated to finally be released from the hellish H2, and set comparatively free on the more lenient, humane G2. We had off-ward privileges, visitors, as many cigarettes as we could smoke, and, best of all, weekend passes.
After a week on this ward, it was possible to get a day pass on Saturday. I'd be able to go home to Mom's apartment and be with her all day, without staff and other patients milling about. That would be heaven in itself.

The walls of G2 were a cheery, bright yellow, instead of the sombre blue of H2, and there were plants and pictures scattered about, giving the place a homy feel. The head nurse was Laura, a slim, pretty woman with long, straight brown hair and an easy smile. The other nurses were outgoing, helpful and not at all encased in the dictatorial shell of the other ward's staff like Sally, Stephen, Eric and Dave.

I was not involved in O.T. anymore, but had been sent to the Activity Group while on H2, a place for patients who couldn't function at the O.T. level. Terri was a twenty-nine-year-old
patient who looked about twelve and was mentally challenged. Lane had most of his brain cells fried by street drugs and was little more than a gibbering kumquat.

One day I was hooking a rug off all crazy things ( as if I hadn't done enough of those things already) in the Activity Group. I suddenly felt my eyes sliding sideways in that chillingly familiar pattern. I thought the nightmares of the past were over, and was trying desperately to focus them forward again. Before I realized what was happening, the rug hook was hanging from my left eyelid. It had somehow gotten caught on the inside of the delicate skin.

The Activity Group staff member went frantically berserk when she saw the ugly sight and immediately called G2 for assistance. Within minutes, two nurses arrived with a wheelchair and I was hastily moved to Health Services, where the attending physician removed the hook after sweating it out for awhile.

The concensus was that I had done this deliberately and therefore would be returned to H2. Thus ended my five days of relative happiness on G2. None of them ever stopped to think that nobody, not even someone like myself with a history of self-abusive behaviour, would stick a sharp, dangerous object into his or her eye with the possibility of blindness. I cannot imagine anyone putting their sight in that kind of peril.

Dr. Harrington upped my Nozinan back to two hundred milligrams and the terrible symptoms increased once more in intensity. Luckily, I'd gotten a chance to see my mother on the day I arrived on G2, so at least I knew that my folks hadn't given up on me. But now the horrendous chasm had opened up again and swallowed me, and I was gone from them for what was to many months.

Life settled into a series of sixteen-day rug-hooking programs in an effort to get me through the H2 regimen and get back to G2. Now it wasn't just a matter of hooking the rugs, however, but unhooking them as well. They had doubled in size, with twice the number of squares, and the pieces of wool had to be picked out of the canvas by hand and then re-hooked when the huge mess was completed.

After a few days of grabbing bits of wool out, my fingers were raw and bleeding. It became necessary to pull them out with my teeth, which produced an aching in my two thousand dollars worth of orthodontia that was very uncomfortable.

When I wasn't engaged in this mindless activity, I was shuttled off to seclusion with the tied hands and hockey helmet, rolling about on the floor and feeling as though my insides were crawling with electrically charged insects. I remembered how my mother had told me how her cat had swallowed a lot of wool, years before, and had gone mad from the pain. That's how I felt with these awful spells. Moans and yells emitted from my gut, spilling out into the silence of the night and keeping the other patients awake.

"Shut up, damn you and let us get some sleep!!" they would holler at me. But I couldn't shut up, or stop my body from rocking from side to side. I rarely slept and was never able to relax. I grew envious of the other patients who could sit for hours without moving and writhing about and could converse among themselves with ease and relative non-chalance.

I celebrated my twenty-fifth birthday pulling apart a giant rug with my teeth. As the sun began to set on the L.P.H., I came running out in the dayroom in the nude, having spun into a chaotic frenzy while getting undressed for bed and landed squarely into the lap of a very surprised Fred. Nurses rushed about in an effort to cover me up as I wriggled and jerked around in clear view of everyone in the dayroom.

That was probably the single most demoralizing event of my H2 career, for I was certainly not an exhibitionist by nature. Those spells were so overwhelming and severe that they transcended any sense of morality and modesty. People's mouths waggled about this spectacle for weeks and I became the ward laughing stock. Wib, however, with his quiet gentleness, took it all in stride and felt compassion and sympathy for my plight and I dearly loved him for that.

Along with my rug hooking and de-hooking duties, I was given a series of chores to accomplish each day in an effort to modify my behaviour. Some of these included mopping the dayroom floor in the evening, making all the patients' beds, scrubbing the baseboards all around the dayroom's walls, pouring the HS drinks, and changing Mildred's urine-soaked sheets twice a day.

Mildred was this rather frightening, outrageously profane, chewed-up old creature, who looked as if she could have been the creation of pulp-horror guru Stephen King. She was small, with spiky grey hair, thick glasses, and a tongue that was several sizes too big for her mouth.

She used four-letter words I'd never heard before, and had a habit of throwing Readers Digest magazines at people, spitting at them, and threatening to kill anyone who looked sideways at her. It was rumoured that she had killed her husband years before and had been determined not guilty by reason of insanity.

She was one of the "regressed patients;" that is, one of four women on H2 who were so ill that they were basically locked in their own demented prisons and could not really communicate with anyone. Darlene, was another one of them, a skinny pretzel who twisted herself into various contortions, and like Mildred, swore continually. She had no teeth, and because of this her nose touched her chin, and the story with her was that she had gone insane when she caught her husband in bed with another woman.

Pris was a Native woman who never spoke at all and wouldn't look anyone in the eye, and Judith sat in a geriatric chair all day, chewing mindlessly on her tongue. These patients were deliberately placed on H2 to show us what could happen if we didn't get out acts together.

I felt sorry for all of them, even Mildred, who turned out to be my roommate for most of my time there. She, like Judith, was locked in a geriatric chair all day, and tied into her bed at night. She always wet the bed, including the two hours during the day she spent there in the afternoon. she had to be restrained all the time because she was extremely violent and could actually physically attack people.

One night, she got out of her restraints and moved over to my bed, whereupon she put her bony fingers around my throat and proceeded to strangle me.

I awoke with a start and tried to call out to the nurses in their station across the hall for assistance. there were two of them in there chatting away and totally ignorant of what was transpiring in our bedroom. finally, one of them clued in, but not before old Mildred nearly choked the daylights out of me.

Mildred despised me and would utter in guttural, hate-laced tones, "Your mother's a whore, your father's a whoremaster, and you're the little bastard." She certainly wouldn't make finalist in the "Loving grandmother of the year" contest.

During my few, lucid times, I was very much aware of the music that came out during that time. I remember enjoying Dire Straits' "Sultans of Swing," Gerry Rafferty's "Baker Street," ELO's "Don't Bring Me Down" and "Sara Smile" by Hall and Oates. There was still a fair bit of disco crap hanging around to make my life miserable, but I managed to filter it out.

I used to spend a lot of time sitting beside the stereo by the pool table, just letting the songs sink into my brain and hoping that they would jolt me back to life and some measure of happiness. I would have been even worse if it weren't for that familiar connection.

Six months had passed since I had had any visitors, and it had been four since I had been at either Activity Group or O.T., The B. Mod. O.T. had been preferable to the one on P1. It was run by Selene and Duncan.

Selene was a pleasant thirty-eight-year-old British woman and had once been a neighbour of Grandma and Grandpa Colerick. I had babysat for her two young sons back in 1969, and had clear, positive memories about the experience. Janet was an ardent, enthusiastic fan of the The Boomtown Rats and even went to see them in concert in 1978, and I liked her enthusiastic verve and vigour.

Long-haired, bearded Duncan was just as cool, with a relaxed, easygoing manner, and I really missed them when I was held prisoner on the ward for so long. I desperately wanted to return to O.T., where I knew I'd be treated with respect and care.

So I spent my days with rugs, chores, Mildred and being constantly harassed by staff and patients alike. The longer I was separated from my family, the more I felt as though I was drifting into some frightening black hole from which I would never emerge.

One afternoon, as I sat picking bits of wool out of my teeth, I was struck with a horrifying thought: Perhaps I had really succeeded in my suicide attempt in November of 1978, and I was now in some dreadful Purgatory, reserved for lost souls who have taken their own lives.

My penance was this never ending torment I had been experiencing since then, orchestrated by Satan in preparation for my eternal damnation in Hell. That must be it; there could be no other explanation for my suffering. I deserved it, and of course I couldn't see my family and friends, for they were still alive on earth.

I felt sick, and then whatever minuscule shred of hope I'd clung to until that moment just disintegrated. I was the Undead, and could never expect to be released from these demonic forces for all Eternity. From that day onward, I gave up, and let the staff abuse the hell out of me, the other patients torment me and I willingly submitted to the pain.

Patricia became my sole ally, as she, too, was endlessly hassled on H2, and understood my devastation. We sat together in misery while around us people came and went, got better, went off to G2 and were replaced by more poor souls who hadn't yet been damaged by the B. Mod. Machine.

People imprisoned in the Nazi death camps during World War II experienced similar psychological patterns when they knew that they were doomed. They stopped fantasizing about being released, and let their captors have their sadistic ways with them.

Numb to the travesties going on around them, the prisoners adapted, in a way, to their situation, clinging to what little they still had to keep them rooted in some semblance of sanity. They spent hours ruminating about food and eating as they were starved, and they played little mind games with themselves to distract them from the abysmal living conditions and the screams of other victims being killed and tortured.

Now I'm not claiming that the staff on H2 were that vicious, but in some ways, their abuse was just as insidious as Hitler's henchmen's. They used fear and dominance, as well as reward and punishment and even though we weren't slaughtered or gassed in ovens, we were robbed of our autonomy and sense of self. I began to regress during my months in seclusion, and with the many rugs I hooked and took apart.

My world had shrunk to the realm of the dayroom, the observation bedroom and seclusion, with no other stimulation or diversion, except to do chores that should have been done by the nurses and the other patients.

I wonder if those people had any idea of how cruel and dehumanizing their treatment of us was, and that it would leave permanent scars on all of our psyches. They couldn't possibly have believed that they were doing the right thing, or what was in our best interest. Behaviour Modification did not work, and what was worse, it was detrimental. I don't hate them anymore for what they did, but I will never get over the anger I feel for putting me through so much suffering for something that was not my fault.

I've discovered since that time that what I experienced with the "staring spells" was a severe reaction to the antipsychotic drugs I was given. I'm extremely sensitive to any kind of medication and drugs like Haldol, Modicate, and Nozinan are very powerful and potent.

I suppose that in the late 1970's, the psychiatric profession did not realize that patients should never be given these drugs without one called Cogentin for side effects. I wasn't given anything like that for the year and an half I was on H2. Dr. Harrington should, however, have realized that my traumatic symptoms could possibly be medication-related before hastily dismissing them as "acting out" for attention.

The other patients were having some difficulties of their own. Roberta had been transferred to G2 early in January and was released two months later. Then one day, late in March, she returned to H2 and was at least twenty pounds thinner.

She paced up and down the outside railing of the dayroom, arms folded tightly across her chest, and slightly bent over at the waist. The overall effect was one of a half-starved sparrow, similar to the image I'd projected in Rhode Island nearly nine years before.

Roberta had told me how anorexic she'd become in 1977, when, at age seventeen, she'd gone from one hundred thirty pounds to mere eighty. I could see that the poor girl was headed for another session.

Beverly had become involved with a burned-out drug addict named Jason, who was at least twelve years her senior and couldn't utter one coherent sentence if his life depended on it. She was crazy about him, even though the guy wasn't even aware of Beverly's presence most of the time.

Sandi went AWOL one night, made it home and slashed her forearm quite severely, making five gaping cuts that needed immediate stitching. She did it so that she wouldn't have to
return to H2, and after discussing her case with her father, the staff let her leave. I don't know the full story, but, given Sandi's terrible home life, she was most likely sent off to a foster home. I never saw her again.

Stanley was still high as a kite, pacing continuously and rambling loudly in endless, run-on sentences, that were punctuated with a great deal of maniacal laughter. He still had a mad crush on me and never missed an opportunity to feed me one of his classic, come-on lines, such as: "Hey, doll, let's you and me go down to the sub-basement and have some fun." Needless to say, I never got around to taking him up on it.

Shane made it to G2 but then got mixed up with some bad dope and returned to H2, mad as hell. He was terribly disillusioned with everyone and everything, especially my outbursts of the past several months. He'd say, "You used to be so cool with your foxy clothes and hair. Then you got real weird on me".

Poor Shane, he just couldn't cope in a world that wasn't totally predictable and unchanging. It made me wonder what he saw in drugs, which are anything but unpredictable.

One Wednesday morning, during that meeting with the patients and the doctors, social workers and staff, I was asked why I didn't try harder to stop my episodes before they got really out of hand. "Once you get going, you really can't stop, and we know that. But we feel that you are able to exert a certain amount of control over yourself at the outset. You shouldn't let yourself get all worked up, because then it's too late to regain your composure." This was spoken to me by Sheila, one of the younger nurses.

I wondered how she could come to that conclusion. Sheila seemed so damned sure of herself, as they all did, including Harrington and Mr. Walters. They sat there like a close-minded jury, convinced that their assessment of me was the right one and that my sentence would be another year of rug hooking, unhooking, chores and belittling comments.

I didn't know where they got their evidence, since none of them were able to crawl into my head and read my mind. It was all conjecture, pure and simple, based on the flimsy theory that all of us on H2 were simply naughty, despicable behaviour problems that needed to be whipped into shape.

I left the meeting with my usual feeling of heaviness, a disappointment mixed with a substantial amount of bitter frustration. I grasped onto little pleasures like drinking a cup of coffee at supper and savouring the caffeine. This was before I knew that all the coffee and the tea in the L.P.H. was decaffeinated.

I greatly anticipated going to bed at night, for it signalled the end of another bad day on the ward. I still had no visitors and no privileges. I craved a cigarette, but knew that the time would likely never come when I'd get even six per day to inhale rapturously.

One particularly dismal day, as I sat on the floor washing baseboards and listening to one nurse say to another that she'd rather be dead than be like me, I was called to the front of the dayroom.

Mrs. Samuels informed me that I was to go directly to Mr. Walters's office. I was curious, because I had no privileges to see him, or anyone else off the ward. Stephen escorted me to the third floor where Mr. Walters's office was.

I walked in and Mr. Walters stood up, extended his right

hand and said, somewhat cheerily, "Hello, Jane. I have someone here who really wants to see you."

I looked sideways and was happily shocked to see Mom sitting there opposite the man's desk. "Mom!" I rushed to her and threw my quaking arms around her waist, kissing her forcefully and saying through choked sobs, "How did you get her? How is this happening? They kept telling me I couldn't have any visitors! Oh, God it's been so long!!"

Mom was as overcome as I, and cried openly. It seemed that Grandma had contacted her friend Selene, and then the O.T. instructor had pulled some strings to get Mom to be able to meet with me, under Walters' supervision.

I was so ecstatic that I couldn't speak very clearly for a few minutes, and tried desperately to catch up on months of separation and silence.

That was the beginning of a gradual upswing on H2 for me. By June, Dr. Harrington had significantly lowered my dose of Nozinan, and, seemingly coincidentally, my traumatic symptoms decreased markedly. I was also on Ludiomil, and Dilantin for my seizures. For the first time in over a year, I wasn't plagued with those severe, frightening and emotionally wracking sessions, at least not to the extent I had been.

The decrease wasn't noticeable at first, but within a few days, the writhing, moaning and unbridled physical anxiety had abated enough to allow me to sit in a chair for several hours and only rock slightly back and forth. My eyes still drifted to the side, which pissed the other patients off, but it wasn't accompanied by those noisy outbursts. When I lay in bed, next to mouthy old Mildred, I enjoyed the sensation of feeling calm and still, with no frantic, obsessive movements keeping me awake for hours. It seemed like some kind of miracle.

Within three weeks, I'd gotten my sessions and staring spells under enough control to actually be transferred to G2. I couldn't believe that suddenly, I was sprung from the terrible Purgatory and back with the vital and the alive segment of the population.

Mom came to visit me during my last two weeks on H2, as well as Dad and his girlfriend. Even Jim came and was intensely relieved that I was able to see everyone again. He hadn't known what was going on all those awful months and I tried to tell him. It came out sounding stilted and wooden, and I gave up after awhile. I sat and looked at my dear brother long and hard, thanking God that he hadn't been lost to me along with the rest of the family.

Then he gave me the ghastly news that he was moving to Vancouver right after graduation from Western. I was heartbroken, thinking of Jim being three thousand miles away, but he'd fallen in love with the West coast during the past two summers when he went to the British Columbia interior to plant trees.

I cried bitterly and was told by Sheila that at least now I had something legitimate to be upset about. I lay in bed and wept for the loss of the only stable force in my screwed-up life. Jim had taken on the role of the "older," more stable sibling during our years at university.

He no longer was my "little brother," but rather, the person I went to for comfort and guidance. Fortunately, he wasn't leaving until September, which was still three months away. I was afraid, though, that I wouldn't be out of the hospital before he took off.

It was a banner day when I got to light up a cigarette for the first time in a year. It would have been wise just not to start up again at all, but my abstinence had been forced and was not my choice, so I felt justified to be puffing away once more. I took that first puff with all the relish and exuberance of someone drawing a deep breath of victory, and I knew that another part of my life was now once more in my control and not somebody else's. When I arrived on G2, I found some familiar faces: Lisa,

Rita, Shane, Harriet and a group of others I had spoken to on several occasions. Unfortunately, I came down with the flu a week later and was sent to bed for three days with clear fluids and no cigarettes.

My roommate was a fourteen-year-old named Patti who seemed normal enough, and we got along quite well. By the end of my third day in exile I was starving, so she sneaked me in some chips and pop.

I got a huge shock one afternoon, as I finished up in the shower, when one of my old familiar staring spells occurred again. Before I knew it, my eyes had slid off to the side and I was lying on the bathroom floor banging the metal garbage can and writhing about. Luckily, it stopped before anyone came in, and I managed to pull myself together and get dressed. I couldn't figure out why that had happened after a month of no incidents, and it worried me. There was no way in hell I could endure another year like that last one. It would be preferable to be dead.

I soon got weekend passes and spent the time with my mom. She was going out with a pleasant, but complex man named Jim Kilpatrick, ten years her junior, and she was very happy. She went out every Saturday night, but I didn't mind spending some time alone. it was great not to be besieged by thirty-five other patients and a contingency of staff members. I played records, watched television, and wrote, mostly short stories. Maybe there was a future for me after all, and I could finally leave my sordid past behind.

On G2, I met a twenty-two-year-old named Sam who had been admitted to H2 a month earlier when he slashed his arms with a knife. He looked a lot like Jim Kerr of Simple Minds, although that's a reference from the present and not the 1980's, as the band hadn't been formed yet.

He was kind, sensitive and I was extremely attracted to him. He spoke softly and explained to me that he had been trying to kill himself when he used the blade, but that he was not certain exactly why he wanted to die. We became fast friends, tied together by fate, it seemed, and each struggling with the negative components of our personalities that drove us to self-destruction and despair.

I had not abandoned my own demons, as I was to learn. Even as my quality of life improved on G2 with the increase in freedom and privileges and though I was no longer being persecuted by staff members, I felt despondent a great deal of the time.

As the weeks progressed, this deadening sensation developed into strong urges to harm myself and I began to formulate plans to begin cutting again. It's still difficult to try to explain this need to camouflage emotional pain with a physical one. Something crucial was missing in my life, and not only that, I felt as though I was constantly grieving for something that was lost to me. This feeling had been with me for twenty-one years, since I was four.

I talked to Sam about it and he said he understood perfectly, as he experienced a similar, mysterious sadness and that may have been the catalyst for his suicide attempt.

We became friends with a girl named Cassandra, who, at eighteen, was extremely angry and bitter at being shunned by her family and dumped in the L.P.H. I was drawn to her self-destructive nature, and when we decided to become blood sisters and cut and cut our wrists together, Sam balked angrily. "That's a really stupid thing to do. I thought you had more class than that".

I retorted that he had cut himself multiple times and had the scars to prove it, but he simply got up and stalked furiously out of the games room.

Cassandra and I decided against the bloodletting ceremony, but the seed had been planted. I needed to slash, to feel the icy cold steel of a razor blade sliding into my skin and producing a warm rush of blood.

My brother had been visiting Mom and I a great deal on the weekends, since He was leaving soon for Vancouver. He was even more protective of me than he'd been in the past, ever since I was kept on H2 for so long. Sam and I went out drinking a lot on our weekend passes and one night I returned home quite inebriated.

Jim looked up from his book and asked, with a look of genuine concern, "Are you okay? What have you been up to?"

I sat down awkwardly, then replied through rubberized lips, "Oh, nothing much. Had a few beers with Sam. No big deal."

Jim frowned for a minute or two, then relaxed his expression and smiled slightly, "You should take better care of yourself. You're just getting over all your problems, so don't create more of them. Anything you want to talk about?"

I thought it was sweet of him to care as much as he did. I would certainly miss him when he moved thousands of miles away. Who was going to look out for me then?

Unfortunately, Mom's relationship with Jim Kilpatrick fizzled after he broke it off unexpectedly. The poor woman was devastated, and cried for days. I tried to console her, but it was futile. I even played Burton Cummings' "Stand Tall" for her, but that made matters worse. Then, on top of that, she got the awful news that she had uterine cancer and had to have a hysterectomy, with no guarantee that she would make a full recovery.

I didn't take this very well at all and was completely unhinged when she told me. She had the surgery and spent a week in Texas with Aunt Elizabeth recuperating in the hot, southern sun and floating around in the Holtz's pool.

Somewhere during this time, I pulled something that caused the relationship between my brother and I to rip wide open and made festering sores that would take years to heal.

I was home for the weekend and Mom had gone out to her singles club on a Saturday night. I sat at home watching "East of Eden" and was overwhelmed by the urge to cut myself. I just felt that I couldn't deal with my sordid past, my mother's problems and facing more time in that horrible hospital. I needed to anaesthetize some of the pain, so I devised a plan.

I would put a razor blade in my purse, walk down to a pub downtown that Sam and I frequented, have a few beers, then hide in the washroom until everyone left. Then after the staff had gone home, I'd slash my wrists and arms to pieces, and by the time someone found me, perhaps I'd get lucky and it would be too late. I wasn't afraid of dying; I'd suffered worse insults than that in the past year.

I just couldn't handle my life anymore. I had grown weary of pushing my depression down into the pit of my stomach and shuddering everytime it surfaced again. My eyes still occasionally rolled off to the side and I greatly feared regressing to the point where I'd been on H2 once more. It was just a matter of time before my freedom expired and I was once again emotionally tortured on that despicable ward.

Now it appeared that Mom could die and I'd have no support system left. Jim was moving away, and Dad wouldn't be able to deal with me. On top of all this was that nebulous sense of despair that gnawed at my soul and chewed my confidence, well-being and zest for life into tiny fragments.

"I can't do this anymore," I thought, walking down King Street toward Richmond, "Enough is enough." I got slightly drunk at the pub and waited until last call. Then, a half hour later, after all the patrons were leaving, I slipped into the washroom, closed myself into a stall, and produced the blade from my wallet. After staring numbly at it for a moment, I slashed repeatedly, making certain to cut as deep as I could, all up and down my arms and violently into my wrists.

I didn't feel any pain, even as the blood oozed out of the multiple lacerations and spilled onto the floor and into my lap, running in rivulets over my blue suede shoes. (I certainly could have done a chillingly Apocalyptic version of that old Presley tune).

I watched with morbid fascination as the cuts gaped open, revealing veins, muscle and yellowish fatty tissue. The next thing I knew, I was sprawled on the floor and conscious of two large feet at my head. Then everything went black.

I awakened in the emergency room at St. Joseph's Hospital, where an intern, looking somewhat green and nauseated, began asking me questions. He wanted to know if I'd been drinking, had I taken any pills If I'd been trying to kill myself and who could be notified as to my whereabouts.

I explained that I hadn't taken an overdose, but he didn't believe me and made me swallow two doses of Ipecac. That was absolutely horrendous, and I puked my guts out for a half hour, feeling sicker than I ever had in my life.

He said that I shouldn't make decisions about my life when intoxicated, and then added somewhat sadly, "Some of these cuts are really deep."

I said nothing, just turned my head to the side and looked away from his judgmental eyes. I didn't want my mother to be called, terrified of her discovering what I had done. This was a very bad mistake, for she was at home worried sick and wondering where I was.

After getting stitched up, with over one hundred thirty sutures, I was made to stay in the emergency room for the remainder of the night, after which an ambulance took me back to the L.P.H.

Naturally, I was put back on H2, and this completely blew me away. I lay in the observation room, crying bitterly and loudly for hours. I couldn't have any visitors or privileges and was told curtly to stop making such a racket and disturbing the other patients.

When I finally staggered out into the dayroom, I was met by a small, bespeckled fifteen-year-old boy named Percy. He was very kind and soft-spoken, and I warmed up to him immediately. I was soon to discover that he was extremely sexually precocious. After telling me I had the body of Kristy McNichol, he asked if he could go to bed with me.

I replied that he was far too young and to get his adolescent mind out of the gutter. It turned out that he was on Behaviour Modification for molesting his nine-year-old foster brother, but I think that little Percy just craved affection and love that he didn't get from his foster parents. I felt sorry for him and his plight helped to draw me out of my own misery.

Mom came to see me a few days later, completely undone.

She was sobbing uncontrollably, shaking violently and stoned on Librium which her doctor had prescribed for her frayed emotional state following my selfish antics.

I felt terrible and well I should have. She couldn't understand why I hadn't called her to let her know I was safe instead of putting her through such tremendous agony.

Jim was livid and wouldn't come to visit me. Dad said little, but felt I was the most selfish and inconsiderate brat that ever lived. He was right on the money there, I had another rug to hook, and spent three weeks on H2, which was much less than I deserved.

I met a quiet, shyly handsome patient named Garon, who, at forty, had been diagnosed with paranoid schizophrenia. He was intelligent, witty and laughed at my stupid jokes. We talked about literature and music and I was happy to have finally found an academic soulmate in the illiterate wasteland of the L.P.H.

I got back to G2 in September, and vowed finally to get my act together and get the hell out of that damned hospital. I had been seeing Mr. Walters on a weekly basis for quite awhile. He told me that my staring spells and all the accompanying frenzy were the result of anxiety, which really frustrated me. They still would not admit that my symptoms might have been due to the medication.

Mr. Walters liked to discuss my sexuality, or rather, the lack thereof, and for the next couple of years I obligated him, oddly fascinated with the way in which he tried ambitiously to steer me away from my attraction to women. Once he found out that I had been to a gay bar and felt drawn toward my own sex, he donned his homophobic Baptist garb and figured he could "save me." It was a little game I played with him, although I don't think he knew I was doing it. I thought he needed to take a different approach to his therapy, and secretly laughed at him.

I had been assigned to work at I.T., or Industrial Therapy, a huge workshop on the hospital grounds where patients did abso-lutely fascinating and mind-expanding things like unwrapping bubblegum, packaging sandpaper and emptying packets of Lik-O-Maid into giant vats. I hated it, and to add insult to injury, we only got paid twenty cents per hour.

After several months of this idiocy, I was sent to a place called the Satellite Workshop, several miles up Dundas Street on Clarke Road. There we got sixty dollars a week and did piecework for companies like 3M. It involved packaging, collating and some carpentry, and I didn't mind it too much. A woman named Donna McManus ran the place, along with someone named Betty and they were decent to us.

Garon worked there, along with a thin, intense young woman named Pearl, a tall, gangly kid with pale blond hair and large, myopic eyes named Ron, and a cheerful, effervescent woman of about twenty-eight named Sharon. We worked well together, for seven hours, five days a week, and it offered a chance to be away from the L.P.H. The workshop was small, clean, and we were treated fairly and with respect.

During that time, I thought I was getting too chubby at one hundred ten pounds and went down to ninety-eight, subsisting on salads, coffee and cigarettes. The G2 staff gave me a hard time about looking anorexic and Mom was definitely not pleased. But still, I couldn't let go of my eating disordered life, and it was forever coming back to haunt me, particularly when things were otherwise improving. It was like a security crutch, an old friend who was always waiting in the wings to let me feel virtuous and somewhat holy.

Sam continued to go out with me, even after my cutting episode. he'd gone to the pub the following Monday to ask questions about what had happened and some waitresses told him that the janitor had found me when he was cleaning up the washrooms.

I would go over to his basement apartment on the weekends and we'd drink, listen to music and engage in a lot of kissing and heavy petting. I wouldn't have intercourse with him, for fear of getting pregnant.

One night, we had a big fight about something so trivial that I've long since forgotten and the two of us broke up afterward. I just stopped seeing him. He'd been out of the hospital for a couple of months and I remember being extremely angry with him. Lisa and Cassandra wouldn't speak to me after that, thinking I was a real bitch for treating Sam like I did. They were probably right, for all I know.

Finally, on November fourteenth, 1980, I got released from G2. I was incredulous; after two full years of being a patient in the L.P.H., I had my ticket to freedom. It hardly seemed possible that they were actually letting me out of that hellhole. Although I still felt depressed and couldn't say for certain that I'd never cut again, the spells were under control and Dr. Harrington could see no reason to keep me any longer.

Mom met me at Mr. Walters's office on that Friday afternoon, and I remember actually feeling scared and panicky about leaving what had been my home for so very long.

I'd continue seeing Mr. Walters every Wednesday and Dr. Sussman would be in charge of my medication. I'd pick it up once a month at the out-patient pharmacy.

As I packed my gigantic accumulation of stuff from G2, I knew in my heart that I would never be back there again. Patients came up to say good-bye and the staff wished me luck, saying that I could come to the ward anytime to talk. I knew that would never happen, but I thanked them anyway.        I walked off the ward and out of the L.P.H., feeling as though I'd been through one of those Turkish prisons. My heart raced as I breathed in the sweet scent of freedom, and felt rather drunk with the knowledge that my life was now in my control.

That very night, I attended a Burton Cummings concert with Karen. I even met the man again after the show, when he thanked me enthusiastically for a book I'd sketched for him and planted a big, hearty kiss on my lips.

"Thank you for doing that picture of my mother! I'm sending the book to her in Winnipeg. We've been looking at it for the past half hour."

Yes, I thought triumphantly, I had my life back. And what a life it was going to be from now on.

## Chapter Twelve

# Goodwill Industries: The Sheltered Employment Trip

After that Burton Cummings concert, I met two guys with the band who were doing promotional work, and Cathy and I got hired on to sell t-shirts and buttons at the show in St. Catharine's the following weekend. Karen couldn't go, but I stayed down the hall from Burton at the Holiday Inn and got a venue pass, met him later and went drinking with him and his entourage afterward. It was the last concert of the tour and we all got pretty loaded.

I got so much into my cups that I kissed him later in the lobby, but declined an invitation to his room where a private party was happening.

One woman, a thirty-year-old groupie with obvious designs on the rock star, got into this heated argument with Burton later and I awoke at four AM to this loud commotion in the hall. I was quite thankful not to be involved, for, years later in 1990, Burton remembered me and treated me with affection and respect.

I may have harboured slight desires to sleep around with rock stars, but the guys have no respect for you and cast you aside like an old pair of worn shoes. Besides, I wasn't on the Pill and really didn't relish bringing Burton Jr. into the world as a single parent.

Burton knew of my less-than-illustrious past with mental hospitals and suicide attempts, and didn't judge me for it. I have a great deal of respect for him for that. He's nothing like the media portrayed him, not at all egotistical and opinionated.

When I got back to London, the realities of being an ex-mental patient with no completed education, no job and no place of my own hit hard.

My mother had met another man, Steve Wendell and I disliked him from the start, because he had an annoying habit of telling me that I shouldn't be living with my mother at twenty-five years of age.

I finally got tired of the endless tirades and moved into a flea-bitten dive in the east end, which consisted of a small, run-down, dirty kitchen, a bedroom with a lumpy old mattress on the floor, a dilapidated refrigerator and only two electrical outlets. It was on the second floor of a slum dwelling on Ontario Street, but it was all I could afford when I went on welfare.

Basically, I was miserable there, with no television, no phone, and nothing much to eat but peanut butter and crackers. Grandpa tried not to express how appalled he was that his granddaughter was living in such deplorable conditions, but he restrained himself.

He was suffering from emphysema and would come huffing and puffing up the steep stairs to bring me thermoses of coffee. That's the kind of guy he was, totally selfless. I grew closer to him and Grandma, especially since they didn't think much of Three either and the three of us would band together and console each other, feeling that Mom was making a very big mistake with the man.

I tried looking for work and found employment at the Beef Baron, a strip joint. I was hired on as a waitress and lasted all of one day. The manager said I didn't have what it took to work with the leering, drooling male customers, meaning that I wouldn't let them pinch my butt constantly. I was glad to be out of that lecherous armpit of the world of slease.

Eager to get off welfare, I went to Christa Richie, head of I.T. at the L.P.H., who got in touch with Vocational Rehabillitaion Services. This was an organization intended to place people with learning disabilities, psychiatric problems and those who were mentally challenged in work settings, or back to school.

I met with a man named Mike Smith, who sent me to Good-will Industries. This didn't exactly overwhelm me with joy and gratitude, as I thought people who worked there were very slow and unable to learn much. "I have two and a half years of university and you want me to work at Goodwill?" I exclaimed to Smith, incredulous that he didn't think me capable of doing anything more intellectually stimulating.

He explained that I would be hired on as a member of the service (V.R.S.) and would complete an internship at the plant on First Street. They'd give me a series of tests to determine what I was best suited for. Some people finished the placement at Goodwill and moved on to other things, while others were then hired on to work at the plant or at one of the Thrift Shops. He assured me that it was nothing to feel ashamed about, and that, since I had little work experience and an incomplete education, I did not exactly have unlimited options.

My first day at the plant was mildly interesting. I met Alan Jackson, a tall, smiling, chipper man who looked over the top of our heads when he spoke, perhaps to pretend we weren't there. He ran me through a number of tests, ranging from screwing nuts and bolts together, pronouncing five-syllable words and doing exercises in math and English.

I was assigned to a counsellor as well, a young, somewhat plump ex-nurse named Mary Jane Kaufman, whose warm smile instantly made me feel at ease. She would be seeing me once a week for the four months I'd be at Goodwill and told me that if I needed anything at all, just to let her know. I liked this dark-haired, large-eyed woman immediately, for she obviously loved her work and cared about all of us.

It was already May of 1981 and I had recently turned twenty-six. After my week-long testing period, I was told that I had a problem with hand-eye co-ordination. (I wondered how I managed to play the piano for nine years if that was the case). I was also informed that I did well with word comprehension and pronunciation, not so stellar in math, and needed some assistance in the area of concentration.

I was sent to work in the plant, a large open area where people milled about in great numbers, sorting loads of used and donated clothing and other items into various categories, pricing them, salvaging the rejected materials, and running a noisy, smelly fork lift.

I was assigned to price clothes for "binning", which meant things like jeans, sweaters, t-shirts, shorts, underwear and night-gowns into various pricing groups. This required a lot of thought, so I was grateful not to be mindlessly tossing torn clothes onto a conveyor belt at least.

I was paired with a pleasant, thirty-eight-year-old woman with grey-flecked hair and a ready smile named Terrie. She'd been around this area for a long time and knew her prices down cold. She suffered from epilepsy and would take grand mal seizures in front of me. I was instructed to lay her head on the side and keep her as comfortable as possible when these occurred. Sharon hated anyone making a fuss over her and warned me not to try to catch her when she fell. "I'd crush the daylights out of you, kiddo," she said, grinning broadly.

I met some interesting people there in the dusty, busy plant. Della. was my age, a tiny, flighty woman who seemed to be off in her own little world and spoke inappropriately most of the time. I liked her, though, for she spoke fondly of her husband and little boy, Drew and asked for my advice on everything. I wasn't used to that.

Judy was thirty-one but looked much older. She was thin, pale and very serious, but every once in awhile her face would burst into a wide grin and she'd let her wonderful sense of humour escape. She had an appalling family life, with an abusive, alcoholic father who hit her so hard once that he put her into a coma for weeks.

Her mother couldn't handle the man and didn't offer any support to Judy. She became anorexic as a teenager and went down to a frightening low of fifty pounds. She still, fifteen years later, struggled with the disorder and was not able to maintain a normal weight. She lived on yogurt and fruit and always thought she was too fat, even though, at five foot six, she was only one hundred pounds.

Judy and I "adopted" Della and took her out to supper at Perry's Restaurant on Richmond Street. Soon the three of us hung together all the time, buoying one another's spirits and sharing stories of our checkered pasts. My life certainly hadn't been as horrendous as Judy's, however.

Gretchen was an extremely enthusiastic, sexually expressive twenty-three-year-old who was very attractive despite being over-weight, and had one exceedingly profane mouth. Lynda was constantly entertained by Joan's promiscuity and I think she really wished she could cast off her strict religious restraints and emulate her.

Doug was one of the oldest of our group, at fifty-five and was small, wiry, bespeckled man who had been hired at Goodwill because of a leg injury that didn't heal properly. "There's nothing wrong with my head, just in case you're wondering," he said quickly, "so don't go thinking I'm some kind of nut case."

Then there was the inimitable, outrageously hilarious Lillian. She's a book in herself. Lillian suffered from cerebral palsy and was confined to her wheelchair, had great difficulty speaking and was quite overweight. But she most certainly didn't let these "incidentals" stop her or squelch her vibrant, insatiable zest for life.

This forty-three-year-old powerhouse laughed so hard she often nearly fell out of her chair. She told raw, uncensored sex jokes, regaled us constantly about how sexually frustrated she was and absolutely refused to feel sorry for herself. She'd been married for years to a man named Jerry and had two daughters, one age eight and the other fifteen, a stunningly beautiful girl named Sara.

Lillian was crazy about her kids and despaired about being separated from them. They lived with their father, also a C.P., in Brampton, and whenever Hall and Oates' song "Sara Smile" came on the radio, Lillian would dissolve into tears and powerful, gut-wrenching sobs would rack her large body.

For all her jokes and laughter, she possessed a tragic side and I just adored her spirit and sense of feisty survival in a world that liked to cast people like herself aside. She worked hard at the plant, even though she'd get more money on a disability pension sitting at home. But that wasn't her style.

The majority of people employed at Goodwill were psychiatric patients and I recognized many from the L.P.H. They made less than minimum wage, under the rules of the Sheltered Workshop law, and I thought this was grossly unfair and exploitive. We had to work at a certain level there and were paid according to how much we accomplished.

The days were seven hours long and by the end of the first week, I was stiff and exhausted from standing for the entire length of time on a cement floor. I could hardly wait for my internship to be over.

However, as the weeks progressed, I began to really enjoy working there at the plant. My supervisor was a tall, slim, middle-aged woman named Doris Sullivan who had a great deal of respect for us and what we had to contend with. I talked to her a lot and listened to her words of wisdom. She was fair, honest and direct, the kind of person I would choose for a boss.

I moved out of my dingy, east end digs and into a semi-slum joint on Elmwood Avenue. It was a two-storey walk-up which had probably been a spectacular home in its day, circa 1920, but had fallen into disrepair in the early 1980's. Still, it had a living room, bedroom, kitchen and bathroom, and it was liveable. I rented a television and inherited some furniture from Mom, but I let the place get hopelessly cluttered and messy.

I began to suffer from my old nemesis, depression, early in July. I found it difficult to get myself up in the morning, and began to call in sick a lot. Judy came to visit quite frequently and urged me to eat, but I'd lost my appetite and was losing a lot of weight. When I reached ninety-three pounds, my mother began to hassle me about looking anorexic again, but I liked being thin and wearing children's clothes.

Mary Jane was getting concerned for my well-being and I talked to her about my past family life and spoke for the first time about how Mom and Dad's divorce had devastated me. I'd never acknowledged it before, but the dissolution of our family, even if it had been slightly dysfunctional, left me feeling empty. Now, with Mom seeing Steve so much and even planning on marrying him, it seemed as though we'd never be close again.

I began gravitating more toward Grandma and Grandpa and spent a lot of weekends with them in their apartment in Berkshire Village. It had been extremely hard on Grandpa when they were forced to move from his beloved childhood home on Talbot Street several years before, but the upkeep had become too much for them. First they moved to Albert Street, nearby, but left a year later for our old neighbourhood of Berkshire, to a smaller, newer apartment building. I don't think Grandpa ever truly adjusted to highrise living, but he got a great deal of pleasure from the television. As his health failed, it became his lifeline and an invaluable link to the outside world that he was denied.

I was still seeing Mr. Walters every Wednesday, which I found totally useless, and I was on the same medication I left the L.P.H. with. In August, Dr. Harrington increased my antidepressant to see if it would lift me out of my despondency that was choking the life out of me.

Mary Jane sometimes kept me in her office for two hours, trying to help me sort out what was making me feel so awful. I remember having no enthusiasm or spontaneity and thinking that I was just frittering my life away.

In September, I was sent to one of the Thrift Shops at 295 Richmond Street and I did not greet this news with open arms.I spent the first day hiding in the basement washroom, refusing to have anything to do with this new work setting. I'd gotten used to the plant and the other workers and always hated change of any kind. I'm one of the most maladaptive people I know, strongly holding firm to the familiar and the comfortable. Mary Jane said it was time to move on, for my placement would be over in a month and it was stipulated that I spend four weeks in a store.

I did get used to it, after several days. The manager was a small, curly-haired thirty-six-year-old woman named Shirley Hardy, who walked with great difficulty and used two canes. She was stricken with polio as a child and it affected her mobility as well as the strength of her feet. She was cheerful. level-headed and gave a damn about us. When Shirley looked intensely at you and asked "How are you?" she really meant it, not just as a flippant figure of speech.

I liked the other workers at the Richmond Street store as well. Melanie was tall and robust, with an infectious, hearty laugh and a wholesome, refreshing innocence. She took me under her wing and guided me through the store procedure, like sorting and hanging clothes when they came in off the truck each day, colour coding the items and assisting customers.

Cindy, a short, chubby forty-three-year-old practically shook the rafters when she laughed, which was almost non-stop, and liked to mother all of us. She, like Terrie, suffered from epilepsy and had the same non-chalance about it. She was wonderful with the customers and Shirley Hardy relied heavily on her to deal with the particularly difficult ones.

Wallace was only a few months away from retirement at sixty-four, and was a big, cheery bear of a man who had been in the psychiatric hospital for a long time and had a drinking problem. He liked to think and act much younger than his years and thought the world of Shirley Hardy. He had a gruff, throaty voice and a pleasant twinkle in his eyes. I knew I would get along well with him.

Linda was nineteen, an eager, pensive girl who worked diligently and possessed a quiet intensity that must have developed from her difficult past. She wanted to return to school in the near future, but was content, for the time being, to work at Goodwill. She never complained about anything, even when customers stayed way past closing time or whined about prices being too steep.

Ruth, forty-three, was terribly thin, with a delicate beauty and an excruciatingly shy demeanour. She chain-smoked and ate practically nothing, and I figured her to be anorexic until it was discovered that she had lung cancer.

The other male at the store was fifty-year-old Johnny, who was a dead ringer for Fred Astaire and had a rapier wit, sparkling blue eyes and a rather humble intelligence. He was well-read, admirably educated and I took to him immediately.

Then there was sixty-two-year-old Pamela, an absolute treasure. She had been born in England and still retained a distinctive British accent. She was tiny, with hardly a trace of grey in her curly dark hair and had deep, thought-provoking eyes that seemed to burrow right into your soul. She was a reliable and capable worker and despite a soft, genuine laugh, I sensed a definite sadness about her. Shirley Hardy told me that a lot of people didn't care much for Pamela because she could be blunt at times, but I never got that feeling from her.

So I settled in quite easily at the store and was just getting on to the routine when my month was up and Mary Jane informed me that my four-month period of assessment was completed.

I met with Mike Smith, who told me that the decision was to have me hired on at Goodwill as a sheltered employee. I was happy about this, for I'd grown fond of working and felt a close, communal spirit with the other employees. Mary Jane had assured me that I could learn a great deal and really needed the emotional support that a sheltered setting would provide.

I was also told that there would be a four-month waiting period before I could expect to be hired on permanently, but I was pleased to learn that I'd be working at one of the stores.

My income was still being provided by V.R.S., so I didn't have to worry about money. I spent the next four months writing short stories, listening to my records and going for long walks. I saw a great deal of Grandma and Grandpa, but little of Mom or Dad.

They were busy with their own lives, and Mom was placed in a rather awkward position by Steve, whose extreme possessiveness and jealously kept her basically barred from her family. But, she really needed the intimacy and security of a relationship, so she let him control and dominate her.

Dad lived alone in an apartment near Western and wasn't particularly happy or fulfilled. He was soon to meet someone, however, and Geogia Wayne would eventually become his second wife in the summer of 1983.

Jim was miles away in Vancouver, making a new life for himself, but was desperately homesick for Ontario. He had met a young woman, Pauline, and moved in with her and her menagerie of a large dog, several cats and two cockatiels.

I was still unattached, but secretly yearned for a boyfriend to fill a definite void in my life. I harboured a bit of regret about my failed relationship with Sam, but had no desire to see him again.

Shortly after the New Year in 1982, I got a call from Goodwill and was sent to work at the store at 908 Oxford Street. My first day was enveloped in a heavy snowstorm, so I left early and arrived before the other workers.

The manager, a short, stocky woman of thirty-eight, with close-cropped, straight, black hair and dark-rimmed glasses, met me at the front door and immediately began giving me a run-down on store procedures. She introduced herself as Elaine Kelsh and seemed very pleasant and easy-going.

I liked her no-nonsense approach and direct way of speaking. I sensed that she would expect a lot of hard work from her employees but would be fair and just.

The other two employees arrived shortly after, forty-year-old Janis and a tall, fiftyish woman who introduced herself as Tyne.

Janis was rather shy and somewhat introverted, but carried her tall, slender body with a certain amount of dignity. She wore her slate-grey hair short and had stylish glasses framing bright, alert eyes. Helen wore no make-up, but I figured she could do a great deal with rouge, lipstick and a new haircut.

Like Janis, Tyne had a dignified air about her, despite being affected by a facial twitch, which acted up whenever she was nervous or upset. She had this savvy way of smoking long, skinny cigarettes and could be very witty and caustic whenever the spirit moved her.

I found out that Tyne had been a nurse in Woodstock but "burned out" as she put it, ending up in the psychiatric wing at the general hospital. She and Helen seemed to get along very well, and I hoped that they wouldn't think that I was planning on interfering with their established friendship.

Working in a very small store was quite different from the large, two-room one at 295 Richmond Street. Our lunch breaks were fifteen minutes longer and there was a lot of time with little to do except fold clothes in the bins and rearrange the paperback books. I got quite bored after a few days, for there weren't as many customers here either and I craved some kind of external stimulation.

Elaine taught me all about cash register procedure, which I'd begun to learn at the other store. I was shown how to ring off and get all the money counted and ready for deposit at the bank each afternoon. This proved a welcome respite from the creeping numbness of standing around idle so much, trapped for eight hours a day in a small store while the snow piled up incessantly outside.

I befriended Janis, going with her next door to the donut shop for coffee and talking about rock music. I was happily surprised that she was so keen on it at her age I was a typical twenty-six-year-old, imagining that anyone forty or over to be stodgy and over the hill; I know better now. I promised to lend her some of my albums.

Unfortunately, Tyne saw me as coming between her and Janis, and took an extreme disliking to me. I didn't know why she was so openly hostile, however, and grew increasingly disturbed at her sarcastic comments.

My depression returned in full force as I felt more and more victimized, steeped in ennui from the deadly slow pace at this store and unhappy with my living conditions on Elmwood.

The landlord let the heater break down and wouldn't get it fixed. He was a drug addict and totally inept at looking after our building, and so I was forced to wear my winter coat, hat, and mitts indoors for weeks while the temperature dropped to the freezing point. On top of that, the gas stove went on the fritz, and I had to buy a hotplate to cook on. Unfortunately, when I plugged it in, the appliance shorted out everything and from then on I couldn't use it.

Dear Grandpa, emphysema, congestive heart and all, came trudging up the steep steps several times a week with hot food and coffee, even though I protested vehemently and said he was going to kill himself. His love for me transcended physical discomfort, though, and he persisted.

Finally, I couldn't take it anymore and made plans to move. I had no idea where I could find a place I could afford on Goodwill wages, but luckily, Grandma and Grandpa found me an adorable little one-bedroom apartment in a highrise in Westmount, just a couple of blocks from our old home on Village Green.

I was ecstatic, and decided to celebrate the victory by quitting smoking. So in May of 1982, I marked my last day of nicotine dependency, or so I thought at the time.

I also began running, something I'd wanted to take up for a long time, and would go over to the Saunders track every morning before work and run around the circuit five times. The first morning, I thought I'd die after making the first mile and a quarter distance and collapsed on the ground with terrible abdominal cramps. I swore I'd never submit myself to that again, but persisted nonetheless and even decided to join the YWCA. I felt good about adopting this new, healthy lifestyle and was beginning to feel like a real jock.

The running was lessening my depression, and I'd even experience a high after a half hour or so. My body got sleek and toned and I lost that nagging smoker's hack. At the Y, I met other runners and we'd all get together, doing four to six miles around the city.

We got together for Sunday Fun Runs and I was in awe of this girl who'd recently completed the Montreal Marathon. "I'd love to do one of those," I thought to myself, "just to see if I could finish."

In July I suffered my first injury and watched in horror as my left ankle swelled markedly and became painful to lean any weight upon. Linda, one of my running buddies, recommended a "running doctor" she'd gone to named Dr. Harris. I limped off to his office on Oxford and Wharncliffe.

Dr. Harris was a pleasant, good-natured man of about thirty-five, with youthful good looks and a curiously eccentric manner. He rattled off some ten-dollar medical term for what was wrong with my ankle and told me to stay off it for the next two weeks. I wasn't terribly thrilled about this, since I'd gotten quite addicted to running, but I obliged anyway.

Life at Goodwill continued to deteriorate. I spent a lot of time with Mary Jane, crying about how miserable I was there and asking if I could return to Richmond Street.

Finally, the tension between Tyne and I got so excruciating that I practically begged Elaine to transfer me. Well, a few strings were pulled and it was a very happy day when I arrived triumphantly at my old stomping ground with Pamela, Cindy, Melanie and the rest. I knew that there would be no personality conflicts here, as there never had been before.

I found out that Ruth had died following the removal of her cancerous lung, only a couple of days before I came back. Linda and I attended her funeral and I cried as her distraught young son stood over her as she lay in her coffin, remaining motionless for over half an hour.

I spent my week's holidays at Grandma and Grandpa's, enjoying their company, Grandpa's jokes, and going for long runs in nearby Springbank Park. They got me hooked on the soap, "The Young and the Restless" as well, and I must confess that I still watch it every single weekday.

Mom married Steve soon after my vacation and Karen came to town for the wedding. It was held in the family room of their new home, and when I cried, it wasn't for happiness, for I knew that not only would Mom's life be miserable, but I'd never get to see her much anymore.

There was certainly a lot more activity and work at Richmond Street than the soporific store at Oxford. Some days were crazy, as a matter of fact, especially the "Bonus Weekends" at the end of the month. Everything was twenty per cent off and the store would simply be crawling with enthusiastic, often pushy, customers. Sometimes I got pretty rattled on the cash register, but Pamela would always come up to help me out.

One day, we got a new employee, twenty-nine-year-old Dennis I was immediately struck by his darkly intense good looks, with large, melancholy brown eyes and shy grin. He suffered from rheumatoid arthritis and had difficulty walking and was unhappy about his condition. It was extremely painful at time and required him to take Valium to relax his muscles. I liked him from the outset, so it wasn't long before we began going out together and engaging in a wild ride of a relationship.

Dennis, like myself, adored music, and regaled me with tales of his misspent youth doing drugs and listening to earsplitting acid rock. He lived in an impressive highrise across from Fanshawe College and the two of us spent a lot of time there, drinking, listening to his vast record collection and talking far into the night.

As our relationship grew stronger, I resisted the temptation to sleep with him, fearing pregnancy as always. Dennis was patient, however, but reminded me every once in awhile that his doctor had prescribed lots of sex for his arthritis.

One night, as we sat kissing passionately on my couch, I let it slip that I was in love with him. Well, this was not a good idea, for it put him on the spot and made him feel very awkward.

Things deteriorated rapidly after that. He made snide comments about my weight, saying that, although I wasn't fat, I was not the prototype of the skinny runner. This really made me angry, and I quickly lost ten pounds and revelled in his dismay. "Well, you told me I was a fat pig," I smirked, "so just shut your face."

Dennis' drinking, which had always been excessive, worsened and the effect of the alcohol was intensified by the Valium. One night, we got into a heated argument after he surmised that I was a brazen slut because I had been on the Pill at university. This was too much for me, so I left. It seemed odd that I did that, however, since we'd been in my living room and I walked out of my own apartment.

After walking around Westmount Mall for a couple of hours, I returned to find him quite inebriated and crying. I felt bad, so we made up and ended up in bed together. Somehow the idea of getting pregnant wasn't as frightening as losing Rob.

Even after we mended a few fences, our relationship was never the same again. We broke up shortly after, but I never really stopped loving him. Then, in 1991, I learned that he had died of alcohol poisoning, alone and in a slum in the east end of the city. He was steeped in booze and pills, evicted from his nice apartment and estranged from his family.

I guess he just gave up after losing these things, along with his job and self-respect. He had been driving a fork lift at GM Diesel and then had slid into a gutter of despair. I felt very sad for such a pitiful end to a tragic life.

Pamela and I spent a lot of weekends together at her place that she shared with her boyfriend. She told me all about her childhood in Britain and how she'd driven an ambulance in World War II during the blitzkrieg, as bombs exploded all around her and people screamed and moaned in the chaotic streets. She was still haunted by these terrible memories, and they permanently scarred her psyche.

She married after the war ended and bore a son whom she adored. He now lived in the states with his wife and Pamela's two grandchildren. Her eyes misted over when she talked about her family, most of whom she rarely saw. Her husband died years before and she hadn't remarried. She met her current sweetheart several years before, but unfortunately, he had a serious drinking problem and she spent a lot of time caring for him. Still, Pamela felt she needed someone to share her life with, so she put up with his alcoholic binges.

We watched our favourite show, "Simon and Simon" together, and I endured her country music. It seemed that everyone at Goodwill loved this genre above all others and I was forced to have my poor eardrums assaulted with the whiny strains of BX-93 (our country music radio station) all day the store.

In the early summer of 1983, I met Dad's girlfriend, Georgia Wayne, for the first time, soon after hearing that he was going to marry her in July. I was somewhat shocked, since I hadn't realized he was that serious about her, but I couldn't help breathing a sigh of relief that he'd no longer be exiled in loneliness.

Georgia was a small, thin woman of forty-one with short, black hair, dark eyes and a friendly, genuine grin. She seemed extremely excitable and was nervous about meeting me, though she needn't have been. She had three daughters, Denise, sixteen, Lorna, fourteen, and twelve-year-old Marianne. They were pleasant, engaging youngsters with three very distinctive personalities and appearances. Denise was plump, strikingly attractive, with long, curly brown hair and a very European look.

Georgia was Armenian, and had a very dark complexion and high cheekbones, which Denise had inherited. She was a rather shy, quiet teenager, concerned about her weight and eager to lose a lot of it. She was politically conscious, concerned about things like nuclear war and the environment, and spent a lot of time thinking and brooding about life and her future.

She had a learning disability, but had overcome it with a lot of patient help from Georgia and was attending H.B. Beal Secondary School. Her mother worried about Denise's obsession with dieting, since she herself had weighed over two hundred pounds at one time. She subsequently lost half her weight through semi-starvation and manic energy expenditure and didn't want her daughter to follow in her footsteps.

Lorna was the introverted, mysterious one, who didn't take to very many people but latched strongly and securely onto Dad right from the beginning. She spent a lot of time in her room playing Dungeons and Dragons and loved to be alone.

Marianne, blonde and blue-eyed, was energetic, perky and a bit obnoxious, but I chalked that up to her youth. She was as outgoing as Erica was inwardly drawn and had a very healthy self-image.

They had two cats, a big grey and white male named Smokey and a sleek, black female called Sonja. They looked almost identical to our two cats from the 1970's, and I did a double take when they came sauntering into the family room. Dad said that he felt that he was living his life over again.

Dad and Georgia got along very well in those days. It was gratifying to see my father looking happy, relaxed and contented, and he even confided to me that he had now found a sense of inner peace" with Linda and the girls.

Just before Dad got married, I travelled by plane to Richardson, Texas to visit my Aunt Elizabeth and Uncle Ray. I had a good time, with my cousin Sue there as well with her three little boys. She and her family were staying there for a month and I was there for two, getting re-acquainted with a woman I hadn't spent any time with since 1971, when I was anorexic in Rhode Island.

Mom was in the middle of a separation from Steve, so while I was in Texas, I was quite concerned about her and it put a bit of a damper on the trip. Uncle Ray sensed my unhappiness and did his quiet, compassionate best to cheer me up. I really did need to get away, though.

1983 was also the summer I met the incomparable Marybeth Skeoch, to whom I would become extremely close. She burst onto the Goodwill scene with a tumultuous flourish, with her fiercely independent spirit, mean sense of humour, and a strong distaste for authority. She went through the V.R.S. machine as I had, and balked at the idea of working in a sheltered workshop.

Marybeth had a learning disability along with an uncomfortable muscle weakness in her legs and after a disastrous experience at the Westervelt Business Schools she agreed to an assessment at Goodwill in hopes of getting into Fanshawe College.

Her learning disability hadn't been diagnosed until her last couple of years at Oakridge Secondary School, where she was ridiculed by students and teachers alike and told she was stupid, inferior and lazy. After the system discovered Marybeth's problem, they sent her to Weable where she was able to learn and comprehend her studies.

At first, doctors thought her weak muscles were due to myasthenia gravis, but later ruled that out. She had been born a blue baby and could not sit on her own without being propped up on pillows as a small child. Marybeth also suffered from hyperthyroidism as well as severe asthma and allergies, but this girl refused to feel the least bit sorry for herself and scoffed at anyone who dared to. Several years later she would be diagnosed with Addison's Disease, which causes the adrenal glands to cease functioning. Doctors put her on Cortisone and she's typically matter-of-fact about this life-threatening illness.

After work, Marybeth and I would drink pop at Perry's Restaurant, where we'd be happy to shed our blue store smocks and talk about things we enjoyed, like music, writing, movies and sailing (she was an avid sailor, spending weekends on her father's boat and learning all she could about the art of skimming a craft over the waves).

She was twenty-one and was shocked to discover that I was seven years her senior, as I didn't even look twenty. I told her I had no hang-ups about having younger friends as long as she didn't mind being seen with an "old broad", and she merely laughed and shook her curly head.

Marybeth had a rough time at Richmond Street, as Shirley Hardy got her to do the jobs that no-one else wanted. The worst of these was colour-coding the winter coats, because not only were there dozens of them, but they were non-descript shades that defied categorization. They were also heavy and awkward, and as soon as she got a few ordered the right way, a customer would come along and move them. Whenever she was given a dumb chore, Marybeth would airily reply, "no problem" but I knew that secretly she was extremely pissed. She wouldn't give Shirley the satisfaction of knowing this, however.

She found that there was one corner of the store that the manager couldn't see from the glass-encased office, so she crouched there a lot of the time and read the books she was supposed to be sorting. I walked by every so often and winked at her, asking with a smile, "Having fun alphabetizing the paperbacks, M.B.?"

She liked this nickname, even though "Marybeth" was all one word. "It either means my name, Milton Bradley or "Made in Britain" she'd say periodically.

She loved the group, The Police, particularly Sting, and

jumped for joy when Synchronicity finally came out. She introduced me this engaging reggae music, along with Duran Duran, whom I'd dismissed as a "teenybopper band" previously.

Things were going pretty well at Richmond Street until I got a nasty stress fracture in my left leg and was off work for a month. Everytime I walked on it, the damn leg swelled up to twice its size and was extremely painful. Dr. Harris said it was from excessive running, for I'd been doing eight to ten miles a day up until the injury.

Then, just as the fracture was beginning to heal, I broke my foot doing aerobics in my living room early one Sunday, to Barry Manilow of all singers, and had to call Grandma to drive me to emergency to have it X-rayed. I knew I'd broken it by the sickening popping noise that ripped into the air when my foot twisted under me. They put it in a heavy cast and I was quite miserable, to say the least.

It wasn't a walking cast, so I couldn't work at the store anymore. Mary Jane told me that if I got a ride to and from work from Paratransit, I could come back to the plant.

The last thing I wanted was to be stuck in that sweatshop again, but I had no choice if I wanted to keep my job. M.B. was distressed that she'd be stuck at the store without me. When her assessment was up in December, she enrolled at Fanshawe College as she'd planned.

I became very depressed at being disabled, even if it was only temporary, and work at the plant was not nearly as fulfilling and exciting as it had been at Richmond Street.

The Paratransit van picked me up late every morning and kept me waiting at least an hour after work. I had to take a reduction in wages with the missed time and fewer hours per week at the plant as opposed to the store.

I worked with Terrie and Lillian in bin pricing, which was something positive anyway. Lillian and I talked a lot, made a great deal of crass jokes and helped one another through various emotional crises. She'd been living with one of the plant employees named Dave, a thin, trembly man with no teeth, a hyperactive, jittery personality and a great love for his "woman".

They complimented one another perfectly, for he assisted her with physical difficulties, and she provided a strong emotional support for him. I loved watching them together and hoped that one day, they'd marry and feel really connected.

It was about this time that I got involved with the peace movement and became politically active for the first time in my self-absorbed life. Camille, the office supervisor at the plant, was a longtime member of Ploughshares and I spent a great deal of time discussing the alarming arms race with her. I'd always feared nuclear anhillation, but now it seemed imminent, and this was reflected in the media. There had been a resurgence of people's fear with regard to the real and possible threat of nuclear war. Demonstrations involving civil disobedience were now erupting all over the world.

I went to my first Ploughshares meeting with Camille and listened while earnest and concerned men, women and teenagers talked openly about what could be done to halt the build-up of the atomic arsenal and make the public more aware of how our government was greatly contributing to the arms race.

Since Ronald Reagan took office in 1981, the situation was becoming critical. He fed the American public's paranoia about the Soviet Union and how they must prepare for a possible confrontation with the other superpower.

I despised everything that Reagan stood for and marvelled at a country who would elect a B-movie actor as President. He was obviously on some bizarre power trip and revelling in the glory of being the most influential human being in the governmental offices of the world. He didn't come across as particularly intelligent or intuitive and seemed to need wife Nancy to do his thinking for him. The guy was an inveterate loser as far as I was concerned.

Canada didn't have a lot of clout and was extremely uneasy about our ineffectual leaders. The world was most definitely going to hell in a handcart.

So, in November, I decided to go to Toronto alone and protest at the Litton Plant. This place made guidance systems for Cruise Missiles and I was prepared to get arrested if necessary to make my point against a company contributing to world destruction.

I was very naive and overly idealistic, and Camille warned me not to struggle if I was attacked by guards or police officers. I wasn't afraid, because I wanted to do something worthwhile for the first time in my screwed up life.

Unfortunately, by the time I got to the Litton Plant, the

demonstration was over, and all the people who trespassed on the grounds had been taken away in a police trailer. I had stupidly taken the subway in the opposite direction and missed all the action.

I began to talk to several of the guards about Ploughshares, and one of them exploded in anger at me, calling me a "fucking lunatic" and a "twisted radical who should be shot". It seems that a group of extremists bombed a building recently where his friend lived and he had been killed.

I tried to tell him that Ploughshares was a peaceful movement and didn't subscribe to any kind of violence, but he refused to listen to me and proceeded to kick the hell out of the fence where I was standing. It's obvious he would have done the same to me if I'd jumped over it. I was still rather shaken by all this anger and suddenly realized that this wasn't a game anymore. It was frighteningly real.

I phoned my cousin Joanie, who lived in downtown Toronto, and stayed at her place for the night. She was pleased that I was becoming politically active, but I deleted my experiences with the hostile guard.

That evening, I watched a twenty-year anniversary special on the assassination of John F. Kennedy and suddenly realized that it was November twenty-second. I cried as I watched the young, eager President giving speeches of hope to his adoring public, and the terrible day of November 1963 came rushing back like a putrid, choking cesspool. What would Kennedy think about Reagan being in the White House and inching toward a global holocaust?

The next day, I went to a church nearby where people from various peace movements gathered to get medication and messages to friends and family members locked up for engaging in the Litton protest the day before. The atmosphere was sombre and subdued, and they all looked like battle-weary soldiers who've seen and experienced too much.

I wanted to go to the prisoners' hearing, but was denied access to the courtroom, so after some time with Joanie's twins, Timon and Emily, I returned to London.

I kept attending Ploughshares meetings after that initiation into the world of peaceful demonstrating, such as it was, but felt we weren't united enough to be effective. There was a great deal of arguing and disagreement among Ploughshares members, and some were quite unpleasant. One woman, a young mother with a chip on her shoulder, wanted to do something to "shake everybody up" like creating a mass riot downtown, all in the name of peace. I thought this was rather ludicrous.

One young man, Darcy, looked like the quintessential 60's renegade, with long, limp hair, a scruffy beard and granny glasses which must have been bought in a pawn shop in 1968. He was my age, unemployed, and wore army fatigues. I liked him, for he had an interest in playing guitar and writing songs about peace. I thought he seemed oddly out of place in the hip and flashy 1980's, but that made him even more appealing to me.

A few of us broke off and went to one another's homes to talk about ways we could change the world for the better, and ran our own seminars. They were mostly young, male and intellectual, many attending Western. I told them I wasn't nearly as dedicated as they were when I was in university, though I wish I had been. Maybe things would have turned out differently.

One of the guys had an album by a band I'd never heard of before, called simply R.E.M. The record was "Murmur" and I liked the refreshing, altogether different sound that went completely against the synthesized-unto-death stuff that assailed the airwaves in late 1983. I borrowed it and played the songs over and over, wondering if 1984 would finally be the year I got it together and changed the course of my rutted little life.

The 1980's had begun with the tragic death of John Lennon,and I remember thinking, on December tenth, 1980, as I wept and listened to "Imagine" playing over and over on the radio at the Satellite workshop, that an era in both music and our consciences, had come to an end. Now it was a new world we were esconsed in and I hoped that it would signal the beginning of a kinder, more gentle time in our history.

There had just been far too many deaths of good, peace loving people during my quarter century on earth, and I didn't know if I could deal with anymore. Perhaps it wouldn't be nuclear missiles that did us in, but rather, we would destroy one another with our bare hands. It was time to look inward at our own sullied souls.

## Chapter Thirteen

# 1984-1987: The Years
# That Live In Infamy

Somewhere toward the end of 1983, I began a vigorous regimen of exercise, rising at four thirty AM, doing an hour of strenuous calisthenics, followed by a ninety-minute run around Springbank Park. I returned to the apartment at seven, totally exhausted, took a quick shower, dressed and grabbed a small breakfast before catching the Westmount bus downtown. Then it was a transfer to the Dundas, which got me to First Street by seven forty-five.

Then, after working all day, I went to the Y for two hours, took the bus home at seven PM, and was often too tired to eat. I would, instead, lose myself in my gigantic record collection and new library of books.

Along with the manic exercising, I'd begun a program of voracious reading. I amassed quite a collection of biographical works from Goodwill, with such illustrious and controversial subjects as Judy Garland, Montgomery Clift, Lenny Bruce, Margaret Sullivan and Sylvia Plath, with her autobiographical work, "The Bell Jar".

With this bizarre schedule of running myself ragged and forgoing eating for book devouring, I began to lose a substantial amount of weight and by the end of November, was beginning to look somewhat haggard and wraithlike. This suited my anorexic mindset just fine, and I made a pact with myself to get down to ninety pounds by the end of January.

Mary Jane wasn't pleased, to say the least, and didn't approve of me reading so many books about tragic and maladjusted people, all of whom had ended up quite dead for one reason or another.

I saw a bit of myself in Montgomery Clift, Margaret Sullivan and Sylvia Plath and got insidiously drawn into their unhappy, psychologically fragmented worlds. I became very comfortable with my self-destructive lifestyle and avoided my feelings of guilt produced by it, by totally immersing myself in the psyches of people much worse off than myself.

Georgia's psychiatrist and friend, Dr. William Kiel, became my therapist at this time as well. He was a big, dishevelled, blustery man with unkempt, whitish hair, an endearingly dissipated face and a manner that was both self-deprecating and engaging. I liked him at once, for he wasn't adverse to using four-letter words to make a point and treated me as an equal, not a subhuman mental case.

I saw him in his office at Victoria Hospital, on the seventh floor, every Tuesday afternoon after work. He told me that patients such as myself were basically a "pain in the ass", because we were difficult to diagnose and didn't fit into any psychiatric category. He was a breath of fresh air from the stodgy, uptight Walters, and I was tremendously relieved to have finally severed ties with the L.P.H.

As my weight dropped, however, Dr. Kiel started getting on my case and told me I looked like something out of a concentration camp. "Jeez, all you need is a shaved head and striped pyjamas," was his witty comment to me one afternoon in early January.

I continued to be a member of Ploughshares, but was tiring of the bureaucratic bullshit. There were too many people vying for control of everything, so my visits to the headquarters at the Cultural Learners Centre were becoming less frequent.

By the end of January, 1984, my eating disorder had spun was out of control and I was read the riot act: "You're coming into the hospital before you damn well kill yourself". Grant was adamant and I knew that I had little recourse. I was eating practically nothing and my face had completely sunk in, making me look older than my twenty-eight years. I hadn't had my period in several months and had made the fatal mistake of relating that to Nelson.

So before I could even spit, I was once again an in-patient, on the seventh floor of Victoria Hospital, and handed over to the care of a Dr. Chandarana, who specialized in anorexia nervosa and bulimia.

I hated it there at first, as they put me on this program that smacked ominously of behaviour modification and was told that I had to gain a kilogram in a week or there would be hell to pay. They had this clever little system whereby you were weighed twice a week, and once a week was called your "anniversary weight". If you didn't reach your goal, you were given no privileges and could kiss any chances of getting released before you reached retirement age good-bye.

I met several other anorexics on the ward. Nancy was twenty-seven, an outwardly cheerful young woman who had reduced her weight from a whopping two hundred pounds to a whippet one hundred and six. She looked very thin and wizened, and I figured her to be closer to forty than twenty-seven.

She had lived on oatmeal and Diet Coke for a year to lose all the weight, and was not terribly excited about having to gain twenty pounds here at the hospital. She despised the notion of eating, and said that it had been sheer hell to starve herself in half. "I'll be damned if I'm going to gain it all back again," she moaned one night in her room. "I work at McDonald's and was so happy when I went from the largest uniform size to the smallest. Everyone there cheered me on, and now here I am being forced to eat six times a day. I won't do it, that's all."

Hope was twenty, a skinny, attractive blonde with terrible acne who lost sixty pounds by bingeing and purging. When I met her, she was attached to an I.V. feeding Potassium Chloride into her depleted body. "They told me they'll take this out when the vomiting stops," she said sadly, "but I don't think it ever will. I used to be a size thirteen and now I'm a five. I like it. I enjoy eating whatever I want and not suffering for it. How do you give that up?"

Donna was the thinnest of all of us, weighing a mere eighty-five pounds. She was a restrictor anorexic, like myself, and was absolutely terrified of eating. She'd been anorexic since the age of seventeen and hadn't been a normal weight for more than a year of the past ten. "I hate being fat," she said, clenching her bony fist, "I weighed one hundred twenty-five two years ago and hated myself. Never again." She was short, had thinning, brown hair and large, melancholy eyes. I thought she was about thirteen when I first met her.

Life on the seventh floor became a series of mind games with the nurses and Dr. Chandarana. He was East Indian, a kindly, soft-spoken man of about thirty-five who genuinely cared about his patients. Still, I couldn't help but be annoyed at the way these staff members tried to control us, monitoring everything we ate, checking our weights religiously and forbidding any exercise.

I looked longingly at the exercise bike in the lounge and thought, "I'll sneak an hour's ride whenever they're not looking."

But they always were.

After a week, another anorexic appeared on the scene, twenty-four-year-old Frannie. She was emaciated and her effervescent personality belied a tortured, anguished soul. She cried bitterly over the phone at night to a husband who continuously dominated and demeaned her. I could see why she was so self-starved: What other control did she have other than the one involving her body size and weight?

I went nowhere with my weight for several weeks, terrified of mushrooming into a hideous blob if I consumed the calorie-laden trays that were constantly pushed in front of me. I decided not to eat any meat, as it was so high in fat, and asked for primarily vegetables and fruit.

Chandarana said that those items were too low in calories, but I assured him that I would consume rice and potatoes if it was demanded of me. So my first foray into vegetarianism had nothing to do with my compassion or concern for animals, but simply my own desire to stay slim. I'm not really proud to admit that, by the way.

Nancy began to eat more as the days wore on, simply because her husband was hassling her half to death about being in the hospital. He even coerced her to consume a half pint of Jamoca almond fudge ice cream, but she balked when he offered her regular Coke. "I do have to maintain some standards," she said curtly.

Her history was not a pleasant one. She'd been repeatedly molested by her older brother as a child, and currently despised him. Her parents were basically useless, being too wrapped up in their own rampant neuroses to be of any support to a tormented girl who felt her life was not in her own hands.

Nancy also suffered from horrendous migraine headaches and was plagued with them during her time in the hospital. She'd vomit continuously for hours and couldn't tolerate any light or noise. I'd had several migraines in my life as well, but not as severe or debilitating as hers. My heart went out to a woman who never seemed to get a break.

Hope was on a real binge/purge cycle, consuming ridiculous quantities of food in the dining room and then immediately retiring to her room to rid herself of every morsel. The nurses soon caught onto this activity, however, and forced her to sit out front with the clerical clerk for an hour after each meal. She began to starve herself after that, and lost even more weight. Her clothes literally hung on her and I feared for her life.

As for me, well, I got a terrible case of the flu one week and threw up for three days, losing eight pounds in the process. I was told that if I didn't start improving, I'd be sent to the L.P.H. I thought this to be grossly unfair, for I didn't know how I was supposed to keep food down when my system was constantly rebelling.

However, after two and a half months, I gained enough weight to be allowed full privileges, but not after a lot of despair about having no control anymore. I really wanted to be released from the hospital and resume my running, so the only way for that to happen was to do as I was told. It was a happy day, indeed, when Dr. Chandarana said I could start doing it again.

I'd been riding the exercise bike for several weeks for an hour at a time, listening to Duran Duran and the Go-Go's on the Walkman I'd gotten for Christmas. When my weight reached one hundred five pounds, I was allowed to run six miles a day, provided I ate enough to maintain and didn't start plumetting again.

The other patients on the ward were a mixed and varied lot. There was a young, nineteen-year-old boy from Iceland who didn't speak a word for weeks and was terrified of everyone and everything. It was gratifying to see him come alive and join the world again. I talked to him a lot, and he wanted me to come to his country one day to meet his family.

There was another young mother who suffered from manic depressive illness and felt extremlley guilty that her six-year old daughter had to be placed in the Children's Village orphanage while she was hospitalized. She was from Britain, had a very pronounced accent and smoked like a chimney. I admired her spirit, and brazen zest for life. She spoke of her psychiatrist, Dr. Max, as if he were some kind of god. I told her I didn't share her enthusiasm for shrinks, although I thought William Kiel was pretty cool.

Then there was Lainie, an overweight, melancholy woman who just couldn't shake herself out of a life long depression and kept herself going by helping other patients. I liked her, but she played a lot of head games and was extremely manipulative with the staff. In retrospect, I believe that Lainie suffered from Borderline Personality Disorder just like myself. It's funny how you don't always see yourself in someone else right away.

I finally got sprung from the seventh floor in April, shortly before my twenty-ninth birthday. I was relieved and felt somewhat triumphant, but secretly harboured some resentment about having to gain twenty pounds and lose my super-thin status.

As the spring wore on, I decided to train for the Kingston Triathlon. This was an ambitious undertaking, since it involved two kilometres of swimming, fifty kilometres of biking and a fifteen kilometre run. I'd been swimming regularly at the Y pool prior to my hospitalization and rode my bike everywhere. Of course, the running was a constant thing, so it didn't seem out of my reach to take part in this endurance test.

I decided to swim two miles a day, which wasn't difficult, and bike at least ten. I returned to running nine miles around Springbank Park each morning and by the middle of June was in top form.

I was extremely pumped for this event and other athletes at the Y encouraged me, saying that anyone with my fierce determination should have no problem finishing the Triathlon and may even have a chance at making the top fifty or so. I doubted this, since I wasn't a fast swimmer or runner, but basked in their admiration and awe nonetheless. It was quite the ego trip for someone who had felt like a total loser for the past seven years.

After some initial difficulties, involving getting my bike on the train in one piece, I made the journey to Kingston and tried to register at one of the residences at Queen's University where most of the other athletes were booked. However, it was full, and since there was a big convention also going on that weekend, I had a difficult time finding a hotel. I finally found a tiny, hot room downtown and left my bike in the lobby.

When I arrived at the grounds at six AM, I discovered that I needed a bicycle helmet, but luckily someone loaned me a hockey helmet as a cheap substitute. I had sworn I'd never go near one of those things after the Behaviour Modification experience, but I was desperate to be entered in the race after coming all that way and training so hard.

I was extremely nervous, trembling and feeling nausasted and fortunately I'd met another scared rabbit like myself before the carbo-loading meal the night before. His name was Mike and he offered companionship and support.

After getting a number scrawled on my upper arms, legs and back with a black magic marker and leaving my bike and clothes in an enclosed area, I made my way down to the shores of Lake Ontario to await the start of the race. The water looked rather choppy, and I wondered if swimming in a lake would be much more difficult than in a pool.

There were hundreds of people in this Triathlon, all looking threateningly capable and self-assured. "What the hell are you doing here?" I thought with a feeling of dread exploding in my gut.

As soon as the starting gun fired, the adrenaline hit hard and I swam vigorously and well, but caught my arms and legs in various clumps of seaweed. Aside from that incident, the swim went well, but left me feeling slightly winded. As I ran toward the area where my clothes and bike were, I realized that I would definitely not be one of the first finishers, as it looked as if almost everyone else had been there and gone already.

The bike ride was sheer hell, as there were many long, steep hills on the highway and the wind was dead against us for half the distance. I looked sideways and caught sight of the Milhaven Penitentiary and wondered if any volatile prisoners were planning an escape at that moment.

During one of my water stops, a woman approached with a microphone and asked me how I was feeling. I replied, "Great. It's a good race," or something to that effect. Then, as she stood watching, I fell off my bike after starting off again, and was extremely embarrassed. So much for fame, I thought morosely.

Finally, after what seemed like eons, the bike race was over, and my leg muscles felt as though they were on fire. God, now I've got to run almost ten miles! I thought dismally.

Well, I nearly didn't make it, for the run, like the cycling, was predominantly uphill. My body screamed for a release from this idiocy. As I climbed a particularly steep incline, another microphone was shoved in my hot, sweat-soaked face.

"Think you'll finish?" a chirpy newsperson asked from a white van.

"Yeah, no problem," I responded. Then, she started interviewing me, asking where I was from and if this was my first race.

I obliged her breathlessly and continued on until I finally saw the blessed finish line. When the race was over, I was doused with several pails of cold water and presented with a gold medal. What a terrific feeling it was! I hobbled around for a few minutes, revelling in the victory that I really wasn't sure would actually happen.

On the train ride back, I sat with a very hyped triathlete, whose whole life revolved around training, training, and more training. "My girlfriend helps me out a lot. She understands how much this means to me," he enthused.

I smiled, and said I just wanted to see if I could accomplish a goal that I'd set several months before. It was one of the happiest days of my life.

In September, I took a plane to Vancouver to spend two weeks with my brother and Sharon. It was a good time, getting reacquainted with Jim and seeing how he'd established a life for himself on the West coast. He was working in a lab at the University of British Columbia after studying pharmacology, but he seemed somehow unfulfilled and restless. Jim really wanted to be a doctor and was disappointed at being passed over for the past four years. I told him that if he wanted it that badly, he should persist, but he was growing rather pessimistic.

Sharon was quiet and intense, a mixture of Canadian and Chinese, who loved my brother and seemed to enjoy looking out for him. I thought that she put a wall up around her, though, and wouldn't really let me in. Her dog, Pippin had just given birth to eight adorable puppies and I spent a lot of time cuddling them. I ran between eight and ten miles a day and went to Chinatown, Granville Island and Grouse Mountain. Running around Stanley Park was breathtaking and invigorating. They lived in Kitsilano Beach and I got drunk with the beauty of the ocean and those majestic mountains.

I met some of their friends, such as Josie, Jason and Mario, as well as Raven, a young lesbian friend of Sandy's, who took a liking to me and to whom I felt drawn. My old bisexual tendencies flared up again but I squelched them out of guilt and shame. "Can't get into any of that," I thought to myself.

When I returned to London at the end of September, my world exploded into horror and despair. Grandpa was hospitalized with severe emphysema and heart failure and for the first time, I was faced with the grim reality that he might not be around very much longer.

He was placed in the cardiac intensive care unit at St. Joseph's

Hospital, where they hooked him up to a lot of tubes, wires and machines. I shuddered when I walked into the room and saw a breathing tube in his mouth and going down his throat. My beloved grandfather was fighting for his life.

Mom was in a terrible state, as was Grandma, and I felt numb and weak in the knees. He couldn't speak because of the breathing tube so we got him a stylus and pad to write messages on.

One night, Mom and I decided to stay all night with Grandpa, and the nurses obliged us kindly. They were terrific, so filled with compassion and caring, and I wondered how they managed to work in such a depressing, emotionally debilitating environment. Mom said the burn-out rate for I.C.U. nurses was very high and I believed it.

We didn't sleep that night, even though a room with two lazy-boy chairs was provided. Mom and I kept wandering into Grandpa's room, watching him and talking, crying, and imploring him to let go. You see, he didn't want to leave his dear family and felt terrible that he would somehow be deserting us if he died. We stood there sobbing and said, "Please, if it's your time, let go. Don't hang on for us. It's not fair."

Grandpa burst into tears, silently, as he couldn't make any sounds, and the salty water rolled down his pale cheeks. Mom and I cried along with him that night as we gave that wonderful, life-affirming man the permission to die.

Doctors removed the breathing tube the next day, after telling Mom, Grandma and I that it would be fatal. He was moved to a room in palliative care, and when we left that night, we had said our good-byes. Grandpa looked lovingly at Mom and said quietly, "Thank you for everything you've done for me."

But he didn't die that night, nor the day after. In fact, for the next while, this phenomenal human being literally thrived, savouring cups of tea, eating with his familiar gusto, and singing, "Happy days are here again."

Jim had come home, ostensibly for a funeral, and instead sat in Grandpa's hospital room while the two of them engaged in non-stop jokes.

The only down side to this was that I got pneumonia and Mom suffered a severe case of septicemia, which we likely contracted when spending that night in the C.C.U. I wasn't too ill, but Mom had to be hospitalized herself and nearly died, Fortunately, she got better, but not after giving all of us a major scare.

Grandpa got released from the hospital after his doctor said it was a "miracle" and I thought happily, "He's going to make it. It's all over. Thank you, God."

Suddenly, my faith in the Lord was restored after lagging for many years. The night we said farewell to Grandpa, I lay in Ingrid's room and prayed for hours, "Dear God, please, please give him one more month. One more month to enjoy life, eat, watch television and be happy."

And it seemed that He had delivered. I was ecstatic, and when Grandpa came back to his home in the Chelsea Park Rest Home, I knew that a miracle had truly occurred.

Well, after five weeks or so, Grandpa started going downhill again. He couldn't catch his breath, and felt extremely uncomfortable and panicky. I visited him a few times and despaired at his anxiety and disquietude.

Then, on November fourteenth, the phone rang at my house. I didn't answer it, for I knew what it was about. I had dreamt the night before that my dear Grandfather had died. It rang again, then again several hours later. I thought that if I didn't respond to it, the nightmare would somehow vanish.

I looked at the telephone as it went off once more and cringed as I finally was forced to pick up the receiver at two PM. "Grandpa's gone" was all Mom had to say. That's all she had to say. The bottom fell out of my chest and I dissolved in tears that wouldn't subside for weeks.

The funeral was excruciating, with Grandpa looking so different and strange in his casket. I stood there, trying desperately to warm his cold hands with mine. I sobbed continuously, while friends and family filed in to pay their respects to a truly unique man who would never laugh, drink, tell jokes or comfort me again.

My Uncle Lin, a loving, dear soul, took me in his lap at the funeral home and held me for hours as I sobbed uncontrollably. I don't know what I would have done without him.

Dad and Georgia were great, very supportive and strong. I even crawled into Dad's lap, something I'd never done as a child, and he held me close with all the loving I'd missed and craved for so long. God I adore him for that. It meant the world to me on the worst day of my entire life.

Christmas was deadly, and Grandma was still in shock from

her tremendous loss. We all simply went through the motions, and didn't even have Jim there for much-needed moral support. I thought that life as I knew it had ceased to exist.

Early in 1985 I bought R.E.M.'s "Reckoning" and let the music sink into my weary bones. It seemed appropriate to be playing the album, as my time of reckoning had arrived. I would either survive or wither away with the winter gusts of wind.

I had told Lillian about Grandpa's death and she burst into tumultuous sobs. She knew how much he had meant to me and it was incredible how sympathetic this woman was to other people's suffering. I hugged her tightly and said quietly, "I'll be okay. Don't worry, kid".

Work became something to distract me from the pain, and I threw myself into it with a vengeance. I hadn't completely recovered from my pulmonary problems and had stopped exercising. I began to gain weight and despised the way I looked. By the spring I was twenty pounds heavier than I'd been when I did the Kingston Triathlon.

I played my records a great deal and had become quite enamoured with Daryl Hall and John Oates. Their music was upbeat and positive to help snap me out of my severe depression. I'd always deemed them to be frivolous and vacuous, nothing like the deep, reflective R.E.M. But maybe what I needed was something frivolous and vacuous

I got back to the Goodwill stores in April of 1985 and worked at the furniture store on Horton Street. It wasn't the ideal setting, since I really wanted to be back at 295 Richmond, but it was a lot better than the plant.

Unfortunately, I suffered a major back injury in July after lifting heavy boxes of asbestos tiles onto someone's truck. I'd been hoisting a great deal of large, cumbersome furniture and appliances, so I imagine that my back finally just gave out. After all, I was thirty now and these things sometimes happen after you've left your cherished youth behind.

What I suffered was a bad lumbar strain and it was exceedingly painful. Dr. Harris put me on Percocet and told me I'd have to take two weeks off work. The pain was almost intolerable, but I sort of liked the slight feeling of euphoria that the narcotic produced. I took so many of them, as a matter of fact, that I even did the London

Triathlon in August, and finished it in good standing.

I'd begun a rigorous program of training a few months before and thought I could handle the race, since it wasn't as demanding as Kingston had been. That was not a good idea, however, for afterward, the pain was so intense that I could barely move.

I got sent to the plant again, but wasn't terribly upset, since I didn't get along very well with the manager of the furniture store and hated the place besides.

I still felt grossly overweight, even after losing eight pounds training for the Triathlon and looked puffy and rather unhealthy from the Percocet. In September I decided to go on another of my famous diets and pare at least twenty pounds from my corpulent frame.

I'd recently gotten reacquainted with M.B. that summer, after bumping into her at the Westmount Mall, and we began spending a lot of time together. She'd taken two years at Fanshawe College, against all odds, and was planning on attending Sheridan College in Oakville in the fall to study journalism.

This amazing girl had gotten herself a job on the college newspaper and had snagged interviews with various rock stars, even getting a gig at the Casby Awards, a Canadian music extravaganza, and talked to Gowan, Dal Bello and Carole Pope, among others. M.B. blushed with embarrassment when she told me that she had lied to her classmates and claimed she'd interviewed Duran Duran, when in fact she'd only attended their show in Toronto.

I told her that it didn't matter, because she'd soon have a spot on Muchmusic, edging out Denise Donlon, to which she replied slyly, "Yeah, I really want her job."

I spent a lot of time watching Muchmusic and felt that I knew VJ's Erica Ehm, Christopher Ward, Michael Williams and J.D. Roberts, since I invited them into my living room so frequently. I adored music videos, and remembered thinking, in 1975, that Supertramp's songs would make terrific mini-movies. Now it seemed that, in the last several years, the industry had finally realized this and we had illustrated lyrics splashed spectacularly across our television screens twenty-four hours a day.

M.B. came over to my place a lot and we spent long evenings drinking, listening to music and talking about the future. She was extremely ambitious and I was totally in awe of her accomplishments despite the educational system's pronouncement,

"This young woman could not function at the college level."

She had a vast knowledge of Canadian musical artists and possessed a keen instinct for what to ask them to draw out their information and expression. I was privileged to be friends with such a go-getter, and couldn't help feeling inferior, as I was still working at Goodwill at thirty and hadn't done anything worthwhile with my life.

I was very angry at that point in time and a woman who worked with me at the plant, Suzanne, pointed that out to me. She said she'd been diagnosed with a "personality disorder", stemming from repeated sexual abuse by her father while she was a child. Suzanne was an alcoholic and had tried to kill herself several times, and I couldn't help but see some similarities in my own behaviour patterns. Still, I couldn't have the same problems as she did because I'd never been abused.

M.B. provided a steady, solid anchor to my drastic mood swings, but it was hard on her to see me starting into the self-imposed starvation that had become so familiar to me over the past fourteen years.

Still, we had a lot of good times together, and one of the highlights of 1985 was the Live Aid Concert in July. We watched most of it when we weren't swimming in my building's outdoor pool, and got completely smashed in the evening, turning the television up very loud and singing to Duran Duran, U2, Hall and Oates and Sting. It felt wonderful and exhilarating to be a part of such a global relief effort by the world's most renowned artists. We knew that this was truly a testament to the power of rock music to really make a difference.

After the Live Aid high, things deteriorated rapidly. I got entrenched in the dismal pit of bulimia late in August after eating an entire box of cereal in a fit of hunger, then forcing my fingers down my throat to vomit all of the unwanted food out of my stomach.

The first few efforts at purging had proved futile, but Hope had told me the year before in Victoria Hospital that the gag reflexes just take over if you kept at it. The release was like an awe-inspiring orgasm. I could hardly wait to try it again.

I slipped over to the grocery store at the Westmount Mall and purchased three boxes of Frosted Flakes, two packages of Dad's Oatmeal Cookies, and several large bags of potato chips. There was no piddling around for me; I just dove right in, foregoing the apprenticeship period of easing gradually into it.

I had been so hungry for so many weeks that I craved to chew and swallow as much food as I could. Hope had told me that some foods were more easily regurgitated than others,and to surreptitiously avoid things like peanut butter, cheese and meat. I wasn't eating meat anyway, so that wasn't a problem. Liquids were essential,so I kept a large stock of mild and juice in my fridge. Bulimia is highly addictive, and extremely hard on the oesophagus and stomach lining, not to mention tooth enamel.

I binged and purged so frequently that it became possible to vomit by simply flexing the muscles of my diaphragm, which saved the backs of my hands from getting anymore scars on them.

Sometimes, as I ate with the ferocity of a woman who hadn't seen food in a month, I feared that something would go wrong and I'd be unable to get rid of all the disgusting calories. This never happened, but perhaps if it had, I would have ceased this destructive behaviour and gotten my act back together again.

My apartment reeked of the smell of vomit, which M.B. mistakenly thought was reefer and accused me of smoking dope. I didn't want to tell her the truth, so I let her think I was steeped in drugs rather than have her discover what I was really up to. I was tremendously ashamed of myself, and wondered what the cashiers at the A & P thought when this scrawny woman put copious bags and packages of junk food on the checkout counter.

Before this nightmare began, I had an encounter with Darcy, my Ploughshares buddy, whom I met for coffee at a little restaurant on Richmond Street called Between the Bread. We talked about music, and he was fascinated that I had met Burton Cummings and sold merchandise at one of his shows in 1980. Darcy was intelligent, insightful and sensitive We probably would have gotten very involved, except that he was having some sexual identity problems and I felt that I couldn't deal with them. I had enough of my own without taking on his as well.

Still, he was affectionate and we spent a lot of time on one another's couches making out to 1960's rock music and discussing world peace. Unfortunately, we were about two decades out of our element, seeming wistfully nostalgic and poignant in the cynical, street smart 1980's.

By September, I was greatful that Darcy and I had broken up, for I had no time or energy for a relationship, what with my distasteful bulimic lifestyle.

That entire month is pretty much a blur, with my days and nights completely submerged in the shrunken realm of kitchen-to-bathroom emptiness. I lost twenty-five pounds by October first, and as the temperature began to drop and the leaves shrivelled into brown deadness, I went walking and cycling in Springbank Park, keenly aware that I was slowly fading out of life.

One overcast afternoon, I walked down Mary Ave, where I'd spent the early years of my childhood, and stood for a long time, staring at our old, red brick house. Making my way slowly and persistently down the street, I was haunted by echoing voices of neighbourhood children, laughing with the carefree abandon of youth. It was as if I was a ghostly apparition, long dead, coming back to reflect upon my living, breathing existence that was forever lost.

That evening, I wrote a poem, the first of many exercises in literary despair, entitled "Desperate October":

Walking through colours
As the tenuous trees
Pluck their dying
Off branches hit
With the Fall's rigor mortis

I stop
To rid my denimed legs
Of the clinging decay

Its pungent odour
Suffocates me
And I can only wonder
Will I be the sustenance
For the next Spring's young?

I filed it away afterward, placing it in the pages of a journal I'd been keeping for several months. I thought that if anything happened to me, my family would find it and know what had gone wrong. It was impossible for me to talk to any of them about my problems, as it always had. It was a long-established pattern, as I suffered silently until a crisis occurred and forced all the ugly spirits out of my dark, dank closet.

M.B. had been accepted into the journalism school at Sheridan several weeks before, and went to live with her aunt and uncle in Oakville. I missed her terribly, but realized that this was a wonderful opportunity for her. She'd had difficulty getting into her studies at first, and called me to say she wished she was back in London and far from the world of academic stress.

In mid-October, she phoned, frantic with glee that she'd be representing Sheridan's newspaper at the Juno Awards on November 4th. M.B. had wanted this assignment intensely and had to do some pretty fast talking to get it. Then she asked if I would accompany her as her photographer.

"You can use my camera!" she said breathlessly, "It'll be a snap, no pun intended. Just follow my instructions and we'll set the Harbour Castle on its ear. Interested?"

Well, I wasn't particularly. For one thing, I had very little experience as a photojournalist, and besides, I was so deeply enmeshed in my eating disorders that I had no stamina for that kind of thing. If I'd been healthier and less preoccupied, I would have jumped at the chance to meet such Canadian music icons as Bryan Adams, Corey Hart, and k.d. lang. But not this year.

"I don't know, kid," I responded slowly, picturing my friend's face falling, "this is awfully sudden."

"Are you serious?! Do you realize what the Junos are all about? Tina Turner's going to be there for God's sake! What the hell's the matter with you!"

Well, she persuaded me, through persistence and her unique brand of enthusiasm, which was extremely contagious. "Okay, I'll go with you. It might be fun."

It was an utter disaster. A week before the awards, I got my hair cut obscenely short and spiked it with a liberal amount of mousse. Darcy bumped into me at Culture's restaurant in the City Centre Mall downtown and remarked acridly, "Hmmm, how things change. Last time I saw you, you looked great. Now you're real skinny and you've lost all your hair."

I told him I was going to the Junos in Toronto and he asked me if I'd put in a good word for his new band, Lowdown. I was amused at his shameless self-promotion.

M.B. wasn't thrilled with my hair either, but kept the snide comments to a blessed minimum. She was incredibly pumped for this assignment and wasn't averse to telling complete strangers on the street what she and I were up to. "I like to be in the limelight," she told me when I chastised her for bragging, "This is something I did all by myself, and I'm proud of it."

She should have been, but we both forgot some essential ingredients for successful interviewing and photographing: Number One: Learn all about your subject and study it thoroughly. We weren't up on who any of the nominated musicians were, what some of them looked like, or anything about their background. Number Two: Learn how to operate the camera first and make sure the flash works. Number Three: Don't act like a couple of wide-eyed, loose-bladdered groupies.

Unfortunately, we blew it completely at the Juno Awards that evening. We got separated soon after the show began. While M.B darted about, in and around the bleachers, I somehow ended up backstage. This wasn't altogether a bad thing, because I got pulse-quickeningly close to such rock luminaries as Larry Gowan, Kim Mitchell, David Foster and Bryan Adams. I even ventured to chirp casually "Hi Larry", when Gowan walked in front of me, blue-tipped hair, impish grin and all, and he replied, "Hey, hello there." I felt suspiciously like a stupid, dumb fan crashing a private party, however.

Then, after readying M.B.'s impressively expensive camera, complete with zoom lens, I blanched in horror when the damn flash wouldn't go off and I missed some terrific close-ups.

Realizing that it was pointless to be backstage with a malfunctioning instrument, I wended my nervous way out and finally discovered my befuddled pal upstairs in the press room with Muchmusic's Denise Donlon and a bunch of chain-smoking journalists who were watching the proceedings on a closed-circuit television.

J.D. Roberts sidled by and looked me up and down, probably trying to figure out what a media type was doing dressed like a fledgling alternative musician (my clothes all originated from Goodwill Thrift Shops).

After the ceremonies were over, all the reporters filed back into the press room, talking a mile a minute and heading for the deli trays. We got ourselves a drink and looked at one another as if to say "Well, what the hell do we do now?"

Just then, a small, pretty young woman approached and

asked if we wanted to meet her band. It was Lee Aaron, but neither of us recognized her, so M.B. said simply, "Not right now, thanks. Maybe later." That set the theme for the rest of the night.

Musicians were everywhere, chatting up the reporters and being besieged by flashbulbs. It was quite chaotic and before I knew it, somebody came up to me and said, "Congratulations". I did a double take, then realized that he was mistaking me for one of the award winners. I tried to explain that I was with the press, but he darted off again to greet somebody else.

This happened several minutes later once again, and then none other than David Foster (I did recognize him) shook my hand vigorously and told me how proud he was of me that I'd won.

By this time I'd stopped trying to argue, since it did no good anyway and just replied with a weak smile, "Thank you very much."

M.B. and I met another reporter, a rather hard-looking woman who seemed somewhat disenchanted, but we decided to stick with her, since she'd been at many of these events before. She worked for a newspaper in Buffalo and appeared pretty streetwise.

I asked her who I looked so much like that everyone was congratulating me. "Parachute Club," she responded, so I let it go at that, even though I didn't think I looked anything like Lorraine Segato.

M.B. and I made the mistake of following the Buffalo girl to her hotel room upstairs, thinking she could teach us a few things, but instead the woman just wanted to get us stoned on pot along with herself and fried boyfriend who languished limply on the bed.

While sequestered in this smokeshop, we missed the party held in honour of Bryan Adams' twenty-fifth birthday. By the time we got to the lounge there was only a half-eaten cake left and a few very drunk musicians milling about and looking to be interviewed. This was one of five parties in the building, so we thought we'd better hustle on over to the others to see if we could get something for the Sheridan paper.

In the elevator, we were tightly squeezed in with Alphie Zappagosta and his band, but didn't know it at the time, and when we got off, Mike Reno from Loverboy , with an extremely
inebriated pal, greeted us loudly and asked if we wanted to do a story on him. By this time, both of us were completely frazzled,and, after the flash failed again, we simply asked Mike for his auto-

graph.

"What? You don't want my autograph," he said with a scoff, then meandered off down the hall.

Earlier, M.B. and I had taken part in a press conference with Tina Turner, but my poor buddie's tape recorder wouldn't pick up anything but a lot of surrounding racket.

"What the hell else can possibly go wrong?" I asked, as everything began to wind down and most of the rock stars left.

"I don't want to talk about it," M.B. replied with an exasperated sigh.

Well, she lost all her equipment after all that and we spent the next two hours combing the entire building for it. Luckily, a security guard returned her valuables, after which we decided to blow the joint and chalk it up to a very, very disappointing and disheartening night.

We stayed at one of M.B.'s Aunt's home in downtown Toronto. I tried to console her, saying that it was her first experience with something as major as the Junos and she could learn a lot from it.

But M.B. had wanted so badly to shine that night and show me that she could excel in something truly significant and respectable, far removed from the Goodwill experience.

We stayed up late watching videos and I was pleased to see R.E.M.'s "Can't Get There From Here" come on after three AM

"No, kid, I thought somewhat sadly, "We really can't get there from here. Not this time anyway."

I got my act together, more-or-less, early in the New Year, after realizing that I would end up back in the hospital on another program for eating disorders if I kept the behaviour going. I didn't totally abandon the bulimia, but kept it in check enough, for a few months anyway, to regain some of the lost weight and a measure of good health.

My back was giving me a great deal of trouble though and I took a great amount of Tylenol Number 3 to keep the pain in check so I could work. I went swimming daily at the Y, doing a modified breast stroke which took some of the stress of my lower spine. Work was gruelling and if it weren't for Maureen and my almost daily sessions with Mary Jane, I would have given up completely.

Then Mary Jane announced she was getting married and leaving Goodwill. I was happy for her, for she had lost a great deal of weight and seemed more relaxed and contented than I'd ever seen her. Still, I regretted that I no longer would have her for a source of emotional support.

I was handed over to Camille, my Ploughshares partner. Everything went well with her for awhile at least.

Mom was having difficulties with Steve, who had verbally abused her and was drinking to excess. He didn't approve of her visiting Grandma and she had to sneak away to see me occasionally. I really missed her support and wished that she could summon up the courage to leave him for both our sakes.
I went over to Dad and Georgia's for supper every Sunday,and developed a close rapport with Denise. She possessed a maturity beyond her years and had a kind and loving heart.

Grandma was having a lot of health problems, as her hiatus hernia was a constant source of discomfort, as well as her right hand which suffered nerve damage when she had broken her wrist awhile back.

I had been on Workers Compensation since my accident at the furniture store, but was only receiving two hundred dollars a month. I began to miss a lot of time at work because of the pain, so Dad supplemented my income by giving me two hundred each month, enabling me to pay rent and buy food. It had been decided that I would go to the Downsview Rehabilitation Centre in Toronto when an opening came up, to assess my injury and discover what the best treatment would be.

Then, Mom finally had enough of Steve and his mistreatment of her and she moved out of their home in Whitehills. She got an apartment at the prestigious Gartshore building on Ridout Street, so I was able to see her much more often.

Dr. Harris assured me that the Downsview centre was a reputable place when I spoke of my reluctance to be sent to another institution, but he admitted that he really didn't know that much about it.

Then, late in April of 1986, I received a letter telling me that I would be going to Downsview in three weeks. I was still sceptical, but tired of the back pain, the heavy doses of Codeine, and losing so much time at the plant.

So I packed my suitcase and took the train to Toronto. A guy on staff at VIA rail was extremely nasty to me when I asked him to lift my suitcase onto the car. I took this as a bad omen of what was to come.

The omen was chillingly accurate. For starters, the Rehabilitation Centre looked like the Milhaven Maximum Security Prison, with a high chain link fence that may as well have had barbed wire on top of it. There were all these long, dismal halls inside the place, dark and dreary, where poor souls limped and hobbled painfully all day long.

I was assigned a bed in a ward with twenty other patients, all of whom were depressed, upset, angry and disillusioned. One young woman had severe tendonitis in her right wrist from working in a textile factory and was desperately afraid they were going to cut the tendon so she could return to work.

Another very vocal, obscenity spewing woman had been there for sixteen weeks and held little hope of getting better. "You want Percocet? Dilaudid? I can get you anything you want," she told me one afternoon.

We had to walk seemingly for miles to get to the dining room, this gigantic area where people butted their cigarettes in lumpy mashed potatoes and talked about their problems. Some cried as they ate, others fought amongst themselves and the overall effect was something right out of the film "Macon County Line".

After a brief orientation, we were informed that there was a strict program there, one that had to be adhered to faithfully and without question. It was an eight-hour per day schedule, including exercises in the gym, lifting and carrying boxes for two hours, carpentry, therapy with TNS, a kind of electroshock for muscles and basic basket weaving, which included activities to keep our flaccid minds and fingers active.

I didn't mind some of the exercises, although the weight lifting hurt tremendously and left me feeling horribly stiff and sore after the first day. TNS was, I thought, rather inhumane because they didn't adjust it properly, so I started skipping it early on.

In the carpentry shop I was told I had to make a cassette case out of wood, then the smiling simpleton of an instructor added that it would be necessary to pay for all the materials. Dutifully, I complied, because I genuinely feared these strange people who seemed intent on making our lives as miserable as possible.

Slowly but surely, the philosophy of the centre crept into my sullied consciousness. These people weren't here to help us, nor were they working in our best interests. They were all part of a hideous concentration camp for parasites of Workers Compensation who had to be punished for having the audacity to get hurt on the job, then demand money for it.

Luckily, I had my Walkman with me, along with some of my favourite tapes. I listened to the Everly Brothers, Hall and Oates, Sting and R.E.M. I'd bought "Fables of the Reconstruction" and it filled me with a sense of hope and beauty that was sadly lacking at this institution. Music, as always, became my link to something better, a world that somehow always eluded me as I was forced into claustrophobic, demoralizing situations that were far removed from my control.

One afternoon at the gym a poor guy collapsed after doing sit-ups and was literally paralyzed in spasms of agony. Instead of rushing to assist him, the staff let him lie there on the plastic mat moaning in agony while they alternately ignored him and hollered to "Get up! Quit putting on a fucking act!"

I was appalled, as were the other patients, but our hands were hopelessly tied. Finally, when it donned on the Gestapo that the man couldn't move, he was lifted roughly onto a stretcher and taken quickly away, hopefully to a hospital where doctors would learn of the atrocities committed here.

I dissolved in a torrent of tears one morning, overcome with despair at the rigorous schedule we were forced to adhere to, and was sent to the medical ward, after people in charge learned that I'd been a psychiatric patient. I guess they were afraid I'd do myself in, but it was even more isolated there than it had been in the open ward.

I shared a room with a quiet, remarkable woman who was practically a cripple from a severe spinal injury and couldn't get out of bed. I talked to her a lot and marvelled at her tremendous spirit and courage. She took great pleasure in watching limited scenes from her bed, like a lighted plane moving overhead at night, and never once complained about her situation. "How do you do it?" I asked her with amazement one day.

"What do you do? I have no choice. You just make the best of it and believe that someday things will get better." I'll never forget her.

One morning, I couldn't get up, as my lower back muscles went into terrific spasms due to the abuse they'd incurred at the gym as well as lifting heavy wooden boxes for days on end.

I lay there for days, while no staff appeared or checked in on either of us. My roommate had her husband at least, but I was cut off from humanity and suffered alone while my mood plummeted to record lows.

One morning I couldn't stand it any longer. I didn't think I'd ever get out of there and figured I must have been forgotten, so I hobbled slowly down to the bathroom where there was a thick rope suspended over the bathtub.

Climbing painfully onto a stool in the tub, I wrapped the rope around my neck, knowing that I could effectively hang myself with no interference. Then, as I tied the rope tightly around my throat, I saw my Mother's face again, just as I had in 1978 when I overdosed in November and I instantly dropped it.

I couldn't give this place the satisfaction of knowing they defeated me this way. Besides, whatever would my family do if they learned I killed myself here?

I made it slowly back to my room, down the long, narrow hospital corridor and stopped by the nurses' station on my way. I told them I almost did myself in, but they were disinterested. All they said was "That wasn't very smart. And we hear you haven't been attending program. That's not very smart either."

I met a young man on this ward, named Shawn, a doe-eyed boy who suffered brain damage when he fell out of a tree while employed as a cherry picker two years before. He had erratic mood swings and spent his days alone in his room, listening to Honeymoon Suite, Neil Young and despairing about a life that was now lost to him.

He had been born and raised in Lark Harbour, Newfoundland, and desperately wanted to go home. I got close to him and we sat together playing each others' tapes and giving each other
back massages. We promised that if and when we got out of that place, we'd stay together and develop a strong relationship.

The staff caught him massaging my back muscles one night and forbade me to see him again. I was very unhappy about this and once more craved a release from my agony.

I was sent to a small, mousy Russian doctor, who was in charge of my case. He informed me that I would no longer be staying there and that I was to return to work. She was displeased that I had, several weeks, previously, become involved with an underground movement, the Injured Workers Union, and had attended several meetings a few blocks away. My pins and paraphernalia had been confiscated and I was branded a reactionary revolutionary; in other words, a "shit disturber".

I was crushed, as my back problem was worse than it had been before I came to Downsview, and knew that I couldn't possibly return to Goodwill under those circumstances.

The doctor was dispassionate and cold. He told me that I had manipulated the system for my own gains and was not a welcome member there.

I returned to London beaten, battered and defeated, and went to Dr. Harris, bemoaning my fate and telling him how awful the rehabilitation place had been.

I had started smoking again there, something I swore I'd never do. But when I was "incarcerated", I totally lost any vestiges of hope. Mom was not happy about this, but understood. Something had happened to me there, for a very significant portion of my feisty spirit had been systematically squelched, perhaps forever.

M.B. returned to London following a triumphant graduation from Sheridan's school of journalism, with an impressive B average. So much for the refuseniks who deemed her incapable of handling work at the college level. Now she faced the task of looking for suitable work in her field, but she decided to take the summer off and relax, something that was well-deserved.

She was dismayed to hear of my disastrous encounter with the "Dachau Disabilitation Crematorium", as I dubbed the poorly-run institution. Likewise, Dr. Grant referred to my Soviet physician as the "KGB" and assured me that matters would be taken care of at the London Workers Compensation Board.

They weren't, however, and after an absolutely excruciating interview with a slit-eyed, pointy-faced ferret of a man at their offices downtown, I left crying and feeling even more defeated. He had told me in a snickery, snarky voice that I had nothing physically wrong with my back other than a slight sprain and should immediately return to work. The W.C.B. would be cutting off my two hundred dollars a month and therefore I would have no other recourse but to tough it out at the plant.

I took vast quantities of addictive painkillers, clamped my teeth on my tongue in order to accomplish that, and sat on a wooden stool in front of the conveyor belt all day. My head swam dizzyingly from all the drugs and the hours dragged horrendously. I lasted a month in that condition, until Karen finally called me into her office to talk about my situation.

In a flat, emotionless voice, she told me that Goodwill was going to terminate my employment because I didn't seem to be able to function very well anymore. She really didn't want to have to do that, but I had missed a lot of time and was clearly miserable there. They didn't want me to work if it was causing me so much grief, so, basically, their hands were tied.

"But I thought this place was supposed to hire handicapped people with problems" I cried incredulously. I felt I was in some perverted comedy of errors. "And now you're telling me I'm fired because I have a disability right now?"

I couldn't see that Camille had no other recourse; I was too consumed with anger that I was being let go because of my injury which I'd gotten working for Goodwill. I packed up the stuff in my locker and prepared to leave for good.

Lillian was amazed and vowed to fight for my case. I said, squeezing her shoulder, "It's not worth your trouble. I'm out of here."

It was the end of July and I had no means to pay my rent. Dad still gave me two hundred dollars a month, but that wouldn't cover it. Grandma came to my rescue and helped me out, however, as did my mom. I hated feeling totally dependent on my family after being self-sufficient for the past five years. It was demoralizing, and robbed me of a great deal of my autonomy.

I hadn't been able to eat much since my days in Downsview, so the familiar territory of extreme weight loss was once again being trodden upon with a vengeance.

I walked with a pronounced limp, dragging my left leg behind me to ease the strain on my lower back and the result was pathetically seriocomical. People stared at me downtown and some even laughed and snorted to see an otherwise ordinary-looking woman walking about like Igor from the 1930's Frankenstein films.

Music became more than a mainstay and a diversion; it took precedence over every other aspect of my life and became absolutely essential to my survival. After waiting a long time for Daryl Hall's solo album to come out, I finally bought it enthusiastically at the mall and rushed home as fast as my gimp leg would take me.

He and John Oates were about to call it quits as a musical

duo,(although they would subsequently reunite a year later) and
this was Hall's second solo effort, a cryptically titled "Three Hearts
in the Happy Ending Machine".

I listened to the album, with a growing realization that the
collection of extremely personal songs was a tremendous departure
from the rather cliche-ridden work he'd penned with his partner. I
strongly identified with the feelings of alienation, psychological
turmoil and creeping despair that permeated the lyrics, and hoped
that Daryl had put all his demons behind him when this body of
work was completed.

I learned that he would be on a Canadian promotional tour for
this album and impulsively called Muchmusic to find out if Hall
would be stopping by their studios at the end of August.

They told me that he'd be interviewed at two PM on Tuesday, August 26th, so I informed M.B. that I was going to take the
early bus to Toronto that morning and secure a place in line to meet
the guy. "Want to come?" I asked, but she politely declined, saying
she had no desire to catch a Greyhound at four thirty AM.

I spent three days and nights sketching pictures of Daryl from
age three to the present, which I planned on giving him as a booklet,
similar to the one I did for Burton Cummings six years before. I had
Muchmusic pumping out songs and videos the entire time, and
intermittently played Daryl's album for inspiration.

One of the songs on it literally blew me away. It was called
"Foolish Pride", and after I had listened to it for the first time, I
whipped out a poem I'd written a week before buying the record. It
was called "Maze of the Minotaur":

A thin, steel-hard wisp of pain
Wraps itself 'round your entrails

Pulling and tearing
Until nothing remains inside
But blood-red pulp.

You are sustenance for the Beast
And its paste-thick saliva
Marks a path for you to travel

alone and stripped bare
Of the frankincense, gold and myrrh

That were your coveted vestibule
And became the mask of idols.

You may have fooled them all
That preening, posturing guise
Could very well have fused itself
to your soul
As whitening scar tissue meshes
with healthy, living skin.

But the Beast knows the truth
He stands laughing at the core of your prison

Waiting

panting

Believing that his convoluted, sanguinary corridor
Will finally lead you home

To where the horns of self-loathing
And sepulchral, draining despair
Impale you with the pointed remnants
Of a misshapen youth

Until you twist and writhe
Until you imploringly beg

for a release

into vacuity.

It was a poem about Daryl Hall, I thought, but it turned out, in the end, to be autobiographical. The line "You may have fooled them all" came jolting back to haunt me as I listened repeatedly to the song. One line went, "If I wanted to, I could have fooled them all" and so I knew I had to insert my poem in the book of sketches.

"Misshapen youth" referred to his childhood, for I had read that he had been repeatedly abused as a youngster and as I drew a picture of him as a five-year-old child I cried openly, knowing that this innocent boy had been hideously violated by older boys. Why hadn't his parents known what was going on? And why did this evoke such a sickening sensation in the pit of my stomach?

The sketches and poem were completed a half hour before it was time to take a cab to the Greyhound station. On the way, I talked to a young businessman from Toronto who seemed somewhat intrigued by what I was going to do. We stopped for coffee and I told him that I really needed to give Daryl  something personal to let him
know that I understood what he was trying to say for so long in his songs.

It must be understood that I wasn't thinking too clearly at that point in my life. I was obviously becoming quite obsessed and preoccupied with matters and people that weren't actually a part of my world at all.

I got to Muchmusic at eight AM and was told that I could wait outside the building if I wanted, but that Daryl would not arrive until five PM. I went down the road for coffee and returned, then sat on the curb, smoking and listening to "Three Hearts in the Happy Ending Machine".

Simon Evans, a staff member with Muchmusic, told me that UB40 and the Bangles were also going to drop by that day, but I was disinterested.

As the morning wore on, people stopped and talked to me, everyone from sad and lonely bag ladies to wandering teens who really just needed someone to talk to who wasn't stamped with a label of authority. I looked about twenty-two, even though I was thirty-one, with my shock of curly hair, creaseless face and thin, adolescent body. I wore black jeans, a black jacket and a white t-shirt with "Rock and Roll" emblazoned across it and two kids dancing around an old phonograph.

I had a black magic marker with me, hoping to get Daryl to sign the back of my shirt. In my knapsack was my camera, the book of sketches, some tapes and several pieces of fruit. I wasn't the least bit hungry, but because of the medication I was taking  for my depression, I  thought I should put something in my stomach once in awhile. There was a good supply of Percocet with me, but I didn't want to dull my senses with Codeine.

This was a significant day for me, for perhaps I would get to talk to a musician I had grown to feel close to through his music, and whom I respected for what he had endured and subsequently overcome.

Early in the afternoon, the UB40 fans began to congregate outside the studio, playing the band's tapes and erecting a banner for them. I talked to many young people that day, all of whom were intent on sharing a few minutes of their lives with people who had taken a chance and made it in the world of rock music.

At two PM, Simon Evans came outside and told all of us that UB40 wouldn't be able to make it, as their tour bus had broken down. The fans were bitterly disappointed and gradually left, leaving the banner intact.

Then the Bangles arrived but I wasn't really into their music so I didn't ask for any autographs or speak to them.

Then Christopher Ward emerged and smiled at us, so I approached him and asked if there was any way I could get into the studio. He replied that it was always absolutely crazy up there. But after I told him that I really wanted to give Daryl Hall something personal I'd created for him, he said that if it didn't look as though he'd be arriving at the front, there was a parking lot around back that I could access by following his instructions.

I thanked him and thought the easygoing VJ was as ingratiating and unpretentious as he came across on television.

Finally, after I'd been hanging around for nine hours, a silver stretch limousine pulled up and a very tall, thin man with long blond hair, Wayfarers, faded blue jeans, blue sweatshirt, a black leather jacket and cowboy boots stepped out and stood directly in front of me.

"Hi Daryl", I said casually, as if the guy was a close, personal friend.

"Hi," he replied, sounding a bit uptight and somewhat wary of me.

"I guess I'm the welcoming committee," I continued, looking around and seeing that I was the only one on the sidewalk.

Well, that dumb comment broke the ice, and, deciding that he had to get upstairs to be interviewed, I pulled out my magic marker and asked for his autograph on the back of my shirt.

"Sure," Daryl obliged, and scrawled a semi-legible signature while I prattled on about how much I loved his new album and God knows what else.

Then I handed him my book of drawings and that bizarre

poem. He grinned at the title and said with a mock dramatic flourish, "This Is Your Life". I had my camera ready and he posed for me, smiling as the rain began to fall.

Unfortunately the shutter didn't open until he'd gone behind the glass doors, so the picture looks quite blurry. So much for a PHD (Press Here Dummy) camera.

I felt pretty euphoric, revelling in the treasured autograph and replaying those precious moments in my head before Daryl emerged again in forty minutes or so. A bunch of people had congregated while he was upstairs with Erica Ehm and clamoured for autographs. I took some more pictures, which thankfully turned out.

I noticed with a sinking sensation of disappointment that Daryl didn't have my project with him and hoped that he had at least looked at it. "What did you think of the book?" I asked, with an edge of desperation in my voice.

He smiled and replied, "I liked it. It's really interesting."

Then I blurted out, "Don't you have it anymore!?"

"Relax. See that woman over there?" He pointed at someone with a bunch of articles, including a Muchmusic t-shirt, an item all the musical guests got doled out when they visited the studio. "She's got it for me. I plan on keeping it, okay? So don't worry."

I squeezed his wiry, leather-swathed arm and sighed with relief. "Okay. Thanks for everything. I won't forget this."

Then he was gone,and I stood on the sidewalk with the rain pelting on my head and knew that the trip, the three sleepless nights working on the sketches and the long wait in front of the Muchmusic building had been worth it. I knew Daryl would soon forget the brief encounter, but I wouldn't. After all, I'd spent most of the past nine years in institutions, had recently lost my job and walked like a pathetic cripple. However, somehow all of that seemed very far away right at that moment on Queen Street at  six PM on that drizzly August evening.

\*     \*     \*     \*     \*     \*     \*     \*     \*     \*     \*

Poor Christopher Ward was soon to regret that he ever met me that day in Toronto, although his second encounter with me was fairly benign. It was via the mail, for I'd sent him a letter and a picture of him that I'd drawn as a thank you for being so courteous to me that day I met Daryl. Also included was a photo of myself wearing the autographed shirt that M.B took and quite to my surprise and embarrassment, he displayed all of these items on the air early in September.

Shortly thereafter, my life started on another downward spiral. I began to keep extremely late hours and only allowed myself four hours of sleep a night. Writing became essential to my existence and I worked diligently on a novella about a video jockey named Jameson Clark. The story involved a jaded, washed-up musician who longed for the limelight again and felt he was wasting his life pushing videos to the public day after day. The character was blatantly patterned after Christopher.

Then a popular rock duo, a la Hall and Oates, visited the station and something quite remarkable happened. These two guys, Brian Nunn and Dale Boyd (caustically witty critics dubbed them "Null and Void") ended up talking a frantic, desperate young female viewer out of killing herself by providing a vocal lifelong to her until an ambulance came.

Because of this experience, Jameson summoned the courage and fortitude to resume his musical career. Brian and Dale decided not to break up and Brian Nunn, a disillusioned cynic, got a new lease on life. It was a rather silly, cliche-ridden story, but I worked at it until it was completed and was blithely unaware that it was eerily prophetic in some respects.

By October, I was hardly eating or sleeping at all and had gradually become aware of something terrifying and atrocious that blasted me violently out of my still waters. It was due, I now realize, by the fact that I wasn't getting much, if any, sleep , as well as amassing a great deal of imagined evidence into a mind deprived of constructive material to work with.

One afternoon, as I watched Daryl's second video from his solo album, "Foolish Pride", I thought I saw a large, angry, vertical scar on his throat. At first, I figured it might have been from a clumsy, amateurish suicide attempt, based on some of the record's lyrics, but then I was violently seized by the dreaded conclusion that it was a scar from the surgical removal of a cancerous growth on his lymph nodes. The songs' words weren't graphic, heartfelt admissions of an emotional  maelstrom, but rather a message of good-bye. Daryl Hall, the kind, considerate man I'd met two months before, was dying.

Well, the evidence was overwhelmingly conclusive: The scar,

the photo I'd recently drawn a picture from that indicated that he was obviously wearing a wig, because he'd lost all his hair from the ravages of chemotherapy and those devastating lyrics, like the lines from "Foolish Pride": You made me feel like the livin' end/But the end came quick/And made me want to die", as well as "Next Step: "We're gonna have more fun NOW" which clearly meant adopting the "Live for today because we don't have much more time" philosophy.

I was inconsolable, sobbing uncontrollably, engaging in wild, spasmodic hand-wringing and despairing repeatedly to M.B. that if Daryl was going to die, then I must as well.

M.B. thought this was absolutely ludicrous, and watched with mounting horror as I sunk ever more deeply into a murky, suicidal chasm.

Then, late one night, I wrote a long, painful letter to Christopher Ward, telling him what I knew about  Daryl's "condition", how, quite suddenly, a "plane had shifted" and I was in some kind of snake-infested Purgatory because I was really responsible for the rock star's health crisis and I would have to pay with my life.

I told him that whoever was orchestrating this monstrosity figured that killing me wouldn't be nearly as bad as having me watch people I cared about dying all around me. It was a painful, nakedly candid suicide note, relaying my emotional trauma and explaining how I'd received "messages" from A-Ha's album "Scoundrel Days" about the impending destruction of humanity by people's evil and crimes against Nature, God and each other.

What had happened was that I had become psychotic from sleep deprivation and by listening to suggestive lyrics over and over for twenty hours at a time, I was locked in a suicidal frame of obsessive thinking.

Recently, two teenage boys had gone into the Arizona desert and shot themselves after playing one the heavy metal band's albums for days on end and had been pushed over the edge from this. Tragedies like these prompted Senator Al Gore's wife Tipper to lobby in Congress for a law that stipulated that warnings would be put on rock albums with "suggestive or profane lyrics" whether they dealt in any way with Satanism, gratuitous violence or excessive use of the f-word.

Personally, I think it is wrong to blame rock lyrics for the unhinging of the young, suggestive and unstable minds, because it is the parents' and teachers' responsibility to instill positive values and a healthy self-image in youngsters, instead of blaming artists for their undoing. Not only that, but some young people become very ill emotionally,and would whether they listened to naughty lyrics or not.

I don't think the general public got the same messages from "Scoundrel Days" that I did, but even though it's been nine years since I sent that letter to Christopher, I can't play that album anymore without having very unpleasant memories come flooding back.

Even R.E.M.'s music got sucked into my cesspool of craziness. After listening to "Life's Rich Pageant" in early November, over and over, I knew without a doubt that it was giving me "apocalyptic messages". I saw the collection of songs as a kind of soundtrack to the dismal and pessimistic book, "Silent Spring" and in my insanity I realized the world was dying because I was still living.

None of the albums I spun on my turntable were particularly upbeat. Peter Gabriel's "So" featured the melancholy "Red Rain", but when "Don't Give Up" with Gabriel and Kate Bush came on, I snatched the needle off the record, thinking that these people had no right to tell me to keep on living after the evil I'd committed.

Corey Hart, one of the original angst-ridden, tortured artists, sang songs about loneliness and being constantly misunderstood, and Billy Idol's "Sweet Sixteen" concerned an unhappy teenager who died, probably by her own hand.

On November fourteenth, I wrote a memorial poem to Grandpa in the newspaper, on the second anniversary of his death. I cried all the time I was penning it:

To my grandfather, Sergeant Edward Henry Colerick, "A True Soldier" in every sense of the word, on the second anniversary of his passing, November fourteenth, 1984.

These thoughts are in fond, loving remembrance/Of a gentle, special man,/Who, unlike no other I have ever known,/Touched the hearts of his family and friends,/With such a sweet, healing balm--/ Indeed/That rare elixir, "Optimism Personified"./Grandpa, had you battled and labelled this wonder drug,/You could have cured the entire world/Of the ravaging scourges of anger and hatred,/Of spiralling depression, and the useless scars/Called jealousy,and hollow-based mortal mistrust./A dreamspun fantasy, I know,/The kind upon which the castles of the idealists are built./But then, you taught me that:/Many nights, when torn from numbing sleep/With horrendous, hideous and devastating scenes/Of that fearsome, final Apocalyptic holocaust,/Screaming its nightmare into my spinning head,/You were always there, a phone call away/ Awakened yourself, and greeted disruptively/By the whimpering, frightened sobs/ Of your "Little Janie"(as you adoringly called me)/I remember what you said to me,/In a voice rich with the character-honing experiences/Based upon a challenging life/Of frightening war upon war,/One in the death-stained European waters/But most of them private./And, my dear, courageous soldier in the army of Hope/It was through your impressive personal conquering/Of these battles with your peace-challenged heart/That you uttered special words of wisdom to me:/"Love your family and your country,/For they're the best in all the world/And consider yourself fortunate, Sweet,/ Just as I do, as I always have,/Despite the scary nightmares,/ Despite the pain that may threaten you/On life's often difficult journeys."/Though two years have passed since you left us/Take heart in the assurance that you haven't really at all./For you left your tools and ammunition behind/In order that I could battle those demons of my own./And I know, in the verycentre of my being/ That you're up there smiling and watching/As I, fumblingly and stumblingly,/Learn to operate and utilize/The tools that are character-builders/And the ammunition, forged out of love, trust and humour/But most of all, Hope./I miss you,and love you so much.

Love, your "no.1" granddaughter, Jane."

I wanted to have hope now, but it eluded me. I chain-smoked, keeping the windows open so M.B. wouldn't choke on the smoke and get seized up with an asthma attack. As it got colder, I began wearing layers of sweaters and several pairs of socks, for, because I wasn't eating, I was even more sensitive to the freezing temperatures.

Something that kept my head above the choppy waves and postponed me from killing myself right away was following the amazing progress of paraplegic Rick Hanson as he wheeled from coast to coast in an effort to earn money for spinal injuries research. M.B. informed me that he would be coming through London late in November and so we made plans to be on the roadside at Wharncliffe

Road and Southdale.

I decided that, since I was going to die soon anyway, I would give him my gold medal that I had won at the Kingston Triathlon. I had been fiercely protective of it, but figured that Rick deserved it much more than I did.

Unfortunately, on the day he arrived, my back went into terrible spasms as we stood in the cold morning air and I had to be driven home by a good Samaritan. M.B. gave the medal to Hanson and later showed me a photo of him on the front cover of the London Free Press wearing it. I had to smile when I saw this.

Back in my apartment, I put my headphones on and began singing loudly and mournfully to the music, so loudly, in fact, that a neighbour rapped at the door and asked if I was alright. Embarrassed and upset, I was later warned that if I caused anymore commotion like that I would be asked to vacate the building.

By the outset of December, a couple of weeks after I sent my sad letter to Christopher Ward, I decided that I would kill myself. I just couldn't live with what I thought I had done and figured that if I died, then everyone would be allowed to live and grow healthy. It was a true Messianic complex, I suppose, thinking my death would redeem humanity and it was all rooted in the way I perceived the lyrics I was listening to and my unwavering belief that Daryl Hall was dying and it was all my fault.

I bought a package of razor blades, had four beers late at night and figured that I would slash my jugular vein, since the wrist-cutting hadn't worked last time. While "Three Hearts" poured out its terrible messages, I held a mirror in my left hand, to see what I was doing and made frantic, hesitant strokes on the left side of my neck.

After several minutes of this amateur hacking, a frightening surge of blood spilled onto my clothes and the filthy, littered living room rug and I fell out of my chair, hitting the floor with a dull thud.

I must have passed out for awhile and I awoke with the sickening knowledge that I hadn't succeeded. In fact, all I did was nick the jugular vein. I was very upset and didn't know what the hell to do next. I lost my nerve when I saw the blood and felt an uncomfortable throbbing in my neck. So I wrapped up the blade and put it back in the medicine cabinet. I had a lot of cuts on my neck, so it was necessary to tie a scarf around it to camouflage my handiwork.

Prior to the acts of self-mutilation, I'd told M.B. that I could no longer go on living, after which she begged and tearfully implored me to reconsider, to abandon such a selfish act and think about my loved ones that I would surely destroy.

One day, she spied an ambulance in front of my building and recoiled in horror at the thought that it was probably there for me. It wasn't, but afterward, she distanced herself a lot to preserve her own sanity. I despised what I was putting her through that fall. I regretted the psychological scars that I inflicted on this dear, life-loving woman who couldn't imagine anything as pitiful as dying by one's own hand.

Then, on December eighth, Mom came over, ostensibly to help me defrost my ice-encrusted freezer, but actually ended up discovering how much her daughter had deteriorated over the past months. She was appalled at my emaciated appearance, the huge bags under my eyes and grew suspicious about my scarves, since I'd never worn them before.

My apartment, never a study in neatness and immaculate order, was an utter pigsty and I seemed strangely distant and uncommunicative for the eight hours she was there.

Then, I must have slipped into a chilling catatonic state, for something sure scared the living daylights out of her. She immediately called Dr. Grant and demanded that I be hospitalized.

Kiel was extremely disappointed in me, since I had gotten so brazenly self-destructive and couldn't seem to pull my life together. He admitted me, but for the entire time I was a patient on the seventh floor, he avoided me and refused to say anything. I missed the affectionate hugs and warm kibitzing, but understood that the man was simply fed up.

When I was admitted on December ninth, I was placed under the care of an earnest, conscientious resident and Dr. Keil's clerical clerk. They spent a couple of hours asking me a lot of questions and I found myself blurting out how Daryl Hall was dying because of me and that I was a deadly force that had to be destroyed.

These young doctors figured that I was totally insane, but didn't realize that I hadn't slept more than ten hours a week for several months. The voices returned with a vengeance and I became lost in my demented world of disordered thinking and frightening delusions.

They decided to put me on another program for my anorexia and bulimia, similar to the one I'd been on in 1984, which I hated and fought ferociously against for the first few weeks.

My neck was carefully examined and I was told how lucky I'd been not to have cut any deeper.

"Glad you think so," I snapped, turning my back on their concern.

The nurses were as receptive and helpful as they'd been the last time. I confided a great deal in them as the doctors kept me confined to bed and I had a lot of free time on my hands.

I had some interesting roommates in the four-bed room I was in. Rose was a tiny, hyperactive bundle of nervous energy, and was excessively whiny. She had lost her beloved husband of forty years to throat cancer and was now thrashing hopelessly about in a world that didn't understand or have any particular use for a seventy-one-year-old hysterical widow who was drowning in loneliness and grief. I took her under my wing, doing her laundry, fixing her wispy hair and listening to her sad reminiscing about a brave soldier of World War II who'd fallen completely in love with "Rosy the Riveter".

June was in a wild, manic state of mind when I met her, and took it upon herself to "will me back to health and happiness". She'd come breezing to my bedside at three AM, rubbing me down with smelly hand lotion, giving me boisterous lectures about starving and chatting non-stop in a loud, raucous cockney accent. I found the boisterous fifty-five-year-old extremely exhausting, mentally and physically.

Then there was forty-year-old Gabby, a plump, dreamy woman suffering from schizophrenia who developed a heavy crush on Eddie, a  darkly handsome orderly and pursued the poor guy relentlessly. Gabby was supposed to undergo an experimental therapy for her illness, but decided against it at the last minute. She simply signed herself out, thinking the doctors were going to do terrible experiments with her mind.

I didn't get to meet any of the other patients for weeks, because I was pretty much chained to my bed. Mom visited frequently and brought me stuffed animals, love and emotional support. It was somewhat of a relief to be looked after now, instead of being trapped in my concentration camp of an apartment.

People on the ward began to stop by my room to catch a

glimpse of the patient who wasn't allowed out of her room. One young man, Cecil, took an interest in me and we spent many hours talking about music, our illnesses, days of drugs and personal relationships. He was the first black man I'd ever been involved with, the only reason being that London is predominantly white, Protestant and middle-class, the Wonder Bread Capital of Canada. We didn't care about the seven-year age difference either, and I told him that my best friend had also been born in 1962 and there was no "generation gap" with M.B. and me.

Speaking of M.B., she wasn't allowed to visit while I was confined to bed, but came religiously afterward. She said that after visiting her brother in jail, the psychiatric floor was nothing, even though some of the patients spooked her at first.

Finally, they released me from the shackles of my bed and I moved freely throughout the floor, talking to some other young women who were being treated for eating disorders. One was diabetic and, after bingeing, she'd refuse to take her insulin and urinate everything out.

I was seen daily by the resident who was pleased to see that my "delusions" had subsided. He chalked it up to a substantial increase in my Nozinan, but I'm sure it was because I was finally sleeping eight hours every night.

The Nozinan made me feel ridiculously sluggish and stoned and I got very dizzy whenever I stood up too fast. My tongue felt too large for my mouth. I became extremely unco-ordinated and tripped over my own feet.

I was startled to see Alice, a young red-headed woman whom I'd met in 1984, strung out on Speed. She had no desire to stop poking and flying high and she was dressed in the garish garb of a streetwalker. She'd left her Native husband to raise her two sons alone and I thought that they would have a very grim future with a Speed freak for a mother.

I was hospitalized for nearly three months. After I'd gained fifteen pounds and didn't look so comparable to a stick figure, as well as coming out of my severe depression with a new drug called Sinequan, I was released to the care of my mother.

It was early March of 1987, and although I still kept my apartment, I lived with Mom in her new building on Springbank Drive, right beside my old public school.

I stopped seeing Dr. Kiel, so Dr. Harris referred me to Dr.

Tad Prince, a psychiatrist at University Hospital. After going to see him in the middle of the month, he asked me if I wanted to learn more about my disorder, then handed me a book entitled, "Living and Working With Schizophrenia".

I was shocked, and nearly fell off my chair. Was this possible? I took the book home and read it privately, despairing over the myriad of similarities between myself and the patients discusses in the body of work. People talked about hearing voices, of blacking out and losing track of time, as well as believing things that weren't rooted in reality.

"Oh God, I am really crazy," I thought. Schizophrenia was insanity, after all, and what was worse, it was incurable. I might never be able to work again, or return to school. And, I'd never get off the psychiatric merry-go-round.

I didn't show the book to my parents for a week or so, fearing their negative reaction. I knew that my great grandmother had died in the Ontario Hospital, a victim of this disease. I must have inherited that fateful gene. I hoped that Jim didn't as well, for I didn't think I could stand it if he had to go through what I had for the past sixteen years.

Ironically, Dad's PHD thesis had concerned statistics relating to schizophrenia, and I thought about the bizarre ways that life had of throwing these nasty little curve balls.

I told M.B., who replied with a shrug, "So? I always knew you were weird. Now everyone knows it. Big deal. I'm not going to treat you any different."

I was extremely grateful for that, because Mom felt that she had to "look after" me and cried about my situation a great deal. I tried to tell her that it wasn't that bad, that at least I had a caring family and a home. Things, after all, could be a lot worse.

There was a certain amount of relief and satisfaction in finally having a diagnosis after all those years and knowing why my life had been thrown into such turmoil for so long. Many questions were answered and I decided to make the best of it and accomplish something.

I had written another letter to Christopher Ward when I got out of the hospital, to let him know I was alright. I wrote quite a few times to him over the next several months, making up musical crossword puzzles and chatting away about anything and everything. He kept putting my silly stuff on the air and seemed appreciative, but I'm sure he figured I was quite the little pest.

M.B. and I went to Hamilton to see the Beach Boys and had a good time at the concert. It felt good to have some fun again and rejoin a world that I thought was forever lost to me.

Afterward, I began my shirt-painting business, when I found out that it was possible to accomplish rather impressive portraits of rock stars on articles of clothing, and best of all, get paid for it. My first effort was a picture of Daryl Hall and John Oates, done as an experiment from a drawing off the cover of their "Live At the Paramount" album.

Mom was very impressed with the shirt and took it to work to show it off to her fellow teachers at the RNA school, where she'd been teaching since 1975.

I painted many of them, including Sting, the Everly Brothers, Burton Cummings, U2's Bono, R.E.M.'s Michael Stipe, and Tina Turner. Over sixty were amassed over a period of five months,and I also sold custom-made shirts of Echo and the Bunnymen's Ian McCullough and Peter Townsend of The Who. I was paid thirty dollars for them and decided to try and sell the others at a flea market at the Western Fairgrounds for several Sunday mornings in October.

Mom accompanied me. It wasn't exactly a resounding success, even though the Elvis and Bon Jovi shirts received a lot of attention. I put the prices too high, taking into consideration the number of hours that went into the designs, as well as the cost of the materials. People who go to these markets just don't want to spend a fortune on something hand-made.

I gave up after a few weeks and chalked it up to an invaluable experience. I still have all the shirts in my dresser drawer and they are a positive reminder of a way to get my troubled life back on track in the latter part of the 1980's.

My brother married Sharon in the summer of 1987, so Mom and I flew out to Vancouver to attend the wedding, which I cannot remember too clearly to this day. Dad took Georgia, who felt quite insecure with so many of Dad's family milling about everywhere.

I hoped that Jim would be happy and fulfilled, but couldn't help wondering if this was what he really wanted. He was extremely thin, which worried Mom and me, and seemed somewhat nervous and hesitant about the whole thing.

Fortunately, I didn't have to see Dr. Prince very often, only once a month for about five minutes each time. This suited me just fine and I told him that I was managing quite well, despite all the Nozinan and Sinequan.

Jim came home for Christmas that year, but without Pauline, who couldn't get the time off. He was a dear and spent a lot of time with Mom and I, joking about married life and calling his mate every night.

Grandma was depressed, for she couldn't get used to life without Grandpa, but was happy to see her grandson again for ten days.

I'm sure that Mom told Jim about my diagnosis, but he wasn't convinced that I was schizophrenic. He couldn't believe that a brother and sister could share so much in common without either both, or either of us having such a major disability. Mom and I just figured that he didn't want to believe it.

After talking for hours, he held me close to his chest and gave me a big, warm hug. That spoke volumes and when I retired to bed, I cried myself to sleep. I missed him so much and he was living so far away. I had no idea what he was up to and how he was managing. He still really wanted to get into medical school and I prayed that September would finally be this hard-working, dedicated man's big break.

1987 ended on a positive note, all things considered, but I couldn't help feeling that something was missing in my life. In truth, a lot was, and, on New Year's Eve as Mom, Grandma and I yelled "Happy New Year!" off Grandma's balcony, I resolved to finish the manuscript of poems I was working on and launch my professional writing career. If I couldn't work anywhere else right now, I could at least utilize my creative skills and make a name for myself.

I'd recently sent off three poems to Mosaic Press, a publishing company in Oakville, including "Maze of the Minotaur", one about mental illness and another, "To Tame the Blue Ox" about bulimia. I hoped that something would come of it, but I realized that the writing field was extremely difficult to break into, even if you weren't schizophrenic.

# Chapter Fourteen

# The W.O.T.C.H. Dimension: Opening Some Doors

Early in 1988, I got extremely itchy to get out of Mom's apartment and surround myself with other living, breathing human beings. Writing was rewarding and provided an essential emotional outlet, but I was very lonely and isolated. I spent my days at my own apartment writing, as I had done with the shirt painting, but it was an austere, reclusive life. I was beginning to talk to myself, and Muchmusic wasn't enough stimulation, since they were only faces and voices on a flickering, one-dimensional screen.

I found out about W.O.T.C.H. from Dr. Harris, who'd been trying to get me to go to the old Heritage home at 57 Ridout Street for months. Finally, in March, I said, "Okay, I give up. I'll give them a call."

W.O.T.C.H. is an acronym for Western Ontario Therapeutic Community Hostel. It was a meeting place for psychiatric patients to engage in activities, get back into the work force, return to school and be with others who understood their situation.

I met with one of the organization's social workers, a chubby, smiling blond man named Jim Cockerton one Monday afternoon. He asked a lot of questions about my hospitalization, diagnosis and my life since leaving hospital a year before.

He told me that there were two programs offered at W.O.T.C.H., the Day Program, involving seven hours of planned activity five days a week, and the Morning Program, which met every Tuesday, Wednesday and Thursday morning from nine AM until noon. I decided to opt for the latter, since I wasn't prepared to invest a great deal of time in an unknown entity.

The first member I met there was Betty, a young woman I'd gotten to know in the L.P.H. several years before. She was pretty, heavyset with melancholy eyes and a penchant for self-destructive behaviour. I latched onto her immediately, as she was a familiar face and had been around W.O.T.C.H. for several years.

The organization had begun in 1970. Dad had actually been instrumental in assisting it in the early years. It was run by a group of dedicated professionals who believed that mental patients deserved to be treated with fairness and respect and really required a place to hang out where they wouldn't be laughed or pointed at by the often close-minded population.

The morning program was difficult to adjust to at first. We climbed up several flights of stairs to the blue attic room of the house and sat around in a big circle.

All of us had to tell our names and what our diagnosis was, as well as what we thought W.O.T.C.H. could do for us. One girl said that she was schizophrenic, had been hospitalized for most of the past five years,and that she hoped eventually to find work.

Another young man said that he was manic depressive and had just gotten released from the L.P.H. two weeks before. He wanted to structure his days, and was later moved to the day program. I was excruciatingly shy and didn't want to say anything. I sat on my chair, shaking violently and staring at the carpeted floor, hoping that nobody would notice or acknowledge me. There were about twenty-five people surrounding me and I could feel their eyes burning into the top of my head.

Finally, I spoke hesitantly, stammering profusely, "Hi, I-I'm, um, Jane and I, um I'm schizophrenic. I'm kind of scared actually."

Everyone greeted me warmly and affectionately and my apprehension melted. The people who worked with us were incredibly compassionate and sympathetic to us, like Wendy Brown, a slim, perky twenty-two-year-old with an incredible capacity for caring and this unique way of making you feel significant and important. She exuded youthful enthusiasm and a fresh-faced idealistic air. I liked her from the start.

Jake Lenders was about thirty-eight, small, grey-haired, hyperactive and quick with a laugh and a comforting word. I knew instinctively that he was not there for the money or prestige, but for what he could do to improve our lives. I thought that he might be gay, based solely on his speech pattern and mannerisms and this made him even more appealing. He would know very well how it felt to be regarded as "different".

Loretta Hayes was very motherly, with a warm, nurturing

way about her and this shy self-deprecating smile. This was coupled with an obvious embarrassment and flustered blush whenever anyone said anything even remotely provocative.

Cathy Pliley was large, boisterous and fun-loving, but I knew from the outset that she would tolerate no bullshit or game-playing. This no-nonsense lady put me off slightly, for she wasn't averse to uttering expletives and telling someone off if they needed it. But I admired her honesty and directness,and knew that I would always be able to trust her.

Two women really stood out in the morning program and would make an indelible impression on me in the weeks to come. One was Estelle, a slightly pudgy but attractive twenty-two-year-old who always took time to put make-up on and had a wicked sense of humour. She was gutsy, spirited, and didn't want to be labelled a "mental patient".

She told us that she suffered from anxiety and depression,and it became obvious early on that she had the beginning of a serious drinking problem. As time wore on, I'd learn of her disastrous home life, sexual abuse by her father and wild teenage years trying to escape the incredible pain. She looked as if she could be any typical young woman just out of her teens and on the threshold of life, but the system was waiting there to flog her into submission.

Moira was truly unique in many ways. For starters, she had a ten million dollar vocabulary and was witty and clever as hell. She was extremely thin, about thirty-eight years old, with short-cropped hair, major bags under her ironic eyes and hands that reached constantly for a chain of cigarettes. Moira was vehemently and ferociously allergic to bullshit of any kind and told it like it was, whether you wanted to hear it or not. A prototypical tragic figure, she was plagued with schizophrenic demons, lived with her mother, brother and three cats, and fervently hoped for a better life somewhere around the next bend.

I was intensely attracted to her fierce determination not to wallow in the dredges of self-pity and loved the way she cursed anyone who administered sympathy toward her. She loved music, particularly Rita McNeil and sang along with Jim Croche's "I Got A Name". I latched onto her immediately. In time, she'd become a close and devoted ally in the war against mental oppression.

After my first week at W.O.T.C.H., I settled in quite comfortably, taking part in Wednesday's project day, going for outings to

Victoria Park, Eldon House and walking along the Thames River in Springbank.

I even grew fond of discussing goals, where we had to write down what we planned to accomplish during the week,and then checked back the following Tuesday morning to show that we carried them out.

Some members had difficulty in making decisions and others were apprehensive about being in the community. I was strongly encouraged to enter one of W.O.T.C.H.'s four group homes for a year and establish some independence from my mother.

I went to visit Piccadilly House, named after the street it was on but didn't like it. The bedrooms were so cramped and small, and I didn't relish cooking for eight people on a regular basis. I told Loretta that I decided against it, but she wasn't particularly pleased to hear it.

Mom had met another man to fill the void that Steve left. His name was Al Pond and he was an affable, fun-loving and gentle man who came from Newfoundland. He was pleasant enough and quite attractive, but I feared losing Mom to him. I was devastated when she announced that she was going to marry and move in with him to his townhouse in Berkshire Village. That was actually pretty selfish of me, for I shouldn't have been so relentlessly petty where my mother's happiness was concerned.

Dr. Prince strongly suggested that I come into the psychiatric ward of University Hospital to adjust to moving back to my apartment, so I reluctantly agreed.

The tenth floor was a lot more luxurious and posh than Victoria Hospital's seventh had been, with comfortable furniture in the common room, lush, carpeted floors and pretty decent food.

I was placed in a room with a thirty-eight-year-old severely depressed woman named Anna Lee, who was darkly attractive, terribly intense and spent her days on her bed, clutching her head in her thin hands. She'd been in hospital for weeks and hadn't ventured out of her room for the first two. She had stayed huddled in a miserable ball, refusing food and never speaking to any of the nurses when they came to check on her.

Anna Lee told me that she'd been a "vegetable lying in bed" at home for six months and didn't understand why she felt so oppressively inert and without any energy or spark for living anymore. She was despondent over the growing chasm between herself and seventeen-year-old son and noticed that her marriage was foundering. My heart went out to her. As the weeks went on, she grew close with a teenage boy on the ward who took her under his wing and gave her what her own child would not anymore.

The other patients interacted a great deal with one another, such as Greta, a forty-two-year-old childless woman suffering from manic depressive illness, who wanted to take in a sixteen-year-old self-abuser with no family or support system outside of the hospital. Unfortunately, Greta had a severe drinking problem and later proved to be an inadequate mother figure for Nancy, so the girl finally left and ended up being readmitted.

I felt guilty being there, since I wasn't displaying any symptoms. People wondered if I was admitted under false pretenses. Greta pointed out that "you don't seem schizophrenic at all. A girl who was in here last month was convinced that God was talking to her through Johnny Carson."

I didn't see Dr. Prince while I was on the ward, but talked to a male resident who assured me that I should be capable of living on my own once my mother marred Al. He said it was time I grew up and learned to laugh my problems off. He was a good-looking young man, but seemed rather insecure about the fact that he was losing his hair.

Anna Lee improved a great deal after they finally put her on Sinequan, the first anti depressant to be at all effective in treating her illness. After a week, she was talking, smiling and even wanted to go for walks with me around the UWO campus. She still had many issues to deal with. At our group therapy sessions held twice a week, she explained that there were still many days when she felt like destroying herself.

One of the nurses, a pleasant, no-nonsense young woman, took me aside and said that I should go back to W.O.T.C.H. during the day,and if I refused, Dr. Prince would release me from the hospital. "You need a lot of structure in your life," she explained, "and if you don't take positive steps to improve, there's nothing we can do for you here".

I returned to the morning program and was glad to have some freedom. After six weeks, I was released, but felt that those forty-five days on the tenth floor had been an utter waste of time.

Then, Mom informed me that she wasn't going to marry or move in with Al after all. So I resumed my schedule of spending weekdays with her and weekends at my apartment.

One afternoon, I got an encouraging letter from a Mr. Howard Aster at Mosaic Press, telling me that he loved my three poems, that I had a lot of talent, and to please send him more. He included three paperback books, one entitled "Words for Elephant Man" which Mosaic Press had published the year before.

I was extremely happy and set about writing a large collection of poems, eighty in all, and submitted them two months later. They were unquestionably depressing, and when Mom read them, she cried through the entire lot. They were obviously written from unpleasant personal experience and spoke openly about the mental anguish I'd endured over the past sixteen years.

Howard Aster wanted even more of my writing and suggested I meet with him at his office in Oakville. I stayed with M.B. and her parents one weekend and gave my friend some much-needed moral support.

She had recently suffered a terrible, spirit-deflating experience after accepting a job writing for Durham's newspaper. M.B. found living in a small, rather incestuous town, far from her family, quite unbearable. The townspeople were close-minded and suspicious of her. She was forced to live in a tiny, dismal rooming house with an eccentric old woman. The weird creature scared the daylights out of M.B. and she was afraid to close her eyes at night.

She had sobbed on the phone every night to her parents and friends and told me brokenly that she finally understood how it felt to want to do yourself in. She sustained by playing Peter Gabriel and Kate Bush's duet, entitled, "Don't Give Up" and finally left Durham to return to Oakville.

I told her that I completely understood her unhappiness and this buoyed her spirit considerably to hear that someone wasn't critizing her for being a quitter, which she really wasn't.

Howard Aster picked me up and drove me to Mosaic Press, where I got the grand tour and was presented with at least forty more books. Howard reminded me a great deal of Woody Alan, with a kind of smallish, pixyish face, diminutive stature and rather rapid, nervous manner of speaking. I felt totally at ease with his self-effacing personality and obvious enthusiasm about my work.

He told me that he wanted me to write a book about my life, which I resisted at first, but then decided to do a fictionalized version of my years at York University and Lakeshore as well as the devastating Behaviour Modification experience.

When I returned home, I immediately began writing and would spend the next five months scrawling pages and pages while my creative mind vacillated in seven hundred milligrams of Nozinan. Concentration was difficult at the best of times and I lost my train of thought a great deal while attempting to bring my characters to life and stay coherent and consistent.

I got a fifteen hundred dollar grant from the Ontario Arts Council, through Mr. Aster and used part of it to purchase a second-hand electric typewriter, since my old one finally gave up the ghost.

Meanwhile, I was developing some strong friendships at W.O.T.C.H. as well as having some major difficulties with Mom. Basically, we got on each other's nerves and were far too enmeshed in one another's lives for our own good.

On top of this, Grandma got very ill that summer and had to be hospitalized at St. Joseph's. She was having terrible diarrhea and the doctors couldn't seem to find out the source of her problem. She lay in her bed, sometimes oblivious to Mom, who visited her every day. We were both very worried about this extremely frail and thin little woman who seemed to be fading away before our very eyes.

With the stress Mom was under and my petty squabbling, we got into many bitter arguments. One night, I flew out of the apartment in a fit of pique, braving a torrential thunderstorm, and walked to the main house where Wendy said, in exasperated tones, "Well, you choose to live there. We're trying to get you to move into one of our group homes, because it isn't healthy to be living with your mother. We don't recommend it."

I was beginning to see her point, but still wasn't comfortable with the idea of giving up my apartment and cramming all of my stuff into a tiny bedroom in a big, old-fashioned house.

Toward the end of the year, I met a rather large, sad-eyed, but extremely kind woman at W.O.T.C.H. named June, who was an aspiring writer like myself. She had been attending meetings with an established author's group and wanted me to join.

There, I met young people who were just starting out in the field and wanted to learn from older, published writers. I attended several meetings, where guest speakers told us about various publications such as London Magazine and what they were looking for. I learned a great deal and was finally beginning to feel like a real writer.

As 1988 started drawing to a close, poor Grandma took a very bad turn and was hospitalized again for the last time. She was going to have surgery to repair her stomach so that she would be able to eat again. She'd been fed through a tube for the past while in the hospital and was definitely not getting any enjoyment out of life.

Grandma had recently been moved into a nursing home and despised it. I didn't blame her, but there really was no alternative. She wasn't well enough to look after herself anymore and needed professional, round-the-clock nursing care.

The day before her surgery, I had this terrible, sinking feeling that I would never see her again. I sat with her in her hospital room and spoke in broken tones, "Grandma, if there's anything I've ever done to hurt you, I'm so sorry. I love you so much."

"No, no, you never hurt me at all," she said kindly, smiling at me, "I always knew you cared a lot about me. It's okay."

I tried not to cry, but I did anyway. I just couldn't shake the feeling, as I walked out of her room, that I'd never get to speak to her again.

I was right. When doctors opened Grandma up, they found cancer and that explained why she had been so sick all that time. They told her afterward and the poor lady just gave up. Two days later, after remaining comatose, she died.

As Mom, Aunt Louise, and I stood at her bedside that last morning, on December third, 1988, I cried out to her, "Grandma, we're all here. We love you."

Then almost magically, she opened her eyes, looked lovingly at all three of us, and then closed them forever. She knew we were there and her last earthly sight was of her sister, daughter and granddaughter, before she went to join her beloved husband in Heaven.

In January of 1989, I took a screenwriting course at Fanshawe College, where Mary Lou Cornish, the instructor, had written many television screenplays and, though they'd all been rejected she'd been given extremely positive feedback about them. She was my age, eager and ambitious,and taught us a great deal about this writing form. We watched a lot of films, such as "Local Hero" and "Never Cry Wolf" and analyzed the scripts.

The other students were eager to learn and were absolutely in love with screenwriting. Randy, a forty-year-old, white-haired, boy-ish man, punctuated nearly every sentence with a hearty laugh and waved his hands around a lot when he spoke. He was intested in learning all he could so that he could make a living as a screen-writer.

Kevin kind of put me off, with his sarcastic comments and the way he downplayed everything I wrote. I learned to expect it from him. However, it turned out that he was more critical of his own work than anyone else's, so I guess it was okay about his negativity.

Marie had had some poems published, was a member of my writer's group and wrote extremely thought-provoking and intelli-gent screenplays. I realized that she would go far in her field.

Sandi was a rather quiet but fun-loving young woman, with a keen, intelligent wit and had set her sights on learning all she could about writing, no matter how she had to go about doing so. I had an unfortunate experience with her later on, one that taught me a lesson about being too utterly naive about people's intentions.

Beverly was a devout Christian writer and was working on a screenplay about Christ's cradle called "The Greatest Gift". She seemed possessed by this amazing serenity and happiness,and I wished I could share her beliefs. I had recently begun to question my faith and would eventually lose it completely for awhile.

Muriel was my favourite of these Fanshawe students and I talked to her a great deal, since we sat together in class. She was two years my senior and thought I was only about twenty-four or so. I let her believe this, after all, I might as well be nine or ten years younger, considering I'd spent that long being locked away from the world. Heather was a rabid trekker and was working on a screenplay about the offspring of the original Enterprise crew. She, like myself, was wildly enthusiastic about music, so the two of us got together and watched videos. She lived only a half block away from Mom's apartment.

We all worked on treatments, a detailed summary of our screenplays and I came up with a story about two sisters, Oriole and Amanda, who grew up in the 1960's, went their own separate ways and then were reunited when Oriole was diagnosed with terminal cancer. It was loosely based on the lives of the Everly Brothers, except for the cancer part, and  stressed the extreme tension be-tween the sisters, especially when they learned that Oriole was dying.

The course lasted six weeks, so a group of us decided to form our own screenwriting faction and meet at one another's homes every week. Mary Lou, Sandy, Beverly, Muriel and I, as well as a young, eighteen-year-old super-brain named Corry, who had an absolutely amazing mind.

I wouldn't have had the nerve or capacity to do any of this if it weren't for W.O.T.C.H. That place gave me the opportunity to interact with people again and develop a sense of self-confidence. I was extremely grateful for all of this.

Sandi found out that I was involved with Mosaic Press and invited me over to her place for supper and to "get to know me better". Her mother was there, a loud, energetic, fast-talking woman who wanted to pump me for information on publishing and get her daughter's "foot in the door", so to speak.

The experience was very negative for me, because I thought Sandi was offering friendship, but instead she just wanted to see what she could get from me. The whole thing left me cold.

In May of that year I went with Mom to Ottawa to take part in a film seminar that was held there every year. It attracted major, established cinema talents from all over Canada and parts of the U.S. to teach fledgling screenwriters, directors and producers the fine art of becoming a success in the business. It cost three hundred dollars but was invaluable, as far as learning the craft from experts and meeting people like Atom Egoyan, who hadn't yet hit it big in the U.S. but was certainly well on his way.

The instructor of our class was Canadian television producer John Frizzell. I liked his informal, relaxed method of teaching, but he had a habit of latching on to one student and concentrating all of his individual attention on her. This year it was a small, complex young woman named Sarah who wrote extremely well despite having suffered some pretty severe personal problems.

I couldn't help but feel drawn toward her sadness, though, as was the rest of the class. It seemed to me, as I'd long observed, that artistic people, for the most part, have a difficult time of it, emotionally speaking. It seems to go with the territory, because we all see too much, feel too deeply and despair over our inability to right the wrongs that we see with the world, and with ourselves.

Even John Frizzell appeared ill-at-ease with everything, despite his rather impressive success. I'm sure that's why I'd always felt so attracted to musicians, the documentarians of society and its ills. Writers share a common bond, no matter what medium we're involved with.

Unfortunately, because of the massive doses of Nozinan I was taking, I couldn't take part in the evening festivities, like the parties, marathon drinking and discussions. I would often fall asleep during the film viewings, snoring loudly and embarrassing myself in front of the other students.

Still, it was a positive experience overall and I even spent the last night with Atom Egoyan at a party, feeling the creative electricity that literally emanated from him. I marvelled at what a far cry this was from my hospitalization periods.

Mom spent the days touring Ottawa and had a wonderful time. It brought us somewhat closer and we developed a strong, mutual respect for one another. We both really needed this time away.

When I returned to London, I was bitterly disappointed that a new film, "Beaches" starring Bette Midler and Barbara Hershey, was strikingly familiar to my screenplay, so I regretfully abandoned it. I began work on another about a disillusioned university professor who becomes romantically involved with a free spirit during an idyllic summer in Florida. M.B. worked on it with me, as she thought it would make an excellent vehicle for Sting, who was desperately in need of a hit movie.

It turned out that this ideal lady suffered from brain damage received when her abusive father hit her and her brother ferociously objected to his sister seeing an older, jaded college professor. The fact that parts of the screenplay smacked of Sting's "Brimstone and Treacle" didn't daunt us and gave us something productive to do when M.B. came to London to visit.

During that summer, it was decided that I would join the day program, as the W.O.T.C.H. staff felt I needed more daily structure than the morning program could provide. I'd begun to get depressed again and had missed a great deal of time there because of overwhelming apathy.

On top of this, I had managed to get addicted to Codeine over the past several months. The pain in my back had long subsided, but I really liked the way the drug made me feel, semi-euphoric and with a sense of well-being that I couldn't seem to get any other way, even with the writing. I lied to Dr. Harris so that he'd give me

Percocet, claiming that my back still hurt and that my migraine headaches were intolerable. In truth, they were manageable with ordinary Tylenol with Codeine that could be obtained from the drug store, but he didn't have to know that.

He only gave me twelve Percocets a weeks, so it became necessary to buy Codeine over the counter. In a short time, I was taking over sixty of them a day. I needed them just to function, never mind the pleasant sensation. Just prior to going to Ottawa, I had been in the hospital because the voices had become disruptive again.

While in there, my Grandpa Wanklin died, but I was so distracted that it didn't hit me at the time. He and Grandma had recently moved from their home in Kitchener to live in Meadowpark Nursing Home, when Grandpa's memory loss, a complication of his diabetes, made it impossible for Grandma to look after him any longer. He had been like an Alzheimer's patient and couldn't do much for himself any longer.

I hadn't really spent much time with them in the past, so I went to Meadowpark on several occasions to visit them, and was disheartened to see how much Grandpa had gone downhill. Grandma cared for him religiously, but it was very hard on her, so when he finally died of a stroke in March of 1989, she realized that he was really better off in many ways.

Grandpa's death didn't sink in for me until I was hospitalized for my Codeine addiction in the latter part of the summer. Dr. Prince decided that I would eventually destroy myself if I kept abusing the drug the way I was, so I was put on a program of gradual withdrawal and monitored closely.

I dissolved into tears one afternoon when I realized that I'd never see my grandfather again. I was having a hard time as my body adjusted to being without the Codeine and the stress was overwhelming for me. The psychological withdrawal was worse than the physical and I didn't know if I could survive without this medication that I had come to think of as my friend and constant companion.

Still, I got off of it, and swore that I'd never touch another Percocet, Tylenol Number 3 or over-the-counter Codeine again as long as I lived. I couldn't imagine going through that nightmare one more time.

My book was finally completed, such as it was, and I used

five hundred dollars of my grant to get it professionally typed. I just couldn't face doing it myself, as I was so sick of the project and when it was done, I mailed it to Mosaic Press. Mom and Dad both read it, flinching with the pain it evoked, but I wasn't satisfied with something I'd created while stoned on Codeine and Nozinan. I didn't hold a lot of hope that it would get published.

Moira was thrilled that I'd written it, though, and said to me, "Way to go! Now the world will know all about that despicable L.P.H. and how demoralizing and cruel it is."

I was thankful to be away from that institution and vowed I would never return under any circumstances.

The day program was long, extraordinarily exhausting and basically useless, in my opinion. I hated being trapped in a series of discussion groups, cooking, cleaning the house, listening to people's problems and card-playing. The only upside was our forays to the Y twice a week, where I took part in aerobics classes, swam, and rode the exercise bikes and stair-master.

I'd met a shy, reclusive eighteen-year-old schizophrenic named Sheila, who looked closer to twelve and saw me as some kind of ideal specimen worthy of emulation and her full attention. I was embarrassed by this, but liked this pretty, dark-haired girl who'd been a classmate of Maryanne's at Central Secondary School and who'd had to leave grade ten when she got sick.

She heard voices, like I did, but seemed more confused and befuddled than I. She lived at Wortley House, another W.O.T.C.H. group home, but wanted to move back home with her parents. Carla went with me to the Y, and we talked a great deal about writing and music.

I had developed the annoying habit of apologizing profusely all over the place, based on rampant insecurity and fear of people turning against me. It drove everyone batty and I was told repeatedly to "Stop saying you're sorry!" I became even more self-absorbed than I'd ever been in my life and got hopelessly lost in my own angst.

I felt I was wasting my life away and had blown my big chance to be a published author before I reached the age of thirty-five. I missed the intellectual stimulation of the film seminar and had started skipping a lot of our screenwriting meeting because I was so tired after slogging away at the day program for seven hours a day, five days a week.

Finally, at the end of the year, I resolved to make the best of my situation. I resigned myself to the schedule, hoping to get rid of some of my negativity and get along better with the other members.

A new staff member had recently joined W.O.T.C.H., named Dave Small, who had known Mom from her work at the RNA school. He was the most positive, sincere and big-hearted man I'd ever met, with flaming red hair, a splash of freckles on his beaming, soulful face,and I was crazy about him. He was twenty-seven, recently married, unfortunately,and had a burning desire to fix up all our lives and make everybody happy again.

I used to kid him that he had an "unrelenting Pollyanna complex", because he always saw the good in every situation and refused to let any of us get down on ourselves. He loved music, which was definitely a plus in his favour and he got me into the songs of Sinead O'Connor and Midnight Oil. He didn't care for the classic rock hits, preferring a more alternative slant to things, so I told him to give a listen to R.E.M.

I listened to their "Green" album a great deal, which, with its heavy political edge, made it sound an awful lot like "Document, Part Two" in many ways. One song really leapt out of my Walkman and hit me squarely in the face. It was entitled "World Leader Pretend" and could have been my theme song. I sat for hours, literally hypnotized by the familiar sentiments expressed by someone else whose career I'd been following from the outset.

Well, 1990 was the year I stopped fighting the W.O.T.C.H. system and agreed to move into Craig House group home that was merely a block away from Mom's Gartshore apartment and a stonesthrow from the main house. Mom was intrigued that this place was only two houses down from where we had lived in 1958 and she took it as a very odd twist of fate. She wasn't terribly happy about me moving out, but basically wanted what was best for me.

I shared a room with forty-year-old Heather and lived with five other people. They seeded friendly and pleasant enough. Ted was a cheerful, outgoing young man who would soon get his own place, twenty-two-year-old Bill, who had difficulties managing his life and needed the emotional support of the house, twenty-four-year-old Shelley, a small, sad girl with a tragic past, thirty-six-year-old Melissa, a flighty, nervous woman who seemed to be in a world of her own much of the time, and twenty-nine-year-old

Frank.

Frank was a strikingly attractive young man, who immediately caught my attention when I arrived at Craig Street. We talked a great deal about music, Suzanna Moody, the Canadian writer, and our unstable futures. He didn't feel he had one to speak of and was extremely frustrated that he couldn't study anymore or keep his job at Cuddy Farms. He'd been raised on a farm and wanted to return to that quiet, uncomplicated life, away from "city folk" who made fun of him for being mentally ill. He despaired over being schizophrenic and felt he would do anything to get rid of this scourge on his formerly agile mind.

Shortly after arriving at Craig house, I suffered a minor breakdown, which had been brought on when I drastically reduced my dosage of Nozinan. I couldn't sleep for nights on end and began to hear voices telling me to destroy myself and that "You know what you've done. You're evil and cannot be allowed to continue living".

I was readmitted to University Hospital, where I spent my days huddled in the common room, refusing to eat, talk or engage in the ward activities.

I met two extraordinary people there, who had arrived about the same time as I. Gina, a tall, heavy-set girl of twenty-one, suffered from severe depression and was admitted to hospital following an overdose. She was a student at the university, away from home for the first time and didn't know why she felt so terrible all the time. She lost herself in science fiction books and Star Trek, and had all the original episodes of the 1960's series memorized.

We talked a lot, since we shared a room and she told me that her mother was manic depressive and Gina had had to rescue her from serious suicide attempts since she was a child. I thought perhaps she'd inherited her mother's illness, until she added that she'd been adopted. Gina grew sad when she revealed that her brothers made fun of her because she wasn't a blood relative.

We started hanging out with another trekker, twenty-year-old Trevor, who impressed me with his intelligence, wicked sense of humour and poignant unhappiness. He had also been attending Western, but had suffered a breakdown and wasn't able to concentrate anymore. Doctors couldn't seem to come up with a diagnosis for him and experimented with all sorts of drugs. It was like looking at myself thirteen years ago.

Trevor spoke with a slight lisp, was chubby and loveable, but some of the other patients made fun of him, much to my dismay. He strongly identified with Supertramp's tortured song, "Rudy" and I understood why. He was heavily steeped in the same kind of music as I was and eschewed the light, simplistic stuff, professing it to be empty and inane.

He was a wonderful kid, who teased me for being "ancient" at thirty-four, but admiring my "youthful outlook". I slapped him in mock annoyance and then the two of us would collapse with laughter. Trevor was very good for my mental health.

I didn't want to leave the hospital this time, as I was unhappy at W.O.T.C.H. and didn't exactly love living with six other people with no privacy and nowhere to write or listen to my records. I used the ward as an escape, once Dr. Prince put me on Perphenazine to control the voices and felt that I was still incapable of functioning on the outside anyway.

Dr. Prince told me that I couldn't hide there at the hospital, for the beds were desperately needed for really sick people. I still felt very depressed so he increased my Sinequan, leaving me feeling puffy and bloated as it did at the higher doses.

I was finding it hard to eat during that time as well. I still wasn't eating meat, so was living primarily on vegetables, fruit and coffee. Trevor was a vegetarian as well and had been for several years, but he was quite addicted to Coca Cola. He'd even drink two cans for breakfast and wouldn't go for more than half an hour without downing one or two.

I started doing some running while I was in the hospital, now that I wasn't so doped up on Nozinan. When I was sent back to W.O.T.C.H. during the day, I ran to and from University Hospital, a total of eight miles. I was pleased to see that I was losing weight and wanted to get down to one hundred pounds by the time I was released.

Finally, I got the boot and returned to Craig house, where I was surprised to discover that Roberta would be moving in. She was a close friend of Shelley's, as the two women had shared a lot in common. Roberta had gained a great deal of weight since I last saw her in 1980 and I barely recognized her.

She remembered me, and felt very bad about treating me so negatively when I was flipping out on H2 all the time. She now realized that I wasn't doing it deliberately and apologized, saying she'd been pretty messed up back then too. She and Shelley spent a lot of time down in the television lounge, smoking and watching movies on the VCR. I ventured down there occasionally when I didn't mind inhaling the cigarette fumes. I'd quit again late in 1988 and was certain that I would never use tobacco again.

Poor Roberta had had her bladder removed several years before and wore a plastic bag attached to a stoma. At night she had to use a large plastic bag fixed to her side with a tube and said it made her feel like a "freak".

She still did a lot of time in the L.P.H. and had been involved with W.O.T.C.H. for the past five years, living at another group home on Frank Place before arriving at Craig Street. As the months wore on, she lost a lot of weight by starving herself. Shelley joined in this activity and neither of them would join us upstairs for supper.

I had to cook three times a week, usually with Frank, but I refused to eat meat. I was forced to live on cheese and vegetables, since the mainstays there were beef, chicken and pork. I told Ron Rook, one of the workers there, that it would cost a lot less if we bought lentils and beans instead, but he nixed this idea. "You can't live on that stuff," he said through his walrus mustache.

We had to go grocery shopping every Thursday, which usually took several hours, because we also stopped at the discount store for dry goods.

Ron was a good head, a chipper and energetic forty-one-year-old who genuinely cared about us but wouldn't take any nonsense. The two staff members never stayed all night, but arrived for several hours during the evening to run our weekly meetings and make sure that none of us were killing each other.

Frank and I grew closer with time, and eventually began going out steadily. We comforted one another when we felt depressed, which was often and went for long walks in Thames Park, holding hands and holding out for something better to happen in our troubled lives.

I went out running at five AM every morning for ninety minutes and kept myself in pretty good physical condition. I weighed one hundred five pounds and was satisfied with that, even though one hundred would have been preferable. But my cerebral fitness suffered at the group home, as my writing came to a standstill and I didn't even crack my typewriter all the time I was there. It was starting to really distress me that my life was so empty and devoid of purpose.

I spent weekends with Mom and was relieved to escape the rather oppressive environment at Craig house for a couple of days a week. Dave Small came to work at the home after several months and that made things a bit more bearable.

While talking to Roberta one day, I learned that poor Angela had killed herself by leaping from her eighth-storey balcony. I was very saddened to hear that the young woman who'd been a friend and support to me on Behaviour Modification had finally given into her vicious demons and listened to the voices that tormented her for so long. I hoped that she had finally found some peace wherever she was now.

Then, in October, I was once again admitted to University Hospital, this time because I wasn't functioning very well in the day program and spent a lot of my days crying in the washroom.

I didn't understand why I was so unhappy and where this pervasive feeling of doom came from that came over me all the time. I was sobbing incessantly while Dave tried to help me and was disrupting the day program by going on about my lousy life all the time.

One young man, Mike, who suffered from manic depressive illness, said bluntly to me one afternoon, "Jane, you are so damned negative." He was right. I just could not climb out of the deep hole that my life had become.

As predicted, my book wasn't published, but Mr. Astor didn't want to give up on me. "Keep it up," he told me on the phone, "Write, and don't stop until you have something we can use. I like your style. We get thousands of manuscripts a week here and your poetry one really caught my attention three years ago."

But I still couldn't write anything. I sat in my garret room, rocking on the hard, narrow bed and feeling sorry for myself. When I got released from the hospital after a few weeks of going nowhere, I felt even worse.

Jim and his new girlfriend, Diane arrived from Vancouver for Christmas that year and I was pleased to see that my brother was putting his life back together again after Pauline kicked him out the year before.

Jim had finally gotten into medical school in 1989 and was right in the middle of some serious studying when his wife pulled that fast one and told him not to come back. Still, I was deliriously happy for him that he'd finally achieved a goal he'd been working toward for years and no-one deserved it more than Jim.

Diane seemed very nice, with a gentle kindness, but when they arrived I was in such a turmoil with my unstrung life that I really didn't enjoy their visit. I hated myself for being so selfish and robbing my brother of the opportunity to learn about his new life.

Then, after a year at the group home, I got the chance to move into one of the W.O.T.C.H. permanent houses on Forest View Circle. I'd be living with three other people, one of them Sheila.

I moved early in May of 1991. It was a huge, modern house, with four bedrooms, a living room, family room, large kitchen, a full bathroom and a smaller one downstairs. I got the biggest room, through drawing straws, and Mom bought me a bed. I moved in my stereo, television, a large bookcase, and a rocking chair. W.O.T.C.H. provided all the other furniture, bought from nearby Patton's Place, plus all the dinnerware, cutlery, glasses, cups, pots and pans.

It was our job to keep the place clean and tidy. Something we didn't do very well I must admit. Sheila was ecstatic to be out of the Wortley group home and settled in quite easily.

The other two members were twenty-four-year-old Tony and thirty-seven-year-old Ruth Ann. Tony was an excruciatingly shy young man, with a severe case of acne and eyes that never met anyone's gaze. He never really talked, but mumbled almost inaudibly. Still, I liked him for his diligence and sense of self-reliance and for this sly little grin that occasionally spread across his face.

Ruth Ann was rather annoying, with this really whiny voice and a pervasive negativity, and none of us got along very well with her. Still, she was capable and fairly stable when she wanted to be. After several weeks we all adapted to this more independent lifestyle.

I befriended a stray cat, feeding him every day and getting a dead mouse for a gift. I noticed one day that he was wearing tags so we called the number of the Animal Hospital and found out his name was Sam. Not only that, but he lived just three doors away from us, so I reluctantly gave him up.

Later, I discovered he had been put to sleep because of a flea problem. I cried for days with the thought of this poor animal having to die for such a stupid reason.

I decided to go to the Humane Society and get a cat of my

own. The best thing I ever did was bring a big, sad, golden-eyed grey Tabby named Julius home with me. He was a year old, with no history and was the most affectionate, kind-spirited feline I have ever encountered.

We became inseparable, even after I had him neutered and declawed (at W.O.T.C.H.'s insistence). I helped get a law passed that the homes could have cats, saying that pets are terrific therapy for mental patients. I just adored that animal, as I do today and vowed I would always take good care of him. I didn't let him outside, as there was so much traffic in our area and I couldn't bear the thought of him getting hit by a car.

Frank and I were still seeing each other and spent weekends together at Forest View. Then, gradually,as it always did, my happiness began to wane and by the end of the summer,I found myself back at University Hospital.

Now Dr. Prince had had enough of my multiple admissions, so he informed me that, even though he knew I didn't want it, I would be going back to the dreaded L.P.H. I was inconsolable, but understood that I wasn't getting any better and couldn't keep running back to the tenth floor everytime I got depressed.

To my horror, I was sent to H2, of all places, home of the now-defunct Behaviour Modification unit. I cringed as I walked onto the ward and the door was abruptly locked behind me.

It was an admitting ward, whose patients came to be assessed and then were kept for a maximum of two months. I was somewhat relieved to hear this, although I really didn't want to know what happened to the poor, unfortunate souls who weren't well enough in eight weeks to be released.

After my initial shock and revulsion wore off, I settled into the routine, such as it was. I was pleased to see that the decor had changed for the better. One half of the linoleum floor was carpeted, the walls were a lighter shade of blue and there was an abundance of greenery and framed pictures dotting the landscape. Smoking was only allowed in one section of the ward, something for which my lungs were very thankful. Best of all, there wasn't a rug, ball of wool or hook in sight.

One of the patients, a small, thin man of about fifty with a narrow, haggard face and nicotine-stained fingers, took it upon himself to "show me the ropes" and explain exactly what went on there, as opposed to what was supposed to. Bruce said that the staff really didn't have much time to spend with the patients,and it was up to us to look after each other. He said that if I ever needed anything, I should call on him, "'cause the damn nurses never come out in the dayroom, except to watch T.V."

Another patient, thirty-two-year-old Amy, was diminutive, pretty, child-like and painfully depressed. She hardly ate and would only speak to Bruce. Gradually, her mood improved substantially,and we became friends, going for walks around the grounds and talking about her family in Lucknow.

There was another Bruce on H2, a young man with only one leg, who lurched about the ward on crutches while his left stub swung haphazardly in the air. He talked nonsense, raging about being possessed by demonic forces and laughed intermittently. He was alternately mellow and frighteningly angry. One day, when he looked at the small chapel on the grounds, he collapsed on the grass and screamed ferociously, uttering a barrage of obscenities for at least a half and hour.

"I think Bruce has a bit of a problem with religion," I remarked to Amy, who stood staring at him with her mouth agape.

Mom looked after Julius while I was in the hospital, although Tony was good about feeding him and changing his litter. She felt bad that I was involved with the L.P.H. again, but I assured her I wouldn't be in too long.

At first, the psychiatrist in charge of my case was Dr. Karunaratne, whom I only talked to once. After a couple of weeks I was handed over to a Dr. Marth. He upset me by saying that he didn't think I was schizophrenic after I'd gotten used to the label. The reason for my peculiar reaction was this: I wasn't
prepared to being relentlessly experimented on in a frantic effort to be saddled with yet another diagnosis. I'd been there, done that, and just wanted to be left alone.

Nothing much was done for me there, although Dr. Marth turned out to be a pleasant, amicable man who applauded my courage and intelligence for some unknown reason. I told him he was grossly over-rating my attributes, but informed him that I might as well be released from the hospital for all the good it was doing. Marth agreed, so after my shortest stay in my psychiatric history, I returned to the W.O.T.C.H. house and tried to pick up the pieces of my life.

That was also the year that I made a significant and crucial decision that would have severe emotional repercussions. I had a tubal ligation.

The reason for this was because Frank and I planned to be married, for we'd grown very close and we were in love; that is, he was in love with me and I was eager to shed my single trappings for a sense of permanence and security. I cared deeply for Frank, but we didn't share a great deal in common, save for our illness and uncertain future. He wasn't particularly interested in music, movies, exercise or creative endeavors, so we never went anywhere or engaged in any stimulating activities.

But still, I enjoyed the closeness we shared and the way he gazed so lovingly at me with those large, expressive brown eyes of his. He wanted the two of us to live on a farm, something that intrigued me because of the availability of animals and the distance from the loud, obnoxious city.

We knew that with both parents being diagnosed as schizophrenic, our children would have a ninety per cent chance of inheriting the disorder,and neither of us were prepared to damn our innocent offspring with the pain and distress we'd endured for so long.

So I entered St. Joseph's Hospital as an out-patient, where Dr. King, my gynaecologist, performed the surgery. I was extremely uptight about going under an anesthetic, but the operation went without a hitch. Afterward, I was in a great deal of pain and spent hours huddled in my bed and biting down on my pillow.

I was surprised at how well I was taking the fact that I was now sterile and had no possibility of conceiving a child. I figured it was for the best, overall,and possessed a certain amount of altruistic satisfaction that I hadn't insisted that Frank have a vasectomy instead. In retrospect, I believe this was just one more example of my misguided martyr complex, something I'd grown very familiar and comfortable with over the years.

Several months later, I became consumed by my old nemesis of severe depression. I began to isolate myself in my room, formulating plans to cut up my arms and distract myself from the emotional pain. I hadn't indulged this urge for a long time, since it was forbidden at University Hospital, but now that I was affiliated with the L.P.H. again, there wasn't much of a deterrent. After all, who could threaten me now? I was already back in the Pit. I put R.E.M.'s "Out of Time"in the cassette deck and listened to the mournful

"Losing My Religion" while Julius, sensing my mood, rubbed comfortingly up against me and purred his little head off.

Ruth Ann had left our house and was replaced by a young Born-Again Christian named Petra. She was thoughtful, dreamy and spoke frankly about her "religious psychosis" and her months of treatment at the L.P.H. She was quite enthusiastic about her new home and made ambitious efforts to befriend Sheila and me. Petra had grown disturbed about my sullenness and silent withdrawal of late. When she opened my bedroom door that evening, it was in time to see blood pouring disquietingly out of a long, crude gash on my left forearm.

"That's it. You're going to the hospital. I can't deal with this." She was very upset, with good reason, and insisted that she and I take a cab to the emergency department at Victoria Hospital to get me sewed up.

I sat glumly with her as the somewhat bewildered cab driver took us there and knew with creeping sensation of dread that this was my blood-stained trail back to the L.P.H. I didn't really care, however, for I'd been feeling so numb and bereft of spirit that it didn't make any difference whether I was living at home or locked up in an institution. I hadn't been able to do anything productive for weeks and everyone at W.O.T.C.H. was fed up with my attitude and refusal to take part in the activities without a lot of petulant whining.

They sewed me up at the hospital, and then shipped me to the "Highbury Hilton" where I ended up on K2 this time, under the care of an extraordinarily compassionate and giving psychiatrist named Dr. Paul Wadden. He was intelligent, soft-spoken and told me that this kind of depression often occurs in women my age and that he was certain I could be helped with the right medication.

I liked this ward better than H2, even if the nurses treated me like a behaviour problem and seemed to be on some kind of power trip. But those were my observations, and not entirely accurate. For one thing, I really was a behaviour problem, with my tendency toward cutting and closing myself off to them and the staff on K2 were just doing their job in trying to protect me from myself. They couldn't just allow unchecked chaos to abound, after all.

Dr. Wadden's patients all thought very highly of him, as did the nurses. He saw me every day, for at least an hour, and talked about my past hospitalization, asked when this last episode of depression had started and did I know what triggered it.

I said I hadn't a clue, that everything was "just fine" and there were no major stresses or upsets at the house, at W.O.T.C.H. or with my boyfriend.

Gradually, as the days wore on, I came to realize that there were indeed some problems between Frank and me, ones that were quite unsolvable. For one thing, I was disturbed by him constantly telling me that "if it weren't for you, I'd kill myself for sure". Several years before, Frank had doused himself with gasoline in an empty field and was about to set himself on fire. Fortunately, he was struck with a dramatic vision and heard God's voice speaking from the heavens: "Your time of rest is at hand," then explaining that he must evaluate his life and not destroy it. This filled him with a certain amount of hope and redemption, so he put his lighter down and went home to get rid of the gasoline-soaked garments.

But Frank despised being schizophrenic, for he felt inferior to his "more successful" brother and thought he was incapable of acquiring any measure of quality in his life. I didn't like being told that I was all that stood between Frank and self-annihilation. It placed a lot of pressure on me and I couldn't really deal with that.

The growing realization that I'd soon be married to a man who never wanted to go anywhere or do anything made me shudder. I couldn't fathom being on some isolated farm with nothing but cows, chickens and wide open, deserted fields. I was pretty much a city slicker and received positive vibes from the fast pulse of the cosmopolitan milieu.

Worst of all, I wasn't in love with him and it was no longer enough just to care and feel affection for him. He had told me after we made love in a cornfield that I had been his first. This didn't surprise me, since he was quite inexperienced. I was somewhat as well, so our lovemaking was awkward but endearing. True, Frank was eager, warm and giving, but I felt I needed a man who knew what he was doing and what I wanted, since I wasn't really sure myself.

While I was on K2, I met a twenty-seven-year-old man named Darren, who struck me immediately with his tortured demeanour and plaintive outcries against his unhappy world. He was a devout Christian, but instead of bringing him peace and personal fulfilment, it filled him with pain that Jesus had had to die for our sins and we still hadn't learned anything. Darren was plagued with inner demons that would not let him rest and he had difficulty formulating thoughts and sentences.

I was drawn into this sphere of angst and before long we began a tumultuous relationship that literally pulsated with intensity and feeling. I was crazy about him, but agonized over the fact that I was cheating on Frank and spoke of this to Darren one afternoon.

He told me that I would have to make a decision, because it was driving him nuts that the two of us had to sneak around and skirt around the outer edges of a relationship. We kissed passionately, out of the prying gaze of the staff and made dream-spun plans to spend the rest of our lives together.

Darren liked my skinny body and I admired his rock star eccentric looks. One day, he shaved his head and it just added to the alluring mystique.

Finally, however, I couldn't live with my guilty conscience any longer. I had to break off with this gentle, tragic figure who loved so deeply and swam in dangerous, shark-infested waters of mental distortion. I despised this decision, for it wasn't following the messages my heart was giving me. Darren was very saddened and looked at me from a distance from that point on.

Two years later, he took his own life, alone and anguished in his apartment. I never forgave myself for not sticking by him and perhaps offering him a chance for happiness and life.

I decided to break off with Frank as well, while I was in the hospital, something I certainly wasn't looking forward to. I knew he would be devastated, but I could no longer keep something alive that just didn't seem to be going anywhere for me. He would come to see me every day. When I stammered for a few minutes, then blurted out that I just couldn't stay in this relationship, that it was my fault and due to my own shortcomings, he became extremely distraught.

However, he handled his emotions admirably and as I watched his tall, straight back walk out of the ward and out of my life, I broke down and cried, soaking my skin with bitter tears of shame and self-recrimination.

I used my guilt as an excuse to plan an afternoon of vicious cutting several days later. I went AWOL from the hospital in a cab and made long, angry vertical slashes on both forearms in the family room at home. Julius howled pitifully as blood ran over the

furniture, stained the rug, and punctuated the air with its feral
odour.

I made quite a mess and did a very poor job of cleaning it up
afterward. Then, after growing alarmed at my inability to stop the
intense flow of blood, I called Victoria Hospital. Then, I was
immediately picked up by ambulance and taken to the now-familiar
emergency room. I hadn't wanted to die, after all, and, following a
stitch-up by a  very sarcastic and sloppy intern, who did a very
unprofessional job, I was carted back to K2.

Dr. Wadden was extremely displeased with my actions and
regretfully sent me to an intermediate unit. He said that I needed a
much longer hospitalization period than an admitting ward could
provide. This began my long-term relationship with G2, another
ex-Behaviour Modification setting and I was determined to despise
it.

Petra freaked when she returned home to the result of my
wild razor blade frenzy, was inconsolable for weeks. Our friendship suffered tremendously because of it. It was a very selfish, cruel
thing  for me to have done and W.O.T.C.H. housing authorities
wondered if I should have the right to stay there.

Mom was informed of what I did and was terribly upset with
me, wondering what on earth was happening to her daughter. She
hoped I'd get the help I obviously needed on G2.

I was put under the care of a middle-aged, Middle-Eastern
female psychiatrist named Dr. Hussain, who said little and offered
no feedback, except to tell me that I would undergo extremely
detailed psychological testing to determine my proper diagnosis.

She, like Dr. Marth, didn't believe that I was schizophrenic,
so I was given pages and pages of questions to answer. These
would then be fed into a computer and analyzed thoroughly. Some
of them were quite ludicrous, such as "Answer yes or no: I do not
believe in the laws of the land",and "I have never ridden in an
automobile". I wondered if this was some kind of sick joke, but
then decided that they were just trying to determine how crazy we
were or weren't. Other questions involved trying to discover if  we
felt very lonely, hopeless, or contemplated suicide a great deal.

When I finished them all, over a period of many hours, I felt I
had answered as honestly and truthfully as I could. I desperately
wanted the doctors to get to the bottom of my problems and fix
them.

I settled down on the ward and got acquainted with some of the patients. Joanne was upset at being transferred here from K2, where, like myself, she'd been greatly impressed with Dr. Wadden. She was on a spectacular high, running about constantly and speaking in a loud, rapid-firing voice. I figured she must be manic depressive and I was correct. She was dark, pretty, a year my senior and liked to help everybody.

Joanne was extremely affectionate to the more withdrawn patients and didn't seem particularly anxious to leave hospital. She refused to take the Lithium that was prescribed for her and was getting a lot of flak from Dr. Hussain. She threatened to discharge her patient if she did not comply with the treatment.

Deirdre was severely obese, weighing over three hundred twenty pounds and was a chronic self-abuser, with webs of scars on both arms. She seemed painfully depressed most of the time, but like Joanne, was very interested in the other patients' welfare.

One afternoon, a tall, thin man with unkempt grey hair, a scruffy, unshaven face and cloudy eyes sat down beside me and gazed furtively at me. His mouth was set in a grim line and his expression flickered a flame of recognition. Suddenly I remebered him as Garon, the man from Behaviour Modification whom I'd spent hours talking to about music, literature and academe. I had greatly appreciated his gentle integrity and shy admiration for a mixed-up twenty-four-year-old who had been lost in a stifling cavern of hopelessness in the other H2 of 1979.

Then, as quickly as he'd arrived, Garon stood up and walked away without speaking a word. He seemed ill-at-ease and desperately unhappy and my heart went out for his dramatic decline over the past thirteen years.

Other patients milled about in a blurred haze and my memories of their names and faces are frustratingly unclear. I was too wrapped up in my own miserable situation to extend myself very much at this time. I spent most of my days with my Walkman and solitary, self-pitying ruminations.

The nurses here were a definite step up from the ones on K2. Judy Carscadden was the head nurse, an attractive, blonde woman of about forty-three who did her best to create a nurturing and pleasant environment for us on the ward. Her staff talked to me a great deal, trying to get a handle on my negativity and self-abusive tendencies. I wasn't terribly receptive to any of them, however, and refused to say much of anything.

One afternoon, a small, dark delicately-featured young woman walked onto the ward, carrying a thick folder. She then motioned for me to join her in the meeting room down the hall. I followed her, figuring I must have done something wrong, but didn't really care at this point. She introduced herself as Dr. Farida Spencer, the ward psychologist, and fixed me with her large, brown eyes and shy smile. She then informed me that she had the results of my test and what followed was nothing short of nerve-splitting bombshell.

"Well, you are definitely not schizophrenic. We checked the results several times, and it's been determined that you suffer from an illness known as Borderline Personality Disorder."

I was incredulous. "That's a pile of crap! What the hell kind of label is that to dump on someone? You make me sound like some kind of pathetic joke!" All of a sudden, I no longer had the "prestige" of being safely insane and worthy of a certain amount of quirky "respect". I was now listed as being on some borderline of a ridiculous sham of a "diagnosis" that made me sound insignificant and disgusting. Personality disorder? "You mean, I'm like, just nasty and stupid, with some defect in my basic, fundamental make-up? Lady, you are full of shit!"

Undaunted, Dr. Spencer continued, saying that the tests showed that I felt empty and devoid of purpose and that out of a checklist of ten borderline symptoms, I displayed a staggering eight. Some of these included severe depression, suicidal tendencies, drug abuse, eating disorders, cutting, and indications of a certain amount of psychosis. She explained further by showing me a hand-drawn diagram of circles touching each other and the symptoms written in the middle of them. She indicated where the borders all met, thus the cryptic name.

"Okay, so what's this personality element?" My hostility was still in full-fledged bristle mode.

"Well, it could be the result of some early childhood abuse. We don't know for sure."

I sat up straight and yelled, practically spitting at the poor woman, "Hey, I was never abused. Never! My parents may have had their problems, but they never took them out on my brother and I. How can you spout all this garbage? There's a family history of schizophrenia for God's sake!"

Dr. Spencer decided that I was worked up enough for one

session. She told me that I would meet with her once a week for an hour to try to "deal with my problems" and look for some solutions to them.

"Thanks a hell of a lot," I snarled, getting up and walking quickly toward the door. "You really made my day". Something in my head didn't want to relinquish my former diagnosis of schizophrenia. It was a devastating illness, for sure, but it didn't involve any therapy and delving into the past. I just wasn't prepared for any psychoanalytic bullshit.

My depression deepened following that unpleasant encounter with the psychologist. I turned into myself and couldn't talk to the nurses. I just wanted out of that hospital and far away from all of these disquieting new developments in my psychiatric life.

My next session with Dr. Spencer involved a lot of "extended Pinter pauses" as I sat glumly, chin my hands and staring at the floor. She must have realized that she had her work cut out for her.

Dr. Hussain took me off the Sinequan, since it wasn't working very well, and put me on another antidepressant, one of the new, somewhat controversial drugs called Prozac. Within a couple of days, my depression had lifted considerably, but unfortunately the medication got me so wired that I couldn't sleep, eat and I was incapable of sitting still or shutting my mouth. I rattled on incessantly, talking basic gibberish. So after being on twenty milligrams a day for eight days, I was taken off.

Hussain put me back on Sinequan and upped the dosage, which appeared to be effective, despite those unpleasant side effectsof bloating and fatigue.

After a couple of months of stabilizing and perking up substantially, I was released and instructed to keep seeing Dr. Spencer on an out-patient basis. I still considered this an utter waste of time, but agreed to go every Monday afternoon.

After my release, I resumed attending the day program and even worked in the cafe downstairs in the main house. We didn't make much money, but it felt good to be doing some kind of work again after so many years. I lived a quiet, uncomplicated life with my roommates and dear little Julius, who had greatly missed me and was even more loving and affectionate than ever.

My contentment was short-lived, however. By the summer of 1992, I returned to my old habits of wallowing in self-pity. About this time, I decided that I couldn't stand being without male companionship, so I got together with Frank again and mended some pretty heavily-damaged fences.

He told me that he had cried uncontrollably for days after I broke up with him and I assured him that it was a momentary lapse of reason and would never happen again. This was extremely dishonest and selfish (sentiments I was well acquainted with, by the way) for I still wasn't in love with him. I just wanted the security of having a boyfriend.

At thirty-one, Frank was physically appealing, adored me and filled an emotional void that W.O.T.C.H., my roommates and my semi-estranged family could not. We got together in my room to listen to records and make love, even though I didn't get a hell of a lot out of it. Julius disapproved of our activity and meowed incessantly as we indulged our primal urges. He must have known more than I gave him credit for.

Slowly and painfully, I became aware of how much my tube-tying had robbed from me. I was now thirty-seven,and found myself staring obsessively at babies and small children. But it could never be for me and as I cuddled Julius' small, furry body to me, I longed for a tiny human who would look to me for love and guidance,and who would love me unconditionally.

Petra eventually moved out, as she couldn't reconcile herself to living with somebody who slashed herself and bled all over the house and we got another roommate, twenty-six-year-old Daryl. He impressed me with his intelligence, musical tastes (leaning toward the alternative), intense love of Star Trek and cyberpunk, and refreshing honesty. He was devastatingly attractive and took a liking to me, speaking kindly with a pronounced British accent.

Nick was a close friend of Trevor's, who he'd met at one of the W.O.T.C.H. group homes, so it was great to have my old friend come over once in awhile. He and Daryl appeared to have a great deal in common.

Unfortunately, Daryl and Sheila didn't hit it off at all and argued incessantly. He saw her as a whiny, immature kid,and she despised his temper tantrums and coarse way of speaking to her. I often had to be the peacekeeper, lest they kill each other.

Daryl wasn't crazy about Frank either and it really pissed him that we'd spend so much time making out in my room, which was right next to his. He wondered what I saw in him and I merely replied that he was a "warm, kind person" then added with a wink, "not to mention a hell of a good lay." That certainly didn't go over big with Daryl, who smirked in disgust and turned his ghettoblaster on real loud.

As summer got into full swing, I decided to stop taking my medication. I thought it was clouding my head up far too much and making me too drowsy. This was not a good idea, for within three weeks, the decision nearly cost me my life.

One afternoon, when I'd just gotten all my prescriptions filled, I bemoaned the fact that my life was useless, meaningless and that everything was over for me. I was trapped in a relationship with a man I only pretended to love, I could never have a child, I was saddled with a ridiculous, nonsensical diagnosis and my writing had dried up and blown away, probably forever.

That had kept me going for so long and now I'd never make a mark as an author. The day program was merely a way to put in endless time, signifying nothing and worst of all, I despised myself. There was a pervading sense that something really awful had happened to me once, and I would awake nights, drenched in sweat and trembling wildly. I couldn't make any sense of it all.

Around seven PM, while Sheila was at her Dad's, Daryl was out with Trevor and Tony was sequestered in his room watching television, I lay out my four pill bottles on the counter, along with a full bottle of Tylenol, and filled a large tumbler with water. Then I stood there in the cluttered kitchen, while Julius looked on morosely, and swallowed over four hundred pills, gagging, choking and overcome with waves of nausea. Those sensations dissipated with the grim satisfaction of knowing that I was soon going to be dead and forgotten.

After twenty minutes or so, the last pill was downed,and I walked upstairs like a condemned person climbing the "39 Steps" to the gallows, lay on my bed, and put the Everly Brothers on the turntable. It seemed appropriate, somehow, for the last sounds heard to be those chilling, soul-searing harmonies of my long-dead youth. Then I waited for sweet nothingness to take over.

Then, just as I was drifting off, the doorbell rang. "What the hell? Who could that possibly be?" I thought rather fuzzily, deciding to ignore it.

The next thing I knew, someone began banging loudly on the front door and Frank's voice yelled, "Hey, Jane! You there? Don't you remember we were supposed to get together tonight? Answer the door! I know you're there; I can hear your record player!"

Oh God, I'd completely forgotten about him. Cursing inwardly at this very unwelcome intrusion, I stumbled awkwardly down the stairs and pulled the door open, hoping I could quickly get rid of him.

Frank stood there, looking somewhat bewildered. "What's the matter? You look awful."

"Never mind," I mumbled, "I don't feel very well. Do you think we could make it another time?" Then I felt myself falling forward, as if I were on a ship that was engulfed in an angry, choppy sea.

Frank caught me and recoiled in fear and horror. "What the fuck did you do?"

My tongue felt too thick to formulate words, so I merely grunted and tried to push him outside. He fought his way back in, which wasn't difficult under the circumstances, and saw the empty pill bottles on the counter. It wasn't a very smart move to leave them there in plain sight like that. Frank was terrified and furious and decided to take me outside in the fresh air and walk the drugs off.

I don't remember much after that, except the pavement rushing up to my face. What Frank did was run to the house to call an ambulance, which arrived swiftly and rushed me, sirens screaming, to Victoria Hospital's Critical Care Trauma Centre.

There, doctors and nurses worked frantically on me for many hours after deciding that a lot of the medication was already in my system and was slowly destroying me. The team was quite adept at handling drug overdoses, so I survived, obviously. I woke up thirty-six hours later, hooked up to wires, tubes, I.V.'s and a breathing machine.

Frank had called Mom after I arrived at the Trauma Centre, and she sat in agony with Dad in the waiting room while a nurse told them that she didn't know if I was going to make it or not. Then the poor woman stayed at my side the entire time, willing me to hang on. I awoke to see her tortured face and swollen, reddened eyes.

Frank was completely unglued by the experience. He returned home with his parents, for he just couldn't cope with the possibility of me dying in front of him.

Once my vital signs had stabilized, after a couple of days, I was transferred to a private room where a male RNA named Dave stayed with me, watching guard. Then, plans were made to send me back to the L.P.H.

I wasn't happy about surviving; in fact, I was pretty damned furious with Frank for interrupting my plans but I said nothing about this to Dave. I made inane small talk with him, hoping he would leave me alone long enough to allow for a hasty retreat from Victoria Hospital and my uncertain future. He stuck by me like glue, however,and in twenty-four hours, another ambulance escorted me to my now very familiar home and into the clutches of Drs. Hussain and Spencer.

When I arrived, everyone was quite shook up about what I had done. Since it had been such a harrowing close call, I was put on CNO (Close Nursing Observation). I was followed everywhere, including the bathroom, where a nurse stood watching me take a pee. It was quite demoralizing, and hoped this "death watch" would be over with soon.

CAME up to me and asked me a lot of questions about my suicide attempt, but I wasn't prepared to discuss it. "Please leave me alone," I mumbled, folding my arms across my chest.

Dr. Hussain informed me that I would be in hospital for a long time, and that I was a fool to stop taking my medication. Dr. Spencer wanted to know what perpetuated my drastic action, but I just stared at her and said quietly, "Nothing".

Several nurses from K2 stopped by and expressed concern, saying that I probably didn't know how many people cared about me.

"Yeah, sure you do," I replied, elevating my lousy attitude to new heights of obnoxiousness.

I was put back on my Sinequan but it took a long time to kick in. After awhile, I emerged a bit from my self-imposed exile of silence and talked to the nurses occasionally and began to take notice of some of the other patients around me.

Shawn was a rather tragic young man, who suffered from a crippling muscular disorder and whose face was contorted in pain and unhappiness. It must have been very hard on this young, 26-year-old man to be sidelined from his life like that. Gradually, we became good friends and he emerged from his moroseness and let his crazy, off-the-wall sense of humour shine through brilliantly. He really was hilarious, even if he thought Al Bundy was some sort of god and figured I was "pretty ancient" and "rapidly approaching middle age."

WAS still there, although I noted that Len had disappeared. Caryn was more-or-less a G2 regular, who preferred the institutional atmosphere to the harder-edged outside world. She was frustrated that her psychiatrist, Dr. Milo, didn't spend enough time with her. He sure didn't look the part of the "typical shrink", for he strode on the ward wearing shorts, running shoes and a wide, self-effacing grin.

"You're lucky to have a cool guy like that for a doctor," I told her.

I was on CNO for nearly a month and even after that period of time, Dr. Hussain was reluctant to give me more freedom. My bed was in the observation room and the office lights shone directly into my eyes when I was trying to sleep. Nobody trusted me, but I guess they had a lot of reason not to. I wasn't eating much and when I was in Dr. Spencer's office I was heavily cloaked in my customary silence.

Mom came to visit frequently and assured me that she was regularly checking in on Julius. I certainly hadn't proven to be a very good mother to that unfortunate cat and vowed I'd make all this up to both him and my long-suffering family.

Several W.O.T.C.H. members visited occasionally, but I didn't have much to say to them. I didn't want to talk about the overdose or any of the events that perpetuated it. They eventually stopped coming.

Frank came every single day, bringing stuffed animals, flowers and touching get-well cards. I tried to tell him how sorry I was for what had happened but he just kept assuring me that I only had to forgive myself. The staff were impressed with his devotion and dedication, but I still felt completely unworthy and was racked with guilt. It was painful to watch him take such a keen interest in an inveterate loser.

Judy tried to get me to talk about my past, including my childhood, as she was certain that I was holding back a great deal. I told her that it had been perfectly normal and that I couldn't blame any of my problems on anything from my past.

One Sunday afternoon, I was overcome with self-hatred and wanted to finish what I'd started that summer with the overdose. I don't have a really clear memory of exactly what perpetuated my actions, only that I'd begun hearing tormenting voices again and desperately feared I was losing my mind. On top of that, I'd been suffering chilling nightmares for the past six months and couldn't cope with them any longer. In short, I felt awful and was unable to see a way out of the pain.

So I took an empty pop can and went into the shower stall in the washroom, tore it into several sharp pieces and tore at my throat with them for over two hours. I just kept hacking and hacking, as blood spilled over me and made a huge puddle on the floor of the stall and hoped that I would bleed to death before someone found me. I was in a total state of unbridled frenzy, while voices hollered at me from a frightening abyss. I couldn't believe how my life had deteriorated and wanted an end to it.

After a couple of hours, Roberta who was on G2 with me, and a warm and loving young woman from Iraq named Adyon, found me in a pool of dark blood and summoned the nurses. A special emergency code was issued and doctors came running, inserting an I.V. and rushing me to the general hospital while patients looked on in horror.

After I was checked in emergency to make certain I hadn't severed anything vital in my throat, I was professionally sewed up and sent back to the L.P.H. The physician who did the suturing said it was "like putting a jigsaw puzzle back together".

When I got back, I was certified for two months and spent that time finally opening up to Dr. Spencer about my unhappiness and those terrible nightmares.

Gradually, by talking to her and spending time with the nurses and other patients, I began to emerge from my dense fog and even gained a foothold on some measure of inner peace. The crisis had somehow made me stronger, as did my relationship with some of the other patients.

Sally was a nineteen-year-old girl from Costa Rica whom I'd briefly gotten to know when she was my roommate in University Hospital. She was struggling with anorexia and had a habit of going AWOL from G2 and overdosing. Marie had been adopted by a Canadian family years before and there were many problems there. She said she suffered from Borderline Personality Disorder and I replied that I was told I did as well, but I believed this to beutterly false. She just smiled knowingly and leapt off her chair to race around the ward in an effort to burn off more calories.

Marie was basically sunny-natured, but possessed an underlying hostility toward people in authority. Dr. Hussain placed her on CNO for three months because of her AWOLing, because her overdosing was seriously endangering her life. I hoped that she would get the help she so desperately needed.

Then there was an angry, despondent Native woman named Gina who refused to talk to any of the nurses and spent a lot of time scratching her arms with sharp objects. She'd had a particularly unpleasant childhood and was adverse to anyone saying that there was anything wrong with her. In time, however, her apprehension and suspicions waned and she became one of the staff's strongest allies, helping other patients and even smiling occasionally. She formed a friendship with Don and the two of them had many heart-to-heart talks, as well as a great many laughs.

Trevor visited me a great deal and this meant a lot to me. He was kind, considerate and said he knew I could overcome my difficulties and really make something of my life.

Dr. Spencer kept trying to delve into my past and I told her that this kind of therapy was not appreciated, nor was it particularly productive. Our sessions mainly revolved around my desire to cut and starve myself, to which I would reply, "It's really no big deal. I can live with it."

The last couple of months I was in the hospital, I did a lot of racewalking in the sub basement, going for six hours a day, up and down the quarter-mile hall many times and receiving curious looks from patients and staff alike. I vowed to keep it up at the Y every day when I got out. It was a great way to lose weight and, of course, I always found that appealing.

I didn't get released until the end of January, 1993, and made a pact with myself to stay away from G2 and the whole L.P.H. building for the rest of my life. I'd gotten over the worst of my depression and there had been no more cutting since the throat incident.

I thought this was the end of it all and that things would finally look up, enabling me to grow and blossom, leaving my repulsive past behind me. I was about to find out differently.

## Chapter Fifteen

# January 1993-December 1994: The Worst Two Years of My Life

Through Judy, I got involved with S.A.F.E.. This is an acronym for Self Abuse Finally Ends and is a support group for people who cut and starve themselves, as well as take overdoses and indulge in street drugs, in an effort to camouflage the pain their lives produce.

When I was still on G2, I'd met Mary Graham, one of the founders of S.A.F.E. and who had been a chronic self-abuser for years. She inspired me with her straightforwardness and absolute aversion to bullshit and game-playing.

Mary was an attractive, husky woman of forty-five, mother of two teenagers, whose behaviour had been the result of repeated sexual abuse and feelings of self-loathing for years. She'd been locked in a prison of cutting herself so badly she sometimes endangered her life and her kids were forced to protect her from herself on many occasions.

Mary made no excuses for what she did, and stated that she now realized that hurting herself was something she'd never do again. She asked me a lot of questions, some of which I answered, but others I surreptitiously avoided. They simply hit too close to home.

I attended my first art therapy group in a building on Adelaide Street, near Dundas, the same centre as the A.I.D.S. headquarters. Here, people suspecting they might be HIV positive could go for anonymous, confidential testing.

I was extremely nervous and uptight, walking into a roomful of strangers and instantly wanting to run right out again. Mary greeted me warmly and explained that everyone there was cut from the same cloth (no pun intended) and would not be judged for anything we had done.

They were a fascinating bunch of women, ranging in age from eighteen to fifty-five and welcomed me unself-consciously. One girl, a painfully thin teenager with a remarkable artistic talent, wasn't afraid to talk about her tragic past, but wouldn't discuss why she refused to eat. Her drawings and paintings were worthy of world-wide recognition and I marvelled at the way she could sit and concentrate for so long without a break.

Another woman of about forty-seven discussed a husband who made impossible demands on her and was dispassionate to her cycles of cutting and drinking to excess. But she was quick to add that she loved him dearly and couldn't imagine a life without him.

Then there was nineteen-year-old Trish, a sorrowful child-like young woman who cried bitterly one day, saying she felt angry and didn't know why. She was sure, though, that she hated herself and deserved to suffer.

Alli, twenty, had been diagnosed with Multiple Personality Disorder and lived in a hideous maelstrom of bizarre black-puts and mysterious, frightening voices. She'd been repeatedly and viciously raped by her step-parents as a small child and it had left irreparable scars. She was quite large, but very pretty, and I felt strongly drawn to her and her unhappiness.

Peg, from G2, stopped by late that afternoon, but didn't care for the atmosphere of a group of adults playing at being artists, so she left soon after.

We were instructed to paint a design on a small wooden box, and depict something unpleasant from our pasts inside. It could be an event or situation which we'd already put behind us, or a negative emotion or stumbling block. We weren't allowed to illustrate anything involving cutting, or pictures of razor blades or knives, or show any pictures of blood.

Mary informed us that if we cut ourselves on S.A.F.E. property, we'd be asked to leave, get stitched up and stay away from the meetings for two weeks. "This isn't a babysitting service," she said firmly, "and we don't tolerate game playing here. This is a healing group, not one to feed off one another's self-abusive tactics."

But despite Mary Graham's sometimes gruff manner, she was earnest, industrious, caring, really wanted to see us get over our problems and achieve some measure of happiness. She knew we were all capable of escaping our self-slavery and punishment for something that wasn't our fault.

Up until now, I hadn't acknowledged even a flicker of any childhood abuse. But one day, after taking a mouthful of salt and vinegar chips from one of the members, something absolutely terrifying happened. As the bitter taste of the vinegar poured over my tongue, I suddenly saw a brief flash of a woman's face and felt a sinking sensation of dread and fear.

"What the hell was that?" I hollered, suddenly repulsed by the potato chips and spitting them out in the garbage can nearby.

"Huh? You okay?" someone asked, obviously seeing that I was white as a sheet, as the blood drained from my face.

"The weirdest thing just happened. I got this----vision, or something. I don't know....I probably just need to get some sleep."

But the scene haunted me for days. Could I still be having flashbacks from acid I took twenty years ago? It hardly seemed possible, but there really wasn't any other explanation.

Our group sessions had gotten extremely involved, psycho-logically and emotionally speaking. As the weeks wore on, we grew closer, tied extricably together by our haunting, troubled pasts as well as tenuous examinations of the present and future.

Although we couldn't discuss actual cutting, we did explore the reasons we felt compelled  to do it and what methods were implemented to "live one day at a time" and keep putting the acts of abuse off. People talked about their multiple admissions to hospital, problems with alcohol and street drugs, eating disorders and the vast variety of medications they'd been submitted to over the years. I cringed with recognition and empathized strongly with all of their stories and felt powerfully drawn to their despair at having to live life this way.

A lot of them had had horrendous childhood experiences and I couldn't relate to that, not until I began to ruminate about a series of recurring dreams that had tormented me for many years and hadn't made any sense until Mary suggested that they might be more than the result of normal rem sleep.

In my dreams, nightmares actually, I'd be very, very young, not even old enough to talk yet. Someone, perhaps my mother, would prop me up in this old step chair in the centre of a hideously lit kitchen.

Then, while I cried continuously in fear and apprehension, the woman would say things like "Shut up, or I'll give you something to cry about! We do this every afternoon, so get used to it". while lifting a cup of some acrid, distasteful liquid to my mouth and tipping it onto my tongue. "What did it taste like?" Mary asked.

"I don't know. Acidy, terrible." Then the reality hit me like a powerful, knotted fist pounding into my face. "Oh, God, it tasted like vinegar! It was vinegar! No wonder I hate it so much! I always have. I even despise the smell of it."

After that moment of revelation, it was as though a door had been flung wide open into my consciousness. With growing horror, I recalled what the woman in my dreams looked like: She'd had short, dark hair, glasses and had a round, youthful face. It was the description of my Mother back then. Could it be possible that my years of supposed dreaming were actually memories of events that actually took place? Why would Mom do that to me? Was she crazy back then? Did she hate me for crying so much?

I shook these horrific thoughts from away, preferring to believe I simply possessed an extremely overactive imagination. Besides, I figured, even if it did really happen, it wasn't exactly vicious child abuse. It wasn't as if she molested me or anything.

I began to wonder if these S.A.F.E. meetings were such a good idea, if they were going to distort my thinking so much. When I mentioned this to Mary, she assured me that I didn't have to explore avenues that I felt uncomfortable with and that I really needed to attend in order to free myself from the cutting sessions and recurrant eating disorders. Besides, I was starting to make friends at S.A.F.E. and had spent far too much time alone at home. I required social interaction with people who understood and didn't make snap judgements.

Gradually, I began to talk to Mary more, despite my apprehension. Summoning up all the courage I could muster, I mumbled, unhappily, "I think maybe my mother has done weird things to me."

"You sure about that?" Mary asked, leaning forward a little and gazing right into my disturbed eyes," You mean you remember being abused by someone? Could it have been, perhaps, a babysitter or something? A friend of the family?"

I shook my head adamantly. "No, I was really young, I'm sure. I don't think I had any babysitters then. Not until we lived in

Halifax. I think Mom would have told me somewhere along the line".

"You should find out for sure you know. Talk to your mother about these things. It's important if you want to get well".

"What?! I can't say anything to her about any of this shit! She'd freak! There has to be another way, Mary!"

But even as I spoke those words of protest, I knew my friend was right. It just seemed impossible. Perhaps I should just walk away from S.A.F.E. after all. Still, I was making social contacts and being freed from my loneliness and isolation. So I stayed. One afternoon, in Dr. Spencer's office, I began talking about my early childhood for the first time, as it had begun to seem rather unusual and abnormal. What opened up this line of conversation was a gradual acceptance of the borderline diagnosis. I couldn't believe that I could have gotten as screwed up as I did without some just cause. People weren't born with the disorder, after all, and I hadn't wanted to leave university in 1977 and plunge headlong into a sixteen-year nightmare of forced institutionalization. Something had to be at the bottom of this.

In a semi-detached, monotonal voice, I told Dr. Spencer about the time when I was seven and had, for some unknown reason, been terrified of going to the bathroom. "I'd sit for hours on our swing set in the backyard on Mary Ave, rocking back and forth and feeling as if I was going to burst. I didn't have a problem with urinating, but was desperately afraid that if I had a bowel movement in the toilet, it would overflow and drown us all. Weird, eh? I'd want to go so badly, but refused until it got to the point where I was really sick. Talk about being anal retentive."

Dr. Spencer wasn't sure what to make of this, so I wrote it out for Mary and handed it to her, saying, "This is an example of how bizarre I was as a little kid. I had all these awful phobias, like our family was going to be engulfed in flames. Dad would have to take me all over the house when I was seven to make sure the place wasn't on fire. I'd be really freaked out all the time."

Mary read all of it and remarked that something traumatic must have occurred to cause a seven-year-old to feel so powerful and potentially destructive.

I became quite emotionally dependent on Mary Graham and S.A.F.E., attending faithfully and gradually weaning myself from W.O.T.C.H. I wasn't cutting myself at all. I even began training for the 1993 London Marathon. I'd completed the Ottawa one in 1991 and felt confident that I could repeat the performance. It had been a tough race, to be sure, but extremely exhilarating to see that glorious finish line and have Ross there cheering me to victory. Even Dad had been impressed.

I began running between twelve and fifteen miles per day and as May approached, did one twenty-mile circuit per week. I had been very discouraged the previous year when I had been disqualified after having a grand mal seizure after three miles of the London Marathon, because I hadn't trained properly. This year was going to be much different.

I developed a substantial amount of muscle tissue from the eighty-plus miles per week schedule and my weight increased because of it. This didn't thrill me a hell of a lot, since I liked to be one hundred fifteen pounds and was disturbed when the scale registered one hundred twenty. I could still fit comfortably into a size five, but when I visited M.B. at her bachelor apartment in Oakville in April, I was distressed when her superintendent said, "Hey, you've gained weight since the last time I saw you." He might was well have driven a wooden stake into my heart.

M.B. knew that this catty comment would have serious repercussions and she was right. Three weeks before the marathon, I began a vigorous weight-loss regimen and pared ten pounds off my frame by the day of the race.

Because of my nutritional depletion and ensuing fatigue, I only lasted thirteen miles into the marathon and was forced to quit. I took this as a supreme symbol of defeat and failure, and it cost me big time.

Still feeling fat and disgusting at one hundred ten pounds, not to mention wallowing in the sensation of being the quintessential loser for only doing half of the race, I announced to Mary Graham that I was going to begin racewalking, working up to thirty miles a day,and become thin, beautiful and victorious.

She wasn't impressed, feeling that I looked just fine and had come too far to regress that much. I ignored her protests. Nearly two months after my thirty-eighth birthday, I started walking with frenetic, nervous energy around Springbank Park, working up to going four times around the five-mile circuit where I'd racewalked in May to earn money for Multiple Sclerosis research.

Springbank was four miles from our house on Forest View,

so between travelling there and back, plus twenty miles around the park, I was doing a rather impressive, if not self-abusive twenty-eight miles per day. It still wasn't enough, however, so within a few weeks I continued down Springbank Drive to Oxford Street, all the way downtown and then home again. I figured this to be about thirty-six miles, six more than my original goal. I revelled in the smug satisfaction of knowing that I was burning at least three thousand five hundred calories, or a whole pound, each day.

The results made me very happy and elicited a certain amount of breathless euphoria. I didn't weigh myself very often, fearing that the numbers would discourage me, but before long my clothes began to sag and bag on me.

The only down side of all this was that it was excruciatingly exhausting. By my third circuit of Springbank, my muscles were literally screaming for relief and much-needed rest. As the temperature rose and humidity blanketed the atmosphere, I was seized with a raging thirst. I didn't have enough sense to buy a water bottle, so instead I relied on the two fountains in the park, drinking with the unabashed gusto of a man trapped for days in the desert. I would feel orgasmic as the fluid replenished my shrivelled cells.

My Walkman was a constant companion. I chose the radio over my tapes, as the batteries lasted much longer and I wasn't exactly rolling in wealth. I listened to FM 96, the rock station, and left the house at four thirty AM and would finish by eleven, before the sun blistered too angrily.

Daryl thought I was crazy, as did Julius, and Sheila worried that I was becoming obsessed with the exercising rituals and would lapse into anorexia again. I assured her that I knew what I was doing, to which Daryl replied, "I'm not so sure you do."

It was completely dark when I left in the morning. It frightened me to be alone in Springbank Park when I couldn't see two feet in front of me until after six AM.

I was utterly exhausted by eight PM and retired with Julius to bed by eight thirty. I still saw Dr. Spencer every Monday afternoon. She grew alarmed at the number of miles I was racewalking and the fact that I'd drastically reduced my food intake.

She tried to get me to talk about what was bothering me, but I benignly replied, "Everything's just fine. I don't have any problems," and ignored her pleas to get me to reduce my ridiculous mileage and eat more.

The racewalking became the centre of my universe. I'd even go out during thunderstorms, never missing a single day. I still spent weekends with Mom at her new home on Wilkins Street, a scant twenty-minute jaunt from my home. She didn't think much of me leaving the house at four thirty AM, but knew there wasn't a lot she could do to stop me.

I'd walk from Wilkins to Forest View, feed Julius, then go on to Springbank every Saturday and Sunday. I would awaken every day at three during the week and watch old "Laverne and Shirley" and "All In the Family" reruns on television, while drinking several cups of strong coffee before braving the elements.

Sometimes, Daryl would arise with me and the two of us spent a lot of time talking and getting to know one another better. I really liked him and felt badly that he was so tormented by his inner demons. He had a great deal of pent-up anger, which exploded periodically, mostly at himself. It caused him to deliberate frighteningly on how useless and stupid he was, even though I certainly didn't see either of these things in him.

I saw Daryl as a very artistic, sensitive young man who was locked in a mental state that often betrayed him. He drew a picture of a cat for me, which I still have on my wall. He showed me his portfolio, something that should definitely have been published. I encouraged him, but he would simply smile and tell me that there was a lot of competition out there and he was just one more struggling artist.

Then we fell in love. It happened gradually, over a period of months. One night, we went up to my room and consummated our relationship. He was experienced, gentle and intense and I desperately craved the closeness of another human being in an intimate way.

We had unprotected sex, which, in the light of the AIDS crisis, wasn't a very intelligent thing to do, but at this point I didn't care if I got the disease or not.

I'd broken up with Frank for the last time several weeks before, as I was no longer able to live the life of a hypocrite and felt I had been using him as an attractive arm ornament. He was devastated all over again, but I knew I was really doing him a favour. Besides, I wouldn't sleep with two men simultaneously, for that went against everything my monogamous heart believed in.

I continued with S.A.F.E., where members implored me to

stop losing so much weight. I was beginning to looked emaciated
and they feared for my life. Mary said that I couldn't continue like
this indefinitely and urged me to see another family physician, as
Dr. Harris wasn't really acknowledging that I had much of a
problem. Like Drs. Grant and Prince, he was getting pretty frustrated with my self-destructive behaviour.

I agreed to see Dr. Bayana at her office at Oxford and Talbot
Streets. She weighed me, told me frankly that if I didn't stop all this
racewalking and starving, I would end up in the hospital. She was
shy and compassionate, but I didn't want anybody preaching at me.
Dr. Spencer was doing enough of that as it was.

By the end of August, the walking had evolved into a dismal,
agonizing ritual that pelted away relentlessly at my stamina and
spirit. Springbank had some pretty seriously steep hills and as I
listened to R.E.M.'s "The Sidewinder Sleeps Tonite" and
"Ignoreland" on the radio, I desperately wanted a respite from the
muscle-tearing activity that so consumed me.

I hadn't yet bought "Automatic For the People", as I was so
consumed with what I was doing in the park and was too tired at
night to listen to any of my tapes.

I liked what I heard on the radio and, one Saturday afternoon
at Mom's, I saw the video for "Everybody Hurts", which absolutely
blew me away. I only saw it once that summer, but the images and
feelings it evoked, of clutching onto some semblance of hope when
your life is slipping into a depressive abyss, stuck with me. As
always, this band reflected just what I was experiencing and offered
some comfort.

Daryl was growing despondent and frustrated at the way I
seemed to be putting my all-consuming racewalking ahead of him.
I was so caught up in my rituals that I began to drift away from his
love and attention. I tried to assure him that I cared deeply for him
despite my apparent actions to the contrary. In truth, I was rejecting
everyone who tried to help me and pointedly avoided social interaction completely. I was so self-absorbed at this time that even my cat
sensed my preoccupation and felt rather neglected.

I wasn't eating breakfast or lunch, except for a diet root beer
at the A&W each day at eleven. Mom cooked vegetarian food for
me, which I ate reluctantly, but assuaged my guilt by figuring that I
needed some calories to offset the ones I was using up with the
manic walking.

She'd grown alarmed at my appearance, which was reminiscent of 1971, and my face grew haggard and old-looking. I suddenly looked my age for the first time in my life and my body shrank to the size of a concentration camp inmate's. I thought I looked great, however, and as my weight plummeted to close to ninety-five pounds, I found I had to buy clothes in the children's department.

Daryl and I went for walks in the evening to a nearby restaurant on weekends, where I'd pick away at salads while he urged me to eat "real food". He was very attentive and I felt I didn't deserve someone like him.

By the middle of the month, my energy started to wane considerably and it was a tremendous effort to do my thirty-six miles a day. I was dizzy and light-headed and began to hear voices telling me I was obese and needed to exercise more.

Dr. Hussain came into Dr. Spencer's office with us one day and strongly urged me to come into the hospital. I refused adamantly, replying with an angry, "You just want to make me fat".

Then the nightmares started with a vengeance, horrific, heavily detailed exercises in despair about being violently attacked with sharp objects. They were forcefully plunged into my vagina and I tried to scream. Nothing came out but muffled sobs. There was always that round-faced woman, surrounded by bright flames as she laughed maniacally at me as the terrible deeds were done.

One afternoon, toward the end of August, I was walking through the Galleria Mall downtown and I heard R.E.M.'s "Everybody Hurts" come over the loud speaker. Suddenly overcome with remorse and despair, I burst into tears among crowds of strangers and barely made it to the Second Cup coffee shop nearby in one piece. Sitting down at a secluded table, I thought about how my life had disintegrated and how much I wanted to die. What was happening to me?

Daryl decided to move to Toronto to make a life for himself away from W.O.T.C.H. and develop his artistic career. I knew I would greatly miss him, but understood his restlessness and eagerness to begin his life over, miles away from a troubled past.

Finally, my health began to fail during the last few days of the month and I could no longer walk without tripping and falling. I was experiencing periods of confusion as well and didn't know where I was half the time. I knew by now that if I didn't get some help, I wouldn't survive much longer.

I took a cab to the emergency department of Victoria Hospital where Mary Graham and Dr. Bayana met me, quite concerned that I had finally gone over the edge. I told them that I couldn't stand being like that anymore and that life had evolved into a hideous nightmare that seemed inescapable.

This absolutely obnoxious, angry and despicable psychiatrist interviewed me, saying with a snarl, "You're not making any sense you know. You come in here, wanting help for something that you can't adequately articulate. Why should I waste my time with you?"

I cried bitterly, imploring him to listen to what I was saying, that my life was out of control and I thought I was shortly going to die.

He left for a few minutes and I begged Mary to talk to him and make him understand that I wasn't some insipid trouble-maker out to make his life miserable. She shook her head and said that her hands were tied. I decided that nobody could save me from myself and that I was shortly going to just fade out of existence. My world came crashing around my ears when Dr. Rude returned and reluctantly agreed to admit me to the psychiatric floor, but said flatly to me, "You're what we call a "repeater". You never get out of the hospital circuit and you don't really want to be helped. I see so many cases like yours and quite frankly, you all turn my stomach".

I was taken to my old haunt on the seventh floor, where I was abandoned to a single room and left for days unattended. I lay in my bed, only partially aware of my surroundings and refused the trays of food that were brought in. No nurses came to check on me and no doctors ever visited to ask any questions or discuss my case. It had been decided that I would be admitted to the L.P.H. when a bed was available and meanwhile I was expected to just sit on my shrivelled up ass and wait.

They didn't want to get involved with me since I wasn't really formally admitted to Victoria Hospital, and so I sank into a deep well of self-pity and despair. "Nobody cares if I die," I thought dismally, "So why should I?"

I was completely overcome by my depression and when a member from S.A.F.E. came to see me, she told me later that she was tempted to give me all her blood pressure pills. She figured that death would be preferable to what I was experiencing there.

My electrolytes went completely out of whack after three days, so I was given sodium chloride intravenously. I'd fallen out of bed and severely bruised my face and lay there for hours, unable to move before anyone came. "God, let me die," I implored, "Please take me now, I beg You".

When my sodium level stabilized, I was finally transferred to the L.P.H. I had been on the seventh floor in relative exile for over six days. I was not particularly pleased when I discovered that I would be placed on L2 instead of G2.

I was placed in the observation room and encouraged to eat. I refused and the next day, Dr. Hussain approached me as I lay flaccidly on my bed and informed me that she was being transferred to H2 and that I would be getting Dr. Milo for my psychiatrist.

"Do you have to leave?" I asked, desperation lacing my voice. I'd grown to like her very much and didn't take well to any kind of change.

"Yes, I'm sorry, but these things happen. Dr. Milo is a very good doctor, and I'm sure you'll like him." I recalled what Deirdre had said about never seeing the man.

"I don't know. I don't like this, Dr. Hussain. Not at all."

The nurses on L2 soon gave up trying to get me to eat, so I spent all my time lying in bed and feeling my life draining out of me. I crawled out one day when Trevor came to visit and he was shocked at how much weight I had lost. I told him that I wished Daryl hadn't moved. He replied that Daryl had felt Toronto would offer him better opportunities. I thanked Trevor for caring and assured him that I would "get my act together and get the hell out of here."

I got moved back to G2 after a week and met Dr. Milo for the first time. He was still dressed in shorts and running shoes and chewed hyperactively on a wad of gum. He told me that I would be expected to eat and follow ward procedure. "Okay, whatever you say," I replied, knowing that I wouldn't.

They weighed me every few days and grew frightened as the numbers relentlessly declined. Dr. Milo kept warning me that if I didn't start eating, he'd see that a feeding tube was inserted into my nose. I scoffed at him and decided that he was making empty threats.

Mom was quite unhinged by all of this and visited me a great deal. She implored me to stop destroying myself and expressed distaste at Dr. Milo's appearance, saying that he didn't look "very professional."

Michael Milo was not, by any standards, your average, typical psychiatrist. He was boyishly handsome at forty-six, with a vital, refreshing zest for life. He possessed a strong, emotional attachment to his patients, of whom he had at least four hundred, and refused to adhere to the strict guidelines of conventional psychiatry.

He didn't hesitate to tell his patients off when they needed it, sometimes quite profanely and couldn't stand to suffer a failure with any of them. He loved music, everything from Vivaldi to Madonna, and his second marriage to a pretty nurse named Rebecca, was fulfilling and exhilarating.

He was never inappropriate with any of his female patients, or male patients for that matter, even though some of them wished he would be and he despised hearing criticism that he didn't care about his charges. He did care and does, and sometimes his devotion to his work cost him emotionally.

By the end of the third week of September, Dr. Milo was truly frightened that I was going to die. He approached my Mother and told her pointedly that I was to be sent to Victoria Hospital to be assessed and, quite probably, be invaded with a feeding tube.

She was slightly put off by his gruff aggressiveness, but wanted to do what was best for me. "She's going to die, you know," he said with an upsetting edge to his voice. "She's suicidal. Not only that, she's incompetent. She can't be going on like this any longer".

So I arrived at the emergency department again. I was interviewed by two residents who felt that I was not yet in immediate peril, but must start eating again or I would be.

Milo was furious when I was returned to the L.P.H. and despaired that his hands were tied by the medical system of the general hospital bureaucracy.

One morning, I heard his voice from the nurses' station asking anxiously, "Did she eat her breakfast?" When the nurses replied in the negative, he threw up his hands and cried, "That's it! I'm recommending a feeding tube anyway. That woman doesn't know what she's doing!"

I pushed my internal panic button and decided to call Legal Aid for a lawyer to allow me to die if I wanted. Suddenly, I was no longer starving myself to be beautiful and aesthetic, but to commit suicide.

The realization hit me with tremendous force. I had botched my last attempt to end my life and I was certainly not going to repeat the performance. Life had become unbearable, with the nightmares and thinking that my mother had tortured me as a baby. How could I keep going with that awful reality? Those nightmares had been a message to me that she had stuck sharp objects into my twenty month-old vagina and I suddenly realized that I couldn't cope with it.

Slowly and terribly, I slid downhill, unable to get out of bed and weaving in and out of consciousness. One morning, I summoned up some strength and tried to escape from the ward, falling and splaying my thin limbs on the linoleum floor. I was picked up then and put in restraints for the first time. When the lawyer came to visit me, my wrists and ankles were bound up in thick plastic cuffs.

I told him that I didn't want a feeding tube, but rather I wished to be allowed to starve myself to death. He said to me that it was against the law to do that. When I brought up the Rodriguez case, where a woman with Lou Gehrig's Disease had gone to court to do just that, he replied that she had been denied the right to starve herself. I pointed out that it was a rational decision on my part, but the young attorney turned me down flat.

When Dr. Milo found out about this, he flipped and said that I would be weighed every day. If my weight dropped any further, it was off to Victoria Hospital and forced nutrition.

It did drop further, but there wasn't really anything he could do about it. I wasn't in a coma, my electrolytes seemed stable enough and I wasn't experiencing any heart or kidney failure yet.

Dave, the RNA who'd guarded me after my overdose, and who was also employed at the L.P.H., approached to inform me that I probably only had about another two weeks to live. This left me unmoved, as did my Mother's tearful pleas for me to "Please don't do this!" and Milo's constant threats.

When my weight reached a low of eighty-two pounds, Milo decided to send me to Toronto General's ward for eating disorders, a world-renowned institution. However, there was a six-month waiting list and he figured I wouldn't last that long.

My days swirled into one another and I was only partially aware of my surroundings. I lay in my bed, too weak to move, while nurses bustled about the station, going about their daily business and sounding so full of energy and life. I was put on

Special Observation Routine (SOR) and wasn't really clued in to the nurses sitting beside me and checking to make sure I was still breathing.

One of them, an RNA named Marie Eccles, took a special interest in me and spent a great deal of time talking to me about what I was doing. She was extremely giving and compassionate, a vital, warm lady, poised and attractive at fifty. I felt very drawn to her concern and unabashed affection toward such a pathetic piece of disgusting humanity like myself.

She helped me out of bed each day, thinking that the dayroom would provide some much-needed stimulation and connect me with other living, breathing human beings. I sat in one of the lazy-boy chairs, wrapped in a thick blanket, while Marie talked about her cake decorating business, her children and the love she had for G2's patients.

"Why do you care?" I asked her one day.

"Because you're worth caring about. I don't think you realize that, Jane." Her eyes filled with tears and she fought the urge to hug me tightly to her loving, maternal breast. I saw her painand didn't want anyone showing me love and affection.

The other patients were scared to death that they were going to see one of their own die soon. Deirdre talked to me a lot, saying that nothing was worth dying for, and she should know. She tried to get me to eat my meals, but I turned away from her, feeling that she was one of "them" that wanted to jolt me back to a life I didn't want anymore. Garon was there, offering friendship and affection to one who had lost everything. He looked so much older than his fifty-three years, with long, scraggly white hair, unkempt, wild beard and a hunched over frame. I wondered what had happened to cause such a regression.

I got a new roommate, a woman named Ricki, who had taken a terrible overdose on a weekend pass and who was obviously very depressed. She emerged from her private hell long enough to implore me to regain a foothold on my life and offered love and support.

Everett didn't understand what was happening to me and stayed away for reasons of self-preservation. Another patient, Reggie, with rather effeminate mannerisms and quiet desperation written all over his round, cherubic face, befriended me and told me I was too good to end up like this.

Reggie was overweight, but good looking and his affable nature belied a severe, penetrating depression. He and Ricki grew very close and I envied their intense relationship. I was pretty sure he was gay, but Reggie was unable to accept it. I wondered if that could be at the root of his disquietude.

One morning, Dr. Milo came bustling in with a wheelchair, announcing that I'd be taken to Health Services for a thorough examination.

"Get out of here!" I protested as he cheerily greeted me. "You just want to make me fat like all the rest. You're not my friend, Dr. Milo".

"Jane, Jane, Jane," he replied, pulling the covers from me hastily. "That's not it at all. We just want you to get better. Come along. It looks like you won't be going to Toronto General. We're in charge of your case from now on and I'll be damned if you're going to starve to death".

I was weighed at Health Services, examined and informed that I had to start eating immediately. I hated the doctor and his army of nurses, imagining that they were all involved in a sinister plot to turn me into a fat, disgusting pig. I had begun to have second thoughts about starving myself unto death, as I'd been experiencing very distressing spasms during the past few days and was slowly realizing that this form of suicide was particularly nasty and insidious.

When I returned, after several heavy lectures, I lay in bed with the covers over my head and felt my hands get cold and clammy. I mentioned this to Marie, who replied sadly, "You're withdrawing. If you don't start getting better, you're going to die. Do you really want that?"

I steeled myself against the incredible discomfort and resolved that death was preferable to a life that I had no control over. "Yes," I told her evenly, "I do want that. Just let me go for God's sake. Don't keep trying to rescue me. I hate this! I don't want to be rescued!"

She ignored me and tried to get me to take a few mouthfuls of Ensure. "No!" I protested, turning my face away from the straw. "Leave me alone, damn you!"

The turnaround came suddenly, two days later, when my Mother came to visit. She tried to hug me, but I jerked away and was repulsed by her touch. "Go away! Just get away from me! I can't deal with any of this sentimental crap!"

She couldn't stand it any longer. Sobbing uncontrollably, she sprang to her feet and ran quickly from my room, completely torn apart. Wringing her hands and stammering brokenly, my mother implored the nurses, "Please save my daughter! I've never seen her like this! I can't stand it anymore!"

They tried to get her to stay and talk about her extreme pain, but she hurried off. I heard all of this and felt terrible that I was causing her so much agony. I'm a selfish, despicable bitch! I thought. What is happening to us?

The day before, I'd drifted in and out of a semi-vegetative state that really scared me and horrified Ricki. That poor girl had enough problems without worrying about a roommate dying on her. I just couldn't keep doing this stuff to everyone. It wasn't right.

After Mom left, I told Marie that I would try to drink some Ensure. Elated, she brought me a can and I took a couple of tiny, anxious sips. It tasted good and I could feel my shrunken tissue reacting favourably to the unfamiliar sustenance. After the initial shock of taking nutrition again wore off, I settled into a regular regimen of Ensure, mouthful by mouthful, until I was finally strong enough to sit in the dayroom.

Dr. Milo was extremely relieved and his positive vibes were encouraging. He came to see me frequently, explaining that I really needed to regain some semblance of health and peace of mind after what I had put myself through. He spoke in a soft, endearing voice and patted my hand as if to say, "Welcome back. We missed you."

Mom was likewise very happy and when she visited, her eyes had lost some of their cloudy sadness. I felt extremely close to her, but still cringed at the terrifying memories of the past atrocities that I was now certain she'd vested upon me.

The road back was not a smooth or effortless one. When my weight reached eighty-six pounds, I panicked and stopped eating again. This did not go over well with Dr. Milo, but he realized that my weight gain wouldn't be linear and decided to give me some leeway. I had begun to consume some solid food, mostly vegetables and oatmeal. I shied away from anything that looked highly caloric.

Dr. Milo put me on Zoloft, an antidepressant of the Prozac family, starting with twenty-five milligrams and increasing it eventually to one hundred fifty. It began to take effect after a week and I attributed this medication to my gradual improvement. Unlike Prozac, it didn't make me hyperactive and fidgety, but seemed to level out the deep depression somewhat.

Dr. Spencer came on the ward twice a week to talk to me, but I didn't say much at first. I was too wrapped up in my eating woes and was incapable of dealing with anything else. She was patient, however, and let me sit silently and motionless in the quiet room with her until I was ready to deal with my other problems.

When the floodgates finally opened, they did so with a tumultuous flourish. One afternoon, I sat curled up in a ball with my hands frantically grasping my head as if to keep it above a dangerously high, imaginary water level. I spoke of my inability to get in touch with my feelings, as if they were locked away in an inaccessible iron vault. It seemed that there was something horrific and ugly, waving at me tauntingly from a distance and daring me to approach and be violently strangled.

"Are you afraid to deal with these feelings?" Dr. Spencer asked, leaning closer to me as I huddled on the chair.

"I don't know. I don't know. Something terrible is happening inside of me and I can't explain it. I've been living in some fantasy world all my life and now it's threatening to burst wide open. I'm scared shitless. I just want to turn it all off and sleep."

"But look what doing that all these years has done to you. You nearly died this time by walking and starving yourself into a very sick skeleton. It's only by facing your demons that you can ultimately defeat them."

"I can't, Dr. Spencer! I can't do it so please don't make me!" I drew further into myself, whimpering like a frightened puppy and pushing my chin into my pigeon chest.

That's how the sessions went for weeks. I felt as though I'd climbed way up into a towering tree and was unable to get down again, just as I had in Halifax so many times. I cried bitterly and despairingly, often afraid to open my eyes. Some of the nurses tried to talk to me, but I couldn't respond. I sat in the dayroom, rocking incessantly and was scarcely aware of anyone around me for weeks.

Marie sat with me often and spent a lot of time talking about her life and how much her job as an RNA taxed her physically and emotionally. She'd missed a lot of time because of illness and had a grave heart condition. I worried about her and, as she French braided my thin hair, I told her that nothing was worth putting her health in jeopardy for.

She smiled and responded that she was seriously considering quitting and launching full-time into her cake decorating business. Marie showed me pictures of her sugary creations, which were in constant demand by a justifiably impressed public. We grew very close over time and she took a special interest in my case. I don't think I would have done nearly as well without her and I am extremely grateful for all the attention she lavished upon me.

Garon and I soon developed a very strong relationship and I got intensely drawn into his touching psychosis. We talked constantly, holding hands and planning a happy life together away from the hospital. We fell in love and would sit cross-legged in our chairs, watching television and listening to the radio.

"We're two Buddhists in love," he remarked one day, smiling and revealing a lot of missing teeth. Garon had studied Buddhism and told me that he'd long been attracted to the peace and contentment that the religion offered him. He also believed that he was in a different, mysterious dimension from the rest of the world and possessed both a penis and a vagina. He took it for granted that I did as well, though I didn't tell him that I had no male genitalia for quite some time. I was afraid it would disillusion him and he would no longer care for me.

Gradually, I began to think as he did. He believed that one of the female RNA's, Wanda Lewis, was an instrument of the devil and I must stay away from her. Wanda was tall, slim and extremely cheerful, but as the weeks wore on I began to distrust her, as Garon told me that she was trying to undermine his sanity and would do the same to mine.

He despaired over our age difference, saying that he was really too old for me, but I insisted that fifteen years was nothing and that I wasn't at all hung up about things like that. I never had been, for it seemed very petty to avoid someone because they were either older or younger than myself.

Ricki grew close to me and told me that she'd spent most of her life in a suicidal depression. It had gotten worse with the death of her young son in a car accident. She said that Eric Clapton's haunting, "Tears In Heaven" always made her think of Blair and I can't listen to that song now without feeling a large lump rise in my throat.

Reggie was quite upset that Dr. Milo didn't seem to be

particularly sympathetic to his case and rarely spoke to him. He said that Milo hated him, wanted him out of the hospital and back into the shark-infested waters of his unhappy life. I could see how tortured Reggie was, but I knew that our doctor wasn't mean or vindictive. This young man was simply experiencing a lot of self-hatred and couldn't really believe that anyone could possibly care about him.

One evening, Reggie, in a particularly severe fit of despair, cut himself and was placed on CNO. The close observation detail offered him some comfort, but to our surprise, he was discharged shortly after. He seemed to take it well, but after his self-abuse, I grew very frightened for his safety and wrote a letter to his primary nurse, Wanda.

I told her of my belief that Reggie was a repressed homosexual who couldn't deal with it and might quite likely commit suicide. Reggie had grown very close to Wanda, so I knew that she would be receptive to my dire predictions. Dr. Milo talked to me about it and assured me that Danny would be alright.

"Believe me, Dr. Milo, I know what it is like to feel like shit about your sexuality, with the guilt and self-loathing, and to keep trying to convince yourself that nothing is wrong."

"Is this something that you want to talk about with Dr. Spencer?" he asked, looking concerned.

"No and I've gotten the subject away from Reggie. You sure he's not going to kill himself?"

"Reggie won't commit suicide. He needs the structure and stability that Cecilia House will provide for him. Don't worry. Get your own life in order before you take on other people's problems."

Well, my life was far from being in order. As my nutrition improved, I became consumed with the emotional maelstrom that had been kept in check with the anorexia. By the beginning of November, I was forced to acknowledge that I had suffered a jolting trauma as a child and that it was really screwing me up.

Although I hadn't divulged much to Dr. Spencer, I was losing touch with that essential spark that makes a person want to keep living. I devised a plan, one that involved smuggling a pop can into my room, tearing it apart and slitting my throat late at night when the eagle-eyed nurses weren't hovering about incessantly.

I remembered the incident during my last admission when I ripped my throat apart with a jagged can and knew only too well what the instrument was capable of. This time, I figured I'd do it right and not be interrupted before bleeding to death. Unfortunately, Blanche, one of the RNA's, came into my room unexpectedly just as I was bending the can in half, which emitted a loud, cracking sound. "What are you doing?" she asked, pulling the covers back and revealing my weapon of self-destruction.

I freaked on her, screaming wildly, waving my arms as she tried to calm me down and she alerted three more staff members. Someone called Dr. Milo at home and got an order to place me in restraints, but I spat viciously, "Damn you! Damn you all to hell!!" and struggled ferociously to escape the forest of arms that descended upon me. Wanda was there and I grew alarmed that she was going to do something diabolical.

Garon appeared at the door, grief-stricken,and cried loudly, "Mrs. Lewis! Mrs. Lewis! Leave her alone! Just get out of there now and let her be!"

There was utter chaos and just then the duty doctor entered and jabbed me with a needle full of tranquillizing solution. The first dose was ineffective, so he administered another, then a third. Then I blanked out, eyes wide open and lay there in a half-conscious, semi-catatonic state until morning.

This was the first in a series of such angry, frenzied outbursts, which would leave the G2 staff, Dr. Milo and myself, completely drained and feeling defeated. I wouldn't discuss the incident with Dr. Spencer, nor what had perpetuated it. I honestly didn't know, but was grimly aware that some deadly beast had been unleashed.

That's what I termed my extreme anger: The Beast. It became my constant companion and would spring from me, seemingly out of nowhere, disrupting the entire ward and causing fear and apprehension in the hearts of the other patients. I grew accustomed to the restraints and would struggle spasmodically to free my wrists and ankles from the heavy, solid plastic shackles that had to be locked with a key.

It was extremely difficult to sleep like that and I was periodically turned from my back to my stomach in an effort to offer me more comfort. I preferred to be on my back, where a nurse would have to feed me in a half-sitting position. This evoked painful memories of my wrist-bound days in seclusion on Behaviour Modification years before.

I grew hostile toward Dr. Milo, who I saw as my captor. I would spit and fume at him when he came into my room. "I hate you!" I sputtered, hollering at him to "Get the fuck away from me!" Sometimes I'd be in the restraints for days at a time, with a staff member watching me closely from the office. I didn't think it was possible for my life to descend any deeper into the snakepit.

During the times when the Beast was in submission, I spent time with Marie and gradually began to talk about my past. One afternoon as I sat with her on the edge of my bed, I felt something well up inside of me like a frantic storm. Then, an image flashed before my eyes of that terrible woman grinning maniacally and laughing at me.

"No, no, no," I moaned, crawling into a tight ball and burying my head in trembling arms. "Stop it! Stop laughing at me like that! Haven't you done enough to me?"

Marie tried to comfort me, but I pushed her away. "Don't touch me! I don't want to feel anything, do you hear me? I don't want to feel!"

I repeated this over and over, rocking back and forth and beginning to whimper softly. Undaunted, Marie placed her warm hands on my shoulder and said quietly, "What's so awful that you can't let yourself feel? What is it that you're pushing down all the time? Can't you just let it out?"

I shook my head vehemently. "No! I can't let the Beast out again! It's too destructive! It'll kill everyone! Get out of here or I'm afraid I'll destroy you!!"

"I'm not afraid of you. You're a scared, hurting little girl. Let me in. I want to help you."

"I don't want to feel!" I screamed, drawing my knees into my chest. "Aren't you listening to me?!" Then I blurted out, before I realized what I was saying, "I hate my Mother! I hate what she did! Oh God, why can't you be my mother!!"

It was out. The deadly, terrible secret I'd been pushing into the dark, murky recesses of my consciousness for so long now had been unleashed upon this loving, compassionate woman.

Marie took me in her arms and held me while I sobbed loudly and brokenly, my tears drenching both of us.

"Now the Beast will kill all of us for sure", I said. I felt very guilty for telling on my mother, who I was certain had abused me. I didn't really hate her, only her actions. But she was probably very sick back then, stuck in a loveless marriage and saddled with a constantly wailing baby. She couldn't help it. Besides, it happened thirty-seven years ago. I had no right to harbour so much hatred after all that time.

Dr. Spencer had something to work with now and she tried earnestly to get me to talk more about the experience. I didn't want to, but simply wished to put it behind me and pick up the pieces of a shattered life. But I could not. And what if Jim had been abused as well? I found that intolerable to think about. Should I tell Mom that I knew? What would it do to her?

I decided to put that off for awhile and concentrated instead on getting out of the hospital. Surely now I'd seen the last of the Beast.

By December, Dr. Milo was once again in my good books and we talked a lot out in the dayroom. Some of his other patients resented all the time he was devoting to me and it made me feel special. I basked in the glow of his attention and chatted to him about matters such as running, music and the philosophy behind the Art of Anorexia.

He had a wonderful sense of humour and I soon discovered that I was falling in love with him. I guess it was a classic case of transference, when a patient becomes dependent on her doctor, but I didn't recognize it as such. I fantasized about him leaving Rebecca and marrying me, even though he spoke glowingly about her and I could tell by the expression in his eyes that he wouldn't dream of divorcing her.

He talked to Mom about letting me have a few hours out of the hospital at Christmas. I'd earned a four-hour pass a couple of weeks earlier and had rushed home to embrace a very lonely and unhappy Julius. The brief foray into the world of freedom was exhilarating after being locked up for over three months.

Jim came home for the holidays, bringing long-time girl-friend, Diane Letourneau. She was a wonderful young woman and I appeared much cheerier to her than the last time she'd seen me during the past summer in Vancouver. Mom and I had gone for a week, stayed in a hotel downtown and I'd been so depressed that I spent most of the time lying on the bed, steeped in self-pity and suffering from a painful back injury.

Jim came with Dad to see me on the ward the day he and Diane arrived, and he told Dad that I was certainly a "Typical borderline". Jim had learned all about the disorder in medical school and felt that we caused a lot of exasperation for the medical profession. He was relieved that I wasn't schizophrenic, however and hoped that I could finally put my life back together.

I weighed ninety-two pounds and looked thin but reasonably healthy. I was glad that he and Diane hadn't seen me at eighty-two with sunken cheeks and protruding hipbones. Jim and Diane came to see me several days before my Christmas pass.

Diane remarked that a friend of hers had been in a similar-looking institution and she understood a little of what went on there. She was a small, pretty girl of French-Canadian decent, with an infectious, hearty laugh and an obviously intense love for my brother. The feeling was mutual, and I revelled in the joy of seeing how happy he was now. Jim really deserved a break after all the tragedies and difficulties he'd endured in the past.

I wanted Jim to meet Dr. Milo, but when my brother came up to the ward several days before returning to Vancouver, I realized I'd gotten the day wrong. We sat together in the dayroom while he looked shudderingly down the dark, institutional bedroom corridor and remarked with a chill to his spine, "How can you stand living here?"

I assured him that I'd be released soon and that I'd make certain that I never had to return. That prediction turned out to be quite premature, however.

As the New Year got underway, the Beast returned with a vengeance, as did my alarming cutting activities. I began to believe that I was trapped in my own self-constructed concentration camp, surrounded by mental chain-link fences topped with curls of dangerous, emotional barbed wire. I could expect to be there for the rest of my life, robbed of any kind of freedom and inflicting pain and torture upon myself. The Beast was the Nazi-like enslaver.

I remembered a chillingly prophetic line from "Maze of the Minotaur": "He stands laughing at the core of your prison". I'd actually been here all my life and had just become aware of it. I told Dr. Spencer this but she assured me that I could, one day, break down the fences and be happy, free and fulfilled.

I didn't believe her. I spent my days hoarding pop cans, tearing them into sharp strips and slashing my arms so badly that many stitches were required to put my flesh back together.

One duty doctor in particular, who was often called late at

night to suture me, remarked caustically, "This is one aspect of people's behaviour I'll never understand. You're going to have really ugly arms before long".

My cutting rituals became an elaborate game I played with the staff, until they forbid me to sit alone with a can of pop and had to throw it away in front of them. This didn't stop me, for I only became more sneaky. I would get them from the canteen and then hide in the sub-basement and cut myself to pieces in private.

The Beast let itself loose with alarming frequency. I constantly lost my temper at the staff, yelling obscenities and saying they were evil conspirators. Alanna, my primary nurse, tried desperately to sway me from my bizarre rituals of blood, but I thought of my actions as coming from something outside of myself and paid no attention to her.

Alanna was a tiny, delicate forty-one-year-old RN who spoke in a soft, somewhat shy voice and looked at me with a pained expression of concern. I treated her abominably, slashing myself behind her back and telling her she didn't really care about me at all, but rather was just "doing her job for the money and prestige." I was a real pip, wasn't I?

Then there was my deplorable treatment of poor Wayne, an RNA who'd been a student of Mom's several years before and who, at thirty-three, was a devoted, fun-loving man with a knack for effectively reaching patients who were deemed to be too remote and ill to be touched. He was ruggedly handsome, with a body to die for and I could have been quite attracted to his virility and charm if I wasn't so messed up. I rode Wayne constantly, screaming at him when he put me in restraints and calling him a "fucking Nazi swine".

One day, I attempted to talk to him and became absolutely furious when he told me that I wasn't really that sick, but basically was a sad behaviour problem who just needed to "grow up and get the hell out of the hospital".

Well, I really lost it and practically tore the guy's eyes out, livid that he would have the unmitigated gall to talk to me like that after what I had been through. After that, I never missed an opportunity to scream obscenities at him. I told him that he just wanted to "have his way with me", that he was a pervert and completely evil.

To this day, I cannot bring myself to look at him. I become totally overwhelmed with shame and regret about the way I acted toward someone who was simply being honest and telling me what I needed to hear.

By March, I knew that I would never get out of the hospital or escape from my miserable concentration camp. My roommate for a long period of time was the sad and self-destructive Roberta, who cut herself almost as often and viciously as I did. She had long ago resigned herself to spending most of her life in the hospital and had recently lost so much weight that she was as thin as I. She never ate and spent many days huddled under a blanket in her room.

Roberta was very withdrawn, unhappy and had visions of herself on fire. One night, she took off with the intention of setting herself ablaze, but was retrieved quickly. She'd recently been diagnosed as suffering from schizo-affective disorder after spending years wondering why her life was such a shambles. My heart went out to her as she lived her lonely, desperate life
full of self-abuse, visual hallucinations and confused and muddled thoughts.

We talked a great deal and I implored her to eat something. Roberta adamantly refused, saying she wanted to get down to eighty pounds as she'd been in 1977. She made it to one hundred before finally starting to take nourishment again, as she was fed up with the nurses riding her all the time about making herself very sick

Deirdre talked to me about her anguished life as well. She was only thirty-three, but because she was so obese she looked much older. She got married very young and had six children before she was twenty-five, but her husband left her and she lost custody of them because of her many admissions to the hospital and emotional problems. Her father had savagely abused her, even throwing a knife at her once and slashing her foot badly. There was a lot that she didn't tell me, but I knew that this sad-eyed, withdrawn woman had suffered more horrors than most people would in three lifetimes. It showed clearly in her face.

Dad, who came to visit a lot after Christmas, liked Deirdre, but noted how depressed she was. They got along very well, as she possessed a sharp wit and was unusually intelligent.

Deirdre was very concerned with my cutting, for she knew only too well the kind of pain that perpetuated it. She cut a lot as well and once got sent to emergency after violently slashing her abdomen. She liked to be on CNO, for the poor woman craved any signs of love and attention and asked Dr. Milo to spend as much time with her as he did with me.

Every once in awhile, she'd emerge from her cocoon of despair and even laugh, with the occasional twinkle in her eye. That was extremely heartening and encouraging to see. She would only last a few days on the outside, then would be readmitted for some kind of self-abuse.

But she had no home, no love or stability and G2 offered her a smattering of that. I understood this and felt thankful that I had somewhere to go when I got out, if that was ever going to happen that is.

Everett, a thirty-three-year-old man suffering from paranoid schizophrenia, was extremely affable, intelligent and sensible. After two years of being hospitalized, he was looking forward to finally getting his freedom. We got along really well, so I suggested that he move into Forest View, since Carla had moved back with her Dad.

Sheila had felt lost and lonely after I was put in the hospital and needed the security and love that her father was able to give her. Everett and I had a measure of fun together on the ward. He was another inveterate trekker and the two of us would watch "Star Trek: The Next Generation" reruns every weeknight at seven, enjoying our own running commentary of the plots and characters.

Gina had returned in March, after feeling unstable and wanting to hurt herself. We got close and she tried to get me to stop cutting myself so badly. "I just scratch, but you have to see veins and arteries popping out all over the place," she told me.
I just ignored her gestures of concern, but had a measure of respect for this Native woman who'd had a difficult time of it
growing up and carried the emotional scars of feeling "different" all her life and the object of a great deal of ridicule and prejudice.

Garon had gotten completely swallowed up in a devastating psychosis and was lost to me now. He refused to take his medication, which patients were allowed to do when the Mental Health Act was instated. I tried desperately to get him to reconsider and let the doctors give him drugs to quell his inner demons. Once I even bodily dragged him up to the nurses' station and literally begged him to swallow the medication, but he wouldn't.

I saw the Patient Advocate, a man dedicated to sidestepping the institutional bureaucracy for the sake of those of us who were hospitalized,and asked to see a copy of this act, which I did not believe was really in the patients' best interests. I wondered if there was anything we could do to modify it. This became my 1993 cause, just as nuclear disarmament had been ten years before.

However, this plan was thwarted by a recurrence of my angry, frightened outbursts which kept me confined in restraints a lot of the time and cutting became more important to me than getting people to take their medication.

On my thirty-ninth birthday, I realized that I was definitely no longer young and felt I had frittered the first half of my life away and would most likely waste the rest of it in the same fashion. It was a disquieting reality. Afterward my cutting became even more regular and violent. A couple of weeks before, I had awakened to discover that Nirvana's Kurt Cobain had killed himself by shoving the barrel of a shotgun into his mouth and pulling the trigger.

Trevor had gotten me into this band's music and I returned to my bed for the rest of the day, overcome with sadness that yet another desperately unhappy soul was unable to cope with life.

That night, I slashed my forearm so savagely that eighteen stitches were required to repair the damage and in the process, I lost a great deal of blood. Dr. Milo was extremely displeased and getting fed up, feeling that I was not making any progress at all.

One evening, I got into a tub full of near-scalding water and cut repeatedly and relentlessly until the water turned a deep, angry red. After an hour or so I was discovered and dragged out, covered in large gashes that bled profusely. I would later implement my now-familiar dark humour and refer to the incident as my "blood-bath".

I got a new roommate about this time, named Darla, an attractive, smiling-eyed young woman of twenty-three who told me she was schizo-affective, but that she could handle it and was optimistic about her future. I thought, as I listened to her, that she was living in a bit of a dream world, because according to Darla, everything was perfect and she really had no problems to speak of. I wondered what she was doing in the hospital if life was so incredibly rosy.

Then she laid a bomb on me one night as I sat in our room listening to R.E.M.'s "Automatic For the People". I'd bought it during a rare day out of the hospital and absolutely loved the poignancy and fresh honesty of the melancholy, world-jaded lyrics.

When I told Darla what tape I had in my Walkman, she said sadly, "Oh yeah...Michael Stipe. It's a shame he's dying of AIDS."

"What?!" I sat bolt upright, yanking off the headphones and feeling my heart lurch sickeningly. "What the hell are you talking about?" I hadn't heard any of this before, but remembered how painfully thin Stipe had looked in the "Everybody Hurts" video.

"Oh, you didn't know? Well he is, I'm afraid. Sorry I had to be the one to tell you."

My emotional state was extremely fragile anyway, but this latest news sent me into a flurry of cutting that night that resulted in all of my sheets becoming saturated with blood. I'd hacked away at the inner elbow of my right arm so viciously that I cut an artery for the first time and lay there in a semi-
conscious fog singing "Losing My Religion" mournfully into my pillow.

Alanna came in, flicked on the overhead light and saw a vision of horror that must have turned her stomach. Fortunately, Jenny had gone home for the night, so she wasn't a witness to all the blood spurting all over the walls. Alanna dragged me out of bed and called the duty doctor, who spoke solemnly to me about how dangerous it was to cut an artery and that I was lucky to be alive.

He looked sad and tried to make me see that this wasn't any way to live my life. I didn't want to hear it and turned my face to the wall, steeped in mental anguish that the lead singer of a band that had written the soundtrack for the past eleven years of my life was dying of that terrible, unspeakable disease. It was a true cata-strophic reaction.

Trevor informed me the next day that Stipe's diagnosis hadn't been confirmed and he was certain it was a nasty rumour. Of course, being the melodramatic individual that I was, I didn't believe him, but figured he was just trying to assuage my pain.

Everett moved into our house and did very well for a few months, before he stopped taking his medication. He was deliri-ously happy to be out of the hospital and living an independent lifestyle. He moved all the furniture around and settled in comfort-ably, although I was rather displeased that he engaged in pulling Julius' tail periodically.

Then a group of patients got transferred from H2 and I got instantly acquainted with them. They had all hung together on the admitting ward and seemed to genuinely enjoy one another's company. Kari was a chubby, baby-faced twenty-two-year-old who suffered with manic depressive illness and was in the midst of a depressive phase of her illness. She was kind and friendly, but overcome with sadness and self-doubt.

She was very much attracted to twenty-five-year-old Simon, a good-looking Native man who took an instant liking to me. I returned his attention and before long we started going together. He was surprised to learn that I was thirty-nine, as he figured me to be about twenty-eight, but it didn't seem to bother him. Simon had a serious drinking problem, had a lot of scars from a severe case of acne when he was younger, but this didn't detract from his ethereal qualities.

His eyes reflected a lifelong sadness and he suffered from something called rapid bipolar disorder, alternating episodes of severe depression with sudden outbursts of anger. He'd been in a lot of fights, but really wanted to change his life around.

Marjorie was a British woman of fifty-nine, who had an endearingly youthful outlook and said if she'd been twenty years younger, she'd go after Simon. She was very sad, with basset-hound eyes and a poignant smile and told us she suffered from manic depression, like Kari.

MaRjorie didn't want to take her medication, however, which angered Dr. Milo. He threatened to discharge her if she didn't comply with his orders, so she reluctantly decided to take steps to help in her recovery. I wished that Len had Dr. Milo as his psychiatrist.

Then there was twenty-seven-year-old Warren, a handsome, charismatic young man who liked to make fun of me, although I think it was a form of expressing affection. We talked about music and he expressed excitement at having biked down to Macon, Georgia. He'd grown very fond of the southern city and he promised that when we got out of the L.P.H. he'd take me there, if Simon didn't mind, that is.

Unfortunately, Simon's illness interfered with our budding relationship and one day he broke it off, retreating to his room for weeks and causing me untold anguish and feelings of inadequacy. I got really angry with him, yelling whenever he briefly appeared for the odd meal and generally made his life miserable.

I even hollered out one day, "You're evil, Simon!" which elicited a hurt, bewildered look from him. If I'd been feeling stronger and more stable, I would have realized that he was clearly dealing with some very heavy-duty issues of his own, but I was too wrapped up in self-pity and plagued with a seriously ruffled ego.

I gravitated toward Warren, who showed a lot of interest and it wasn't long before we were a couple. I seemed to need to be around men constantly to sublimate my feelings of sexual confusion and had gradually been horrified to find myself attracted to women again as I had been years before.

I didn't want to believe that I might be gay or bisexual and had told Dr. Milo that this was driving me crazy. He said that some of his best friends were homosexual and that it was no big deal. I didn't discuss it much with Dr. Spencer, feeling she would feel awkward and uncomfortable in my presence.

Warren turned out to be incredibly complex, with a great deal of barely-concealed anger that exploded at me with growing frequency. He thought that I was inordinately possessive and played terrible mind games with him.

In between the outbursts, we spent a lot of time in the sub-basement, making out with lusty abandon while a friend of Warren's played guitar and sang Soul Asylum's "Runaway Train" in the distance. He was damn good with his hands and tongue and I craved the physical contact, practically ripping his clothes off on several occasions. We planned to spend a weekend at my place, consummating our relationship.

We spent a Saturday afternoon in my room and made love as R.E.M. played "Low" on my old stereo system. I thought about my heavily-scarred, defaced body as Stipe sang "I can see your lines" and wished the room had been cloaked in darkness. However, Warren didn't seem to care and was patient, loving and kind. We didn't use protection, but Warren assured me he didn't have AIDS. My mind drifted to thoughts of my dalliances with Daryl and hoped that I didn't either for Warren's sake.

But he said that condoms ruin everything, so I squelched my apprehension and went ahead with the process. I really didn't exercise good judgement, and in the coming months, I would come to realize that you just can't engage in unprotected sex with a relative stranger in the 1990's. It's stupid and irresponsible and I'm not proud of myself at all.

Our relationship deteriorated quickly after our tryst that afternoon. Warren grew darkly morose and erupted in cataclysmic fits of rage at me regularly. I wasn't entirely blameless in this, for I was insecure and felt pangs of jealousy when he went for long walks with Kari. One night, as he shoved pool balls into the side of the table, he bristled, "Get away from me! I'm ballistic!"

When I asked him why he was so furious he spat, "You won't even let me go anywhere or do anything with any other woman! You want to keep me on a tight leash and I can't stand it! Come into the lounge. I want to tell you a few things."

I followed him into the deserted, carpeted room, where he proceeded to march up and down, hollering loud enough to split my eardrums. "You bitch at me about Kari, but then you go sucking up to Garon like some pathetic little tail-wagging dog. You say it's long over between the two of you, but you sit together and look adoringly into each other's eyes! I despise you for that! You're such a little hypocrite!"

I dissolved into tears, crumbling onto the floor and crying, "I'm so sorry! It doesn't mean anything. Garon and I are old friends, that's all. He was really good to me when I was so screwed up. I like him as a friend and that's all. I love you Joe. I want to spend the rest of my life with you. Please don't hate me!" I felt as though I was bottoming out, that this wonderful young man was rejecting me and imagining that I was cheating on him.

Later, we made up and returned to that same lounge, where he told me how much he loved me and that he wanted to marry me. I was ecstatic, thinking our troubles were behind us at last. They weren't, though.

One day, Warren found out that I had cut myself while he was out on a pass and returned to see me tied up in restraints and a staff member sitting with me. He was crushed, wondering why I still needed to do that when I had this positive relationship going for me. It caused a rift that would never really close again. I tried to tell him that I'd felt really bad that evening and that cutting was the only way to blot out the emotional pain.

Part of me wanted his sympathy and more love, which I figured could be gotten if he felt sorry for me. It was a familiar pattern, trying to insure someone's undying devotion by making myself look pathetic and helpless. I'd been doing this for years with family, friends and lovers. It wasn't working and I should have seen it long ago.

We talked about my self-abuse, how he was trying to comprehend it and somehow felt that part of it was his fault. Finally, one night, he exploded with rage after another slicing session and said he could no longer cope with it. He refused to touch me afterward. Slowly we drifted apart until all he had left for me was anger and revulsion.

Warren started going to a bar near his home and searching out female companionship that was less complicated and tragic. I realized that my cutting had cost me more than it ever had before and I resolved to try to put an end to it.

Judy began to spend a lot of time with me, telling me I should definitely go back to S.A.F.E. when I got released and come to grips with what my childhood abuse had taken from me. When I grew frantic and wanted to hurt myself, she'd tuck me in bed and give me one of my stuffed animals to hug tightly. "Do you feel safe?" she asked gently, stroking my hair. "Just lie there quietly with your little white cat. Feel the peace, the sense of being protected. Let go of some of the pain."

But I couldn't let go of it. It was too familiar and it gave me an excuse to slash my body. One day, I took a used razor blade, purchased from a seedy-looking man in the canteen and cut my stomach. The wounds didn't go very deep but they made thick, angry scars because I didn't tell the staff in time and they weren't stitched up. Now another body part was mutilated, banning me forever from bikinis and halter tops.

I finally got moved down the hall to Gina's room. The two of us spent a lot of time listening to "Automatic For the People" on her portable CD player. The songs sounded clearer and more potent on compact disks. I lost myself in them for many hours. When "Everybody Hurts" came on, I told Gina the song made me feel very sad and regretful.

"It's a message of hope," she replied, "I think it's very inspirational. It gives me a good, warm feeling inside. "Take comfort in your friends." There's a lot of truth in that. Listen carefully to it and don't be afraid of the sadness. It's part of living."

One afternoon, as Gina lay on her bed sleeping, I heard a voice coming from the CD player, telling me to cut my legs. I hadn't heard any of these diabolical sounds for a long time, but instead of feeling frightened or repulsed, I felt as if an old ally had come back to me. There was no music playing and I nixed an urge to drown the voices out in case the noise woke my roommate. I remembered that I still had my used blade on me, so I sat on the floor and sliced three deep gashes into my right leg for the first time.

Gina suddenly woke up and recoiled in horror, running frantically for the nurse. Afterward, she refused to speak to me, then screamed one afternoon, "I don't want you in my room anymore! I can't stand the thought of coming in and finding you dead on the fucking floor!"

After a few weeks of this silent hostility, I wrote a note to Gina and put it on her bed. It read simply, "I did a terrible, selfish thing. Can you forgive me? You offered me hope and friendship. I'm so very sorry."

Our friendship was renewed then, although we were never roommates again. We watched the Animaniacs cartoon every morning at seven thirty and she would tell me that I looked as though I hadn't slept.

In truth, I hadn't been sleeping much. I started writing again, a book about a southern rock band, heavily based on R.E.M. I was incredibly hyped about it and wrote for six hours every night, often until after three AM. Marjorie was my roommate now and she didn't mind me keeping the light on as she couldn't sleep herself.

Suddenly, I had a purpose again and accomplished over three hundred pages while I was still in the hospital. Writing offered a welcome distraction from what was going on around me. My life was still fraught with a certain amount of angry, explosive outbursts and a great deal of cutting, something from which nobody could deter me.

Several times, I tried to ask Mom about our checkered past, but always stopped myself, not wanting to upset her. Dr. Spencer reached into my tortured heart and extracted some information about the abuse and how it was affecting me now, many years later. I'd been requesting a lot of PRN's, or, medication given in times of stress and emotional upheaval or when experiencing psychiatric symptoms. One day Dr. Milo informed me that I was to have no more Atavan, Nozinan or Chlorolhydrate.

"You can't do this!" I protested, thinking that I took up to eight PRN's a day and relied on them to keep my demons in check.

"Yes I can," he responded firmly, "You're far too dependent on them and as long as you're taking medication to push down your feelings, you'll never get any better. It won't be easy, I know, but you'll be closely watched. You will probably experience some scary flashbacks and go through a great deal of pain. But we're here for you. We'll get you through it. And afterward, you'll start to get better, I promise. Have I ever steered you wrong before?"

"No," I had to admit, "but I'm absolutely terrified, Dr. Milo. I may fall apart and never get back together again."

"I don't think so. You're a lot stronger than you give yourself credit for."

So, in Ocotober of 1994, I was denied anymore PRN's and went through a positively horrific ordeal, the worst I'd experienced so far during this admission. First of all, I launched into a full-fledged love-hate relationship with Dr. Milo that threatened to put up an impenetrable barrier between us. I accused him of not caring about me and of avoiding me because I was twisted and loathsome. "You never talk to me anymore! You think I'm a terrible person just like the nurses here do and you don't care about me at all!"

"That's horseshit", he replied in annoyance, walking toward the door with his black knapsack flung over his muscular shoulder. "I've spent a lot of time with you."

"Yeah, only because you were afraid I was going to croak and it would put a smudge on your perfect fucking record!"

He disappeared off the ward, leaving me convinced that he now despised me. I loved him so much and he wasn't reciprocating my feelings. He was acting like Dr. Kiel, I thought, first showing friendship and concern, then switching them off when I became too much of a nuisance.

The nurses tried to explain that Dr. Milo had a deep caring for all of his patients and thought of me as a friend in a way. "Yeah right," I grumbled, "Then why does he walk away from me all the time? First he takes away all my PRN's and then he hasn't got the time to speak with me. I hate the prick."

I didn't hate him, though, but rather, I despised myself for acting like a jealous lover. What was the matter with me that I sullied everything good that happened to me? Why couldn't I just accept the fact that Dr. Milo was doing the best he could for me without getting sucked into my insecurities and self-defeating attitude?

Several days later, as I sat rocking hyperactively in the rocking chair and listening to my faithful Walkman, I was seized with a frightening torrent of wild, uncontrollable activity, and ran down the corridor, blindly fighting off invisible assailants who came at me with knives and other sharp implements.

The nurses let me run up and down for a few minutes, while I felt as though I was going to be torn apart and left to be pitifully bleeding on the floor. Voices tormented me, screaming, "I'll give you something to cry about!" and I cringed as ugly hands reached to grab my hair and pull me under a sea of certain death and destruction.

I was placed in restraints again, while the voices became so bad I couldn't hear myself yelling. I imagined that evil persons were forcing me into a suffocating box and I fought against iron hands that attempted to secure my flailing arms and legs. "I need a PRN! Please give me something!!"

"No, Jane. Dr. Milo gave strict orders that you weren't to have anymore." Marlene F., a patient, sensible forty-five-year-old RN told me firmly. "Just try to settle down and get some rest. Things will look better in the morning."

Marlene had been extremely exasperated by my repeated cutting episodes, telling me that I should be ashamed of my actions and that I'd be fifty years old and still hospitalized if I didn't get a hold on my problems. I hated her for saying that and felt she was belittling me and making a mockery of my suffering.

After a sleepless, sweat-soaked night, the restraints were removed and I resumed my agitated rocking, cranking my Walkman up to its full volume and clamping my teeth hard onto my tongue. I couldn't eat, for any appetite I might have regained over the past year had completely vanished.

I was volatile and extraordinarily angry, lashing out at patients and staff and causing people to gradually drift away from me. Begging constantly for Atavan to mellow me out a bit, I was told repeatedly, "You know what Dr. Milo said. No PRN's, period. Learn to face your feelings and overcome them with your own inner strength. It's there, just summon it up and you'll finally be able to leave this place."

One afternoon, I sneaked off the ward and walked over to Herbie's Drug Store, a few blocks away, to buy one hundred Tylenol with Codeine. I'd done this twice before during this admission, overdosing, wandering around then returning to the ward to inform the staff and subsequently being sent to emergency to swallow the ghastly thick charcoal mixture and puking my guts out for an hour. They hadn't been suicide attempts, but merely an expression of my inner turmoil and need for attention.

This time, I simply wanted to knock myself out for a few hours and get a much-needed respite from the feelings and sensations that violently haunted me. I purchased the medication, then swallowed sixty of them with a bottle of Diet Coke.

I was listening to R.E.M.'s "Monster", letting the aggressive, stabbing lyrics and music feed into my agitation. I hadn't actually meant to take that many and after I realized what I had done, the panic set in with a vengeance. I hurried back to the L.P.H., certain that I was going to pass out on the street before I got there.

The staff were quite upset with my behaviour, as this overdosing was becoming a habit. After a quick examination at Health Services, I was shuttled off to St. Joseph's to undergo another hideous charcoal experience.

They kept me at St. Joe's for three days with a guard sitting at the foot of my bed and an I.V. drip. I knew that I'd be thoroughly chastised when I returned to the L.P.H. I assured them that it would never happen again and that I had finally learned my lesson. They weren't convinced, however, particularly after I began hoarding pop cans again and cutting myself late at night when the other patients were asleep.

Then came the period of the strip search. This was horribly demoralizing and demeaning, for Shelley, a large but gentle RN, would make me remove every article of clothing while she stood, arms folded on her chest, watching me intently. Then all my clothing would be examined and several times I was even asked if I had anything hidden "up there".

"What? You think I'm that crazy?" I shouted incredulously, "Is this a hospital or a fucking prison?"

Actually, this wasn't the first time I'd been forced to strip naked while my clothes were rifled through. In August, Everett had gone completely psychotic at the house, threw out all of our electrical appliances and kitchen knives, then let Julius out. He forbid my cat to come back in and when I went home to discover that my dear little pet was missing, I went crazy, wailing, wringing my hands and crying, "My baby! Everett's destroyed my baby!"

Poor Everett was gravely ill, ranting that people were out to get him and that he had let Julius go because he thought the animal was dying.

I got permission to go out searching for him every day. I spent hours combing the neighbourhood, calling his name and asking people in the area if they'd noticed a grey tabby wandering about the premises. I was heartbroken, wondering if I'd ever see his furry little face again or feel his gentle purring next to me. How could this be happening?

Each night, when I arrived back on G2, I was told to disrobe while Shelley made certain that I wasn't concealing any razor blades or pieces of glass. I'd been so unstrung by the disappearance of Julius that Dr. Milo and the staff feared for my safety. I finally found him in the woods, terrified and hungry, after five days and nights of pure hell.

I lured him out of the bushes with tuna, which he hungrily devoured, then scooped the trembly animal up in my arms. I was never so thankful and elated in my life and vowed to stop cutting now that God had delivered my beloved cat back to me. So much for that "paper promise".

So the strip search had begun then. I figured it was a temporary measure and would cease now that Julius had been found and a crisis had been averted. But it had just begun and would continue for as long as I was a patient on G2. I really couldn't blame the nurses, for I'd cut myself so many times that I had scars over scars, over more scars.

Doctors had trouble puncturing my skin with the anesthetizing needles because of the toughened scar tissue and my arms looked as if they'd been through a terrible war. I was rarely seen without bandages covering both forearms, so precautions were taken to make certain that I never held a pop can in my hand. I had to pour my Diet Coke into styrofoam cups and I'd remark bitterly, "Yeah, make me contribute to the thinning of the ozone. You shouldn't have this styrofoam shit here."

"Anything to stop this ridiculous slashing," the nurses would reply. All pop cans had to be placed in a huge barrel at the front of the dayroom and patients weren't allowed to carry any cans down to their rooms anymore. If anyone was caught handing me a can, he or she would lose all privileges for twenty-four hours. I felt like a creep and was often met with angry, remorseful glances from the other patients.

Finally, after several weeks without PRN's, I began to feel stronger and more emotionally stable. The turning point came with the ecstatic revelation that it hadn't been my mother after all who'd molested me as a baby. One weekend, during some time at home after getting a couple of passes at last, I got up the nerve to ask Mom if she'd ever made me drink vinegar when I was little. It was hard summoning up the courage to bridge this harrowing subject, but she stared incredulously at me and exclaimed, laughing nervously, "Why, whatever would make you think that?!"

I replied that I knew that someone had and could it possibly be a babysitter if Mom had honestly been innocent, as it seemed she was from the expression on her face. "Well did anyone else ever babysit me besides Grandma and Grandpa?"

Mom gulped hard, paused for a moment and then said slowly, "The only babysitter we had for you was from three PM until Dad got home at five but surely she wouldn't do that....and besides, you were only twenty months old! How could you remember something like that at such a young age?"

"Well, I couldn't tell you at the time because of that fact, that I was so very young. But I sure remember what she looked like. Oh, Mom, she looked just like you, with this round face, curly, dark hair and glasses. I was so certain you had done that! So it really, honestly was some demented babysitter??"

Mom went on to explain that she had put an advertisement in the paper and a woman had answered saying that she was a nurse, but couldn't work anymore because of bad feet. She told Mom that she would be happy to babysit for a few hours a day. "Where did you work before?" Mom had inquired.

The woman told her that it had been the Egerton Street Nursing Home, which Mom recognized as the same place her friend from training, Helen Martin, owned. It was in the industrial East end of London.

Mom had phoned Helen to make certain that this woman was reputable and her friend remarked that she was a nurse's aide and had just left the Home without notice, but as far as Helen was concerned, the potential babysitter would be "okay". So Mom had hired her, content that all would be well and there would be no sorts of problems.

After I'd confided to Mom about the vinegar incident, she anxiously phoned up Helen Martin, who now resided in Collingwood. Mom hadn't seen her friend in years but figured the situation warranted contacting her to "get all the goods" on this bizarre babysitter.

Helen said that the woman had not returned to the nursing home to collect her last pay cheque, so after several months Helen took it to the address they had for her. This was after the woman had stopped working for Mom. Evidently she had rented a room in a deplorable district and when she had "started acting crazy" one day, the landlady called the police. Then Helen dropped a bombshell on my mother when she added that the police had "taken the woman back to the Ontario Hospital", which was the original site of the present-day L.P.H.

"Oh God, you mean she had been a patient there before?" Mom had cried over the phone. Yes, it appeared that when Helen went to her former employee's residence, the place had slid into utter ruin and it was obvious that the poor creature wasn't caring for herself or functioning very well. According to Helen, she'd even eaten food off of patients' plates at the Egerton Home even when she was assured that she could have her own meals. Mom figured this should have clued her old buddy in that all was not right with this person.

This devastated my poor mother, who realized she'd unknowingly hired a mental patient to care for her child. I told her over and over that it wasn't her fault and that she had had no way of knowing any of that, especially in late 1956 and early 1957.

It was a strange, mentally-unbalanced babysitter who'd been hired to care for me when my parents went to work in 1956. No wonder she'd done those other deeds with the sharp objects: It was painfully obvious that the woman was extremely ill and probably a paedophile as well. I thought that I should probably pity more than hate her for what she did, but the whole revelation just made me angry.

I felt terrible that I had mistaken the babysitter for mom, hated myself for thinking what I did and despising her for it. I held her close and hugged her until I nearly cracked her ribs, secure again in her love for and devotion to me. However, there was no way in hell that I was going to tell her about the sharp objects and where they had been inserted into me.

I got much better after that, although I hadn't come to terms with the trauma that the troubled woman had brought into my life and how, thirty-eight years had been devastated and practically destroyed because of the things she did. I wondered if she regretted any of it, or if she was ever plagued by images of a screaming infant who was unable to speak about what she was doing.

I was once again seized with blind rage, erupting spectacularly on the ward and fighting like a wild animal when burly staff members were brought in from other wards to place me in restraints. I'd twist myself into a writhing pretzel while Paul and his cohorts fought to secure my wrists and ankles, while I spouted obscenities and  spat in their faces.

One morning, I couldn't take it anymore, so I raced off the ward and out of the hospital, still clothed in my pyjamas and bare feet. It was early November, before the first snowfall, but it was very cold and damp. Panic-stricken and crying uncontrollably, I made a beeline for Highbury Avenue, a busy, transport-ridden highway where I wanted to be hit by a semi and splattered all over the asphalt.

Then I saw Dr. Milo out of the corner of my eye, who'd just emerged from his car in the parking lot. He went after me and I was caught and secured by his strong, powerful grasp before I made it to the road. Confused, extremely upset and choking away sobs, I let him take me back to the ward where he ordered restraints for the next three days. I shuddered to think what would have happened if he hadn't been right there. I realized then that I had to pull myself together,and fast.

I'd been in the hospital for fifteen months. I knew that if I didn't change my behaviour and attitude, I'd be in for another fifteen, if not more. I worked diligently and steadily with Dr. Spencer, talking for over two hours a week about my rage, depression and compulsive slashing. "I can't go on like this anymore," I said, staring at the floor. "I'm sick of it.

Everyone's sick of it. That woman took thirty-eight years from me, and I'll be damned if she'll rob me of anymore. This sucks."

"I've been waiting a long time to hear you say that," Dr. Spencer said, smiling at me. "So what are we going to do about it?"

The Zoloft had been seriously upsetting my stomach for months, so Dr. Milo put me on Paxil instead. It had fewer side effects and lifted my depression to the point where I was finally able to stop all the cutting. I figured that I had over eight hundred stitches from it and was tired of mutilating my body. Dr. Milo was pleased with my progress and set the date for my release at December twentieth, five days before Christmas.

I couldn't go back to my house, because Kari had moved in and gotten pretty messed up, calling the Humane Society to take Julius away. I was furious at her for months afterward. Now I realize that the woman wasn't well and was being driven frantic by the cat's incessant meowing to be let out. I wanted out of the W.O.T.C.H. housing anyway, though, for it was too unpredictable and unstable. I hadn't exactly thrived there over the past three years.

So on December twentieth, I somewhat apprehensively walked out of G2, my home for sixteen months, after promising to continue seeing Dr. Spencer twice a week and checking in periodically with Dr. Milo. He didn't usually see patients once they left hospital, but said he'd make an exception in my case. He knew how dependent I was on him and that I really didn't want a new doctor. That made me very happy.

Julius and I moved in with Mom, who'd recently acquired a feline of her own, a feisty, rambunctious female named Champagne. Mom wanted the opportunity to care for me in a way that she hadn't been able to in previous years. I knew that I would finally have some stability and security in my very troubled, vacillating, and mentally blurred existence.

Maybe the long, tortured nightmare was finally over forever. I'd come a long way, but still had a few obstacles to overcome.

# Chapter 16

## Internet Immersion: Taking the Superhighway Back to Life and Rewarding Interpersonal Relationships

First of all, I don't really care for the description of the Internet as merely "that information Superhighway", for it's much more than an incredible source of data, statistics, trivia and everything else that can be displayed on a computer screen. But that will be explored later on in the chapter.

I first heard about the "net" on January twenty-third, 1995 from two teenage girls whom I met while waiting for wristbands to get tickets for the R.E.M. concert on June thirteenth in Toronto. I was extremely excited when I heard that my favourite band would be touring again after five years and couldn't wait to finally see them perform live.

I'd never made it to any of their shows in the 1980's, for I was either sick, there was a death in the family, or I was unavailable because of my many hospitalizations. Nothing was going to stop me this time, however. Rachel, Melissa and I spent seven hours a day for three long, freezing days, hoping that Ticketmaster would finally start giving out the treasured wristbands.

As I talked to seventeen-year-old Rachel, a bright, outgoing R.E.M. fanatic who enthused about the band and spoke rapturously about finally, perhaps, getting to meet her hero, Michael Stipe. I discovered that she'd been involved with a computer organization that allowed her to communicate, indirectly with the band and other R.E.M. fans. I felt totally ignorant, since I'd been out of touch for so long,and so caught up in my own miserable, knotted net that I'd never heard about the mysterious world of cybernauts. I tried not to appear too stupid, but I did anyway and asked Rachel how someone went about accessing this intriguing medium.

"You have to have a computer," she replied, "and you pay a monthly fee. If you get on through the university, it's free, although you have to be a student".

I'd made tentative plans to return to Western and finish my degree, but wasn't quiet ready, since I had only been out of the L.P.H. for a month and was just getting over a paralyzing fear of walking about in public.

We finally got the wristbands, after acquiring frostbitten toes, early Wednesday evening. The manager of Sunrise Records and Tapes, the downtown headquarters of the Ticketmaster outlet, seemed pleased that our diligence and innate stubbornness had paid off.

I got a third row centre seat the following Saturday morning, and was positively elated. I'd learned long ago that if you wanted something badly enough, you had to suffer some discomfort and stress to get it.

After meeting a young computer salesman at Big Byte Computers early in February, I arranged to purchase his second-hand machine for nine hundred fifty dollars. That drained my account completely, but I didn't care, for this was something I really wanted. It wasn't just because of the Internet but to acquire a word processor to replace my archaic typewriter.

Mike brought the computer, one that was IBM compatible, over several nights later. He hooked it up with a modem and got me connected to Online Systems of Canada, a local Internet provider that he used. It was a good thing he knew what he was doing, because I would have had a difficult time figuring out the software. I'd never done anything with a computer before. I learned to use WordPerfect at the L.P.H., but was basically computer illiterate.

Then I plunged right into the 'net and subsequently got hopelessly entangled in it. Everything began innocuously enough, as I stumbled upon Usenet and found the R.E.M. newsgroup listed as rec.music.rem. Usenet isn't actually on the Internet itself, but is a huge group of five thousand plus categories of music newsgroups, television shows, past and present, support groups and any other quirky subjects that any cybernetic heart could possibly desire. I avoided the very sick-minded groups, such as alt.sex.bestiality but read a lot of the messages in alt.support.depression, alt. sexual-abuse.recovery and misc.writing.

But the R.E.M. newsgroup really captured my attention and rampant enthusiasm. I "lurked", or read messages without posting any, for several days, taking in everything from  personal reflections on the band and its thought-provoking lyrics, insightful analyses of song meanings, to vituperative complaints about concert ticket prices and denouncements of R.E.M. as having "sold out".

One afternoon, I posted my first message, an upbeat, giddy introduction of sorts, talking about how excited I was about the upcoming show in Toronto and explaining that I'd been an enthusiastic fan for twelve years. I was pleased to get a large number of responses, sent via e-mail to Internet Private Conference 1000, an area of Online Systems that dispensed and gathered messages from people all over the world.

E-mail ranged from the silly ("Tell me your best Michael Stipe dream") to the friendly and personable ("You got a third row centre seat? Fantastic!"). All of them warmly welcomed me to the newsgroup and I felt a sense of communal spirit that I'd never experienced before. I'd been basically living the life of a fan in a vacuum all these years and now there were real, living and breathing human beings sending letters from as far away as Germany and Australia.

Then I stuck a monkey wrench into the whole machine when, one Saturday night as I sat alone listening to "Everybody Hurts", I posted a message that would reveal me as a very disturbed, tragic and messed up individual, one who had spent half her life hospitalized, and one who still dissolved into dark, reflective fragments whenever that R.E.M. song was played. I just couldn't shed the trappings of the victim, it seemed.

I don't have a clear recollection of everything I wrote, but it offered a painfully detailed description of my life with Borderline Personality Disorder and how I'd been robbed of my youth, productivity and any long-term, meaningful interpersonal relationships. I almost aborted this message at the last minute, but ultimately sent it, then ruminated over my decision for the next few hours and how I'd tainted my promising relationship with these exuberant, life-affirming R.E.M. devotees.

What followed truly surprised and heartened me, for within several hours, messages came pouring in from all over the globe, offering hope, compassion and understanding for a life that had somehow taken a bad turn and gotten overly complex.

But the letters that touched me most were the ones from people who opened up their souls and told me their personal, heart-wrenching stories, everything from a young man who'd lost a beloved girlfriend to suicide, another woman who'd been plagued for most of her life with eating disorders and feelings of worthlessness and a university student who nearly didn't make it through 1993 without "Everybody Hurts" keeping him above a life-threatening despair.

Their pain bit into my self-absorbed heart and helped it heal, in a strange kind of way, for I realized that I wasn't alone and that there were so many others who had stared into the abyss, and most importantly, had stepped back out of it again.

One woman, forty-five-year-old Val Hill, spoke to me of her long-time love of R.E.M. and how their music sustained her through a long period of despair. I smiled sadly with recognition, and then she went on to speak about her life being wonderfully renewed with her marriage to a kind, supportive man and the unconditional love of her two young children.

One young man, Sam, wrote and said, "Well, I don't know if I would have written such a personal post to the newsgroup, but I read it with interest and hope you're doing okay now." His posts to the group were extraordinarily insightful and brilliant, with an in-depth analysis of the songs' lyrics and an unabashed enthusiasm for R.E.M. in general. He made me smile, and his shy appreciation for a stranger's words gave me some semblance of hope.

Despite all the heart-warming e-mail, I felt rather remorseful for what I'd written. I posted another message apologizing for being so nakedly candid. Jake, the unofficial "guru" of rec.music.rem, handling the FAQ (Frequently Asked Questions) and speaking with eloquence and intelligence, wrote to me saying, "You shouldn't apologize for what you wrote."

Then he added somewhat sarcastically but with a substantial amount of kind humour, "Well, we wouldn't want a sincere, heart-felt response to get in the way of arguments about ticket prices, after all."

His address showed that he was affiliated with Cornell University, which didn't surprise me, given his wonderful way of articulating and analyses of the band's lyrics.

I decided to write to him and ask if Michael Stipe was okay. Although I'd recently discovered that he really wasn't dying of AIDS, I feared that he might be anorexic. Ron wrote back and gave me a long, detailed explanation of Stipes' extreme thinness, saying that it was because he was a vegetarian and consumed very little fat. "He's always been skinny," Jake assured me, "and besides, remember that the guys are in their mid to late thirties.

When you get older, your face gets more haggard and lined. I should know. I'm their age and look in the mirror and think that I am not a kid anymore. The teenagers say the same thing about R.E.M. They forget that the guys are close to their parents' ages. The band is in a strange position because they are getting older and their fans are getting younger." He continued to say that I was one of the few that attributed Stipe's appearance to anorexia. "Most people think that it's due to AIDS, because of his bisexuality."

I didn't realize he was bisexual, nor did I particularly care, for it definitely has nothing to do with the band's music, but when Ron told me this, I felt curiously comforted. The fact that someone whose work had been so strengthening to me for so long had the same feelings as I did and that it was okay, made me feel much better about myself. Then I made a real stupid "newbie mistake", one which had serious repercussions for me.

I wrote to Ron, admitting that I was pretty certain that I, too was bisexual and that it suddenly didn't seem to be such a big deal anymore. I could accept it now and get on with the rest of my life. But instead of sending it privately, I accidentally posted it to the newsgroup and discovered this devastating fact a few hours later when someone wrote, quoting my message and writing, "Be very careful when you send a follow-up to someone. Did you really want this to be posted in rec.music.rem?"

I was positively transfixed with horror. How could I have made a mistake like that? Now tens of thousands of people were going to know something that not even my friends and family were aware of. I was riddled with guilt and tremendous shame. Then I reached, in a moment of black despair, for my bottles of Paxil and Risperidone, an anti-psychotic medication prescribed by Dr. Milo for my voices. Fortunately, I realized that killing myself wasn't the solution, so I retired to bed for the next twelve hours, huddled under the protective covers. I swore that I wouldn't go back online for at least a week.

One young man who'd written to me recently, a university student from the U.K., sent a message of hope, along with an interview with Michael Stipe from the Athens-based magazine, "Flagpole". I responded by saying that my life was over and that I felt like doing myself in. He kept writing, saying that if Michael saw my mistake he'd understand and that he wished he could be with me to help me through the crisis.

I posted another message to the newsgroup, saying how sorry I was to have made such a terrible mistake and that I felt so awful, I'd nearly swallowed all my pills.

Jake wrote, saying, "It's only a newsgroup after all" and that nothing really horrible had happened. Another young woman named Meredith J. Fine, wrote an exceedingly compassionate, caring letter saying she would willingly listen. Unfortunately, I didn't answer any of my e-mail during this period, but figured I'd respond to her after the storm had died down somewhat.

One Tuesday afternoon, I climbed into the bathtub while Mom was out and slashed my left forearm vertically with a razor blade. I called a friend, Marilyn, whom I'd met on G2 and knew from 1977 on P1, and she then phoned the police, fearful for my safety. The cops came and, when they saw my bloody arm they insisted that I go to the hospital to get stitched up. Reluctantly, I left with them and was sutured by an intern I'd met months before when I was anorexic and who said morosely, "You aren't really getting any better, are you?"

I was then transferred back to the L.P.H. where Dr. Milo kept me on L2 for seventy-two hours of observation. During that time, I became overcome with guilt at upsetting my mother again and telling Andrew just before the police led me off what I had done and that I'd probably be gone for a few days.

Dr. Milo realized that I was under a great deal of stress, but decided after three days that I was no longer in any danger of hurting myself. I found out that when I was hospitalized, so was R.E.M.'s drummer, Bill Berry, who suffered a sub-arachnoid aneurysm. "God, I hope he doesn't die," I thought unhappily, "What the hell else can go wrong this month?"

Luckily, Bill recovered and so did I. The crisis passed and

while Berry was recuperating in the hospital, I resumed my life on the Internet, exploring the writing newsgroup as well as the two support groups I'd lurked about in previously. I still wasn't answering any of my e-mail, or even reading it most of the time, since I was intensely afraid of getting "flamed" by people who were disgusted and repulsed by what I'd admitted publicly and who would probably tell me off with plenty of expletives.

I met a young Internet enthusiast named Paul Balaga, an open-minded twenty-nine-year-old whose father was dying of cancer. He told me that he was gay, and that he had a difficult time dealing with it. He'd read my mistaken message and looked at me as a kind of kindred spirit. A great deal of our lives revolved around our computers and modems. I liked him and felt very bad about his father's grave condition. Dad thought it was a bad idea to meet someone on the Internet and said to me, "What if the guy turns out to be an axe murderer?"

"Dad, he's just a person like you and me. For all you know, his family thinks the same thing about your daughter."

Paul and I had a lot of emotionally-charged and intense discussions about life, death and what it all meant in the "grand scheme of things". I was finally getting some personal contacts in my solitary universe. We went out for coffee and visited one another's homes as well as talking online.

I posted an introductory message to misc.writing and received a lot of welcome messages from other aspiring writers and some established ones, like Ken Goddard. I was enthraled with the whole Internet dimension. It was encouraging me to write again, since it is strictly a writing means of communication. My sentences became less run-on and I felt myself brimming with enthusiasm to be creating again.

I began working on my music novel again, but I still had an annoying habit of making sentences far too lengthy, sometimes entire paragraphs long. Still, it was better than sitting in a hospital, cutting myself all day and night.

Andrew never wrote back to me after I told him I'd slashed myself. I figured I'd likely scared the daylights out of him. That disturbed me and I thought a lot about how damaging and negative the whole process of self-abuse was, especially how deeply it affected others.

I wished that I'd responded to all the people who'd sent me

such encouraging, heartfelt e-mail during the month of February. I lost contact with most of them and really regretted that. I should have been more thoughtful, but then, my self-pity overcame any despair I might have felt for anyone else.

By the middle of March, I decided to try to communicate with some of the R.E.M. newsgroup members who wrote the positive, upbeat posts. I thought that if I couldn't re-establish contact with my soulmates, I could make friends with these people. I wrote to twenty-five of them.

None answered my e-mail. I felt hurt, rejected and overcome with self-doubt. So one night at the end of the month I sent an angry, scathing message that even employed the f-word and didn't even star out any of the letters. I complained that people shouldn't ignore each other on the Internet and that they were acting like famous individuals when they didn't answer their letters. "You're just as bad!" I fumed, and went on to tell them all off, no holds barred.

It was really immature and nasty. I entitled it, "Is This a Virtual Vacuum????" and when I posted it, I knew with a certain amount of dread that people were going to flame the hell out of me. The fact that I was being an utter hypocrite didn't dawn on me then, as I was so caught up in waving a huge, knobby club at everyone's computer screen.

Well, unbelievably, I only got flamed once, by a university student who wrote, "What the hell was that all about? Jesus, take some fucking Valium!" The rest of my mail was much more than I deserved.

One student from the University of Oregon named Ian Best, started off by saying, "Had some pent-up aggression there, huh? I read some of the other posts with disinterest, but yours blew me away."

He went on to explain that he understood where I was coming from, that people on the Internet were basically insensitive and not willing to get too close to one another. He added that he admired people who weren't afraid to speak their minds, saying, "I'm more into Nine Inch Nails and Faith No More than R.E.M., but to each his own." I wrote back to him, thanking this kind soul for being so generous and complementary to someone who really needed a swift kick in the ass.

We wrote back and forth constantly after that. I eventually

told him about my past. Ian said some pretty revealing things to me about his own life. I marvelled at how someone so young could be that courageous. This nineteen-year-old certainly had a great deal going for him.

That's something else of which I was quickly becoming aware: How intelligent, articulate and world-wise teenagers of the 1990's were. Not only that, but people in this age group and in their early twenties possessed a sense of community and elevated consciousness that drastically went against individuals in my generation, the so-called "boomers", who believed that Generation Xers "Are all a bunch of whiny little brats. What do they know about anything? And what the hell have they got to complain about?"

I'm ashamed to be a part of that maligning demographic group, because they are so very, very wrong. The teens and young adults really do have something to be upset about. After all, there aren't any jobs for them to speak of, as my generation has taken up so much of the world's work resources with our burgeoning population, and the eldest of the boomers won't retire for another fifteen years or so.

Not only that, their sex now has the ability to kill them, thus drowning out the previous idyll of the "sexual revolution" and grinding it to a complete halt. There's been a rapid increase in teen suicide over the past ten years and the music of today reflects a prevailing sentiment of hopelessness and despair. I don't call what Generation X does whining, but rather, weeping for their lives and futures that have been cruelly snatched out from under them.

I don't divulge my age on the Internet, except to several people I've gotten close to. The reason for this is that I don't want the young people to feel awkward and flustered around someone who's old enough to be their mother. I don't really feel a sense of kinship for people my age because of the fact that I lost my productive years to illness and institutionalization. I feel as though I'm in a similar position to the younger folks, with regard to the future and opportunities.

The other letters that responded to my "Virtual Vacuum" drivel were equally positive and kind. One young man named Brent started out with a rather caustic, "You are so full of shit" and then went on to express how he felt and that I had no right to expect people to feel sorry for me. This may seem rather mean, but the gist of the message was this: Go out and get some real friends and make your life worthwhile. Don't expect an R.E.M. newsgroup to be the solution for all your difficulties. You can do better."

I was encouraged by the way that he talked so frankly and honestly to me and it gave me some hope to know that not everyone feared speaking the truth or felt they had to walk on cybernetic eggshells in my presence, for fear I'd fall apart and destroy myself.

I wrote back to Brent, thanking him for "having the guts to speak to me like that" and we've communicated ever since, much more positively. We've both come to the conclusion that life really isn't all that bad after all, for either of us.

Peter Vonder Haar, another university student in the States, said he applauded my forthrightness and wanted to get to know me better. He mentioned that my posts were refreshing and offered something more for the thought processes than the incessant bickering that often went on in rec.music.rem. I still write to him too, and he's a wonderful, enthusiastic and intelligent guy. Not only that, he argues extremely well, using logic and common sense when all about him are losing both of these.

Then there was a short, sad letter from Meredith Fine, who'd written to me three times but I hadn't responded to her. She said simply, "I've written to you several times but you never answered and I lumped you in with all of those who don't reply to e-mail. Maybe, after your latest post, you finally will communicate with me."

I cringed with remorse, realizing that I'd hurt her and instantly sent her a letter saying, "Thank heavens. I have your address now. I lost it a month ago when my server deleted all the online addresses. I'm so sorry for snubbing you. Please write again and I promise I'll answer you."

M.J. turned out to be a wonderful, complex nineteen-year-old from Pennsylvania, attending American University. She was fighting a lifelong feeling of despair and struggled constantly toward the light of hope by way of R.E.M.'s music. Her father had died when she was younger and her mother suffered from periods of severe depression. M.J. also felt drawn toward the murky well of hopelessness but refused to give in, believing that some day her life would improve and she would write something "that will touch a lot of people". I have no doubt that she will. It surprised me to find out she was so physically young.

Buoyed by these messages, I delved into the   newsgroup

again, after issuing a contrite apology, and wrote to some other
long-time regulars like Zachary Ralston from the Athens-based
University of Georgia, where the band had attended school, and a
virtual friend of Sam's, Cleaver, who said he liked my posts but
commented that they were "really long".

I didn't fare as well with the writing newsgroup, for after
posting something entitled "Why We Write" I received some pretty
nasty criticism of the personal nature of the piece. Upset and hurt, I
submitted "Could Have Predicted This..." and explained that I
didn't understand why writers would so roundly trounce another's
work when, after all, we were all pretty much in the same boat.

A few members responded, one named Jack Mingo, a long-
time regular who said I should get used to bad reviews but that he
understood my negative reaction. Several other writers sent encouraging e-mail, saying they also wanted a forum where they could
write and exchange ideas. We planned on beginning our own
writing group but, unfortunately, it never came about.

I read the Nirvana newsgroup, as well as alt.fan.courtney-
love and was appalled at the way some people talked about Kurt's
suicide as a "cowardly act" and that they were glad he was dead. I
didn't see how I could reach any of these individuals, although I did
post an "anti-suicide" message and got an angry response from a
nineteen-year-old girl who told me not to preach on the Internet or I
was going to get flamed.

She and I exchanged e-mail several times, after talking about
our traumatic lives, but she left one weekend for a trip home and I
never heard from her again. She'd attempted suicide a year before
and I was really worried that something had happened to her. I hope
she's okay, for she was an extremely compassionate and fiery
person, made stronger by what she had been through in the past.

Then I delved into the sexual abuse recovery newsgroup, but,
unfortunately got no responses to an intensely personal and painful
post about my experiences with The Babysitter. I felt crushed and
defeated, feeling that no-one wanted anything to do with anybody
like me who may well have asked for the abuse she got.

This coincided with my fortieth birthday, a negative day that
brought me face to face with the grim realization that I had not yet
been published. It had been my goal to achieve success as a writer
before this milestone.  When it arrived to find me still on a Disability pension and with no completed manuscript, I sank into a feeling

of overwhelming sadness and self-pity.

Jim called me the next night, but I wasn't able to say much to him. I talked in a hesitant, monosyllabic voice, while he tried to make light of the situation and assure me that "I'm right behind you." Cousin John also spoke to me from Vancouver, and grew concerned at my moroseness. "Are you okay? Want to talk about it?" I didn't, but appreciated his love, which had never failed me.

Once my mid-life crisis had passed, I was beset with another trauma: The selling of my fiercely-guarded R.E.M. ticket. I'd been suffering from a series of overwhelming anxiety attacks whenever I ventured outside, so my parents convinced me that I couldn't possibly travel alone to Toronto and put myself in the midst of sixteen thousand excited music fans. I finally saw their point, and so I advertised my ticket in the newsgroup and received a response two days later from a young, eager woman named Lisa.

I sold the ticket for what I paid for it and felt a twinge of regret as it slipped from my hand into hers. I'd recently joined an online writers group called, appropriately, "Writers" and had sent in a bio telling of my plans to write my autobiography and that I hoped it would help people.

The ticket evaded me on a Friday and the following Saturday night in May, I sat in my room, drinking too much wine and bemoaning the fact that I'd sold a piece of my freedom and happiness with that R.E.M. ticket. Mom had gone out for the evening and as I drank, I grew more and more depressed.

Finally, the thought hit me with bone-numbing force: I just can't live like this anymore. I pictured the carving knife in the kitchen and how desperately I wanted to slice my throat with it. It scared me to think this way, but at the same time offered some reassurance and  comfort. It was familiar, this drive toward self-destruction and tragedy.

I continued drinking until I was quite intoxicated. Then, I posted another message to the Nirvana newsgroup. I started off, "Please read this. I have something to say to all of you, probably the last thing I will say to anyone. Don't malign Kurt for committing suicide, for sometimes it's the only answer. He was overcome with pain and despair. Please forgive him, and forgive me." I also posted a farewell letter to my friends in rec.music.rem, then finished the bottle of wine.

Before I headed downstairs toward the kitchen, I thought

about my new pals at Writers. Partly out of fear for my own precarious state of mind, and partly out of a strong desire to talk to someone, I posted a short, terse note, ending with, "I can't keep living this way. I don't think I'll be alive when my Mother gets home".

This Listserv operates out of the University of Massachusetts, with Mike Barker as the main directing force. He must have read this desperate message, because within twenty minutes, it was distributed to everyone on the mailing list.

Very intoxicated and having a great deal of difficulty thinking clearly, I went online for what I figured would be the last time and checked my e-mail. There was a frantic, concerned letter from someone named jc who implored me not to kill myself and leaving his home phone number. He said, "People aren't around tonight because they're out doing the laundry and things. They care believe me. I care. Please call me collect if you want, and hang on".

I was very surprised that the message had gotten distributed so rapidly and somewhat heartened by the earnest response that sparked with hope. I read the next one, from a man in Israel, telling me that I should talk to him immediately and that he would not stand for me to commit suicide like that. I didn't know what to do. Why the hell did these people care about someone at a computer thousands of miles away? And leaving their phone numbers? What was going on?

Encouraged by the thought of complete strangers taking an interest in such a pathetic excuse for a human being, I decided to stay online and then received more urgent messages imploring me to reconsider. Suddenly, it wasn't just me alone in a bedroom in London,Ontario anymore, having had too much to drink and a carving knife nearby. It was a person who meant something to someone. There were real people out there who didn't know me and wouldn't even recognize me on the street.

Then Mom came home, much earlier than expected, and the melodrama was ended. I didn't tell her anything, as it didn't seem necessary now that I was safe once again. I vowed long ago that I would never kill myself in front of her or while she was in the same house.

I tumbled awkwardly into bed and drifted off into an uneasy sleep, while Julius purred at the foot of my bed. It was over, thanks to several people who simply wouldn't let a fellow writer and human being take her life in a state of alcoholic malaise one Saturday night in the spring of 1995. I awoke to find at least thirty messages from Writers members and my heart broke. I felt so terrible about what I had almost done and buoyed up by these people's thoughtfulness and kind messages of encouragement and hope. I had to get a hold of my life, once and for all. Too many individuals were involved now, from all over the world.

Within several days, messages came from members of rec.music.rem and alt.music.nirvana, saying that they read my posts and grew very alarmed.

One young man, Anthony Kibort, told me touchingly, "I've been reading your posts in the R.E.M. newsgroup for the past three and a half months and have grown to love your honesty and courage. Please write and say you are alright. I'm so afraid for you." I wrote back right away, assuring him that I had weathered the storm and felt badly about scaring him.

We've been corresponding ever since and he's shown himself to be wise beyond his twenty-nine years, as well as very astute, gentle-natured and with an intense love of life and the music of R.E.M. Recently, he made a pilgrimage to Athens, Georgia and was enthraled with the R.E.M.-permeated landscape and Weaver D's restaurant, where the title, "Automatic For the People" originated.

I received about ten messages from the Nirvana group, ranging from the desperate plea, "Just think of one thing that makes you happy!" to a sad, reflective letter from a thirteen-year-old nicknamed "coolboy", who at first thought I was "some kid using her dad's computer" then commented that he could relate to my feelings of despondency and hopelessness.

I wrote to him frequently and he regaled me with witty tales about his life and friendships as he struggled with the pains of adolescence. Letters came from as far away as Norway and all spoke of the futility of suicide and how much devastation it wreaks on those left behind. I know in my heart that I will never entertain thoughts of it again.

Those people gave me something vital that was missing in my life: The opportunity to communicate with real people, instead of being isolated in my room with Julius, Champagne and my music. Perhaps I could once again venture out and make some kind of a life for myself at the not-so-tender age of forty.

A week before the R.E.M. concert, I sent a message to the

newsgroup asking if anyone had an extra ticket for the show in Toronto. I realized that it was a long shot, but I had made up my mind that I really wanted to go and would cope as best I could with any anxiety attacks that occurred at the Molson Amphitheatre.

As luck would have it, someone in Niagara Falls wrote back a day later and informed me that he had a ticket for the four hundred section and would sell it to me for one hundred dollars. I sent him the money by courier and got the ticket, then stayed with M.B., whom I hadn't seen for nearly two years. The show was incredible, even though the seat wasn't anywhere near third row centre, and I came away absolutely mesmerized by R.E.M.'s performance. It was everything I'd imagined it would be for the last twelve years and when Michael Stipe sat crouched and huddled alone on the stage and wailed plaintively the lyrics to "Let Me In", I was over-come with emotion.

I actually did cry when they sang "Everybody Hurts" but didn't care who saw me. I had painted t-shirts for all four band members and gave them to a security guard, hoping that the guys would eventually receive them. M.B. figured I was way too old for this sort of thing, but I just laughed and told her I had a terminal case of "Peter Pan Complex". The concert was a true victory for me, for not only did I remain anxiety-free, but I proved to myself that I could actually get out in the "real world" again and not make an absolute fool of myself.

In July, I met Selene MacLeod, a student at Wilfred Laurier University, who'd written to me several times and was an enthusi-astic member of Writers. She wanted to interview me for a school project, saying she was writing an article on the personal aspect of the Internet and that my experience with the suicidal impulses, as well as the subsequent involvement of the Writers group, would make an intelligent, thought-provoking story.

She came to London by Greyhound bus one Saturday morning,and I was pleased to see a smiling, out-going young woman of twenty who had a definite "alternative look" and had a hip, savvy connection to the whole so-called "Generation X" mentality of music, philosophy and world vision.

Selene came upstairs to my room with me, where I keep my computer, and we talked for several hours about the state of the world, Canadian rock music, writing and  our prospects for the future.

She's an extremely gifted and intelligent writer and has a very astute, dead-on set of observations about people, the media and what drives individuals to put thoughts and ideas on paper. I had just begun work on this book and told her that I finally planned on finishing it and moving ahead with my life. Selene was encouraged that I'd overcome my depression, which I'd actually suffered from for most of my life, and told me I had potential as a writer.

Then we went downstairs and Selene interviewed me for her article. She asked a lot of questions about my psychiatric past, and I complied, feeling very much at ease with her self-effacing manner. I spoke honestly about that Saturday night two months earlier, and then remarked that I might not have been there on this July afternoon if it weren't for the "Internet intervention". When the interview was done, she felt that there was a lot of material to draw on.

I hoped that maybe, for once, my experiences could be of some use and benefit to someone else. We planned to get together again, when Selene would take me to rock concerts and get me "back into society". I was very grateful and assured her that I was out of my "self-destructive period of emotional hibernation".

One young university student, who attended Baylor University in Waco, Texas, had been writing to me for several months. He had responded to something I'd posted about Michael Stipe, saying that Stipe was "pursued relentlessly by the media and people on the Internet who wanted to know intimate details about his personal life". Chris Neal sent me one of his poems, entitled "Dehumanizing Michael", an extraordinarily well-written and very sad piece of work that spoke of his love for the man's music, the way he so strongly identified with the pain often depicted and that he agonized over the way that some wanted to pick his bones clean.

Some of the lines, like, "human beings are to be and not to do", "And another day has passed, And I wonder why I question the safety of your quest" and "So what if you are wearing an artist's disguise?" tore into my heart and told me that this special young man knew what it was like to feel preyed upon and lost in despair.

Chris was an incredibly complex twenty-one-year-old who desired to elevate his life from it's painful roots. He had lost a beloved father, and his mother was awash in her own troubled waters. He loved to write poetry and was extremely prolific. He adopted the "Stipean tortured stance", not to be a clone of the world-renowned musician but because he saw in the man a lot of his own characteristics.

Interspersed with the darkly reflected writing were poems that echoed beauty and hope, and I knew that one day he would find some happiness and fulfilment. I correspond with Chris more than anyone on the Internet, and we keep each other afloat in this increasingly complicated world.

\ In August, Mom and I took a plane to Vancouver for Jim's wedding. It was a beautiful experience, with Diane looking absolutely gorgeous and radiant, like a young Joan Collins and Jim obviously happier than he'd ever been in his life. I knew in my heart that this marriage would be permanent and awe-inspiring, for they just couldn't stop gazing rapturously into each other's eyes.

Jim and I had a lot of time to talk and do the "sibling bonding thing", getting together one afternoon at the UBC campus for several beers and a lot of soul searching. As we talked, Jim and I came to terms with the past, particularly my disquieting part in it, and I knew that he had finally forgiven me for everything I had done to myself and our family.

"I realize I did some pretty bad things," I said slowly, sipping on my Coors Light, "and you spent years wondering what the hell was going to become of me. But I think it's finally over".

Jim looked pleased and responded with a comforting smile, "Well, you did make us all wonder at times. But it doesn't matter that much what happened in the past. Just don't screw up the next forty years".

I assured him that he would be portrayed as the seemingly older, more level-headed one us in my book, and added that I had always thought of him that way.

He let out a short, bemused laugh. "Oh no you didn't! Remember when we were little kids? You loved to flaunt your authority in front of me."

"True. But I got over my authoritarian, domineering phase in time."

He talked about the immense satisfaction he received from his residency in the St. Paul's Hospital ER and his blue eyes literally shone when he described the intense, life-and-death atmosphere of having to make decisions that truly mattered to someone's mortality.

"I hope you can eventually work there permanently," I said, catching the electrical energy that emanated from Jim as he spoke.

"We'll see. It doesn't seem terribly likely right now, but I've beaten the odds before."

"We both have." Jim and I sat there for several hours, discussing our parents, his doomed marriage to Sandy and the way his heart had been gloriously opened by the loving gentleness of Diane. As the afternoon waned, I knew that our relationship had been reaffirmed. Not only that, but no matter what the future held for either of us, we'd face it together, even if we never lived in the same town again.

I returned home a stronger person with some concrete plans for the future. After I finished my autobiography, I wanted to return to university part-time and finally get my Honours degree in English. I know now that I would be able to cope with the stress of the workload and look forward to mingling with the academic faction again.

I also threw away my Codeine supply, for in the months since my release from the L.P.H. I had become addicted to the drug again, as I had in 1989. I liked the feeling of well-being that it gave me, but I had been using so much of it that I was very sluggish and apathetic much of the time.

The little bit of pleasure derived from this narcotic is certainly not worth the vague feelings of nausea, slowed metabolic rate and thick-headedness, not to mention getting hooked and needing to take more and more just to feel normal.

I began to read the online support groups again, not for what they could do for me, but how I might be able to help some of those courageous but anguished people who were constantly plagued with depression, self-abuse and eating disorders because of being sexually abused in the past.

I realized how selfish I'd been in the past with these groups, taking all the time and never offering any hope or encouragement to anyone else. It was time to turn things around and use some of my life experiences to benefit someone else who had not yet found the way back.

Val Hill sent me a package of R.E.M. articles, a photo of herself and her children, and a thoughtful, insightful letter via "snailmail", or the regular post office as opposed to the Internet postmaster. She, like myself, doesn't feel terribly connected with the "boomer generation" and still clings to the raging idealism and blurred thought processes of her radical youth. Together, we're going to change the world, a bit at a time.

The Internet has been harshly criticized as "an escape from the real world", as well as a rather one-dimensional view of life and personal interaction. I do not believe this, for a person can easily get beyond the constant barrage of information flying across a computer screen to the real, flesh-and-blood human beings writing the words.

The 'net has allowed me to emerge from a deep, solid shell, reach out to an often loving, caring community and feel more at ease around people. This computer community saved my life last May, it released me from loneliness and allowed me to share thoughts and ideas with individuals who are now my friends.

Jim said that meeting a companion on the Internet is a "kind of geeky thing to do" but what better way to connect than through written words, spoken from the heart? The Internet attracted me because of the fact that it involved the communication of ideas, feeling, thoughts and opinions through writing and that is what I do best.

You can learn a great deal about someone by the way he or she formulates sentences, composes poems and reaches out with direct, heartfelt phrases. Sometimes, there are more accurate ways of feeling someone's joy, achievements and pain than by being right there in the same room with them. You don't have to worry about self-consciousness, shyness and feeling that somebody's eyes are boring right through you. The Internet is really a blessing for shy people like myself, and can really aid in re-integrating a reclusive individual back into the mainstream of society in safe little bits at a time.

Today, it can honestly and truthfully be said that I have put my unfortunate past behind me. What occurred in the past happened, unfortunately, but it doesn't have to taint the rest of my life. I'm finally ready to turn the page and create my own happiness and fulfillment. At long last, after forty years, it's time to start living.